THE POLITICAL ECONOMY OF INNOVATION

STUDIES IN INDUSTRIAL ORGANIZATION

Volume 4

The Political Economy of Innovation

by

William Kingston

1984 **MARTINUS NIJHOFF PUBLISHERS**
a member of the KLUWER ACADEMIC PUBLISHERS GROUP
THE HAGUE / BOSTON / LANCASTER

Distributors

for the United States and Canada: Kluwer Boston, Inc., 190 Old Derby Street,
Hingham, MA 02043, USA
for all other countries: Kluwer Academic Publishers Group, Distribution Center,
P.O.Box 322, 3300 AH Dordrecht, The Netherlands

Library of Congress Cataloging in Publication Data

```
Kingston, William.
   The political economy of innovation.

   (Studies in industrial organization ; v. 4)
   Includes index.
   1. Technological innovations--Economic aspects.
2. Technological innovations--Government policy.
3. Marketing.  I. Title.  II. Series.
HD45.K557  1984      338'.06      83-21942
ISBN 90-247-2621-2
```

PRINTED IN THE NETHERLANDS

To Mary

"The bourgeoisie cannot exist without constantly revolutionizing the instruments of production... during its rule of scarce one hundred years (it) has created more massive and more colossal productive forces than have all preceding generations put together... – what earlier century had even a presentiment that such productive forces slumbered in the lap of social labour?"

The Communist Manifesto

"The laws of property have never yet conformed to the principles on which the justification of private property rests. They have made property of things which never ought to be property and absolute property where only a qualified property ought to exist. They have not held the balance fairly between human beings, but have heaped impediments on some, to give advantage to others: they have purposely fostered inequalities and prevented all from starting fair in the race. That all should indeed start on perfectly equal terms, is inconsistent with any law of private property; but if as much pains as had been taken to aggravate the inequality of chances arising from the natural working of the principle, had been taken to temper that inequality by every means not subversive of the principle itself; if the tendency of legislation had been to favour the diffusion instead of the concentration of wealth – to encourage the sub-division of the large masses instead of striving to heap them together; the principle of individual property would have been found to have no necessary communion worth the physical and social evils which almost all Socialist writers assume to be inseparable from it."

J.S. Mill: *Principles of Political Economy.*
Book II, Ch. I

Contents

Preface

Innovation is the turning of ideas into concrete realities. To the extent that this process is an economic one, it must also be subject to political decisions, and these determine which ideas are to have resources made available for their innovation. This book attempts to trace the relationship between ideas, resources and politics.

Chapter I deals with the way economic innovation depends both upon markets and upon interference with markets. Schumpeter taught us how market power is essential for innovation. This chapter stresses that the inverse is also true: Innovation can take place wherever there is market power. A most important corollary of this, is that failure to develop any particular type of market power, need not prevent innovation from happening. It will then take place under the protection of whatever market power there is, and it will be geographically located wherever that market power is effective.

Chapter II identifies and seeks to fill a major gap in the literature on innovation, by showing how important modern marketing has become for providing the conditions under which money may be rationally invested at high risk to get new things done. Marketing monopoly, or Persuasive market power, is now at least as important as the market power of Capability, or as the several types of Specific market power, in interference with market forces. It is therefore equally important for innovation. Once marketing is given its proper weight, it becomes possible to deal with innovation according to a definition that is wide enough to do justice to reality; in particular, the distortion of limiting the discussion to *technological* innovation is removed.

In Chapter III, attention is turned to tracing the various sources of the market power which underwrites economic innovation, and it is shown that in every case, the root can be found in some aspect of positive law. The innovation which results from Capability market power therefore depends directly upon the great burst of legislation for deployment of capital in the mid-nineteenth-century; marketing-protected innovations go back to Trade Marks Acts: some technology depends upon the Specific market power of Patent law; and market power becomes global as a result of various International Conventions.

Chapter IV shows that because all this legislation was not based upon a consistent and humane vision of property rights, the resulting pattern of economic innovation has become increasingly incapable of dealing with challenges from without, as well as of inspiring enthusiasm and approval from within. The external challenges from OPEC and from Japanese capability are being poorly met, and many people in Western countries have become disillusioned with a pattern of innovation which is thought to be all that a private property system can produce. Consequently, in greater or lesser degree, they have turned towards collectivism. This is incompatible, not alone with innovation, but also with Democracy. This is why the contemporary crisis in the West is political as well as economic.

In Chapter V, practical proposals are made for social innovations to deal with this crisis. These begin with extensions of the principle of Patenting which could rejuvenate Specific market power. The resulting innovations would cope with the immediate external challenges, and the associated investment would make a large contribution towards reducing unemployment. However, dealing with the problem of internal rejection of the patterns of market power and innovation will require much more thoroughgoing reform of the laws of property. It is only possible to outline the shape such reform might take, but its underlying principle is clear: Market power should be permitted only to the extent that it contributes explicitly to innovation, because there is no other justification for it.

In writing, any attempt to break new ground is an exact parallel with building a prototype in technology. And just as no prototype can possess the elegance which only incremental innovation over a long period of time can bring to the embodiment of any concept, neither can any genuinely new formulation of ideas. I am only too well aware of the shortcomings in the present case, and can only hope that others will be sufficiently interested in my general thesis (that is, that they will agree that the prototype *works*) to take up the work of filling the gaps. In particular, the bulk of my examples and references are drawn from the English-speaking world. The thesis, however, is equally valid for Continental European countries. Some of these, indeed, were the originators of the ideas of Intellectual Property which I am convinced have still such potential for development. Consequently, nothing would please me more than if one of the results of publication of this book from The Hague, were to be quick redress of this imbalance.

I owe particular debts to the Staff of the Library of Trinity College, Dublin, for their response to unceasing demands, and, as always, to Miss Wyn Sheerin for typing.

William Kingston

CHAPTER I

Innovation and market power

To invent is to find a new thing; to innovate is to get the new thing done. In all but the exact form of words, the definition is Joseph Schumpeter's, and it was he who also first called attention to the way in which the difference between the two functions is even reflected in the sociological and psychological types: Some people are good at producing ideas but less good at turning them into concrete realities, whereas others are noted for their ability to carry into practical effect, ideas which they have not originated themselves. Both activities, as discussed in *Innovation*, are most intelligible as related aspects of human creative activity, but this leads to a further important distinction: Creativity on its own can give us Invention and Art almost irrespective of material circumstances. One has only to think of the poverty out of which Clarence Goodyear produced vulcanized rubber, or that of Schubert in Vienna, making music worth more than all the gold of all the Hapsburgs, to realize this.[1]

But *economic* innovation (getting new things done when the innovator needs to mobilize resources other than his own) involves dependence upon the environment. If that environment is altogether hostile, there can be no innovation at all. What kind of innovation, and how much of it there will be, depends upon how supportive of innovators, and in what ways, the environment is. Since the economic environment is shaped by political activity, we can properly speak of the political economy of the particular kind of creativity that goes into economic innovation. Politics and political institutions cannot fail to affect any kind of 'getting new things done', or turning ideas into concrete realities, which has an economic dimension. Like all political economy, of course, the special political economy of innovation relates only to countries where there is a substantial degree of economic freedom, where economic activity is responsive to demand, and where the economy is not centrally directed. These are the countries (and it is no coincidence) which in any event have accounted for the vast bulk of economic innovation.

Paradoxically, economic innovation requires simultaneously, both markets and interference with markets. It therefore requires economic freedom, which

2

is the precondition for markets to exist, yet if there are no limitations to that freedom, there will be very definite limitations to innovation. Economic freedom, in turn, is rooted in the institution of private property, so that much of the political economy of innovation is concerned with the nature of property rights. Human creativeness can only express itself in business activity to the extent that positive law makes this possible. Only laws that represent a considerable social achievement can arrange for that energy to flow in the direction of economic activity. It has to be channelled towards business, and the channel is provided by private property. The energy, for example, which in a more barbaric situation might have gone into preparing to fight for the acquisition or defence of goods, can now be directed into their exchange. More importantly, it can be directed into the discovery, obtaining or production of goods which were not available before; nor does it any longer have to produce an immediate result, because private property extends the time-scale with reference to which men are prepared to act. The energy to plant a stand of oaks, for example, is called forth by a positive law of property which convinces a man that his descendants will own and enjoy the mature trees.

Any positive law of property directs creative energy into economic channels, but different kinds of positive law define the precise economic channels into which that energy will flow. It is the positive law of copyright, for example, which creates property in works of art and writings. Where there is such a law, other things being equal, more authors can gain from producing such things than if there is not. Conversely, in the absence of such a law, the energy of pirate publishers will frustrate the energy of writers by undermining the capacity of legitimate publishers to pay them. It is because its laws of private property have been developed, refined and extended to an unprecedented extent, that Western civilization has been responsible for an unprecedented amount of innovation. Therefore, its power to make innovation possible, constitutes a most important justification of private property. Since creativeness is business is what causes economic innovation, the link between innovation and private property is fundamental. History confirms the existence and importance of this link: The societies organised on a basis of private ownership have emphatically been those in which most innovation has taken place.

The *kinds* of innovation there will be, therefore, can only reflect the positive law which creates private ownership in the first instance, and the same law will also determine the *amount* of innovation. For example, there has never been an effective law in any country making scientific discovery of the more abstract kind, into private property. It is no doubt possible, it has been proposed in the past, and it is being discussed again, but it has never been done. No great exercise of the imagination is needed to conclude that if positive law had developed in this way, the amount of innovation there has been would have been different, and the ideas which would have emerged as new concrete realities would also have been different, from what has actually taken place. The innovation there has been is simply the innovation which one particular pattern of positive law has made possible. Another pattern of positive law would have produced another pattern of innovation in the past. It could do so in the future. There is not just one law which creates private property. There is a complex of specific enactments, each of which creates private property in specific areas of human life, and which therefore make it certain that there will be innovation in those areas. It is the United States Patent Act of 1952 which at present creates private property in certain kinds of ideas coming from the minds of American citizens and others, by ensuring to them a monopoly of the use of the embodiments of those ideas for seventeen years. This law makes it possible for business to pay some attention to turning those ideas into reality. Without that Act, business might have to ignore those ideas altogether, however brilliant or worthy they might be in themselves by any other criterion, because there would be no property in them. The U.S. Patent Act provides for monopolies to be granted only in respect of certain types of ideas, and it grants those monopolies in a certain way, thus providing for only one pattern of innovation. It would be equally possible, constitutionally, for Congress to make the Patent term seventeen months or one hundred and seventeen years. Each of these, being a different kind of property in ideas, created by positive law, would result in a different pattern of innovation.

All markets depend upon the existence of private property, and the minimal requirement for any market to exist, is that there is some effective guarantee of private ownership, most frequently, from the State. Confirmation of this is forthcoming from the Eastern bloc countries, where the tentative re-emergence of markets in certain fields reflects a relaxation of strict collectivist thinking in favour of limited private property. However, a State can opt to protect ownership of one kind of thing and not another, and from time to time it can change the laws which make ownership possible, thus creating or removing the basis for the existence of markets. Slave markets disappeared once private property in human beings was eliminated from the range of things which the State would protect in many countries, during the nineteenth century. During the same century, there was a remarkable trend throughout much the same list of countries in the opposite direction, towards extending the range of things in which the State would recognise and protect private property ownership. The legislation providing for Limited Liability Companies, for example, created a new type of ownership which enabled men to act together in business matters in a way which was not possible before, taking risks in common which they could never afford to take separately, each taking only part of the success or failure upon himself, instead of the whole responsibility, as he would have had to do under earlier laws of property. At least an equally important aspect of this trend was the way in which legal arrangements were extended to a whole new dimension of life, so as to make ideas and information relating to business effectively into property for the first time. Hardly any legislation of the nineteenth century can have been more important for the twentieth than that relating to Intellectual and Industrial Property.

4

However important by absolute standards the things of the mind may be, they do not become property unless the law makes them so. They are also very difficult, if not impossible, to protect by any means other than law. A man's effective ownership and enjoyment of the apples in his orchard may owe far more in practice to his reputation for ferocity or to the broken glass embedded in the top of his wall, than to the protection given to him by law. He cannot protect his ideas in the same way. Once free, these can spread with the greatest ease, to be used with impunity by anyone who comes in contact with them. In business terms, information is expensive to produce, but cheap to re-produce. It is also hard to make money from it. No matter how 'good' an idea may be in the abstract, it can never be an investment opportunity on its own. It only becomes so when the law makes provision for private ownership to exist in it. What is true of ideas in the sense of 'bolts from the blue' is even more true of those ideas or packages of information which require investment *before* they emerge in any sort of shape which can be acted upon. Investing money in the development of ideas or information is simply out of the question unless some adequate form of private ownership attaches to the outcome, and it is this form of ownership which is brought into being by the positive law of intellectual and industrial property. This generates entirely new markets, precisely because it *interferes* with markets.

The essence of a market is that *anyone* can come to it either with something to sell or with money to buy. To 'make a market', as brokers do with stocks or commodities, is to set up arrangements so that this can happen with complete freedom. Market forces are the pressures that are generated by this freedom of entry. They always work to push prices downwards. To have power over a market, then, can mean nothing else than to be able to control its essential characteristic, which is freedom of entry. The effect of that control can only be to weaken downwards pressure on price. Paradoxically, therefore, market power is not power to make a market. It is power to "unmake" it. It is the power to escape from the constraints, especially in terms of price, which the market always seeks to impose. It is always about erecting barriers to entry to a market. It acts by keeping others out.

Market power is indispensable for innovation, because others simply *have* to be kept out if innovation is to be possible. Investment in innovation must always be at above-average risk. Consequently, it can only be undertaken rationally if there is prospect of an above-average reward. In a market where complete freedom of entry pushes price down as far as it can go, innovation is simply impossible. If there is to be innovation, there must be means of interfering with the market, of erecting barriers to entry, of keeping would-be entrants out, so that price can be kept up. Market power does not enable a firm, in the technical sense, to do anything different from what it could do if it had no market power. But having market power enables it to do it more or less alone. It enables it to devote some of its resources to innovation. By definition, this demands that the firm goes into a situation as a lone investor. Market power holds out the prospect of emerging from that situation as a corresponding-ly lone seller, the technical term for which is a monopolist. This will give above-average returns, and this is how market power makes investment in innovation possible.

If necessity is the mother of invention, therefore, market power is the mother of innovation, and market power in this context is strictly a man-made thing. The fact that there is so much innovation to-day is due to the fact that there is so much market power to-day; this in turn is due to a series of extensions of the law of property a century ago; and the form that this innovation takes reflects the nature of those extensions of the law and the market power they confer.

Few things are more striking than the ignorance of those who benefit from them, of the very existence of these laws. In practice, all business men feel that they are subject to constraints that are unnecessary, sometimes imposed by law, more frequently these days by what seems to them like Government harassment. Either way, business men feel that with more freedom — from the Federal Trade Commission, from Trades Union strength sanctioned by Law, from D.G. 4 (Competition Policy) in Brussels — and were left to get on with the job, they would be able to benefit society and themselves much more than they can do now. *Laissez-faire* is supposed to have been originally Laissez *nous* faire, and in this form it represents a deeply ingrained attitude of business men.

Yet, if it were possible to take them at their word, and give them their freedom, no one would be more shocked at the consequences than they. The business of the man who feels restricted by the results of positive law, is itself the result of positive law. His stake in it exists at all only because of laws which give protection to individual property; he is saved from having his entire fortune and family at risk in it because of enactments for Limited Liability; he can raise money from outside through Joint Stock Companies' legislation; and if it involves Patents, Designs or Trade Marks (and many businesses could not run without one or more of these) it rests upon a foundation of specific legislation providing for the existence of Industrial Property. Destroy all these, and the business man as the human type with which we are familiar to-day immediately becomes extinct.

It is not even as if all these kinds of positive law were ways of distorting the free market, this free market being regarded as some sort of irreducible substratum on which different economic constructions could be built. The free market — any market — itself depends upon a positive law by which the State gives protection to private property. It is not the transfer of goods which makes a market, but the uncoerced exchange of titles to those goods, guaranteed by a political authority. There is undoubtedly transfer of goods where jungle law prevails, but it does not constitute a market; equally, goods are transferred in a collectivist economy, but to the extent that the controlling element is command, not demand, there is no market. A market only exists when the State can and does guarantee to individual men, freedom to use or not to use goods which are associated with them personally by some defined set of criteria, to offer them to others or to withhold them, as they please. There is nothing 'natural' about even the freest of free markets; every market is an artifact, a creation of positive law.

Without a positive law of private property, many different types of human activity remain possible, but one does not: The activity of manipulating and exchanging titles to property, which is the characteristic activity of a business man. Typically, however, such a man will think and act as if his work and objectives represented 'natural', 'free' economic activity, always in danger from those who want to distort the free market by imposing constraints of one kind or another. It comes as a considerable shock to most business men to learn that their economic world is a man-made thing, the result of positive legislation which arose out of specific historical circumstances, which could have developed in a different way, which could now be changed or even abolished, still within a private property system. Business men have no difficulty in seeing the positive law which restricts them, but they are almost totally blind to the positive law which puts them into business in the first place, and keeps them there.

It is wrong, therefore, to think that private property can only develop in one direction, or that 'the market' can have only one meaning. Private property exists because the law protects it, and in the form in which the law protects it, not otherwise. A 'market' exists because of these legal titles to property, and consists in nothing else except the free exchange of these titles. No matter how 'free' a market may be, it can never escape being the exchange of State-granted or State-guaranteed monopolies. There are only two alternatives to the law of the jungle — 'la raison du plus fort'. One of these is collectivism, where some authority distributes resources according to its own criteria of value; the second is a market economy, which depends upon authority guaranteeing ownership to individuals, but limiting its function to this, so that resources are distributed according to the utility individuals find in the property of others as compared with their own. To speak of a market, then, without specifying the nature of the titles to property which are exchanged in it, is almost meaning-less. Exchange where farmers sell their cattle to dealers for money is a market. The State protects the farmers in their ownership of cattle and the dealers in their ownership of money, and the titles to both are freely exchanged, according to the utility a farmer finds in the dealer's money and the utility the dealer finds in the farmer's cattle. Such a market is quite close to the traditional description given by economists, where there are many sellers of products that are identical for all practical purposes, there are also many buyers, and price is the variable which reflects the relative balance of utilities between them. But a quite different type of exchange, where the property guaranteed to the seller by the State includes information (possibly in the form of Patents) and reputation (which may be attached to registered Trade Marks); where consequently products are so highly differentiated that there is only one seller of each for all practical purposes; where price remains fixed and no longer measures relative utility. This, too, is a market.

Members of a Bourse or Stock Exchange, by their activity of buying or selling, enable supply and demand for stocks to be kept in equilibrium by means of variations in their prices. Exactly the opposite takes place in the market for a modern advertised product. Here, all the effort goes into *preventing* price from being the variable which brings about equilibrium. When price is the determining variable, it always means that the goods in question are being traded as commodities, each being undifferentiated from the others, as individual stocks and shares of the same issue are. A market where price is the variable factor is the only market possible as long as the State limits its protection to real or personal property. When the State also brings industrial property into being through positive legislation, new types of markets become possible, and in these the constraint of price no longer operates at all, or has its force attenuated.

The characteristic activity in this new type of market is thus to maximise the advantage due to one type of property, and to weaken market forces, which always work to push price downwards. Advertising's most important function, for example, is to create uniqueness of advantage in psychological terms, for goods which are otherwise identical, or very nearly so. That is, its job is precisely to enable these goods to escape from the constraints, especially in terms of price, which the market would impose upon them if they were traded as commodities. What is true of advertising is also true of other forms of sales management and promotion, so that the techniques of modern marketing are most intelligible if they are seen as means of *evading* the discipline of the market. This is not to say that the markets where these techniques are practised are not competitive; indeed they are, but their rules are not the rules of the free market. Moreover, by escaping the constraints which the free market would impose, even the least successful players under the new rules are at an advantage compared with those who will not, or cannot play at all. Ironically, therefore, 'marketing know-how' is not knowledge of how to make a market, but how to make *monopoly*.

All monopoly can be described in terms of 'uniqueness of advantage'. Cournot's mineral spring which is on one man's land and no-one else's, and Adam Smith's 'the product of certain vineyards in France' can mislead as examples, because they look on monopoly from the producer's point of view. From this aspect the entire product *is* unique: There is only one spring producing mineral water; there is only one Clos Vougeot. Looked at from the other point of view, however, that of the consumer, and considering the satisfactions a particular product, rather than any other, is capable of giving, this uniqueness is found to be very much circumscribed. Even if there are no other mineral springs, there are other ways of quenching thirst; however great a wine Clos Vougeot may be, there are other great wines, and some people in any case prefer Bordeaux to Burgundy. But when all such allowances have been made, there remains some residual element which is a particular product's own, not shared with other products, and if it is something that can give a satisfaction of some kind, then this residual element amounts to a product's uniqueness of advantage as compared with other products. Such a uniqueness of advantage can be in almost anything, and it can always be equated with monopoly. It can be in knowledge – the origins of the Rothschild fortunes are believed to owe much to the superiority of their information over that of other bankers. It can be in timing – the Haloid Corporation were actively searching for an investment opportunity related to their business just at the time when Xerography was ready for large-scale backing. It can be in 'resonance' – the way in which some people have a special sense of how particular groups will react to certain circumstances. Survival in the highly competitive world of *haute couture*, for example, depends upon having 'resonance' of this kind with one or more of the groups of women who set trends in dress. The 'uniqueness of advantage' or monopoly is this case is the instinctive awareness of what this group will like.

We do not have to think of uniqueness of advantage simply in terms of the man who owns a piece of land at a crossroads, and who can therefore build a filling station to serve two lots of traffic instead of one. All that is needed for monopoly is any form of advantage that is not shared with others, whether this advantage is physical or psychological. It does not matter, either, how much of a product is shared with others, how close we come to complete similarity, as long as there is *one part* that is not shared; the uniqueness of advantage, or monopoly, then consists in this unshared part. Pure competition excludes any such element of monopoly, by definition, since it assumes products which are exactly alike in every way. The economists' concept of perfect competition adds a further dimension to this: That information is complete, on the part of both buyers and sellers.

Any kind of private property will cause creative energy to be directed into economic activity, but it needs a special kind of private property to cause it to flow into innovation. Only private property which confers some unusual form of uniqueness of advantage, something which is an individual's particular right, not shared with others, can do that. Historically, it has been the marriage of individual energy with monopoly in the institution of private property which has been the most fruitful source of innovation. This must be insisted upon, especially as Russian power to innovate in weapons and Space is frequently pointed out as an example of what collectivism can achieve in this field. Four points are relevant. Firstly, Russian technology had a much broader and sounder base under the last Czars than is often admitted, and Soviet technology has built upon this. Next, their innovation has taken place in relatively narrow areas by Western standards, leaving other areas virtually untouched. However distorted the pattern of innovation in the West may be, it is manifestly a great deal more homogeneous – less 'patchy' – than the Russian one. Thirdly, the Russians have built to a large extent upon Western advances, and have relied heavily upon Western fundamental research.[2] Like

Japan, it has got far more out of the publication provisions of the international Patent system than it has put in. Finally, in order to achieve their innovation, the Russians have had to introduce a system of incentive payments and privileges to direct their best minds into applied science, and these, in the Soviet context, approximate very much to the *results* of private ownership in Western countries. As a class, considered against the backgrounds of their respective societies, the holders of Russian Inventor's Certificates may be better off than individual Western holders of Patents for invention. It is indeed open to Communists to denigrate the pattern and shape of innovation in the West, and to decry the way this is frequently meretricious, mindless, irrational and philistine; but they cannot deny that it is all of these things out of plentitude, not scarcity: Individual creative energy released into economic activity by market power in the institution of private property, has proved itself to be extraordinarily productive of innovation.

The political decisions which affect economic innovation, therefore, are primarily those which establish or modify market power. As long as rate of return on investment is what measures success or failure in economic activity, innovation carries with it the need to escape from the constraints which the market seeks to impose. As pointed out earlier, rationality demands that anyone who enters any situation as a lone investor, only does so in the prospect of emerging from it as a lone seller, and the technical term for a lone seller is a monopolist. For a firm to receive an above-average return on its investment in a particular product, its costs must be lower, or its selling price higher, or both, compared with its competitors. For this to happen the firm must possess some advantage, or combination of advantages, which are uniquely its own, and not shared with its rivals. It is the ability to keep rivals away from any sharing in the feast, that constitutes market power.

Market power is therefore not so much a capacity to do something, as the ability to *prevent* others from doing it also. In this sense, it is a negative force. It is perhaps best illustrated by the power which Trades Unions have over the market for labour. It is not their ability to withdraw their labour, nor even their ability to withdraw it in concert with others, that gives power to unskilled workers organized in a Union; it is the fact that by custom, by picketing, by violence or in some other way, they are able to prevent their employer from recruiting other workers to fill their places. Market power of whatever type, is always "the power of the picket". If there is no such power, if any one factor of production is no better and no worse than whatever can be substituted for it, if entry is free, so that substitution is altogether unhindered, then the effect of the economic forces at work is inevitably to drive the price down to just the level that will cause all the goods on offer to be bought to "clear the market". Any one of the many sellers, if he looks for more than this price, will sell nothing at all; if he offers to take less than it, he will be overwhelmed by orders for more goods than he can supply. Any one of the many buyers is similarly constrained by this unique price, which he has no power to influence. Thus, the constraint which the market seeks to impose always consists of pressure in the direction of more buyers and sellers, of substitutability as between products, of unrestricted entry (capacity on the part of a new supplier to offer the same product for sale if he wishes) and of a price which is out of range of influence by any of those involved.

This price is critical to the question of economic innovation. It is clear that when a market is operating, economic forces drive price down to a level which is equal to the unit cost of the typical producer, the cost of the capital required being a component of this, charged at whatever rate capital is generally available to all producers. Since this price excludes any rate of return above the average, it cannot justify investment with any risk above the average. As a consequence, assuming that investors are rational, *economic innovation is rendered altogether impossible.* Only in so far as there are opportunities to escape from the constraints which the market seeks to impose, can investment in the face of the risks of innovation be undertaken rationally. Since it is the capacity for such evasion, market power is therefore a necessary condition for economic innovation. It is indispensable if investment in the generation of new information (necessary for innovation, but which may well turn out to be worthless) is to be more than gambling. Economists have shown with elaborate theory that a private enterprise system must always invest less than the optimum in basic (fundamental) research as compared with applied research. The truth is that such a private enterprise system in their sense (which would be a system operating under perfect competition) could not rationally invest *anything at all* in *either* type of research. Since, by definition, all participants are to have complete information, any investment in the development of new information would be to the immediate advantage of all those who had *not* made it. Investment in R & D by private enterprise, therefore, is only rational to the extent that steps have been taken to generate imperfections in the market which will prevent "free-riding". In any actual system, the balance between basic and applied research will reflect the type and extent of such market imperfections, as means for earning the above-average return that investment at above-average risk demands.

In any attempts to understand the economic aspects of innovation, therefore, it is first necessary to understand market power and to develop a vocabulary for handling it. Once this is done, since all market power is rooted in positive law, and since law is so largely shaped by politics, it will be possible to move towards a valid political economy of innovation. The contributions of professional economists that will be found useful in relation to market power, mainly arise out of such concern as they have had with monopoly and oligopoly. Economists are no more free than anyone else from being influenced by their time and their environment, and this applies even to the greatest of them. Both Marx and Schumpeter saw innovation as of great importance, but Keynes was largely uninterested in it. Something called 'technical change' does come up in his writings from time to time, but it is never at the centre of his thought. Significantly, too, we do not think of Keynes as having added anything memorable to our understanding of market power, which is the key to economic innovation. Some weight must surely be given to the way in which the thought of both Marx and Schumpeter was formed in periods which were prolific in innovation. Marx was clearly deeply impressed by the innovative power of Europe in the railway age and at the beginning of precision manufacturing and use of interchangeable parts; Schumpeter's impressionable period was in Austria during the years when the new electrical industries were dragging economies everywhere out of the great slump of 1873-96. For Keynes, the comparable 'fertile' time was the 1920s, when innovatory activity in Britain was at a low ebb – was it not for a static economy, after all, that he produced his most famous prescription?

In a similar way, through and beyond the thinking of Adam Smith and the other classical economists can be discerned the social arrangements of the era before the full force of the industrial revolution, when markets were the markets of peasants and merchants. Though merchants were a minority, even they were often too numerous for any one of them to be able to have a major determining influence on price, or for collusion to be very effective – monopoly, always longed for, was hard to come by. Then came industrialisation and with it concentration of economic power through transport and technology – and concentration means monopoly. Consequently, during the nineteenth century and the first third of the twentieth, the question of monopoly received increasing attention, the line of thought passing in this period from Cournot through Jevons, Edgeworth and Wicksell, to Joan Robinson. This kind of monopoly, however, was based upon objective factors intrinsic to industrialised *production*. In the present century, the reality which obtrudes itself has increasingly been the growth of a different kind of monopoly, based upon the manipulation of *demand*, which is, of course, most clearly reflected in the growth of advertising; in this, the pedigree of our knowledge and ideas contains the names of Sraffa, Chamberlin, Harrod and Galbraith.

Theory, however, is always well behind reality, and the men of action who make the real world do so largely unaided (and un-encumbered) by theory. In Britain, for example, if there is one date which marks the beginning of what we may call the marketing revolution, the starting date of monopoly based not on manipulation of productive resources, but of *demand*, it was when W.H. Lever registered the name "Sunlight". This was within months of the 1883 Trade Marks Act, on which this revolution depends, yet it was 1926 before Sraffa's article, *"The Laws of Returns Under Competitive Conditions"* appeared. Even then it took many years for its importance to be seen.[3] E.H. Chamberlin's great *Theory of Monopolistic Competition* came out in 1933, exactly half a century after the Trade Marks Act, and when the marketing revolution was in full spate. Clearly, if W.H. Lever had waited for even a partial theory on which to base his action, there would have been no Unilever; can we say of him, as of any man of action, that he was only able to do what he did, because in at least one sense he did not know what he was doing?

It is easy to be impatient with the way in which theory lags behind reality in time, just as it is easy to be impatient with the way it has to simplify reality even when it does finally attempt to cope with it. This is to ignore the necessary "ageing process" which seems to apply to ideas as to liquor:

> 'A new idea does not come forth in its mature scientific form. It contains logical ambiguities or errors; the evidence on which it rests is incomplete or indecisive; and its domain of application is exaggerated in certain directions and overlooked in others.'[4]

The way in which Economists' thinking about monopoly has developed illustrates this clearly.

For Adam Smith, the important thing in economic theory was competition, and how it established price. In actual economic life, this had come, over a long period, to replace the medieval 'administered' price approach in business matters. Monopoly related to a later world than Smith's, but he did not altogether ignore it. He thought of it in terms of articles for which the supply was fixed and could not be expanded. 'The price of monopoly' he said, 'is upon every occasion the highest which can be got' and from this point of view, the thing to be feared was collusion: 'People of the same trade seldom meet together, even for merriment or diversion, but the conversation ends in a conspiracy against the public, or in some contrivance to raise prices'.[5]

For Ricardo, too, goods in scarce supply sell at a monopoly price, which is entirely determined by demand. In the thought of Cournot, there is, in 1838, as well as a theory of pure monopoly for the first time, the idea of monopolists in competition with each other. Limiting his analysis to two such competitors, Cournot assumed that neither firm ever tests the other's reactions, that is, each firm assumes that no action it takes will influence what the other does. In this, of course, it is wrong, but it never learns that it is wrong. To a business man, indeed to anyone who has ever played any kind of game, this assumption may appear to remove the analysis a considerable distance from the real world, and it does. Cournot was a professional mathematician, and the tradition of mathematical economics, of which he is one of the founding fathers, has always remained faithful to his use of simplifying assumptions. He thought of his two monopolists as each owning a spring producing mineral water of identical quality, supplying the same market. (It is intriguing to see his example in a modern form in the world-wide competition between Coca-Cola and Pepsi-Cola. This is a new kind of competition between monopolies, where the brand name is all-important. There is a sense in which the development of economists' thinking on monopoly represents their attempts to give theoretical explanations for the differences between Cournot's and modern monopolies, both in scale and in kind).

The concepts of 'pure', 'perfect' and 'imperfect' competition emerged in the 1870s. Pure competition becomes 'perfect' when full information is added; 'imperfect' competition is when suppliers can influence the price because they are sufficiently few, that is, when specialisation in one way or another, enters in. However, as the factory system became the normal way of producing goods, 'pure' and 'perfect' competition theory became increasingly irrelevant to real life:

> 'Given the existence of fixed cost in the plant, competition is necessarily imperfect.... Perfect competition can exist only when production at every level of output is carried on under constant returns to scale.... Thus perfect competition, rigorously defined, is wholly a matter of technology...'[6]

Differences of scale in plants were, to begin with, a product of the transport revolution, of the canals and railways that made manufacture of goods for distribution to a wide area possible, and of the harnessing of steam power. Thus, the evident fact of competition between units that were also in some way *insulated* from competition began to impress itself on economists in the 1870s, although it was a further generation before the widespread existence of imperfect markets got its first and sketchy treatment from Knut Wicksell in 1901, still another before Joan Robinson's definitive treatment in 1933.[7]

In a similar way, although changes in Trade Mark law which will be discussed fully below began to bring about product differentiation in the modern sense as early as the 1880s, it is only with E.H. Chamberlin that the incorporation of their results into theory begins. The fact that Chamberlin's and Robinson's books both appeared in 1933, and both contained some very similar insights, led many people to wonder why Chamberlin held so vehemently that his concept of monopolistic competition was not (or not 'just') imperfect competition. What was really going on was that Chamberlin was trying to express in theory the reality of a later stage of historical economic development than that which interested Joan Robinson. The 'real world' counterpart to Mrs. Robinson's book is the industrial world of most of the nineteenth century, when the spread of technology had made indivisibilities (which are the heart of imperfect competition) the rule rather than the exception in manufacturing. In the twentieth century, on the other hand, the communications revolution, based, as we shall see, on the Trade Marks Acts, began in earnest, advertising came into its own, the manipulation of demand through product differentiation developed into a most important factor in economic life – and it is this reality which Chamberlin undertook to make intelligible. To illustrate the contrast: Robinson's *The Economics of Imperfect Competition* goes a long way towards explaining the hundred soapmaking firms in England, each with its own local franchise which was often a local monopoly or very near it, that was the pattern at the outset of W.H. Lever's business career; but it takes Chamberlin's *The Theory of Monopolistic Competition* as well, to begin to make sense of the position as it had become at the end of Lever's life, when his own brands held three-fifths of the British market through an advertising appropriation which was an eighth of their total sales value, and national distribution had become a virtual condition of survival for such firms as remained in existence.[8]

Chamberlin's book is needed *as well*, because monopolistic competition theory does not *replace* that of imperfect competition, but rather extends the theory to a new area of reality. For example, if in some way product differentiation could be eliminated from the British detergent market, this would not change the fact that a 70,000 ton/year blowing tower has an operating unit cost which is half that of a plant with an output of 28,000 tons. Since returns here are not constant to scale, competition is equally imperfect. Clearly, the amount and nature of imperfection is changed by whether or not product differentiation is also present. In the present example, without it (in the form of mass-advertised brands) there could hardly be the concentration of the detergent industry into a few large firms which could use blowing towers of anything like 70,000 tons annual output; indeed, because of the link between modern branded products, concentration and innovation, there would probably be no synthetic detergents at all. The steel business, because of the importance of scale economies, operates very much in an environment of imperfect competition, but because branding is of small importance, hardly at all in one of monopolistic competition. For cosmetics, branding is virtually everything, so the proportions are reversed. Shaping up to such reality, the theories overlap, and Chamberlin himself referred to 'that portion of the whole subject matter that the two theories exploit in common'. Nevertheless, there remain major conceptual differences: Imperfect competition is primarily about goods, about the differences imposed by the nature of technology; monopolistic competition is primarily about what goes on in minds and hearts, about *information*, about product differentiation, that is, differences built into a product which are 'of consequence to at least some buyers' – even if these are largely subjective. Imperfect competition takes demand as given; monopolistic competition regards it as there to be manipulated.

The thought of these two giants of economists' monopoly can be reconciled if the differing real words they reflect are kept in mind. For Mrs. Robinson, this real world hardly included psychological differences between products, and these were not of great importance to her. To Chamberlin, on the other hand, they were of great interest. The use of marketing techniques has long been more obtrusive in the United States than in England, and even in England, if Mrs. Robinson had been writing from industrialised Oxford instead of from Cambridge, she might have been less able to ignore the 'marketing' aspect of economic reality. The difference in the pressure of promotional techniques in their respective cultural environments must have caused Chamberlin to be so much more concerned that his theory should take account of them than Joan Robinson was, even though they were both writing at around the same time.

This also explains another point of controversy between them – the importance of the *industry* as opposed to the firm. For Mrs. Robinson the idea of an industry made up of firms producing substantially homogenous products is the starting point. (Any other approach would hardly have been possible for an economist in the tradition of Marshall). Chamberlin, it is fair to say, was never quite sure what an industry was, but in any event his thought began not from it but from the firm – 'like the atom in physics, it is fundamental'. This, at heart, is because Mrs. Robinson's view of the firm is production-oriented, whereas Chamberlin's is customer-oriented. Her 'firm' is organised primarily to *make* something; his to *sell* something. Both economists refer to the 'entrepreneur', the business man who is the agent of economic change, but is is clear that they see him quite differently. Her entrepreneur is really a jumped-up Works Manager; his came up through the marketing side of the business. A Works Manager is dominated by technology, he has his being in a world where other firms make much the same kind of things by much the same techniques, where change is a slow and laborious business, always subject to frustration by the intractability of matter. In this world, it is as much as a man can do to know how to make one thing properly, and a steel man does not expect to find himself transferred into the textile industry. In contrast, a marketing man has for his stock in trade an awareness of what people want or can be made to want, coupled with knowledge of how to use the available techniques of persuasion. His world is therefore a more dynamic world than that of the Works Manager, he is not 'industry-bound' in the same way, and may move from selling detergents to electrical applicances to beer without feeling very much more or less at home.

The contrast between the two situations finds theoretical expression in the books of Robinson and Chamberlin and in the traditions which these books have inspired. Of these traditions, the Chamberlinian is the more important, in that it explicitly takes account of marketing (in the modern sense) as a fact of economic life. In Donald Dewey's words,

> 'work in Chamberlin's tradition is more difficult to assimilate into axiomatic economic theory than is work in the Robinson tradition. But I believe that this difficulty can be taken as conclusive evidence that when the object is to understand how competition works in the real world, axiomatic economic theory is not enough.'[9]

Even with no knowledge at all of economists' jargon, it is not difficult to grasp Chamberlin's central idea. For any product, the relationship between what it costs to produce a unit and the quantity produced, can be plotted. It is common experience that it is relatively cheaper to make a lot than a few, and so what is known as the unit cost curve starts high, and moves downward as output increases. The older economists thought that average costs began to move upwards again once a certain output was reached, because of the problems of organizing large-scale production. This was because they were thinking of family businesses. Modern thinking is that over a very wide range of output indeed, unit costs can be prevented from rising, but for the purpose of understanding Chamberlin, the U-shaped cost curve may be accepted for the moment.[10] Corresponding to supply is demand, and it needs no effort to grasp that less of any product is bought if it is expensive than if it is cheap. Graphically, therefore, when price is plotted against quantity, the curve must run from a low quantity where price is high to a high quantity where price is low, that is, no demand curve can escape from being negatively inclined.

It may not *seem* so, however, to an individual who can only see a small part of such a curve. Consider 'pure' competition, for which two things are essential: That the number of producers is large, and that there are no differences which matter to any buyer between the output of one particular producer and another. An example is the milk from many different farms which may be collected and pasteurized in the same plant. When an individual producer looks at the demand curve for such a product, *he cannot see the slope in it*, because the quantities which affect the price in either direction are so much greater than those in which he himself deals. The earth *looks* flat to us because of the closeness of our perspective; the demand curve *looks* flat to him for the same reason, although the earth's surface *is* curved and the demand curve *is* always sloped.

In such a situation, no single producer can do anything about the price. Whether he puts his goods on the market or not makes no difference, when identical goods from a multitude of other producers, are available. Consequently, in so far as it affects this single producer, the demand curve *is* flat; it is in fact a straight line at the market price, because this is what this individual producer will get for any quantity he cares to offer. The only part of such a demand curve that matters to a producer – the part he can see – can now be related to his cost curve to find out how he will react to this situation. It is not difficult to see that he will organize his production in such a way as to make his own unit cost equal the going price. The aggregate effect of all producers doing this is that the demand curve is tangent to the cost curve.

This is how the world of buying and selling is organized, according to the competitive model. Chamberlin looked at it and noted that everything the ordinary man means by competition – selling, shading a price, advertising and so on – was not only absent from it, but *could not be included in it*: 'The principles of such a market seem so unreal when applied to the "business" world.' To replace it, he developed his theory of monopolistic competition, and illustrated it by what is now one of the most famous diagrams in the history of economics. (*Fig. 1 on page 17*) 'It is not true', said Chamberlin, 'that in the "business world" a producer is faced with a demand curve which appears to be horizontal (because of his partial perspective of it) nor is it true that those who buy from him are indifferent to what he is producing compared with alternatives available to them'. In so far as his product is at all different from that of others, he, and only he, can supply whatever market there is for it. Moreover, he sees the whole of the demand curve he faces and is aware that it is not the flat line of pure competition, but is negatively inclined. This curve is DD' in Fig. 1. If this and the unit cost curve PP' do not meet somewhere, there is no level of demand which the cost pattern can satisfy. Consequently, for the good to be produced at all, the demand curve must either be tangent to the cost curve PP', or intersect it, as in Chamberlin's diagram. In the first case, it will just pay to

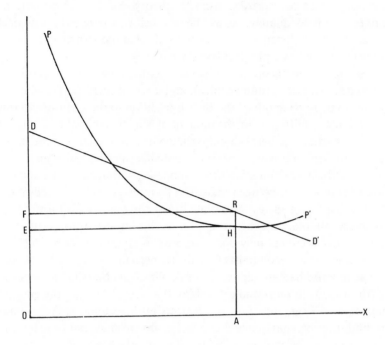

Figure 1

produce the goods in question. However, because the producer controls the supply of the product, he can also decide at what price to sell it. In Chamberlin's diagram, this is represented by R. At this point, monopoly profits will be made. These are represented by the area EHRF (Unit profit multiplied by quantity). To the extent that the product is not replaceable by another identical product from another producer, the mechanism which operates under pure competition to drive the demand curve and the cost curve to tangency is weakened; as a result, monopoly profits of one level or another are present.

Although the demand curve which faces a producer is 'individual' to him, others are free to make more or less close substitutes, and so gain some of his market. The effect of this 'entry' will be to move the demand curve of the first producer downwards to the left. Monopolistic competition, then, is about the adjustment of economic forces between a *group* of competing monopolists, all trying to satisfy much the same demand. Such a group is always small, i.e. the situation is technically known as one of *oligopoly* or few sellers. In such a group then as 'industry'? The question caused much difficulty. Chamberlin never really made up his mind fully on the subject, and this emerges in the treatment of groups in his theory. His assumptions regarding these were that the firms composing them were producing homogeneous products, but he later moved to the view, because of the unreality of these assumptions, that the group concept must be discarded from his theory. Yet he had nothing with which to replace it adequately. As will be seen below, Chamberlin's difficulty arose from the incompleteness of his own insight that modern products have a psychological as well as a physical component.

The next important theoretical advance was therefore to be found in an attempt to deal with this group problem, and it was Robert Triffin who made it.[11] He did so by moving out of the British tradition to the Continental tradition in Economics, shifting from the thought of Marshall to that of Walras and Pareto, from partial to general equilibrium theory, from picturing the firm-in-an-industry to firm-in-a-world. Alfred Marshall's thinking can stand for the British approach. It was limited to firms competing within industries and never extended to competition *between* industries themselves. Yet this kind of competition is a big factor in real economic life – for example, a farmer has to make choices all the time between putting his money into fertilisers or machinery, and a secretary may opt for more new clothes instead of a holiday in the sun. Continental economists had always been more aware of this side of reality. Chamberlin had attempted to break out of the Marshallian stockade, but Triffin was much more radical, taking the step of making the costs and demands of each firm, functions of *all* firms in the economy. According to Triffin, both the cost and demand curves for any product can be affected by *any* other product, not only by products in the same industry (Robinson) or by substitutes close enough to form a recognisable 'group' (Chamberlin). Because he saw competition as essentially a *global relationship* between firms and products, Triffin developed the concept of 'cross-elasticities' between products. These show for example, how the secretary switches her spending to clothes when the price of holidays goes up. At one limit there can be a situation where the quantity of one product bought is quite independent of the price of any other – such a product, in fact, is the output of a monopoly. At the other limit, a product gets the whole market if it can reduce its price without being followed by competitors, but correspondingly loses all its sales if it increases its own price. This, of course, is pure competition – or 'homogeneous competition' as Triffin called it. Between the two is what he calls 'heterogeneous' competition, which he equates – uncritically – with both Robinson's imperfect competition and Chamberlin's monopolistic competition. Where this applies, there is freedom of entry to the market because there is freedom to produce substitutes, and so power to 'enter' is universal.

If Joan Robinson's entrepreneur was at heart a Works Manager, and Chamberlin's a salesman, we can say that with Triffin the Advertising Agent walks on the stage of economics. An advertising agent is concerned with psychological factors even more than a salesman is, because, even though his job is persuasion, the salesman's work is always anchored in the particular *things* his firm is organised to make. Behind him is a *plant*; it may be a plant which makes one thing or a range of things, but it does not make just *anything*. The advertising agent is not constrained in the same way, since he is developing images or 'selling propositions' which often *can* be applied to anything. Sex in advertising, for example, is used to sell cosmetics to women. As any machinery magazine shows, it is also used to sell earth-moving equipment to men. 'Prestige' and humour can also be used effectively in advertising quite different products. For Triffin, then, 'heterogeneous' competition robbed the old concept of the industry (or the Chamberlinian group) totally of significance. His theory therefore added a new dimension to thinking about monopoly, but lost touch with reality by trying to explain all economic facts of life in terms which really only apply to the psychological elements in economically-rooted behaviour. An advertising agent may use sex very successfully in the promotion of bulldozers − but the bulldozers will only sell if they work as well and as economically as those made by competing firms in the earthmoving machinery industry. As one of Triffin's critics put it,

'if we are willing to make Chamberlin's behaviouristic assumptions, forget asset structure, leave out dynamics and ignore coalitions and institutional imperfections, then cross-elasticities would also indicate the form that would be taken by the market behaviour of the competitors.... (these factors)... must be included if a market-form classification is constructed for any applied purpose.'[12]

A modern 'product' is made up of two ingredients, one physical, the other psychological. 'Sales promotion (is) considered as being another product sold to the consumer and enhancing the sales of the advertised product sold jointly with it.' Mrs. Robinson's theory of imperfect competition almost completely ignores the psychological ingredient, Triffin's almost completely ignores the physical product with which this ingredient has to be associated if it is to be turned into money, and Chamberlin's tries to deal with them in combination, even if it is not completely successful. The next major step forward in monopoly theory involved another shift in perspective, made by Lawrence Abbott.[13] For him, 'Chamberlinian monopoly competition theory is a branch of price theory, and therefore excludes a second dimension of competition, which is quality competition.' In his view, the 'exchange process must be regarded as the outcome of desires to satisfy a given set of wants, not the marketing of a given set of goods'. This involves choices by consumers on the basis of quality, but quality choice is unanalysable as long as market preferences are ultimate data for the economist. The analogy is with the geographer, who takes the contours as data, not the geologist, who sets out to explain them. Abbott is an economic geologist. The basic want is desire *for an experience*; a derived want is the good which gives it. Derived wants are a function of basic wants and information about ways of satisfying them. Theoretical work, Abbott claimed, had dealt with uncertainty about quantitative matters, prices, costs, interest rates and incomes, but not about the want-satisfying power of goods, or an entrepreneur's uncertainty as to how far his product suits his customer's needs. Chamberlin had concluded that the position of each producer was monopolistic too early, because he took products, and not *the experiences to which they lead*, as datum.

Concentration on experiences leads Abbott to the idea of 'constellations of wants'. This is needed because 'a want for an experience is in truth not a single want, but a complex of related supplementary wants, usually consisting of a major want plus numerous minor wants.' The 'constellation of wants' approach allows, for example, flavour as well as power to nourish to be taken account of in economics as well as in eating. It is precisely because products are alternative ways of achieving an experience that they can be substitutes for one another. All this has a definite real-world resonance, and enables us to make the inference – since Abbott himself is not explicit – that marketing in the modern sense is changing a 'basic' want into a 'derived' want, or want-for-a-product. Competition is a contest between sellers to deliver an experience in the form of products, in which buyers are the judges. Effective quality competition needs fewer numbers than effective price competition. There can be quite effective quality competition even with only two competitors, as the party-system in politics illustrates. Another stimulating point is that since brands are necessary for *quality* competition, this would be lessened if they were abolished, whatever effect that might have on *price* competition.

For Abbott, monopoly is 'solitariness', and this can be in relation to the psychological or to the physical aspects of a product. Clearly, if no one else can make a physical product which 'performs' nearly as well as that of a particular firm, that firm is virtually alone *in the industry*; but if others are also able to make substantially the same product, then its 'solitariness' is limited to the preferences it can build up amongst consumers *for its brand*. Abbott illustrates this in the following way:

Where little 'solitariness' and little or no power to exclude others from entering the market are found together, there is some approximation to pure competition. Equally, when they are both together and at a maximum, there is monopoly. An innovator rates highly on 'aloneness' (because he is out ahead of the field) but may only have limited power to exclude others from copying him. Where monopolistic competition exists, there is high power to exclude others, coupled with fairly low 'solitariness', because of close substitutes.

All that Abbott claimed for his theory of quality competition was that it is the 'other half' – with price theory – of a complete theory of competition. It was later refined by Kelvin J. Lancaster.[14] And Abbott stressed that

'it deals only with economic conduct that occurs when consumers are to some substantial degree successful in forming and maintaining their own tastes and values, in informing themselves about products, in making use of their reasoning powers, and in avoiding being victimized. If producers can in fact create basic wants and manipulate value systems virtually at will, or if rational calculation of the best means to given ends is an insignificant element in consumers' choice, or if consumers 'information' bears but little resemblance to the objective facts, a

different sort of theory would be needed to explain predictable behaviour.'[15]

This is the real issue of 'marketing' monopoly, as will be discussed in the next
Chapter.

So far, the transport revolution, resulting in specialised production in
factories with clearly identifiable fixed costs, has been seen to be reflected in
theory in the work of Joan Robinson on imperfect competition; next came 'the
substitution of salesmanship for workmanship', which Veblen had noted in the
nineteen-twenties, and which was the real subject-matter of Chamberlin's monopolistic competition. This was refined by Triffin into what was really an
analysis of what Veblen called 'absentee salesmanship' – advertising.[16] The
factors relating to the production of the physical products to be sold (which are
the whole of Joan Robinson's analysis, and still bulk importantly in Chamberlin's) are reduced to virtually nothing in Triffin's book. All three thinkers had
one thing in common, however: They looked at the problem of monopoly from
the standpoint of the firm. It was Abbott's and Lancaster's distinctive contribution to look at it from the point of view of consumers, and to show how
monopolistic organisation appeared from that angle. Paolo Sylos-Labini tried
to view monopoly in a still wider perspective than that of the firm or the
industry, on the one hand, or even of consumers on the other.[17] His objective
was to understand it in the context of the whole economy. Ever since Keynes,
and particularly since his work was fleshed out by that of Simon Kuznets and
others who made national accounts statistics a vital part of the political process
everywhere, what is known as macroeconomics, or the study of economies as a
whole, had developed prodigiously. In one sense, it was a rogue growth, since
only at very few points did it seem possible to link it with the older theories
which concerned themselves with the units which go to make up an economy,
now grouped together as microeconomics. One of Sylos-Labini's main objects
was to bridge the gap between the two disciplines;

> 'by finding some common ground on which they could meet and com-
> bine. The problems of market form, which concerns individual firms,
> and that of effective demand, which concerns the economy as a whole,
> have always been discussed separately. The two questions have been
> tested by two different methods of analysis, microeconomic in neoclas-
> sical, and macroeconomic analysis in Keynesian theory.'[18]

Sylos-Labini calls attention to the independent discovery by Hall and Hitch in
England and Sweezy in America, that the demand curve, *as visualised by an
actual business man*, has a 'kink' at the existing price.[19]

This is because he takes the view that his rival's actions would not be the
same if he increases his price, as they would be if he lowers it. He thinks that in
the first case, they would not follow him, and he would therefore lose
customers to them, but that if he lowered his price they *would* follow him
down. Price, therefore, is not fixed by any elaborate reconciliation between
costs and revenue; the prime factor is the business man's concern with the

actions (or possible actions) of his rivals. This preoccupation obviously depends upon there being few sellers. In pure competition, the sellers are so many that watching them can tell an individual business man nothing; in monopoly there are no rivals to watch; when there are few enough to make watching profitable, there is oligopoly. It was one of Sylos-Labini's most important insights that it is not fewness of numbers in itself, but concern with rivals, which is the heart of oligopolistic behaviour. He distinguishes 'concentrated oligopoly', which is substantially Joan Robinson's imperfect competition situation, in which 'the fundamental objective element of price determination is technology' from 'differentiated oligopoly', which is very much that of the Chamberlinian 'Group'.[20] 'Live and let live' is the rule by which business men operate (here is another point at which theory checks with common experience). Price tends to settle just above the entry-preventing price of the least efficient firm which it is to the advantage of the largest and most efficient firms to let live, and the absolute size of the market is an important determinant of what this price will be. In the long run, this same price both eliminates the least efficient firms from the market, and prevents the entry of outsiders. Because of this 'implicit collusion' between the larger firms to prevent small ones from existing and growing, the profit rate of medium-sized and large firms is well above the minimum and this high rate cannot be eliminated.[21] Sylos-Labini makes the point, echoing Sraffa in his famous article, that within each group of firms, barriers between firms are 'determined by the selling costs involved in acquiring an adequate circle of customers'. These he calls 'installation selling' costs and they are comparable with fixed costs in the plant. If product differentiation also involves a different technology, or vice-versa, then both types of oligopoly exist simultaneously in the same firm, 'thereby accentuating the degree of monopoly.'[22]

At much the same time as Sylos-Labini was writing, J.S. Bain produced empirical endorsement of his theory in a major study of barriers to new competition in the U.S.[23] The most important conclusion from this was that Goodwill is a more important barrier than scale economies, or that scale in advertising is more important than scale in production. Product differentiation is at least as important an impediment to entry as scale economies in production and distribution. The greatest entry barriers owe most to product differentiation. Surprisingly, he found advertising is not the main key to this, less surprisingly, that Patents are unimportant. Patents, resources control, know-how and management expertise are all distinctly less important − absolutely and relatively − than product differentiation and scale. Sylos-Labini's view of restrictions on entry is very much the same as Bain's, and he summarises it in terms of the necessity for potential entrants to have to count from the outset on a relatively large volume of sales. 'Ultimately, the (entry) barrier lies in the size of the market itself'. Linked with this, the firms already in the market do not aim at maximising profits, but look for a target rate of profit. This Sylos-Labini thinks, is the one 'in which no individual firm tries to grow to the detriment of the other firms, so as not to provoke acts of retaliation'. This is evocative of Galbraith's comment that when a business man takes into account the reactions of his competitors, he is thinking of 'what is good for the industry' and this is monopolistic thinking.[24]

Sylos-Labini advanced technical monopoly theory, in the first place, by showing how concern with rivals, and not just fewness of numbers, is the essence of oligopoly, and then by stressing the way in which collusion, implicit or explicit, to keep outsiders from entering a market, is a real factor. Two further aspects of his contribution, relating to innovation and to the effects the existence of oligopoly has upon the economy as a whole, however, are at least equally important.

Schumpeter had been the first to articulate explicitly the dependence of innovation on monopoly, since nothing else can offer the prospect of high profit from high risk investment. Innovation, in turn, is the 'powerful lever that expands output and brings down prices'.

Sylos-Labini took Schumpeter's thinking a stage further, noting that the effects of innovation are by no means always translated into more output and lower prices. More often they are reflected in higher wages or profits in firms when the oligopolistic mechanism of few sellers prevails. In agriculture, on the other hand, where competition in the 'pure' sense of many sellers is the norm, the situation is quite different:

> 'In industry, the prevailing tendency is for the fruits of technical progress to be distributed through rising money incomes rather than through falling prices, in agriculture the prevailing tendency is for prices to fall. The exchange ratio between agricultural and industrial prices thus tends to deteriorate for agriculture, and this is precisely the opposite of what would happen under the classical mechanism (of pure competition) and what in fact did happen during the whole of the nineteenth century.'[25]

The same, of course, can apply to industrial raw materials, to the detriment of the Third World. Perhaps the most important aspect of this distortion is the way in which profits become transformed into executive salaries, which

> 'are not a mere remuneration for the services of men of outstanding or even exceptional ability, nor are they in any way related to some fictitious "marginal productivity" of these services; these salaries do, in effect, incorporate part of the extra profits of oligopoly and are a status symbol (as the sociologists say) of business managers. As such, they are almost a necessity of the system...'

To capture a substantial share of the profits in this way requires that there be implicit collusion between managements, in their own interests rather than that of shareholders, but as noted earlier, Sylos-Labini sees this type of collusion everywhere in oligopolistic organisation. The introduction of innovations, he considers, is also greatly affected by this factor, to the extent that there is a bias in the system in favour of investing in new things which save costs on the existing pattern of output, rather than on things which expand output. This is because of the prevalence of 'live and let live', as the working philosophy of the group or industry. Only when the reward of getting a new thing done is so great as to tempt a firm to 'break the line' will investment be made in output-increasing innovations. In technical terms, except with regard to innovations that greatly reduce marginal cost, oligopoly exerts a selective action against output-increasing and in favour of factor-saving innovations.

What effects does the existence of widespread oligopoly have on the economy as a whole? For Sylos-Labini, by far the most important is what it does to employment, and on this point his work was remarkably prophetic. Theoretically, under pure competition, any improvement in productivity should be balanced by an increase in consumption and total money demand which keeps the number of jobs stable. In practice, of course, this has never happened, and full employment, being associated with the height of the boom, has been a feature of unbalanced situations, not stable ones. Historically, average unemployment in Britain from 1850-1914 was 5.5% of the labour force, in the U.S. from 1890-1914 around 7%. These levels, however, are low compared with those reached during the period between the two Wars, when at one time the U.S. figure was 20%.

Sylos Labini's first hypothesis to explain this is that

'the forces tending to absorb unemployment were weakened because the field of action of the oligopolistic mechanism expanded at the expense of the classical mechanism of competition...What it all comes to is that in modern conditions any economy based on private enterprise is likely to go on expanding only if private enterprise is stimulated from the outside. Yet these economies must go on expanding lest increases in productivity be translated into rising unemployment'.[26]

During the inter-war period the external stimulation was inadequate, but the War (and then the Cold War) later raised government spending to such a level as to prove what Keynes had called his 'grand experiment'. U.S. public expenditure, for example, which has been 7.4% of Gross National Product in 1903, is now heading for 40%. For Sylos-Labini, there is no difference between the chronic unemployment of the advanced countries before the War, and the structural unemployment of the underdeveloped countries. Both are due to the process of concentration, which accentuates the discontinuities of technology and generates oligopoly, so weakening the forces tending to reabsorb the workers displaced by new machines. In any agricultural economy, he holds, investment only causes inflation.[27]

'The social problem which oligopolistic concentration creates, Sylos-Labini concludes,

'is not that the individual large oligopolistic firms stand in the way of technical progress, for when all is said and done, in this respect they deserve Schumpeter's praise. Nor is it that they pay their workers low wages. The social problem of oligopoly.... resides in the oligopolistic firms' price and cost policies, in the particular way in which the forms of technical progress achieved by oligopolistic firms are distributed throughout the economy, and in the imbalance which this distribution creates.'[28]

If Sylos-Labini is right that the most important thing about oligopoly is that business men are more concerned with the way their rivals will react to something they themselves do, than with the reactions of consumers, then it is this activity, rather than demand in relation to oligopoly, which should yield to study. Concern with what a rival or rivals will do is of course the essence of playing games, and in 1944, von Neumann and Morgenstern had produced their famous *Theory of Games and Economic Behaviour*. However, it was not until the appearance of *The Theory of Imperfect Competition: A Radical Reconstruction*, by Donald Dewey, in 1969, that many of the practical implications of game theory for monopoly were drawn. Dewey's main thesis is that oligopoly is intrinsically *an unstable state*. In the U.S., for example, it is 'largely a product of the American antitrust laws. There is nothing natural about the stable co-existence of the Big Three in automobiles, Big Four in cigarettes, and so on. A rapid consolidation and rationalisation of such industries would follow the repeal of the American legal restrictions on mergers and cartels'.[29] In the absence of external forces, then, competition as a *process* will destroy competition as a *state*, and history confirms this. Dewey develops a convincing geometry to describe the interactions of businesses operating a number of different plants, by which he is able to show that once entry of new firms can be prevented by some means, then the industry will move, *in the absence of some legal restriction on freedom of contract*, to a technically efficient monopoly. This will take the form of a profit-sharing cartel. Sensible firms opt for the levels of price and output which keep other firms out, no more, no less. 'Stay-out pricing *is* the competitive process in operation'.[30] The only way to be sure an industry will consist of more than one firm is to ban war between firms, joint maximation of profits and stay-out pricing.

If this is rational conduct for firms, why then does entry ever occur at all, as it so evidently does in the real world? This happens, in Dewey's view, because of uncertainty about the future. Uncertainty, indeed, is the other factor, apart from the anti-trust laws, which keeps oligopoly from turning into monopoly. Risk for statisticians is when all concerned believe they have all needed information, have full confidence in it, and all act upon the same data. But business men are in uncertainty, have different tastes for it, different amounts of data, and different degrees of belief in their data. This is where games theory comes in, because the estimate of the cost of entry made by the managers of the established firm may differ from that of the challenger from outside. Various strategies are open to the parties, and according to good game practice, they will choose out of a number which promise the same maximum gain, the one which also offers the highest minimum. But since business men are not in a statistician's risk situation, but in a situation of uncertainty, they must operate by decision rules or 'rules of thumb'. Because of this, an established firm may set output too low and the 'stay-out price' too high in relation to the decision rules of an outsider, who then enters the market. For another outsider, the judgment of the established firm may have been right, and the price and output in question do in fact cause him to sheer off. Yet a third outsider may put off a decision, by investing in additional information. Dewey claims that once we accept that in objectively similar circumstances, business men will behave differently when a decision involves uncertainty, we can no longer assign much meaning to the assumption, widely used in economics, that 'maximising profit' is their primary objective. Competition is better viewed, he thinks, as a search for information, since all definitions of competitive activity that are applicable to the real world carry the connotation of exploratory behaviour designed to produce information about the market and the reactions of rivals in it. The corollary of this is that 'the preservation of competition necessarily requires the maintenance of a constant quantity of uncertainty in the system'.[31] This marries with the conclusion arrived at from a quite different starting-point by another writer, that 'uncertainty and risk aversion are the reasons why small firms exist alongside the giants'.

Now, the fulcrum about which the lever of uncertainty moves the market is entry, and this leads to the overwhelming importance of potential competition for drawing the sting from monopoly. As long ago as 1907, J.B. Clark had praised

> 'monopoly in form but not in fact, for it is shorn of its injurious power, and the thing that holds it firmly in check is *potential competition*. The fact that a rival *can* appear and *will* appear if the price goes above the reasonable level at which it stands, induces the corporation to produce goods enough to keep the price at that level. Under such a nearly ideal condition the public would get the full benefit of the economy which very large production gives, notwithstanding that no actual competition would go on'.[32]

Free entry, Dewey himself says, will bring price and unit cost as close to equality as demand and optimum size of plant allow. Entry is linked with uncertainty, and information is the opposite of uncertainty. For this reason, he also uses modern information theory to throw light on monopoly.

This equates uncertainty with 'entropy' or disorder in the system, and information is what removes uncertainty. The *information content* of a message is thus different for different people; in the case, for example, that an individual already possesses the knowledge, the information content of a message is zero. Modern information theory thus always equates information with *news*. Under perfect competition the cost of information is zero and there is no uncertainty. In the real world, on the other hand, there *is* uncertainty and information does have a cost. Firms will therefore cease their information-gathering at a point which stops short of eliminating all the entropy that it is theoretically possible to remove. There are many forces at work to *destroy* information, countering the gain in information as production continues through time. These include death and forgetting, change in consumer tastes, and *innovation*.[33] This deterioration tends to restore the uncertainty which 'learning by doing' removes, and so balances the trend to monopoly which is the inevitable result of information gain, by opening up possibilities for new entry to the industry. Competition, indeed, can never be separated from information, and the cost of market information is always a factor, – it is zero only in perfect competition, one reason why this cannot exist in the real world.

Most of these thinkers share a common liberal tradition to one degree or another, but what of the Marxist view of monopoly? One valuable statement of it is that of Baran and Sweezy, which is concerned to show that

> 'an output the volume and composition of which are determined by the profit maximisation policies of oligopolistic corporations neither corresponds to human needs nor costs the minimum possible amount of human toil and suffering'.[34]

Marx himself had not seen much of a future for monopoly because, like the classical economists, he thought of monopolies as the remants of feudalism. He certainly did not foresee the effect which capitalist technology and research and development would have, so that his prophecy that capitalism would wither away because of a falling rate of profit has been completely confounded. In contrast to Marx, Lenin was alert to where monopoly could lead – he called imperialism 'the monopoly stage of capitalism' – and it is this, according to these authors, which accounts for the contemporary strength of the Leninist-Maoist forms of Marxism. Traditional Marxist social science has stagnated, they think, because it has accepted the assumption of a *competitive* capitalist economy through relying too much on the Master's thought as expressed in Capital. Marx's followers are, nevertheless, still able to use his concept of surplus value, which includes primarily profits plus interest plus rent, and secondarily elements such as revenues of Governments, of churches, of the financial sector, and of unproductive workers – once can easily sense that all these groups have something in common. According to empirical studies made by J.D. Phillips for these authors, total surplus value in the U.S., which was significantly under half of national output in the twenties, is now significantly *more* than half of it. Within the total, however, the secondary elements have grown at the expense of the primary ones. Monopoly capitalism, in the Marxist view, has 'a chronic inability to absorb as much surplus as it is capable of creating' and is therefore self-contradictory. It turns the economic problem on its head by making it, not how best to use scarce resources, but how to dispose of the products of super-abundant resources.

Population growth in itself is no answer, since it does not create investment outlets fast enough to absorb its contribution to the employment pool. Nor will invention and innovation fill the gap, because modern business can finance all or nearly all of the costs of these from depreciation allowances without the need for new investment at all. (It is interesting to recall here that Sylos-Labini claims that it is only *major* innovations which require an increase in the total volume of investment). And foreign investment, if properly done, *creates* wealth rather than absorbing it – the oil firm of Jersey–Standard had one third of its assets abroad by 1958, but these produced two-thirds of its profits. So, according to Baran and Sweezy, the enormous power of surplus-creation inherent in monopoly capital, has to be absorbed by the costs of salesmanship in all its forms, of government, and of militarism and imperialism, and they are not at all impressed by the kind of society which this produces. In their view, it only confirms Marx's contention that capitalism generates wealth at one pole, poverty at another. And, as monopoly capitalism develops, they hold, there will be less demand for low grade labour and so people like Negroes will be worse off. Thus the Marxist criticism of monopoly in practice, centres on precisely those aspects of society that worry many people to-day. It is, of course, possible to give all due credit to Marxist diagnosis without agreeing with Marxist cure, as Chapter V will attempt to demonstrate.

Reference to the concept of economic rent are scattered throughout the economic literature on monopoly, and are of great importance for understanding it, and the innovation which it makes possible. This concept is in fact an essential component of the political economy of innovation. Rent is the financial aspect of monopoly and oligopoly. Joan Robinson calls it the surplus earned by a particular part or a factor of production over and above the minimum earnings necessary to induce it to do its work; alternatively, in her view, it is due to 'inelasticity'. Stigler defines it as the excess of the return from the best use of a productive service over the return from other possible uses.[35] An illustration often quoted compares the very high earnings of an individual who happens to be a film star, with what he would obtain in the ordinary job which may be all that he is fitted for otherwise. Marshall restricted the application of the word 'rent' to the free gifts of nature which are clearly limited in amount, and he invented the term 'quasi-rent' for application to productive devices made by man. Dewey prefers to use 'rent inherent in the fixed costs of the plant' as an alternative way of describing what is often called 'monopoly profit', to convey that the difference achieved between total cost and total revenue 'is neither accidental nor temporary'. Marshall's use of 'quasi-rent' was precisely to indicate when the nature of the income flow *was* temporary. *In the long run*, Marshall believed, all quasi-rent would be changed into costs. Indeed, he was ahead of Dewey in seeing the greater part of what are commonly called the profits of a business as quasi-rent, partly the earnings of ability:

> 'In some cases and for some purposes, nearly the whole income of a business may be regarded as quasi-rent, that is, an income determined by the state of the market for its wares, with but litle reference to the cost of preparing for their work the various things and persons engaged in it.'[36]

In the light of this analysis the word 'profit' loses much of its meaning when it is applied to the modern corporation. So much so, that an economist of the standing of Milton Friedman does not use the word at all, but only refers to 'actual and expected non-contractual costs':

'Finally,' he says, 'there are payments whose amount depends upon the actual receipts of the firm; these we shall call "Non-contractual costs." The actual non-contractual costs can never be determined in advance... It is therefore important to distinguish between actual non-contractual costs and expected non-contractual costs. The difference between actual and expected non-contractual costs constitutes "Profits" or "pure profits" – an unanticipated residual arising from uncertainty. Expected non-contractual costs on the other hand, are to be regarded as a 'rent' or 'quasi-rent' to entrepreneurial capacity. They are to be regarded as the motivating force behind the firm's decisions.'[37]

The truth of the matter seems to be that for the investment under uncertainty to which any given flow of income is to be referred if this flow is to be called profit, a longer time-scale than is common must in general be used; it is necessary to look further back into the firm's history, even to its very origins. As so often, Schumpeter saw this point earlier and more clearly than anyone else. 'It is not' he said, 'the running of the business according to the new plan is the source of profit; it is getting it to run on the new plan in the first place'. In Schumpeter's theory, the most important kind of innovation always meant a radical break with past ways of doing things, which is different from the marginal improvements over time that are part of any technical process. For Schumpeter, innovation is always a jump, a discontinuity in the measurable aspects of the activity under examination, often involving a change in direction. Such a new way of doing things creates an immediate degree of uniqueness of advantage or market power for the individual or firm which is first off the mark, and this will last until all competitors have adopted the new method. While it lasts, the innovator will receive an extra income because of his uniqueness of advantage, and more or less proportional to it. Can this be attributed, in each accounting time-period, to a return from investment under uncertainty in that period? Hardly. It makes much more sense to regard it as the *continuing* financial results over time of the original 'jump'. In so far as this 'jump' involved uncertainty, or uncertainty reduced to its calculable elements, which is risk, this related to a possible flow of money in the future, over a number of accounting periods. This flow can be regarded as being potentially there, though unrealized, at the single point in time when the translation to the new and advantageous method of working was made. Theoretically, at least, it could have been capitalized at that time. The increase in the money flow over time is therefore a rent attributable to the uniqueness of advantage – market power – achieved at one point in time *by the innovation*. More precisely, it would be a quasi-rent, following Marshall's usage, because it will only last for a limited time. Some future innovation will eventually render it obsolete in its turn.

Information concerning the fruitful organisation of resources is an asset of any firm – perhaps its most valuable one. A firm can invest (under considerable uncertainty) in the production of new information concerning the way to deploy its resources. Once the new way of using resources – Schumpeter's 'new plan' – has been devised and proved to work, there is henceforward much less uncertainty about operating accordingly, yet the gap between revenue and costs widens, as the firm 'moves along the learning curve'. Consequently, the surplus return from such use cannot be called profit. Theoretically, the same resources could be combined in a different way – say the way of the 'old plan' – with a smaller return. The difference between the two returns is a rent attributable to the use of the information available to the firm in its best way rather than in the next best way. In other words, this difference is a rent or quasi-rent of information. Schumpeter regards the establishment of a new monopoly as the true activity of the entrepreneur. Once this is done, the same individual may concentrate on management, which amounts to *maximising* the rents arising from the monopoly, but he is then no longer exercising his entrepreneurial function in the strict sense. Profit from founding a business and permanent return are distinguished in practice; the former is the capitalized value of the monopoly, the latter is just the return in accounting periods from the monopoly condition – 'attributable to those natural or social forces on which the monopoly position rests'.[38] Schumpeter regarded economic life as a circular flow, and in this flow, there is no room for any 'profit' over the value of the services of labour and land it incorporates – due to competition and to imputation of returns to the various factors used. As soon as producers realize a permanent profit, they must value correspondingly the means of production to which they owe it.

Note that Schumpeter recognized that a monopoly position could rest upon 'social' as well as a 'natural' forces. Such social forces, to be considered particularly in Chapter III, are invariably expressed in terms of positive law, such as the laws which underwrite Patents for invention, or the registration of Trade Marks. Schumpeter's point will be expanded to the claim that much of the excess of sales over the cost of sales in any business, should not be thought of as 'profit' but as rent attributable to, for example, a Trade Mark or Brand. The establishment of a new business, as he saw it, had as its essential characteristic the element of uniqueness of advantage or monopoly, rather than any form of organisational structure. In his earlier writings, he saw the new monopoly as being expressed in a new firm, and in his famous theory of 'creative destruction', 'the competition from new firms strikes at the very life' of the old ones. This was because his thought was formed in the hey-day of Patents, which then lent themselves to a pattern of economic expansion through the formation of new firms. However, he lived into the era of the multi-product firm, which relied much more upon innovations which were protected by 'capability' or 'marketing'. In later years, therefore, he recognised that the change was so fundamental as to require a modification of that original formulation of his ideas. To sum up, then, all successful innovation results in rents or quasi-rents, which produce a continuing flow of funds over time. Much of what the Stock Exchange counts as 'profit' is really the rent for a period (say a year) arising from some past innovation. As innovations increase in numbers, as they do in the multi-product firm, the fluctuations from year to year are damped down; only unexpected *variations* in the aggregate of these rents has any claim to be truly called 'profit'.

This has never been put better than by G.L.S. Shackle, after a lifetime devoted to reflection on the nature of uncertainty, of profit and of business success:

> 'Not necessarily wholly rejected in expectation, profit must be something surprising... expectation must consist in a range of diverse possibilities for every envisaged outcome. Profit is the registering of the failure of that range to be capacious enough. Profit is history's irony'.[39]

In contrast, the underlying continuing reality of returns on investment, is the largely predictable element of Rent. Rent is market power in action; it is the dynamic aspect of the reality that, looked at in static terms, is market power; rent is the *process*, market power the *state*. It is rent, not profit, that modern business is all about, and the only economic point of innovation is the generation of rents.

This shift in perspective from profits to rents in respect of a modern firm's surplus of revenues over costs, is vital to understanding how innovation is related to politics. Because of past innovations, the world of the modern corporation is a world of rents. Governments are enabled to expand their areas of involvement because rents lend themselves to being taxed. Employees wrest a share of the firm's rent from its owners, with the result that there is now a large growing element of rent in all wages and salaries. This rent element, in its turn, provides the purchasing power for innovations in products that depend upon discretionary income, and so on. Any modern economy is therefore a high-rent, high tax economy, with a pattern of economic innovation which reflects these characteristics. When, however, this pattern no longer corresponds to the innovation which the times require, the result is economic crisis, and the contemporary version of this will be discussed in Chapter IV.

One reason why economists in general may have not made more of rent in relation to monopoly is that a rent has to be imputed to some productive factor, and it has not always been immediately clear to them to which factor the rent which they could see to be inherent in monopoly profit was to be attributed. They tried hard. Marx has the idea of rents being earned by superior management, and Marshall spoke of 'the quasi-rents of ability.' But Joan Robinson would not allow that rent of entrepreneurship was part of the expenses of production, rather it was part of monopoly profit – as W.J. Baumol also held. R.J. Hawtrey tried to reconcile the differences by regarding all business incomes as the 'rent of ability considered as selling power. Selling power is the co-efficient on which the profitmakers' income above all depends'.[40] But what gives 'selling power'? It must be a special kind of monopoly, since it produces rent. It is *marketing* monopoly, and the missing productive factor, as will be shown in detail in the next chapter, is to be found in *legal protection for reputation*. Monopolistic competition, as Chamberlin insisted, is the result of product differentiation. Whenever this is involved, it will be found that the resulting rent can be explicitly imputed either to a Registered Trade Mark or to an exact equivalent, on which this differentiation is always based to-day. Although Chamberlin did not formally link rent, monopoly and Trade Marks all together, he did realise that there was a connection between them. He observed that Goodwill, not competition, is the fundamental legal right. In *The Theory of Monopolistic Competition*, he devoted a complete Appendix (E) to the monopolies created by industrial property legislation, and also referred to them in the body of his book:

> 'Both Patents and Trade Marks may be conceived of as pure monopoly elements of the goods to which they are attached: The competitive elements in both cases are the similarities between these goods and others.'

He also saw which of these 'social forces' was the more important:

> 'merely to suggest such a comparison is to raise serious doubts as to whether the monopoly element in Patents is even quantitatively as important as that in Trade Marks.'[41]

He understood that the possibilities of monopolistic profits are increased by the presence of advertising, although he did not advert to how much the presence of advertising is due to the Registered Trade Mark. Chapter III will explain how this is what effectively gives a monopoly in the supply of advertising for a particular product.

Chamberlin saw all selling costs as the result of attempts to create a new scheme of wants by rearranging the consumers' motives; 'those made to adapt the product to the demand are costs of production; those made to adapt the demand to the product are costs of selling.'[42] By developing differentiation, these selling costs make one product less óf a perfect substitute for another:

> 'In monopolistic competition there can be freedom of entry only in the sense of freedom to produce substitutes; and in this sense freedom of entry is universal, since substitutes are only a matter of degree.'[43]

But if as a result of selling and differentiating activity, perfect substitutes are not available, demand curves will be to the right of their tangency point with cost curves, and profits will be 'supernormal'. 'This is the explanation of *all* monopoly profits of whatever sort'. Imperfect competition always involves fixed costs in the firm − sometimes represented by plant, sometimes by erecting and maintaining non-physical costs of barriers to entry by others, or 'installation selling expenses', as Sylos-Labini called them. And just as Dewey prefers to replace the term 'monopoly profit' by the phrase 'rent inherent in fixed costs in the plant', when talking about imperfect competition, so in the monopolistic competition case, it is equally possible to speak of rent inherent in the fixed costs of the 'installation selling expenses'. Another way of putting it is to say that the firm, insofar as it is making something, is in a situation of imperfect competition, because there are fixed costs in its plant. It also has to sell its output, and if it does this in a pure competition situation, it incurs no selling costs. But if it seeks to escape from the discipline of pure competition, by building differentiation into its product so as to make it attractive to one segment of consumers rather than another, and *at the same time* taking steps to make those consumers prefer the product to others, then the firm does have selling costs. Moreover, these selling costs are of such a nature that a large proportion are independent of the absolute volume of sales. On advertising, for example, which is one of the most important ways of building product differentiation, H.R. Edwards concluded from his study of the British soap and detergent industry, that

> 'where buyer preferences are built mainly on advertising, there is in general some *necessary minimum* of advertising expenditure which must be undertaken if the firm is to remain effectively "in the market" − a sum which is thus independent in the main of any particular firm's volume of sales, and which is large in absolute amount'.[44]

One way of regarding monopolistic competition, then, is as the special case of imperfect competition when the imperfection relates to the 'psychological ingredient' of the product, i.e. to the way people think and feel about it. At the level of the physical product, in pure competition, even more in 'perfect' competition, which assumes full knowledge in addition, there is no 'psychological ingredient', and all that consumers can think about any individual product is that it is just the same as any other. This being the case, they can hardly *feel* differently about it either. But there can be a good approximation to pure competition at the psychological level, whilst at the physical level, competition may be very imperfect. Cement is a good example of this. It is a homogeneous product, generally made to a public standard specification, nobody gets very emotional about it, there are substantial economies of scale in its manufacture, and it is not cheap to transport to where it is required. These last two factors make the market for cement an imperfect one, in spite of the fact that its homogeneous nature and the number of plants might seem to make it a candidate for pure or perfect competition. As Chamberlin put it, the cement industry in terms of numbers, is highly competitive, but once the spatial element is introduced it is highly imperfect. If firms in the cement business now seek to introduce an element of manipulation of demand, for example, by putting persuasive salesmen on the road, to the extent they are adding a degree of monopolistic competition to the imperfect competition which is already there. Most real life situations are combinations of imperfect and monopolistic competition, because most real-life 'products' are combinations of physical and psychological ingredients. Both types of competition have their appropriate fixed costs, and these fixed costs form a barrier to entry to the market from the outside, because any potential entrant has to be able to meet them in his own operation. Investment in plant of big enough capacity may be the barrier in the case of steel, since marketing costs are low; in contrast, plant costs are hardly a barrier at all in the case of cosmetics, but the investment in advertising and promotion is correspondingly greater. In both cases, the barrier to be overcome lies in scale. In one case this is in manufacturing, in the other, in selling, and in both of them the rents earned by those inside the barrier, are attributable to the fixed costs which have been incurred in achieving a particular scale of operation.

With the outstanding exception of Schumpeter, the relevance of market power to innovation has often been missed by economists. This is because so much of their attention is directed to the way in which resources are used and distributed in an economy whose existence is taken for granted. The dominant naoion of equilibrium carries with it the connotation of a snapshot of the economic process or machine at a particular instant in time, with the slowest-moving parts being the most clearly defined. This is especially true of the welfare economists, in spite of the fact that their static measure

> 'is not the only or necessarily the most important criterion; and in particular, that a market situation must also be evaluated, among other possible criteria, in terms of the extent to which it affords a stimulus to continuing technological progress – the *dynamic* criterion... it is apparent from the very arithmetic of growth that even a small but cumulative gain over time in the productivity of a given quantum of productive resources may contribute substantially more to increasing economic welfare than any conceivable reallocation of given resources with unchanged technique in accordance with the conditions of the static welfare criterion'.[45]

What is vital, therefore, is the combination of markets and interference with markets that will give such a growth in welfare over the long term. As the Harvard Program on Technology and Society put it:

> 'Corporations foster their own growth by generating demand both for their existing products and for new products, while at the same time exploring new ways of producing their existing products and developing the technology for producing new products. In other words, following the original ideas of Joseph Schumpeter, the process of growth is the process of innovation.'

And the process of innovation, of course, can do no other than reflect the processes which generate market power so that investment in innovation can be a rational act. All such processes can be categorized in three ways.

Firstly, there is the market power which arises from investment in productive assets, which may be called the market power of capability. Next is the type of market power (or capacity to exclude others from entering a market) which arises from some identifiable ordinance of the State. It may be a Patent for invention, an exploration licence, a planning (building) permission, or any similar piece of protection. This type of market power may appropriately be designated Specific. Thirdly, there is the market power which results from investment in changing consumer preference or shifting the demand curve. Sylos-Labini's phrase for this type of investment, it will be recalled, is 'installation selling expenses'. Its objective and result may be called Persuasive market power, or marketing monopoly. Economic theory has so far been able to contribute very little to the understanding of this type of market power, and consequently even less to that of the innovation which depends upon it.

One cause of this gap has undoubtedly been the use of a definition of innovation that is too narrow. All economic innovation must be understood in the very broadest sense of "getting new things done". In particular, it must not be restricted to *technological* innovation. The years since the last War have seen an unprecedented number of 'new things' that are outside the technological area. They are the result of marketing, and the capacity to 'unmake the market' that makes them possible is the market power of persuasion. The results of this type of market power are now so important, and yet so little understood, that it will be necessary to devote the whole of the next chapter to an attempt to fill some of the gaps in economists' thinking in relation to it. Only when that has been done, will it be possible to present all three types of market power – Capability, Specific and Persuasive, in terms of their respective roots in positive law, and consequently of their place in the political economy of innovation.

Notes

1. cf. Kingston W.: Innovation. London: John Calder, (1977).
2. Sutton A.C.: Western Technology and Soviet Economic Development. Stanford, California: 1968-73.
3. Sraffa P.: In Economic Journal XXXVI (1926) 535.
4. Stigler G.: Essays in the History of Economics. Chicago (1965) p. 14.
5. Smith Adam: The Wealth of Nations, Book I Ch. 10 (ii).
6. Dewey D.: The Theory of Imperfect Competition: A Radical Reconstruction. New York (1969) p. 191.
7. Robinson Joan: The Economics of Imperfect Competition. London (1933).
8. Chamberlin E.H.: The Theory of Monopolistic Competition. Cambridge (Mass.) 1933. 6th ed. London 1949.
9. Dewey op. cit. p. xi.
10. Edwards H.R.: in Oxford Economic Papers (1955) p. 113.
    Worcester Jr. D.A.: Monopoly, Big Business and Welfare in the Post War U.S. Seattle (1967) p. 83.
11. Triffin R.: Monopoly Competition and General Equilibrium Theory. Cambridge, Mass. (1968).
12. Shubik M.: Strategy and Market Structure. New York (1959) p. 32.
13. Abbott Lawrence: Quality and Competition. New York (1955).
14. Lancaster Kelvin J.: in Journal of Political Economy (1965) p. 133.
15. Abbott op. cit. p. 214.
16. Veblen T.: Absentee Ownership. London edn. (1924) pp. 72, 312.
17. Sylos-Labini Paolo: Oligopolic e Progresso Technico. Milan (1957).
    English Trans: Cambridge, Mass. (1962).
18. ibid. p. 213.
19. In Oxford Economic Papers (1939).
20. Sylos Labini op. cit. p. 35.

21. ibid. p. 52.
22. ibid. p. 56.
23. Bain J.S.: Barriers to New Competition. Cambridge Mass. (1956).
24. Galbraith J.K.: American Capitalism. London (1952) p. 42.
25. Sylos-Labini op. cit. p. 125.
26. ibid. p. 214.
27. ibid. pp. 160, 20.
28. ibid. p. 170.
29. Dewey op. cit. p. 59.
30. ibid. p. 128.
31. ibid. p. 184. cf. R.A. Jenner in Economic Journal 76 (1966) p. 786.
32. Clark J.B.: Essentials of Economic Theory. New York (1907) p. 380.
33. Dewey op. cit. p. 113.
34. Baran P.A. and Sweezy P.M.: Monopoly Capital. London (1966) pp. 18, 114, 109, 142.
35. Stigler G.J.: Theory of Price. New York (1946) p. 99.
36. Principles of Economics Book VI Ch. VIII Sections 8-10.
37. Friedman M.: Price Theory – A Provisional Text. Chicago (1962) p. 99.
38. Schumpeter J.A.: Theory of Economic Development. Cambridge, Mass. (1934) p. 152.
39. Shackle G.L.S.: On the Nature of Profit. London: Woolwich Economic Papers (1967) p. 26.
40. In Economica (N.S.) X (1943) p. 222.
41. Chamberlin op. cit. p. 61.
42. ibid. p. 123.
43. ibid. p. 201.
44. Edwards H.R.: Competition and Monopoly in the British Soap Industry. Oxford (1962) p. 29, n. 1.
45. ibid. p. 12.

CHAPTER II

Marketing and the power to innovate

In the literature of innovation, marketing might just as well not exist. There are a number of reasons for this. Economists' treatment of marketing itself has been very patchy, especially when compared to the amount of effort they have expended on economic growth and technical change; the bulk of the literature on marketing deals with techniques, and is notoriously shy of the definitions and vocabulary that would enable it to be placed in the wider context of economic discussion. Marketing men themselves like to justify the way in which they make their living by a particular description of their trade. They say that it is the activity of finding out what people need and then seeing to it that products are developed which satisfy those needs. This largely false description then becomes accepted by many others. There is almost total lack of awareness that marketing as we know it, is rooted in specific legislation and international agreement. These were touched upon in the previous chapter, and will be discussed further in the next one. Marketing is not, as many business men think it is, in any sense part of the natural structure of the universe. It is a by-product of one particular system of property rights. Specialist students of innovation, for their part, are still grappling with technology, on the emergence of which there is all too little empirical information. It is hardly surprising, therefore, that the added complexities of marketing have been neglected by them.

Yet marketing is one of the most important of all sources of innovation today, both in itself and in the way in which it reinforces other types of market power. This arises from the manner in which it enables products to escape from the constraints which the market seeks to impose. Marketing is emphatically about "unmaking" markets, not about making them. It operates by erecting highly effective barriers to entry, which in turn generate economic rents, and wherever rent is in prospect, innovation is a possibility. Where large rents can be foreseen, investment at above-average risk (the kind of investment that is inescapably associated with innovation) can be considered rationally. An investor can see that to the extent that he is alone in being involved in R & D and/or product development, he will emerge alone when there is a developed product ready to be sold. That is, he will be some sort of monopolist, and will earn Rent. Modern marketing is a most fruitful source of rents, and consequently of innovation.

Some of this innovation is of a special type, reflecting the special kind of market power − the market power of persuasion − that has brought it into being. However, marketing also underwrites innovation by the way in which it reinforces the market power of capability, the type of market power which results from investment in productive assets. When combined with secrecy, capability and persuasive market power together offer a means of "unmaking the market", and thus rendering innovation possible, that is more comprehensive and more reliable than all but the very strongest kinds of Specific market power. Certainly, for a large and increasing volume of technology, and over most of the present century, this threefold combination has been replacing Patents as the means of erecting barriers to entry to markets, and therefore justifying risky investment. Where innovation is in prospect, this combination is increasingly the one that business men take most seriously as means for justifying their investment.

Marketing, then, is most intelligible when seen simply as a particular way of exercising economic power. The authors of its textbooks are as notoriously reluctant to accept this as they are to define their terms with precision. This applies especially to the words 'market' and 'marketing', and to the areas of 'disposable' or 'discretionary' income and 'development' of markets. The existence of the money which marketing techniques are aimed at tapping, is taken for granted, but little or no attention is paid to how this 'disposable' or 'discretionary' income arises in the first place. Also, whilst discussion of the techniques is likely to take it for granted that they are used in 'developing' markets, this discussion frequently lacks any rigorous analysis of where precisely the differences are, between an 'undeveloped' market on the one hand, and a 'developed' one on the other. These gaps must be filled if the way in which marketing augments the power to innovate is to be properly understood.

On the question of discretionary income, the first point to be made is that it can only be income which contains a substantial element of rent. Those who own property will obviously be collecting rents from it, possibly in the form of royalties or dividends. An even larger class of people, however, will be those whose salaries or wages contain a rent element, thus giving them discretionary income. What is the source of this rent? It can only come from the firm or other undertaking in which they work, and then only in so far as that undertaking itself generates rent. Since the source of all rent is market power, we can speak of the *Primary* market power of the undertaking, and the *Derived* market power of its managers and employees. Just how these two types of market power are related will be discussed further below. At this stage, however, it will be helpful to introduce another element into the vocabulary that is being developed. This is also drawn from economics, and is the concept of *Surplus*. Producer's surplus is equivalent to Rent. Consumers' surplus is just the opposite: It is the difference between what a buyer pays for something, and what he would have been willing to pay if forced to his limit. Another useful definition of Marketing is therefore that it is the activity of transferring consumers' surplus into producers' surplus.

Consider now a subsistence economy in which pure competition prevails, so there is no market power, no rent, no surplus of either kind, and, of course, because of the absence of all of these, no innovation. In the circular flow of economic life, what is paid to all the factors of production is exactly matched by what these factors pay for whatever is produced. Say's law, that supplies in general are demands in general, simply two different aspects of a single reality, is dominant:[1]

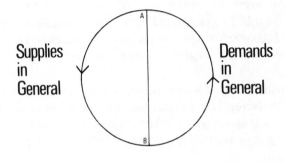

Figure 2

Next, introduce innovation, which necessarily involves simultaneously bringing in both market power and rent (without market power, there can have been no prospect of return at above-average risk to enable the innovation to be carried through, and the success of the innovation generates rents or quasi-rents). The flow of economic life now ceases to be circular. It first of all becomes distorted on the supply side, and then on the demand side, into the beginnings of a spiral:

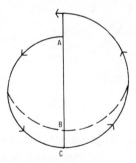

Figure 3

40

As long as the only market power is of the primary type, according to the vocabulary which is being developed, this will be an investment spiral. For example, the Duke of Bridgewater's innovatory canal opened up his coalfields, thus making Britain measurably richer. Almost all the resulting rent accrued to the Duke and his heirs, and most of this was re-invested in ways that contributed further to the industrial revolution.[2]

At that time, derived market power was virtually non-existent. Specialist factors were certainly needed to build the canal, but did not go very much further than the expertise of James Brindley. The labour force it entailed was expressly forbidden to combine for the sake of getting a share of the primary rent by laws which were effective until 1824. Even a century after the building of the Duke's canal, derived market power was weak compared with primary market power, as the records of the Guinness brewery illustrate. Between 1871-6, this firm had aggregate profits of just over £1 million. It was most progressive, so £400,000 was ploughed back into development. The Guinness family took out £600,000 for their own use, much of which was invested in land and in buildings. But the aggregate wage bill over the period was only £300,000.[3]

With the growth of derived market power, however, as a result of increasing specialization of factors of production, but even more from legalized combination by non-specialized workers, the rent accruing to the primary market power is greatly reduced, and the spiral changes from being primarily an investment spiral:

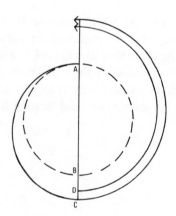

Figure 4

AB remains the indicator of the pre-innovatory situation, and BC that of the increased wealth generated by the innovation made possible by the primary market power. But instead of remaining in the hands of the owner of this power, much of the rent is captured by the derived market power, as indicated by BD, leaving the primary market power only the proportion represented by DC. This capture of primary rent means that workers now have a substantial rent element in their salaries and wages. Since rent is defined precisely as surplus over what is necessary to cause the emergence of a necessary factor of production, this means that employees now have discretionary incomes. It also means that the nature of the spiral has changed from investment to marketing. This is because the existence of mass rents means that there is now much consumer surplus available to be translated into producer surplus. The techniques for this are the techniques of marketing, which by 'unmaking the market' prevent the elimination of the rent element in the prices charged for products. The success of these techniques mean firms with high rent accruing to their primary market power, much of which rent is again captured by derived market power, so that with each turn of the spiral, the aggregate amount of rent in the system grows.

Moreover, the character of innovations progressively evolves in the direction of those types which will be most effective at extracting discretionary income, rent or consumer surplus from those who possess *derived* market power. This means in the direction of *marketing* innovations. It is also worth noting that the marketing spiral is the reality to which Schumpeter was adverting in his altogether remarkable insight that 'large firms create what they exploit'.[4]

In addition to the effect of derived market power, the rent of the primary market power is also eroded by taxation. The State thus comes to have a vital interest in market power, because a high-rent economy is a necessary prerequisite for a high-tax one. Taxation also accelerates the growth of the marketing spiral, and the trend towards innovations of a 'marketing' type. When part of the rent acquired by the owner of the Primary market power is taken by taxation, the Government uses much of it to pay its own employees, so augmenting the amount of disposable income in the system. By any definition, by far the largest part of Civil Servants' salaries is rent. Another major tranche of what is collected in tax is re-distributed in social welfare schemes, and ends up almost completely as disposable income. In so far as a government possesses the ultimate sanction of force for its tax-gathering, and also because it guarantees the financial aspects of publicly-owned enterprises, the derived power of employees of the State or where it plays an important role, is inherently greater than wherever its role is more restricted. It should be stressed again that what the marketing spiral illustrates is nothing more or less than how the amount of rent in the system grows. Each cycle provides more rent in the form of discretionary income of consumers, which thus becomes available to be captured to increase the rent of producers. It is not *necessarily* related to the well-known inflationary spiral, since it is possible to conceive of a system in which the rent element is growing strongly, combined with stable money and prices. In the real world, however, the existence of marketing does exert inflationary pressures via the political system, and this will be discussed in Chapter IV.

So far, then, it has been established that every successful innovation increases the funds available for investment in further innovation, that the existence of rent is due in the first instance to the same positive law which makes innovation possible, that discretionary income owes much in its origin to the laws protecting Trades Union power, and that the amount of rent in the system is also the greater according to the importance of the State's role in economic life. It has also been seen that the growth of derived market power must have the effect of changing the type of innovations that it is economically attractive to carry through, in the direction of those types which relate to the exploitation of discretionary income. As the latter grows, all the factors needed for innovation, that is, brains, imagination, commitment and money, necessarily become progressively attracted to consumer-oriented rather than capital-oriented innovation.

What are the characteristics of these consumer-oriented innovations? The point has already been made that every modern product has two parts, one physical, one psychological. The proportions differ according to the product, but there is no product, however 'physical', that is without some psychological ingredient, and vice versa. Consider for example, the contrast between cosmetics and computers, in which the proportions of each ingredient are inverted:

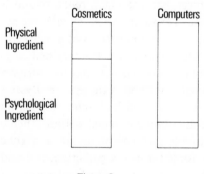

Figure 5

In cosmetics, many of the raw materials of the physical product are trivial in cost, and the cost of manufacturing is minimal − rarely involving more elaborate equipment than mechanised versions of the mortar and pestle. The marketing costs − advertising, sales promotion, packaging and distributional costs, salesmen, retailers' margins, rents of counters or floor space in department stores − are correspondingly high. Moreover, the whole cosmetic market rests on promises to women that no product can in fact fulfil by standards that are completely objective. Successful marketing depends upon the plausibility of the 'selling platform', the story told by the Advertising. Such selling platforms or believable stories in this area are hard to come by, since there are many firms in the cosmetic business, all searching for the same thing – a way of differentiating their own product from others. The "psychological ingredient" is virtually everything. Even though this is not the case with a completely different type of product, Computers, these, too, will be found to possess "psychological ingredient". Although they are considered to be "hardware", the psychological ingredient enters in because decisions concerning them are mostly made by people who are not spending their own money. In large organisations, recommendations to install one make rather than another are invariably made by men who are concerned above all to minimise the risk to their career path in terms of job-security and prospects, that any large decision taken under one degree or other of uncertainty, must involve. In this case, marketing's importance lies in its power to reduce that uncertainty. For example, computer salesmen will produce data from comparable installations elsewhere, to demonstrate in concrete form what the potential buyer will get. Everything possible will be done to ensure that taking a decision to buy a particular make, cuts the visible risk to the careers of the individuals involved in the buying decision to the barest minimum. Similarly, the salesmanship will try to show how a decision to buy alternative hardware requires that someone stakes his own reputation to some extent, on the judgment which favours it. The most successful sellers possess large resources to make the taking of decisions favourable to them largely easy and free of personal career risks to the individual concerned. If the client firm has to pay a premium for the relief of its executives from risks in this way, through higher price or rental, this is rarely an item which comes under perceptive or detailed scrutiny. The persuasive resources thus deployed are marketing resources, the power they give over the decision-making process in customer firms, is marketing power, and the uniqueness of advantage which the firms which use them, possess over their competitors, is the power to *sell* even more than it is the power to *make* – persuasive market power even more than the market power of capability.

Indeed, there is no theoretical reason which would prevent such firms from growing into areas that have nothing whatever to do with computers on the basis of the same set of marketing resources as they already have; exactly the same need to reduce personal career risk in decision-making within the bureaucracy of large firms is present in relation to all kinds of expensive hardware, and not only computers. The reflection leads back to Donald Dewey's insistence, referred to at length in Chapter I, that without anti-Trust laws, monopoly is the normal condition towards which business tends. The tendency towards concentration is as evident with persuasive market power as with any other kind. The way in which this type of power reinforces the firms' associated capability to exclude new entrants, in fact, can throw some light on the economic Law of Proportional Effect (Gibrat's law). The consequence of this law is that 'the concentration of any given industry will increase over time, for the larger firm will possess the same probability of a given proportionate growth as the small firm, and thus the logarithmic variance of the distribution of firms sizes about the mean will tend to increase over time, and, in the limit become infinite'. One explanation for this may be that once the level of static returns to scale on the physical production level is reached, the dynamism of a growing firm is given by increasing returns at the psychological production level, i.e. on the marketing and communications side. Incidentally, this explains some of the inconsistencies which give economists so much trouble in their studies of growth rates of firms and of the relationship between profitability and firm size. These are due to lack of preliminary screening of their data according to type of market power. Both U.S. Steel and Procter and Gamble come into the same list of the largest 500 firms in the U.S.; both have market power, but the source of this power (on which they both depend for their rents) is different. In the case of U.S. Steel, there is overt oligopoly, since the number of producers is limited, and power depends upon satisfying objective requirements of the market, whose imperfection is brought about by fixed costs in the plants. In that of Procter and Gamble, the market power comes partly from overt oligopoly in so far as there are certain objective requirements in the detergent and associated markets that have to be satisfied, and not many sellers can do this. Even more, however, the firm's rents come from persuasive market power, depending upon delivering a unique psychological ingredient or subjective element together with the physical product, its brand name, 'unique selling proposition' and 'brand image'. It will be explained below how this is another –"covert" –type of oligopoly.

The world-wide change in the direction of more important roles for marketing power, is the meaning of the shift from being 'product-oriented' to 'market-oriented', which Management Consultants everywhere are so actively promoting. A 'product-oriented' firm takes the requirements of the market as given, and tries to manufacture so as to meet them as best it can. If it is particularly sophisticated, it may search for individual segments of markets which it can satisfy especially well, and so achieve some degree of capability market power. Such firms are characterized by being local or national in scope, by having their output splintered over a large number of products, for each of which the production run is comparatively short, and by flexibility and a short time-scale in forward planning. Firms that are 'market-oriented' in contrast, direct themselves, not towards those elements in the market which are objectively expressed, but to those which are indefinite, to the 'uncertainty' of buyers rather than to their knowledge. They bring information to bear to reduce this uncertainty, and in doing so achieve some degree of power over customers, or marketing power. When there is some element of advantage from the marketing power thus achieved that is unique, and not shared with others, there is a situation of 'marketing monopoly'. It is characteristic of market-oriented firms to be international, either actually or potentially (the special reasons for this will be explored later on) to have fewer products but longer production runs for them, and to be slower to change direction and to take a longer view in their planning for the future, than product-oriented firms are. All this is because of the nature of the 'uncertainty-reducing' process, which has become a major activity of this type of firm. Indeed, no matter what they make, all firms which are market-oriented in this sense, can say that they are 'in the information business'. Information is always uncertainty-*reduction*, and it is uncertainty-reduction that gives marketing power. The market imperfection in this case, is brought about by the use of communications. Not alone are there great economies of scale in the use of the techniques and means of mass communication, but the standardization of output which they make possible produces major plant economies and thus more capability market power also. Clearly, the effect of both types of market power combined can more than counterbalance diseconomies of scale, increasing inefficiency of management and other disadvantages as the firm grows. Scale economies in the use of communications, scale economies in the plant, and scale economies in the use of research and development – these are the rewards of persuasive market power. On its own, this capacity would be enough to account for the trend towards concentration in industry. By studying size, growth and profitability *within type of market power*, therefore, we are dealing with coherent and intelligible groups. There is more in common between a large and a small firm, both of which are built on persuasive market power, than there is between either of them and firms of identical size, as measured by assets which exist to satisfy objective requirements of markets, or to keep rivals out through capability.

It will now be clear, that 'getting new things done' or turning ideas into concrete realities, or innovation, has exactly the same economic consequences whether it relates to physical or psychological ingredient. From the point of view of the investor in innovation, the objective is the same: To transfer consumer surplus into producer surplus, or to maximize Rent. Since economic innovation is impossible without investment, it is of vital importance to be clear-sighted about what motivates those who control the financial support that innovators cannot do without if they are to be successful. The extent to which contemporary economic problems are attributable to neglect of this point will be discussed in Chapter IV. What matters for the present argument is that *for achieving the objectives of investors*, persuasive market power is at least as valid a means of underwriting innovation as are capability or specific market power. In some cases it is significantly more effective, meaning that it is a better way of generating rents.

Although persuasion is most frequently associated with the psychological ingredient in products, it can also be concerned with the physical ingredient. What decides the issue is the progression from need, to want, to demand. Human needs are always non-specific and inchoate, and as such, are *never* satisfied. Need, however can be articulated into want, which is *always* specific and can be satisfied only by a particular product. When purchasing power (money) is added to want, there is *demand*, and it is only at this final stage that any type of market power can produce the required results. Now, to the extent that individuals articulate their own inchoate needs into specific wants, they are invulnerable to persuasion and to the type of market power associated with it. But if they cannot or will not do this for themselves, they provide an opportunity to marketing people to step in and do the articulation for them, naturally in the direction which suits their firm. This is achieved by manipulating 'wants'. Women, for example, have an innate need to be beautiful, but they cannot articulate this into wants for specific products because they simply do not know what it is that can give them beauty. It is therefore open to cosmetic firms to articulate this need for them, which they do through the information and the promises their products offer. Inability or failure on the part of the buyer to articulate his or her needs into wants for specific products occurs much more frequently in respect of a product's psychological ingredient than of its physical one. However, it does happen, too, in respect of physical ingredients. Conversely, buyers sometimes themselves articulate their own need into a want for a psychological ingredient in a most precise way. When they do so, there is no option for those who want to sell them products but to comply as best they can.

The posture of a firm's management must therefore vary according to the degree to which needs are already articulated into wants. Where this has been done by the buyer himself or herself, the only stance possible for the firm is one of reverence towards the precise instructions which are reaching it from its customers. All it can do is adapt its product as perfectly as possible to the instructions, and any Rent it gains will be as a result of its market power of capability in doing this. The firm's capability is a barrier to entry, because it has to be matched by newcomers if they are to be able to meet the customer's requirements equally well and so get into the market. But where the buyer has *not* articulated need into want for a specific product, then it becomes possible for the firm to adopt an aggressive posture, taking positive action to ensure that the instructions which reach it from the market are of a kind that can be best complied with by the products which, as it happens, the firm produces and offers for sale. In this case, its market power will be the market power of persuasion, and its strength will depend upon two factors: Firstly, how shy or incapable the consumer is of articulating his or her own inchoate needs into a want for a specific product; secondly, how capable any competitive firm may also be of "bending" the instructions coming from the market in a direction that is advantageous to itself.

On the principle that precision of vocabulary and definition is essential to understanding, there are advantages in using the word "market" in all cases where the stance is one of reverence to instructions from the market which cannot be changed, and 'marketing' when the posture reflects a readiness to fill, by persuasion, a vacuum left by the market's failure (whether from inability or neglect) to articulate its inchoate needs into specific wants. In this terminology, for example, market research is concerned with establishing concrete facts about the market, and its own precise specification of wants, whereas marketing research is directed towards inchoate needs, with the object of identifying opportunities there for modifying the market's instructions.

Market research is frequently, then, the intelligence-gathering function of capability market power, and marketing research tends to be the same in respect of persuasive market power. In a way, the distinction which is being sought after in using the two words is the distinction between imperfect competition in the Joan Robinson sense, and monopolistic competition in the Chamberlinian sense. The idea of influencing demand is absent from the theory of imperfect competition as such; the requirements of the market are taken as given. This idea, however, is part and parcel of monopolistic competition, because it is inherent in product differentiation, which, as Chamberlin always insisted, is the core of his theory. Implicit in it also is the idea that the requirements of the market are capable of being modified by the seller.

To illustrate this point, consider for example a set of firms all extruding aluminium rod in different diameters. For this work, the major element of fixed cost is the extrusion press, the various dies (or tooling) used to vary the size of rod being relatively inexpensive. Suppose that a demand arises for rod of 14 mm. dia., which none of the firms is already supplying. One firm obtains tooling to enable it to extrude this size and so satisfy the new demand. Clearly, at this stage, this firm is a monopolist, since it is the only one which can satisfy this particular special requirement. But its monopoly is very circumscribed, since the only barrier to entry by competitors who already own extrusion presses is the small cost they would incur in obtaining a similar extrusion tool. A second firm, however, might adopt a different approach. Instead of getting a tool to extrude 14 mm. dia. rod, it might spend money in changing the demand, by sending a salesman to persuade the users that by making minor design changes, they could use 15 mm. diameter rod, which all members of the group can produce. In that case, the second firm's advantage lies in the fact that its claim to be able to offer the best quality control and delivery is believed. Again, its position is insecure, since the only barrier to entry is the cost involved in matching the investment it has made in persuasion. If 15 mm. is extruded by all firms, it is possible that counter-persuasion from a rival salesman may gain entry to the market for yet another firm.

In both cases the uniqueness of advantage or monopoly derives from investment, in one case in the 14 mm. extrusion tool, in the other in persuading users to change to 15 mm. diameter. The barrier to entry represented by the first case is quite straightforward; it depreciates at a more or less constant rate, and any rival firm that wishes to overcome it must make a comparable investment in a similar tool. With persuasion, however, depreciation has to be at a much faster rate; people are apt to become unpersuaded again more quickly than a tool wears out. The rival who wants to overcome the barrier, too, may not have to make the full investment in persuasion, which the first firm did. A buyer who has once been persuaded to revise his design so as to use 15 mm. rod instead of specially extruded 14 mm, is now open to persuasion from all the firms in the group about their respective merits in supplying 15 mm. Marketing power can therefore be more expensive to maintain, and may give a lower level of barrier against entry by newcomers for a given capital cost, than 'capability'. Against this, however, marketing power contributes to the efficiency of the plant, because it is a force tending towards the realization of whatever scale economies in operation are available – it reinforces the firm's capability market power also. Capability market power works in the opposite direction, by attempting to conform the plant's output to the range of objectively different requirements of the market, resulting in short production runs. In the aluminium rod field, a firm which operates on a basis of this type of market power will look for its uniqueness of advantage through having a special tool for every possible diameter the market could demand, which means willingness to extrude small quantities to individual requirements; the firm which operates by marketing power will have a limited range of tooling and will seek to achieve long production runs by spending money on persuading potential users to abandon their special requirements and move to one of the standard sizes offered. So there is market research and marketing research, market power and marketing power; capability and persuasion as barriers to entry by others. In every case, the first describes a static situation in which the producer does little more than react to the requirements of the market; there is a substantial equality in status between buyers and sellers. The second refers to the dynamic situation, in which the producer has some degree of power to bend the requirements of the market in his own favour; there is a definite degree of superiority of sellers over buyers. There is more Rent, and therefore there can be more innovation.

It is probably this sense of the subordination of customers to producers that lies at the heart of Galbraith's thesis that consumer sovereignty is no more than a myth to-day. He points out that control of the market by giant corporations is made necessary by modern technology, since huge investments over many years can only be justified by a high degree of certainty about disposal of the eventual output. He illustrates this by the contrast between Henry Ford's first car and the modern Ford Mustang. In the former case, from start to completion was a matter of a few months, and if it had been decided to abandon the project half-way along, the simple tools used could all have been just as effective for making something else. In contrast, several years' work went into the Mustang from original plan to first production model, and the prodigiously expensive tooling to make it, was fit for no other use: It either made Mustangs or it was scrap. Galbraith points to the great success of the Mustang, and claims that this shows that the Ford Company, like other giant firms, has a degree of control over customers which matches the scale of their investments, in plant, men and time.[5] It is significant, however, that he picks for his comparison the Ford Mustang and not the Ford Edsel: All the elements in the comparison with Henry Ford's first car are just as valid in the case of the Edsel, yet it was a resounding failure. This was because, although Ford's spent an un-precedented amount of money upon the identification and delivery of psy-chological ingredient, the car was a mediocre piece of engineering, and was identified as such by *Consumer Reports*, which has strong readership in the target market. Ford's stance was not reverent enough to the instructions arising from their potential customers' willingness and ability to articulate their needs into wants for themselves; the firm over-estimated the corresponding 'vacuum' left for them to fill with psychological ingredient. The control of even the largest firms over the market is nothing like as complete as Galbraith thinks it is, and consumer sovereignty is by no means all myth.

Any true position of uniqueness of business advantage seems to be the result of a combination of both market and marketing power in the senses given above, i.e. a combination of response to the objective requirements of the market, with purposive moulding of these requirements to what it suits the seller to produce. The balance between the two types of market power in any concrete business situation will depend on the particular market. Evidently, in selling turbo-generators for power stations, the objective requirements of the market are precisely and expertly defined, and there is limited room for *marketing* power, because of the amount of objective information that exists about both demand and supply. Market power, of course, can still exist in such areas, because it is perfectly possible for one supplier to be alone in capacity to supply a particular segment of the market. Once one firm has proved its capacity to make turbo-generators which produce more electricity than any other, then, because of the economies of scale these offer to power-situation operation, it possesses a major degree of market power. This power, of course, is of a temporary kind, since competitors will be struggling hard to overtake the originator and to get into a position to offer plant of the same capacity.

Markets where there are few objective requirements, or where buyers are unable or unwilling to define them, display the contrasting balance between the two kinds of entry barrier: In these, market power is low, marketing power is high. Buyers of cosmetics have no idea (and indeed *can* have no idea) of how their felt requirements can be translated into a specification for a product. There can be little or no *market* power, because it is almost impossible to find a segment of the market which offers a chance of investing in plant which is uniquely related to production for this segment. Since both types of monopoly go back to investment, either in the plant or in the apparatus of persuasion, then, if requirements of a segment of the market cannot be translated into fixed costs in the plant, there can be no capability market power. Cosmetics offer next to no scope for uniqueness of advantage in fixed costs in the plant, and the scope for investment in technical research and development is also limited, by the nature of the problems, and by the difficulty of protecting any discoveries effectively from imitation. This very lack of objective requirements in the market makes it fertile ground for persuasive market power. Since consumers have almost no fixed ideas of their own, they are most vulnerable to persuasion; since uncertainty is high, there is need for information to remove it; since there are in fact only extremely partial solutions to consumers' problems, everything depends upon the reputation of the brands offering such solutions as there are; the lack of market requirements which can be defined objectively means that the extent to which claims can be tested is extremely limited. There is therefore scope for large-scale investment *in the apparatus of persuasion*, which provides the fixed cost element that is always associated with monopoly, for the cosmetic industry.

Although the balance between capability and persuasive market power, between the 'static' and 'dynamic' responses to a market, can fluctuate widely, in all true business situations, neither is ever entirely absent. However minimal the element of persuasion, information, or reduction-of-uncertainty may be in the selling of turbo-generators, it is nevertheless there. A firm's capability is rarely so dominant even in heavy industry where plant and research and development fixed costs are almost everything, that it can dispense with salesmen entirely, and sell merely by sending out catalogues in its own language. Equally, although the important factors in cosmetic marketing are almost all psychological, there nevertheless remains a minimal technical level that must be attained if the product is to be acceptable. Actual market power in business, is made up of a combination of types of entry barrier. Uniqueness of advantage can relate to advantage over customers, or over competitors, or – in the case of an absolute monopoly – over both. To possess capability market power is no more than to be able to satisfy one or more segments of a market with some form of uniqueness of advantage. Frequently, this uniqueness of advantage arises from the narrowness of the segment itself, in that there just is no other supplier who offers a product that is specifically designed for this segment.

As long as any degree of monopoly or uniqueness of advantage depends upon there being a single source of satisfaction of a particular combination of articulated needs, it is impossible to speak of both parties in the transaction as being in a position of complete equality. Such an equilibrium, or balance, is only to be conceived of in terms of the abstract pure competitive situation, and without it the producer will earn some 'supernormal' or 'monopoly' profits, that is, Rent. At the same time, as long as what is produced is controlled by objectively defined need, and all that the producer does is respond to the specification of this need, then the balance is not shifted too greatly in the supplier's favour, even if he is the sole source.

In the case of persuasive market power, however, the advantage shifts more decisively in favour of the seller. To begin with, he is not subject to the constraint of conforming to a need which is precisely and objectively defined. Whether this is because the buyer cannot define his requirement or fails to do so, his position relative to the seller is weakened. Next, it is the seller, not the buyer, who decides what the segments of the market are to be, it is he who chooses the ground on which bargaining is to take place. Thirdly, by using persuasion to group the wants of buyers into larger segments, standardisation and economies in production are achieved. This increases the average size of producing firms − and thus the barriers to entry by newcomers − without any necessary corresponding increase in the size of consumer's orders. What Galbraith called the 'countervailing power' of buyers as against the 'original power' of sellers is thereby weakened. The initiative in the economic process passes from the consumer to the producer; supply, not demand, becomes the driving force. Everything points, then, to the conclusion that the uniqueness of advantage which can be attained through persuasive market power is now intrinsically stronger than that achieved through capability. This means, in turn, that there are more possibilities for innovation in those areas of economic life where marketing is important.

This view is reinforced by reflection on the respective levels of profits which may be expected from each form of control over the market. Market power of any kind arises from having some specialised capacity to make something which corresponds to a demand. Marketing power arises from some extra element in the specification of the demand which has been introduced *by the action of the producer*. Now, whereas with respect to the independent elements in the demand specification, the producer is most likely to be in a situation of oligopoly, one of few sellers, with respect to the element he has introduced into the specification himself, he is the only one who can supply this, and is thus a true monopolist, a *single* seller. If W.H. Lever had just decided to buy a soap boiler, he could have gone into the soap business, say, in Liverpool. As such, he would have been just another of the roughly 100 soapmakers in Britain at the time. He could perhaps be said to have a monopoly position in Liverpool itself if there was no other soapmaker there, to the extent that people were loyal to their local producer. At at time when communications were poor, he was certainly closer to being a monopolist there than an oligopolist, because transport difficulties effectively eliminated competition from any firm that was not geographically close to him. He would have nothing to fear from the soap-boilers of Exeter or Ipswich, but possibly something from those of Runcorn or Manchester. However, once he introduces a new element into what the market specifies to producers as being what it wants, adding to the pre-existing requirements for a piece of soap that it also be wrapped and be called 'Sunlight', he is no longer one of few sellers, but, in respect of these new elements, a single seller, a monopolist in the strictest sense. He has the correspondingly higher Rent of a monopolist as compared with an oligopolist, and this Rent will be further reinforced as his sales expand and bring him economies of scale in production, even though at this level he remains one amongst several. His 'plant' therefore consists of two parts: The 'productive' plant, making the good in so far as it is specified by consumers or users themselves, independently of anything he does, and the 'persuasive' plant, which both creates an additional part of the market's specification, and satisfies it. Both parts of the plant have fixed costs, to which the market's imperfection corresponds, but it is clear that the return to the 'persuasive' plant is higher, since competitors can approach less closely to it with their products which attempt to satisfy the same 'constellation of wants'. At the 'marketing' level, there is pure monopoly since Trade Mark registration law (of which much more later) grants this explicitly to the brand name. At last it is possible to see clearly where the downward-sloping individual demand curve which fascinated Chamberlin, comes from. It is the resultant, in the two-part product, of the vertical curve of the psychological ingredient (the brand, which is a pure monopoly) and the near-horizontal curve of the physical ingredient (produced oligopolistically, or even under virtually pure competition).

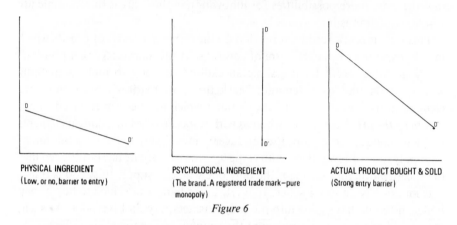

PHYSICAL INGREDIENT
(Low, or no, barrier to entry)

PSYCHOLOGICAL INGREDIENT
(The brand . A registered trade mark – pure monopoly)

ACTUAL PRODUCT BOUGHT & SOLD
(Strong entry barrier)

Figure 6

It should now be clear how wrong it is to think of economic innovation as limited to technology. It was, of course, largely so throughout the first and second thrusts of the industrial revolution. From roughly the 1780s to the 1880s, the ideas which were turned into concrete realities were predominantly those which could be protected by the market power of capability, that is, by investment in physical production capacity. In the next period, roughly until the Great War, Patents were a significant additional method of protecting investment in innovation, but, by definition, this also was protection for technology. The years before and after the War saw a considerable upsurge in derived market power – indeed, one partial explanation of the Depression of the 1930s is that because of this power, wages were 'sticky downwards'. As potential investors saw it, the combination of derived market power and taxation had exhausted investment opportunities. This was indeed true of opportunities of the traditional type. New opportuniites, however, were offered by the rent element in wages and salaries which resulted precisely from the derived market power, which was so troublesome in respect of investment in technology. This rent element received a massive boost after the last War from the widespread adoption of Keynes' ideas, which led to the growth of State intervention in economies, and thus inevitably, to massive bureaucracies. Rent in wages and salaries is discretionary income, which is the target of marketing; consequently, the new investment opportunities were in the marketing area, relating to the delivery of psychological ingredient in products. In the new consumer, consumer-durable and services markets, advertising was the main instrument for delivering this psychological ingredient. Because it could be related to a registered Trade Mark, it was found to be a most effective means of protecting innovation in the development of psychological ingredient, and in delivering it. In the third thrust of the industrial revolution, therefore, the ideas which offered the best investment opportunities, were typically related to marketing rather than to technology; or, where they were technological, the technology was subordinated to marketing.

To grasp fully how and why this change took place, it is first necessary to understand how advertising works, and to this end, the way in which innovations are diffused throws light upon how innovations in psychological ingredient are generated. This is illustrated in Rogers and Shoemakers' well-known diagram:[6]

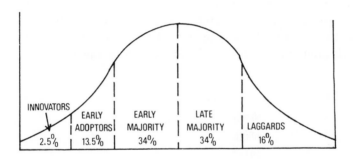

Figure 7

If the number of individuals accepting an innovation is plotted against time, the diffusion of the innovation is found to follow the normal curve. When a standard deviation is marked off either side of the median time period, this will include the early and late majority. A second standard deviation brings in the "early adopters" on one side. At the very outset of the diffusion process is a small group, never more than 3% of the total, who are of quite disproportionate importance. These are the innovators, who tend to be younger and better educated, and to have more spending power than others. Even more important, they have a special interest in the type of product to which the innovation belongs. This may make an individual an innovator in respect of one type of product, even though he does not have any of the characteristics of innovators generally, such as youth and education, and though he may be anything but an innovator in respect of other types of product. A member of the buying public who is an innovator as far as the classical record companies are concerned may well be a "laggard" when it comes to buying "hit singles". Innovators are particularly characterized by having an unusually high level of confidence in their own judgment about the subject-matter of the innovation. This, and their special interest, are the reasons why they are the first to try out the new thing in practice, and why they are very likely to take steps to try it out, whether by buying it or otherwise, once they learn of its existence. They will act on information about a new thing which reaches them through a print medium, for example, and so they respond *directly* to advertisements. In contrast, early adopters, the early and late majorities, and laggards, have progressively less interest in, and knowledge of, the product group, and less confidence in their own judgment about it. Consequently, they tend to take purchasing decisions only when they are reassured by reports from others of actual satisfactory experience with the product. This is what makes the innovators so important in the process of diffusion of innovations, and especially when mass communication, notably advertising, is involved. So much is this so that those who make up this group of 2 or 3 per cent of the total, are called in this case "gatekeepers", because they open the way for others to move in a particular direction. As long as the only advertising available is in print media, such as newspapers and magazines, a simple two-stage model gives a useful insight into how advertising works. In the following diagrams of information diffusion, gatekeepers are represented by circles and others by squares:

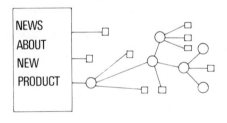

Figure 8

The very first person to learn of the new things is more likely to be a 'gatekeeper', whose satisfactory experience with the product influences (let us say) three others in its favour. One of these influences another one, a second (who also happens to be a 'gatekeeper') influences three more, and so knowledge of the new thing spreads. It will be seen that the speed at which information is diffused through the population depends very much upon how quickly the 'gatekeepers' obtain it, because each of these, by his special interest in the innovation, influences more people than an ordinary member of the population does. He also tends to have more contact with others who share his own heightened interest in the type of product. Without advertising, the speed with which the 'gatekeepers' learn of the new thing is no greater than that of the general spread of information through the population. Information transfer then takes place largely by a process in which the probability of any particular piece of information becoming "accepted, is mainly a function of previous transfers. What advertising does is to extract the gatekeepers from this process, and bring them to the beginning of it in terms of time, as is indicated in the second and third diagrams:

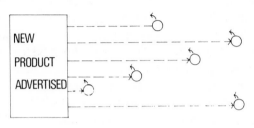

Figure 9

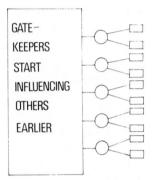

Figure 10

Advertising thus 'telescopes' the diffusion process over time. The 'gatekeepers' are no longer dependent upon a chain of person-to-person informational contacts, with all the possibilities inherent in such a chain of the original information being attenuated, distorted or lost completely; instead, the time factor is eliminated for them, and they are immediately placed in possession of the information they want in all its original freshness. Because it is their heightened interest in the area in question which makes them 'gatekeepers', they are more likely than others to act on this information which reaches them in a form which is impersonal (for example a newspaper advertisement); but once they have done so, their experience is transferred to others in a personal form, and so people who would never react to advertising alone become influenced in turn. By picking the gatekeepers out of the crowd and bringing them to the front of the time-scale, advertising accelerates the whole diffusion process tremendously.

This view (of advertising as an *accelerator* more than anything else) explains the universal experience with advertising, that no amount of it can sell a bad product. If advertising is indeed only an *accelerating* force, this will be so because in the case of a bad product, there is nothing to accelerate. What is more, this also explains why advertising actually speeds up the destruction of a bad product, or why advertising which is built upon what Rosser Reeves calls 'the deceptive differential', a miniscule difference which the consumer cannot observe in actual practice, also does so. In the first case, the advertising is selecting out of the crowd to experience the product, the very people who will broadcast their dissatisfaction with it; in the second, because the difference is unimportant, the number of 'gatekeepers' will be few to begin with, and then they will have little power to exercise their function because nobody else regards the difference as significant. In both cases the advertising has picked out just the wrong people to get further sales. The way in which mass print media advertising works, then, may be somewhat different from what is frequently thought, even by people in the advertising business. It is not by having a direct influence on a great many people, but by selecting out from the mass, those individuals who have a special interest in the product and causing them to get actual experience of it. It is these who directly influence the mass through personal contact by their reports of that experience. The advertising, however, has to be to the mass from the start, because it is impossible to know in advance who are the 'gatekeepers' for any product or for any particular advertising approach for it.

'I know half my expenditure on advertising is wasted, but I never know which half' – the saying has been attributed to Lever as well as to many others. It should now be clear why it is true. It is that advertising has its effect upon certain members of a particular population, who in turn influence others, but there is no means of identifying in advance who these key individuals are. Of course, media research is widely used and can contribute much to breaking down the total population into segments which can be reached with some degree of precision, so that expenditure can be concentrated. Nevertheless, no matter how far this goes, the identified group is large in absolute terms, and within this we are unable to pin down the individuals who will be the first to bring the new thing into their range of experience and to influence and persuade others as a result. The advertising must cover the whole group, because this is the only way to reach the key individuals in it.

Another fact of advertising life which is explained by this theory, is that if a choice has to be made between 'coverage' and 'intensity' it pays to choose coverage. If a given expenditure is used to deliver the advertising message to a large number of people only a few times, it generally gives better results than if it is used to deliver the message to a small number many times. This could be because once the 'gatekeepers' from any section of the potential market have been brought to try the product through the advertising, the further diffusion of the product through the population depends more upon what they have to say about it, than upon repetition of the advertising message. Consequently, once the advertising level has reached the minimum 'threshold' necessary to get the 'gatekeepers' moving, repetition is a less productive use of advertising resources than reaching the same 'threshold' level – i.e. more gatekeepers – in a larger population. There can, of course, be no point in spreading the advertising effort so thinly over a wide audience that it never reaches the minimum level needed to get the gatekeepers to buy. This view of what determines the 'floor for advertising expenditure', referred to by H.R. Edwards, adds a dimension to Edwards' conclusion that 'there is a minimum amount which can be spent for effective advertising and that this amount is in general, large'.[7] The parallel with Sylos-Labini's identification of monopoly with 'fixed costs in the plant' does not need to be stressed. There is clearly a reality which can properly be described as 'fixed costs' on the marketing side of a business also.

The concept of threshold levels for effective advertising expenditure is of the greatest significance for market power and thus for the relationship between marketing and innovation. It will be obvious that the existence of such a threshold level constitutes a barrier to entry by others, and if the level is inherently high, it is a major barrier. As such, it will make innovation possible, because the prospective Rent to be earned will justify investment at high risk. There will naturally be a bias towards "new things" in terms of psychological ingredient, but incremental innovations in the physical aspect of products will also be encouraged, because they can be protected by marketing, especially when combined with secrecy. It should be noted, however, that this type of entry barrier is much less able to underwrite A-phase or originative innovation. This bias, as will be seen in Chapter IV, has important consequences for economic growth and employment.

However effective the barrier to entry of a substantial advertising appropriation may have been in the pre-television era, it became vastly more so once television advertising became widespread. This is because television enables an advertiser *to generate his own gatekeepers*. The immediacy and power of the T.V. medium is such, and people spend so much time watching it, that it has become the main source of 'significant' information for most people in the advanced countries, and the sole source for many. 'Significant' information is the only type of information that has a bearing upon action, because emotional "weights" have become attached to it. Everyone acts selectively to reduce the constant and overwhelming stream of data with which he is deluged every day, to manageable proportions, by adding such 'weights' to each bit of incoming information. Only the bits with most 'emotional weight' attached, get past the 'filter' to earn further attention. The result is that information which comes from TV, including advertising, is 'personalised' in the same sense as information from a 'gatekeeper'. Because there is some sort of personal relationship between an early adopter and a gatekeeper, the gatekeeper's experience is trusted; because the emotional inputs to TV viewing are so strong, the information coming from TV is similarly regarded as trustworthy. It is believed to reflect experience with the product on the part of someone whose judgment is sound, and it has the same effect in clearing away psychological obstacles to the buying decision, as a "gatekeeper's" endorsement. This has enormous advantages for any advertiser who can afford the large extra expense of TV advertising. He no longer has to rely upon "live" gatekeepers to 'personalise' his selling message, with all the possibilities for attenuating or distorting it which this involves. Instead, he can act directly upon the much larger numbers of early adopters, and have complete control over both intellectual and emotional aspects of the information they receive. A medium which can select 16% of potential adopters of an innovation out of the total (all early adopters) and bring *them* to the front of the time process, is obviously much superior to one which can only influence 3% at most (the gatekeepers). Television, however, is an expensive advertising medium, so these advantages favour the largest advertisers, making the barriers to entry to their markets even harder for outsiders to surmount. The Rents their firms earn are bigger, and they become responsible for an even greater proportion of whatever innovation takes place. For these reasons, Television has intensified the bias in the innovatory pattern away from the big, fundamental innovations and in the direction of innovations in psychological ingredient. In the U.S., President Carter commissioned the Baruch Report to recommend how the country's slowing rate of innovation could be reversed. Some members of the Commission expressed surprise that against this background, no less than $18 million could be invested in the launch of a new deodorant. There is nothing surprising about it, however, if a wide enough definition of innovation is used, and if the way in which innovation patterns faithfully follow the patterns of market power, is understood. It is simply because modern marketing can erect such high entry barriers that so much innovation in products that can be protected by them, can attract any investment it needs.

Another important aspect of TV advertising is what it does to product life cycles. It will be recalled that in the hypothetical case without advertising, information about the product passed through the population slowly, since the gatekeepers, on whose 'personalising' of the information the early adopters and the majorities depend, only received their information about the new product as a result of chance contacts between individuals, the overwhelming bulk of whom have no particular interest in the product. The introduction of press media advertising accelerates the whole process, by getting the information quickly to all the gatekeepers, so that they will personalise it, and then it is able to have an effect on the others. Television speeds up the process still further, by acting immediately on the early adopters, as well as all the gatekeepers. It should be noted that these effects take place whether or not the information about the product that is personalised is positive or negative. Bad news about a product will be accelerated just as much as good news. Thus, whether or not the product is successful, the curve of acceptance in relation to time, changes its shape:

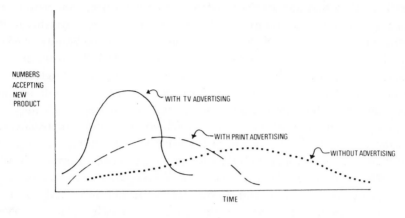

Figure 11

The shortening of the time taken by a product to be adopted by all who are going to adopt it, naturally intensifies the pressure to develop its replacement. However, technical innovation follows its own logic, which is not necessarily in phase with a firm's requirements for new products as a result of the use of advertising. The pressure from shorter product life cycles therefore adds still more weight to the other factors which are pushing the firm's innovatory effort in the direction of new things that are limited to psychological ingredient. This is particularly reflected in the growth of what is known as Sales Promotion.

Promotion, as von Clauswitz might have said if his business had been advertising instead of War, is the extension of advertising policy by other means. A good enough working definition of it is marketing activities other than advertising and personal selling. Among such activities for consumer goods are couponing (generally a gift of some form of entitlement to a discount when buying a product, sometimes given with an earlier purchase); banding packs of related products together and selling them more cheaply than the items separately; offers of goods other than the product in question on special terms (these are said to be 'self-liquidating', if the revenue from the public covers the cost of the goods offered); free gifts, of course, linked with buying the product; and competitions of various kinds. A good enough rule for deciding whether something is Promotion or not, is according to whether the advertising agency is paid by commission or by a supplementary fee to its client. Generally, when there is such a fee, it is more likely to related to Promotion than to advertising. This type of activity depends completely upon the existence of property in brand names, through registration. Without this, it could not exist at all, because Promotion as we know it is possible only in the case of modern mass markets, where advertising has done its work, and where it is the symptom of market maturity. As long as there are real differences in products, there is no need for Promotion, since advertising can do all that is necessary. But when products have become identical or very nearly so, then there is need to find new ways of differentiating them from competitors, of reducing consumer uncertainty as between products. These ways amount to Promotion, and they depend completely upon ownership of a brand name in a way which would be quite impossible without Trade Mark Registration.

Of course, it is only in the absence of innovation in the physical ingredient of the product, that the activities that have been called Promotion become important. If, at the physical level, something new arrives which makes a product different from others in a way which consumers can appreciate, up goes the advertising budget again, at the expense of Promotion. In the advertising world, one principle is unquestioned: If you have a story to tell, you tell it. When women have learned everything that is relevant to them about synthetic detergents, firms will compete with free artificial flowers and tea-towel offers, but when their technical people have come up with enzymes or phosphates or liquid soaps, and they want women to change to them, they use communications media and forget the candy-floss. If a new additive to petrol were discovered to-morrow which improved it as much, say, as tetra-ethyl lead did in its day, then, until this became standard and in every brand, Promotion would be of secondary importance to advertising.

Modern information theory throws light on marketing power mainly by helping our understanding of advertising and promotion. In turn it illuminates economic innovation, which depends upon the barriers to entry which these techniques erect. It will be remembered that information is what removes uncertainty, and the amount of uncertainty removed is the measure of the information content of the message transmitted. Conversely, 'entropy' is the amount of uncertainty there is to remove. Looked at in this way, information is equated with 'news', and a message which merely tells someone what he already knows, has an information content of zero. From this it seems that the definition of his trade given at the beginning of the century by the advertising man, Albert Lasker, that 'advertising is *news* about a product' may be truer than even he realised. The problem is that there is a limit to the amount of 'news' or information that there is to give about any product, and this limit is quite soon reached. "The more you tell, the more you sell" is an old adage in the advertising business, but for most products, a single advertisement can contain everything that is relevant about it. Certainly, many advertising men would be very happy if they could be sure that everything they could put into one advertisement would reach and be absorbed by their target audience. This explains why they know from experience that the word 'New' is the most powerful in their vocabulary. It is because in many advertisements it may be the only word that removes any uncertainty at all and is therefore the only word which has any informational content. Consumers know everything else there is to know about the product from earlier advertising, and even more from experience of it. So the information that the product has some 'new' aspect, or that 'something new had been added' to it, does tell people some-

thing they did not already know; it does reduce 'entropy' (the amount of uncertainty), it is 'news'; and it justifies the use of advertising media and the advertising mens' effort.

The main advantage of looking at advertising in the light of modern information theory is that it removes the unreal distinction between advertising
which is 'informative' and that which is 'persuasive'. This distinction is most
frequently used by people who dislike advertising, the implication being that
'persuasive' advertising is bad, whereas 'informative' advertising is good, or at
least harmless. The British Labour Party report on advertising made much of
this distinction and held that the resources absorbed by advertising cannot be
justified in terms of information only. This is an inadequate view of information. Persuasion *is* information, once information is defined as that which
removes uncertainty. A gun in the hand of a discovered burglar is highly
persuasive in getting obedience to his orders; the persuasion, however, comes
from the information the gun gives about his capacity and intentions. To the
extent that uncertainty remains about his willingness to shoot, about the
accuracy of his aim, about whether the gun is loaded, or about whether the
safety catch is off, or not, persuasive power is reduced.

Defining information as what removes uncertainty makes all information
persuasive, which is in line with the common-sense view that the first step is
persuading someone to go a particular way is to show him what the way is.
There may still be a great amount of uncertainty in his mind as to whether or
not he should go that way, and further information may be needed to remove
this, but the whole process from start to finish involves information (from the
information theory point of view) and persuasion (from the advertising point
of view). All advertising is information, and all information is persuasive. The
roots of marketing power are always to be found in the opportunities there are,
and the resources available, for the use of persuasion, that is, for the removal
of uncertainty.

Three further points emerge clearly from a look at advertising in the light of
modern information theory. Firstly, this approach forms a bridge between
experience and that part of economic theory which has observed the importance of the time factor in the changes which take place under imperfect or
monopolistic competition. What has been noted is that in contrast with the
situation in perfect competition (pure competition plus information) instead of
immediate change, there is *change with a lag*. When a customer can get better
value for his money from one supplier rather than another, in a situation of
pure competition there are no quality differences to prevent his making a
change immediately, although he can still fail to change because he does not
know of the price advantage available to him. With perfect competition he has
this information as well, so that he will certainly switch suppliers immediately.
If competition is imperfect, there are both quality differences and inertia,
which work to delay the switch, but it does take place eventually. When monopolistic competition is present, because deliberate steps have been taken to

reduce the buyer's uncertainty in regard to one particular brand, attachment to this makes for a still longer delay. What is known as the 'demand transfer period' is zero under perfect competition; under imperfect competition it is short; under monopolistic competition, it is longer. In every case it will be observed that the length of the demand transfer period is decided by the balance of uncertainty as between the product being bought and the alternative offered: In perfect competition, there is full balance, and so a zero period; in monopolistic competition, the balance of uncertainty is most in favour of the present product, and so the demand transfer period is at its longest. In developed markets, where there is intensive 'informational' competition between brands through the use of advertising, there may be a virtually complete balance again, which is the situation which marketing men describe as being one of low brand loyalty, and which they seek to change in their own favour by the use of sales promotion techniques. In modern markets which are fully-developed, there can be a demand transfer period which is close to zero, which gives an illusion of perfect competition. It is an illusion, because transfer can only take place to another brand whose 'information' content is the equal of the present one; there may be low brand loyalty as between brands of detergent, but at the same time high consumer loyalty to the use of synthetic detergents as such, as contrasted with the alternative of using bar soaps.

A similar illusory picture can emerge from the way a modern developed market is reflected in the brand's profits. None of these may seem excessive when compared one with another, but all contain a major element of rent when contrasted with products which are outside the exclusive 'club'. Likewise, illusion as to the source of new things in our world is also widespread. An enormous pressure towards novelty is exercised by the very existence of advertising. It is often argued in favour of advertising that without it, new products would either remain in the laboratory or be so expensive as to be available only to a few, and that what advertising does above all is to make mass markets, and consequently, mass production, possible. The implication is that the process of scientific research and new product development operates only under its own stimuli; and that advertising only comes into the picture when the practical results of these stimuli have the potential of satisfying a wide demand. In practice, since advertising's function is fulfilled once a story which is inevitably limited in content and interest has been told widely enough (which, as media become more powerful and ubiquitous, takes less and less time) those concerned with it will constantly be asking the research and development people to produce something which will allow them to use the magic word 'new' again and so revive their proper function of transferring information. It is even better, of course, if the Research people can put them in a position to tell a story that is *completely new*. The stimuli to research and development, therefore, are anything but independent. They come from the marketing side, and so the direction taken by Research is mapped out for it by the requirements of the marketing and advertising men. It is from the marketing men, therefore, not the R & D Scientists and Engineers, that the major stimulus comes to new product development in all product fields where discretionary income is important to the purchase.

Moreover, this pressure from the people who are concerned with information, and who want what they are spreading around to have a genuinely informational content, remains at a high level whether or not the research and development people are able to produce anything new in response to it. In the nature of things, real technological advance of a major kind can be made only infrequently. Since the filled bar soaps, for example, there have really only been the soap powders in the twenties, the synthetic detergents in the forties, the enzyme products in the sixties and the liquid soaps (probably of lesser importance) in the seventies, in a field which is recognised as being in the forefront of new developments in mass marketing. Between bouts of real product innovation at the technical level, therefore, there are periods, more or less long, when the information content of advertising will be reduced virtually to zero because every possible buyer in a particular market knows everything that he or she needs to know, wants to know, or indeed that there is to know, about a product. There is little or no uncertainty to remove. Yet the elaborate organisation remains in being – and must be kept in being, because it is impossible to tell when the next innovation will need it. The last word about this particular stage in the product's evolution has been said, yet the wordsmiths have to be reluctant to admit it, for to do so would mean they were no longer needed. Also, they *will* be needed again, to herald the next advance in the product's technology, so it is unthinkable that the carefully assembled team of specialists should be disbanded. A gap opens between what the informational organisation related to the product (which includes the money appropriated to the advertising budget as well as the advertising department and the advertising agency) is set up to do, and the actual work there is for it to do. This vacuum is filled by Promotion. Since uncertainty does not exist, it must be created, so that the informational organisation of the firm can justify its existence by removing it! This is what most of the activity of product differentiation in practice is all about. It is making news about the product once this is no longer news in itself, because the organisation is set up to disseminate information, and information is news. All the packaging changes, special offers, free goods and competitions have one over-riding object: To give the advertising something new to say about the product. This often leads to straining after miniscule differences, 'leading to the distortion, exaggeration, fake claims, and hucksterism that have given all advertising a bad name'. If the ordinary man's image of advertising is largely based upon his experience of Promotion, this is because Promotion, in the most precise sense, reflects advertising on its 'off days'. Although the statistics are inconclusive, the view is widespread amongst practical marketing people, that Promotion as a whole is increasing its share of total marketing expense. If this is right, it can only confirm that in more and more markets there is no new technology, and that for many consumer goods, firms are working close to the 'production possibility frontier'. More and more of the monopoly power generated by marketing is used to finance what have been rightly called "pseudo-innovations".

It is easy to see how strongly the informational organisation of a firm presses for promotional activity to be intensified during the intervals between physical developments in products. This is a kind of pressure which is likely to meet little resistance from top management, because of awareness at this level of what are the sources of the firm's uniqueness of advantage and its power to escape the constraints which the market seeks to impose on it. Nothing is more important to the firm's survival than this capacity to 'unmake the market' in its own favour. This capacity, it should now be clear, can depend upon maintaining a high level of fixed costs on the marketing side just as much as on the production side. Fixed costs are the barriers to entry to a market by new competitors, making for imperfect competition when they relate to the production plant, and making for monopolistic competition when they are in marketing. One major element in the fixed costs of marketing is the advertising budget. Management is pushed towards keeping the level of this budget up, even at the times when there is little work for it to do in the strictly informational sense, because this budget is the major part of the barrier against new competition which the firm has built up on the foundation of its registered Trade Marks. It is this barrier which provides the firm with a level of financial return on capital which would be out of the question if it were subjected to the discipline of the market.

This way of looking at the relationship between Promotion and advertising can be tested in the light of our knowledge of how barriers to new competition do in fact get broken down, and it stands up well. The evidence on this points clearly in one direction: Even very strong barriers to entry in the form of large advertising appropriations are vulnerable to a genuine advance in product technology (or physical ingredient). With this, the informational content of the new product's advertising is vastly greater than that of the existing products, and its effect, in terms of money spent, is correspondingly greater. The advertising also gains from being about the core of the product itself, rather than about peripheral adjustments to the product, which will be the case if – as is likely – the older products have moved into the stage of Promotion. Procter and Gamble's destruction of Unilever's near-monopoly of the British washing products market was based on two such waves of real product innovation – the soap powders in the 1930s and the synthetic detergents in the 1950s. By being 'ahead of the game' technologically in both instances, Procter and Gamble, although starting from a very much smaller base, were able to make their advertising more effective than Unilever's and so get a very much higher return on capital employed.

Something more needs to be said about the effectiveness of a large advertising appropriation as a barrier to entry by others. Once consumers have come to accept a given level of psychological ingredient in a product, their *definition* of the product comes to require at least that level in new products, before they will consider buying them. Say, for example, that the amount of psychological ingredient delivered by the main brands in a market is the result of aggregate spending on advertising at the rate of 10% of their total revenue. This means that to be taken seriously as a product in the field according to the definition which consumers use in practice for their purchases, a newcomer must, *from its launching date*, deliver psychological ingredient to all potential customers at a comparable rate. The Nielsen marketing research firm found by empirical study of large numbers of new product introductions, that a necessary (but by no means sufficient) condition for success was spending on advertising *from the outset* at a rate that bore the same relationship to the total amount spent by all products in the product class, as the share of the market which it was eventually hoped to achieve. Thus, for a target market share of 15% it would still be necessary, during the period when brand share was only 3%, 5% and so on, to keep advertising expenditure up to the level of 15% of the total. Clearly, not only must the newcomer be a firm with mastery of the necessary marketing techniques, it must also have very large financial resources indeed, to be able to contemplate investment of such a scale and such a level of risk.

It is, of course, true that the effectiveness of advertising varies considerably, so that with a particularly good campaign, a firm may be successful in gaining entry to a market with a relatively low investment, whereas another firm, whose advertising is delivering less well-tuned psychological ingredient, or whose physical product does not give the satisfactions which the advertising claims for it, may fail in spite of much larger expenditure. Nevertheless, in spite of great advances in techniques of testing advertising campaigns, the uncertainty surrounding an actual launch remains so great that in practice firms rely on the scale of resources for advertising even more than on the advertising's quality. The point is obscured by the technical literature on the subject, which naturally concentrates upon techniques of advertising, but the truth is that in many markets the real barrier to entry is nothing else than the sheer scale of the advertising and promotional expenditures of the firms that are in the market. No matter how good some new campaign may be, it can happen that the amount of money that would have to be put behind it to make a sizeable impact on the market, would be too great for *any* outside firm to commit at a single throw. This point is reinforced by the contrast between the level of risk in investment to enlarge capability, and that to increase persuasive market power. Buildings generally retain much of their original value; unwanted plant will always realize some part of its cost; but money spent on advertising a product which fails is *totally* lost.

Once inside the barrier, with a successful product, however, the rewards are extremely high. They are highest for the brand leader, which has the largest share of the market, and which is consequently able to reap the large economies of scale that there are in all communications media, and not only scale economies in physical production. The brand leader also has the advantage of deciding upon price changes of such magnitude and at whatever time helps its commercial policy, in the confidence that other firms in the market will follow suit. They will do so, because the whole point of their advertising appropriations is to be in a market where competition is in terms of factors other than price. Being in such a market, indeed, is being a member of an informal Cartel, with none of the disadvantages which Cartel membership can bring with it. Every Cartel exists to limit competition, but the history of Cartels shows that they have always been difficult to operate. Even the strongest ones have generally found that trying to include those firms which account for about the last 15 per cent of the market is not worth the effort needed. Also, a cartel is difficult to maintain in being, since the short-term rewards for "cheating" are so tempting to any firm in difficulty, or which is simply greedy. Ever since the Sherman Act in the United States in 1890, overt Cartels have been progressively hounded by the authorities in most countries, and they are also decidedly unpopular with the public. Contrast with them, the 'covert' cartel brought about by marketing power. This requires no secretariat, no policing, no meetings in smoke-filled rooms, no danger of going to jail for price-fixing. Yet it involves collusion to escape from the constraints of the market, which has a degree of effectiveness that few overt cartels can ever have achieved. The entry fee to the 'club' is substantial and there is no escape from paying it. It is set by the existing level of persuasive activity, and hence by those who are already in the market. Any potential entrant must have the resources to deliver psychological ingredient at the level which is considered 'significant' by consumers. If he does not, he will merely be contributing to the "noise" in the system, and his advertising will have no acceleratory effect.

Investing in persuasion in this way, also means accepting that price will be determined in practice by the Brand leader, and that competition is to be in terms of factors other than price. Succumbing to temptation to "breach the line" is self-defeating for a firm which can use persuasive market power, because it is merely putting itself outside the "club" which earns high Rent. Further, regulation of advertising by governments is restricted to the area of the claims which may be made for specific products, and is unable to come to grips with the real issue of firms' capacity to controle entry to their markets. And, generally, advertising is well thought of by the public, since the claim of those who use and practice it, that it is the means of bringing the benefits of mass-production to the public at large, is widely accepted. It may seem odd that the authorities devote so much effort to the regulation of capability market power by Anti-Trust action and the like, when persuasive market power establishes groups of firms whose capacity for implicit collusion is inherently so much greater than that of any cartel for open collusion. This can only be due to Governments' lack of understanding of the business practices which they attempt to control. With all the possibilities for generating Rent through membership of the informal Cartels that are made possible by modern marketing, it is hardly surprising that the effect on innovation of this type of market power is in the direction of new psychological ingredient or incremental changes in the physical product, rather than towards basic innovations.

Although the detailed argument is more appropriate to the next chapter, it is essential for understanding of the relationship between marketing and innovation, to explain at this point why Trade Mark *registration* is fundamental.

It will be immediately clear that in respect of any kind of investment, continuing business is only possible if there is legal protection of *reputation*. Goodwill, the propensity for customers to come back to the same source when they need to buy again, is the only possible justification for spending money in ways that will only be paid back by many purchases, spread over time. Who would invest to put something on the market, if others could benefit from customers' liking for the product, by pirating their reputation? So, if the law did not recognise reputation as something which it has to protect, piracy would be rife. Consequently, all legal systems protect reputation. For example, 'Passing-off', that is, selling goods under the pretence that they have come from a source which has a particular reputation, was actually made a criminal offence in mid-nineteenth-century England. In the Common Law systems of the English-speaking world, protection also came to include marks used to distinguish their products by manufacturers, because these were part of 'reputation'.

The 'Civil law' system of Continental countries adopted a different approach to Trade Marks.[8] They established registers for these, so that once a Mark was on the register in a particular firm's name, that firm had an absolute property right in it, in most cases irrespective of whether or not it actually used it in trade. The Common Law countries eventually added Trade Mark registration to their laws, whilst maintaining the principle that a Mark could be protected as 'reputation', even if it was not registered. Thus, in Britain and America a Trade Mark can be a carrier of reputation, protected by law, either through use or by registration; in countries such as France and Germany, the tendency is for protection of a Mark to be obtainable through registration only.

Why this is so important for advertising is because of the way in which legal protection has to work. To the extent that 'use' alone is relied on, a Court will look for evidence that the public does in fact associate a particular mark with a particular maker. If the only protection that is available for reputation depends upon being able to offer that evidence, then by far the most important function of advertising must be to ensure this ability. It would do so by developing awareness in the public's mind of the source of the goods it is buying. With Trade Mark registration, in contrast, a Court can accept the evidence of the entry in the Register that a particular Mark is the property of a particular firm. Advertising no longer has to be concerned with the link between Mark and maker. This leaves it free to articulate needs into wants for specific products, to build up an 'image' of the brand, to offer a 'unique selling proposition', to be concerned with 'positioning' or any of the other activities which have been generically described earlier as 'delivering psychological ingredient'. Note that advertising cannot perform *both* functions effectively at the same time. All experience with it, as well as empirical research, and aspects which are now understood through modern communications theory, confirm that a necessary if not a sufficient condition for good advertising, is that it tries to get across *one message, and one only*.[9] If a second theme is introduced, the effect is greatly diminished, and the advertising only contributes to 'noise' in the communications system. For this reason, therefore, as long as advertising had the task of linking a Mark to a maker in the mind of the public, it could never have developed as it did. Consumers to-day will know the 'selling propositions' or the 'images' of countless products, but they will not know who makes them. The difference is due to Trade Mark registration, which transforms the function of advertising.

"Getting new things done", as has now been seen, is not limited to new technology, but also includes novelty in the psychological aspects of products. Yet another important aspect of economic innovation is doing the same thing, but on a new plane. This is characteristic of the trans-national and multi-national firms, which are in fact most intelligible when they are seen as vehicles for exploiting their own innovations on a world-wide scale. 'Trans-national' is a word coined by economists to designate firms which operate over up to five countries. However, since in terms of innovation and market power the number of countries is irrelevant, both types will from now on be designated as multi-national Corporations (MNC).

When a firm moves into the international field, the problems of satisfying *objective* market requirements are multipled many times because of the differences between countries, as well as language and communication-over-distance difficulties. In contrast, those of using communications media to shape demand into patterns which it is profitable to satisfy, remain far more manageable, thanks to the International Convention for the Protection of Industrial Property, (widely known as the Paris Convention).[10] Under this, since 1883, a firm in one member country has the automatic right to be treated in any other member country in every way as if it was a local firm, in the matter of Industrial Property, i.e. Patents and Trade Marks. This does not at all mean that there has to be standardization of industrial property law in all member countries, although in practice a great deal of such standardization has come about. What it does mean is simply that whatever the local laws are, they will be the same for citizen and foreigner. The historical pattern seems to have been that the most advanced countries adopted a particular pattern of Industrial Property legislation in their own interest, and this pattern was much the same in most of them, because they wished to have reciprocity in trade. Registration of Trade Marks, for example, was urged on the 1862 Select Committee of the House of Commons so that British manufacturers could obtain protection in Prussia and France on a reciprocal basis. The less advanced countries then modelled their own Industrial Property laws upon the more advanced ones, presumably because they thought that this was the way to progress. The existence of the Convention (and even more, of the Permanent Secretariat of the Convention in Geneva) has contributed greatly to the standardization process, even though the basic principle of the Convention would remain even if this process had never taken place. The net result in practice is that, to all intents and purposes, the Convention brings about one legal world for industrial property. All the possibilities of monopoly which have been found to exist within a single country as a result of the power to register Trade Marks and obtain grants of Patents, are now available on a world scale. In spite of all that is being said and written at the present time about the multi-national Corporation, many examples of which dispose of more resources than a medium-sized state, there is one glaring omission: It is scarcely realized at all that the cause of the existence of many firms of this size and with these international ramifications is positive law, as expressed in the International Convention. What would be impossible without the Convention becomes inevitable with it. When physical products become substantially the same, the key investment a firm makes is marketing investment, especially in ways of differentiating the product from its competition. Product development means far more than development of a mere physical product; it covers development of the whole bundle of satisfactions the consumer buys, including the essential psychological ingredients. Among these, of course, is information about the product, using the word in the strict information theory sense of 'what reduces uncertainty'. This, as was stressed earlier, makes it unnecessary to distinguish between 'information' and 'persuasion' in the communication process. The search for psychological ingredients to which consumers will respond, the testing of many approaches to get the right combination of size, price, packaging and above all, advertising platforms − with the right balance between various media (the 'media mix') − all this is voracious for expensive skills and energy. As a result, even the products that get to the stage of test marketing already represent major investments at high risk. But, great as these investments are, they are small when compared with what comes afterwards: Full scale test marketing cannot be done without spending heavily, and the historical record is that of fast-moving consumer goods, only a fraction ever gets beyond this stage. When a firm has a really successful new product, therefore, one which comes through all the tests and is successful in a full-scale national market, it possesses an asset which is quite rare. The innovation has enormous potential value in terms of earning power, and it has to have, since the firm can only rely on it and a few other successful products like it, to pay for the many unsuccessful developments which have to be written off at different stages, as well as its overhead costs, capital charges and dividends. In the firm's balance sheet, what is not to be found is often worth more than what is; goodwill is rarely counted at more than nominal value, and, more importantly, know-how about developing goodwill for a particular product does not appear at all. Yet it is these which generate the cash flow when innovation based upon marketing is involved.

There is still more to having a successful product with a strong marketing content. As discussed earlier, there is a 'threshold level' in the use of communications media which has to be achieved if this use is to be successful for marketing, and this volume is large by any standards. It is particularly large when the risk element in it is taken into account. This is why no asset a modern firm has, remotely approaches in value the capacity to invest large sums of money in advertiging and other types of sales promotion, at a *subjective* level of risk which is not too much higher than that which applies to investment in fixed assets.

Under the Convention, a firm may obtain immediate registration and legal protection virtually all over the world for its Trade Marks. A few of these will become its well-known brands for which it will possess the know-how of successful investment in advertising and sales promotion. But know-how is not enough; business is a matter of making decisions, not of assembling information. The decision to invest in this way has to be made, and everything depends upon making it. Nothing is more difficult than making a decision on abstract and theoretical material alone. It is through experience that decisions become easy to make. The power to take such a decision comes from actual experience with the brand in the home market. When registration of the Trade Mark in other countries is possible, then the risk of investment in communications to develop a market for the product in those countries becomes little more than the marginal risk of doing so at home, once the product has proved itself. Through its provisions for Trade Mark registration, the International Convention turns foreign markets for products in which the psychological ingredient is significant, virtually into extensions of the home market. Since the firm knows that investment in a certain type of advertising, certain promotional methods, and so on, really 'work' in the case of this product, its management can have the confidence to invest freely. This confidence alone often marks the difference between success and failure. Success in advertising depends upon reaching the 'threshold level' (which is akin to 'critical mass' in certain physical reactions) quickly, and this in turn reflects decisiveness in making the investment in it. It is possible to burn box after box of matches and never light a lump of coal, because no match will stay alight long enough to raise part of the coal to the temperature where combustion becomes self-propagating. In the same way, if decisiveness and confidence are lacking, investment in advertising will be too small and too slow, so that the threshold level is never reached.

Here again the existence of Trade Mark registration is of vital importance. Without it, protection of the international brand in a new country could only depend upon use, and would therefore build up only slowly, as the brand's sales developed. With Trade Mark registration, however, protection is *immediate*, and any desired investment in advertising can be used to break into a market, all at once, without fear that a competitor could pirate the brand name. The advantage which this gives a multi-national firm from the aspect of reaching the 'threshold level' in advertising is enormous.

It is hard to overestimate the value to a company which is built on persuasive market power, of the knowledge its management has that a particular product sells, and of all the aspects of promotion, packaging, price and other factors which make it sell. This knowledge, thanks to the International Convention, can be used freely abroad, in almost any country in the world where there is worth-while purchasing power. Say, for example, that in a fast-moving consumer goods field, a particular successful product has reached a share of 15%. Depending upon the nature of innovation in them, some markets of this type tend to have an outstanding market leader, with second, third and often fourth products also having important but progressively reducing shares of the market, and with the rest nowhere; other markets tend to split more evenly between a number of brands. From its knowledge of the market pattern in which it is operating, together with what it knows from the product's own behaviour, the management may conclude that diminishing returns will set in rapidly after the 15% market share level. Looking abroad, on the other hand, it sees a foreign market in which conditions are sufficiently similar for the same 15% share as at home to be a reasonable target. Using the Nielsen rule of thumb, this implies investing in advertising during the first year at a rate of around 15% of the total advertising expenditure in that market in the foreign country. If that country is of any size, and if its market is well developed (we can assume it is, since our hypothetical firm has selected it for its first venture abroad on grounds of similarity to its home market) this means a single decision about the once-for-all expenditure of an amount of money that is both absolutely and relatively large. If the decision happens to be wrong, there will be nothing saleable left over from the wreckage.

Clearly, the power to make such a decision with all the odds being in favour of making it correctly, is an enviable one. These kinds of decisions depend completely on the existence of the International Convention. If immediate Trade Mark registration in the foreign country were not available, no decision to spend heavily and quickly could be made, because unfair competition protection for the brand would only become gradually available over time as the public began to associate a particular product with a particular producer. Moreover, the very basis of this type of protection might be of negative value to the foreign firm, since chauvinism in business is a factor to be reckoned with in all countries to a greater or lesser degree. Under the present law, the Brand is given an existence of its own, and its connection with the foreign owner is hidden in the records of the Trade Mark Office, where consumers never enter. It is therefore perfectly possible, and it is common practice in countries where strong local feelings affect buying habits, to spend money on advertising and public relations with the specific objective of spreading the idea that the brand is a local brand. But the difference between the genuine local brand and the international brand which is enabled to be in a particular country because of the provisions of the International Convention, lies in different powers of management decision about the investment of major sums of money in intangible assets, which lie behind them.

For the local firm putting a new product on the market, the decision to invest in advertising and sales promotion generally, is fraught with all the uncertainties that surround even the most thoroughly researched product until it has been seen actually generating cash flow. Decisions of this type, therefore, are necessarily cautious and slow, which is a drawback in anything to do with mass media. Yet anything else would not be prudent management, but gambling. In contrast, management in an international firm, of no better ability and judgment, and no more inclined to gamble, can take decisions in respect of the same country on a grander scale and very much more quickly, because it is reaching them out of actual experience with cash flow generated by the product in its own home market. What may appear to be daring, is in fact not so, because in the case of the international brand, it has all been done before. It must be clear that even if equality is assumed in every other respect, the international firm must beat the local firm, if only by virtue of its enhanced power of making marketing decisions. What to the local firm must be a venture into the largely unknown, involving a relatively high degree of risk to its investment, is to the international firm the further exploitation of already proved potential, by investment whose alternative use at home would be running into diminishing returns. It cannot be stressed enough that it is the International Convention, which effectively makes a single Trade Mark registration law for the world, that makes all this possible.

The 'marketing spiral' is also helpful in understanding how great are the advantages to international operation in the case of branded products which make use of advertising. The number of turns in the spiral, it will be recalled, is a measure of the amount of rent in an economic system. Some primary rent is in turn captured by derived market power, and by taxation. When it comes to be spent it is discretionary income, which in turn is the raw material out of which firms with persuasive market power extract consumer surplus and change it into their own producer surplus, or rent. The number of turns in the spiral therefore also acts as a measure of the proportion of psychological ingredient in products. The following diagrams indicate the differences from this point of view between a Third World country, a 'poor' OECD member country and an 'advanced' OECD country:

THIRD WORLD COUNTRY   'POOR' OECD COUNTRY   ADVANCED COUNTRY

Figure 12

In the Third World country, the spiral has scarcely begun to be formed. In so far as there is an exchange economy at all, it is so close to the subsistence level that there is virtually no consumer surplus. Since this means scarcely any possibility of extracting rent from consumers, it is not worth while for any firm to devote resources to articulating need into want for its product. As money is lacking, the final, essential step of adding it to want so as to form demand, cannot be taken. At the other end of the scale, in the 'advanced' OECD country, there have been very many turns of the spiral, and consumers' income so far surpasses what will purchase their basic requirements, that the bulk of it is discretionary, capable of being spent in any of a large number of ways. The psychological ingredient in many products in such a country is now generally more important than the physical ingredient. This offers immense opportunities to firms which are successful in articulating inchoate needs into wants specifically for their own products, for transferring consumer surplus into producer surplus. The 'poor' OECD country is between the other two examples, although because there is a significant amount of rent in its system, it is much closer to the 'advanced' OECD country.

Why the spiral is so instructive, is that it shows that contemporary differences between countries in terms of the development of their markets, are mirrored in the way the rent element has grown in an advanced country over a long period of time. For a firm in a country with a developed market to start selling its products in a country where there have been fewer turns of the marketing spiral, is just as if it was repeating an earlier exercise in its own home market, with all the advantages of knowing, from experience, how to avoid the mistakes which were made the first time. For such a firm, moving from the national to the international level can therefore be described as 'a re-run with hindsight'. Marketing in the most advanced countries to-day is very much like steam engine technology at the end of the eighteenth century, in that theory is well behind practice. But just as a mine owner who needed to keep his mine pumped free of water, could not afford to wait until Clausius had developed the science of thermodynamics enough to explain why steam power was able to do this for him, so marketing decisions in advanced economies have to be made largely in the dark, and mistakes and failures on a large scale are inevitable. The Ford Edsel and Du Pont's Corfam are typical examples. In retrospect, however, much that was obscure becomes clear, and it almost always becomes possible to see why things happened in particular ways in the course of a brand's development. There are several ways in which this can be particularly helpful in exploiting a brand in a foreign country. The first is in knowing 'what comes next'. If one is working at the current frontier of the market's development, this can be a terrifying question, because an enormous amount may depend upon a correct judgement of where the market is going. When the Polaroid camera and stainless steel razor blades came out, the market leaders did not consider them to be a serious challenge. We know now that they were, but only a few years ago, even to some of the most experienced and capable marketing men in the world, the answer was nothing like so obvious. In contrast to this type of uncerainty, working in less developed markets, rather than on the frontier of marketing technology, always means working in an environment where the demand is for products at least one stage back, and very often several stages. Nothing can be surer than that for such markets, the completely new product need not be reckoned with. Confidence in spending on advertising can be very much greater, because the unknowns are limited. In place of the multitude of questions facing a firm which is working on the frontier of the market, there is really only one question facing the firm which is expanding abroad. This is: Because of the differences between the two countries, how far back into our own 'Corporate Memory' do we have to go to find similar conditions in our home market? This is a tremendous advantage. What for the international firm in the poorer country is a 're-run' of previous experience, for the competing local firm means working right on its own frontier of marketing experience.

It is hardly surprising, then, that so many marketing areas become denuded of local firms, and why international firms are so much in evidence where persuasive market power is the characteristic pattern of business. Given the different levels of uncertainty with which they are dealing, even a mediocre management of an international firm in a foreign country has a head start on the most capable and resourceful management of a local firm. Often, of course, the local firm's marketing management is not as good as the local management of the international firm either. The main advantage of the firm from the advanced country in extending its marketing power to the poorer one, is elimination to a large extent of uncertainty regarding the future. Another example of this is a situation in which a brand's growth at home had been sharply checked at one time by the introduction of a competitive brand whose selling proposition was more attractive to many consumers than its own. If the second brand is not yet in the foreign market then the first brand abroad may adopt its rival's better approach. In all of this, of course, poverty is relative, and what is true of the advantages to a firm from a rich country exploiting its marketing power in a poor one, is equally true of a firm in the poor country doing the same in one that is still poorer.

A firm in an advanced economy will be working in markets which have been broken up into numerous sub-markets, or "segments", chosen so as to reduce consumer surplus to the minimum. For the same reason, the firm will almost certainly be marketing a range of products, so as to be able to compete in each segment. This range would be quite inappropriate for a market with less consumer surplus capable of being absorbed, and consequently with less segmentation and also presumably lower prices. However, the firm has not forgotten the time when its own home market, too, could be satisfied by simpler and less expensive products, and its corporate memory will produce the information necessary for success in the less developed market.

The effect of marketing on the power to innovate at the national level is therefore extended to the world level by the International Convention. More investment in R & D at home can be justified, because successful innovation can be exploited all over the world, and not just in a national market. The advantage of "lead time" as a barrier to entry to the new product's market by competitors, is all the greater when launches of the product abroad are "reruns with hindsight" of its introduction at home. Any advantage that persuasive market power combined with secrecy has for protecting innovation in a national market, is all the greater when marketing is carried on internationally.

Since U.S. companies operate in the country which has had most turns of the marketing spiral, there is nothing surprising about the extent to which multinational firms whose products contain a lot of psychological ingredient also tend to be American. In the same way, because of the way in which marketing reinforces the market power of capability, which the Japanese now possess in such a high degree, it is inevitable – given the pattern of existing industrial property law – that Japan should now dominate so many world markets in which incremental technical innovation is important.

To sum up, therefore, some of the strongest barriers to entry to markets are now provided by the techniques of marketing. These, especially advertising, depend upon national Trade Mark registration law, and its internationalization by means of the Paris Convention. Barriers to entry equal market power, which generates economic rent. Wherever there is rent there is the possibility of rational investment at above-average risk, in anticipation of above-average returns. This means that there can be investment in innovation. The type of innovation, however, must reflect the nature of the barriers to entry. In this case, therefore, the innovations will be in the areas of psychological ingredient and of incremental changes to existing products, rather than in those of radical technological advance. 'Marketing' innovations are no more than a rational response on the part of business men to the increased proportion of rent in the economic system, as illustrated by the marketing 'spiral'. The barriers to entry raised by marketing are not of the kind that can lead to radical technological advance. In fact, to the extent that they are more effective than other types, they will draw the resources that are available for innovation away from concern with radical change. This is not the least important result of the connection between marketing and the power to innovate. It might nog be dangerous as long as there are no great shocks from external sources to disturb the economies which emphasize marketing innovations instead of those in technology and basic science. When there are such shocks, however – as have been delivered to Western countries by OPEC and by the rise of Japan – marketing alone cannot provide solutions. The imbalance in favour of marketing innovations at the expense of those in technology then becomes a life-and-death issue, which will be considered in Chapter IV. Before this, however, it is first necessary to examine more carefully how all market power, and therefore all economic innovation, is rooted in positive law.

Notes

1. Say J.B.: Traité d'Economie Politique, Paris (1803) 1,179; "Les produits s'échange contre des produits; Ils trouvent toujours un marché". cf Hutt W.H.: A Rehabilitation of Say's Law, Athens (Ohio) (1974).
2. Malet Hugh: Bridgewater, the Canal Duke. Manchester, (1977).
3. Lynch P. and Vaizey John: Guinness's Brewery in the Irish Economy, 1759-1876. London 1960.
4. cf. Capitalism, Socialism and Democracy. New York (1942) p. 82.
5. Galbraith J.K.: The Affluent Society. London (1960).
6. Rogers E.M. and Shoemaker F.F.: Communication of Innovations. New York (1971).
7. Edwards H.R.: Competition and Monopoly in the British Soap Industry. Oxford (1962) p. 29, n. 1.
8. Beier F.K.: Basic Features of Anglo-American, French and German Trademark Law *in* Information Review of Industrial Property and Copyright (1975) p. 285.
9. Reeves Rosser: Reality in Advertising. New York (1961).

CHAPTER III

The legal roots of innovation

Since innovation in free economies depends upon market power, its roots will be found in whatever gives rise to market power. This will invariably be found to be some provision of positive law. As discussed in the first chapter, laws establishing and protecting private property are a necessary condition for markets to exist at all, even in the most primitive form. Markets as we know them to-day, however, have been brought into being by much legislation which has extended the reality of property far beyond its original limits. This legislation reflected a process of attenuation of the effect of medieval law on business which had been progressively evident since the Reformation. The Common Law, which is so important in Anglo-Saxon countries, has its roots in the Canon Law of the medieval church. Consequently, its reduced influence in these countries can be seen as an aspect of the waning of ecclesiastical power. Since property means the capacity to prevent others from doing what the property owner can do, any new legal means of limiting the range of activity of others, can represent an extension of property rights. Such an extension may be seen in the changing attitudes of the civil courts towards agreements in restraint of trade. Such agreements obviously extend the market power of those who make them, at the expense of others. The attitudes of the Courts to them evolved from partial suppression during the period up to the seventeenth century, to tolerance in the nineteenth and twentieth centuries. The resulting effect in practice of Judge-made law was extension of property rights. For Adam Smith, as for the Scholastics earlier, it was freedom of trade or 'natural liberty' which should regulate business activity. It did this by excluding all forms of exclusive privilege or monopoly. Smith's disciples in the Manchester School developed his teaching into pure *laissez faire* theory, and their influence must have contributed greatly to the growth of 'hands-off' policies in law and in the Courts: 'The value of common law remedies in cases of restraint of trade and in actionable conspiracy has been gradually and continuously eroded during the past 400 years.'[1]

This is only one side of the coin. The other is the emergence of the idea of property without corresponding responsibility. In the middle ages, although property existed in theory and was defended by the Church, it was hedged around by so many qualifications that its power to direct creative energy towards economic activity, was limited. Gradually, under various influences, more and more property became 'full' (in the sense that a man could dispose of it in virtually complete freedom, without regard to the effect that disposal might have on others). This evolution played a vital part in preparing Europe for leadership in the enormous forward strides in economic terms which were made in the last few centuries.[2] But at the same time, it also created tensions which have already come close to destroying Europe and much more besides, and may yet do so. The first way in which this new type of property affected innovation, was through the market power of capability. This is probably inseparable from any type of private property system. However, as long as the property guaranteed by law was widely diffused, and held in small individual or family units, the related market power of capability was so restricted that there was in reality little scope to escape from the constraints which the market seeks to impose. This situation was first changed radically by the remarkable social innovations of the Joint Stock Company and Limited Liability, both intimately linked, and both brought about widely by legislation within a few years of each other. Before this legislation, when prison was punishment for debt, no division of labour between investors and entrepreneurs could develop to any significant extent. The risk of becoming saddled with the harsh results of another person's business failure was too high to be widely borne. There is no need to stress how much of an obstacle this placed in the way of entrepreneurs seeking capital on terms which would still leave them in control of their own projects, as well as a substantial share of the profits. The new social innovations swept away this obstacle. Limited Liability allowed investors to abdicate from performing a management role in respect of their investment, and thus to parcel these investments out. Entrepreneurs now had access to funds, even if these funds were available in small individual amounts which needed to be aggregated in order to finance a project. The vehicle for this aggregation was also to hand in the Joint Stock Company. Together with Limited Liability, this even made money available for innovation. For the first time, individuals could each prudently invest a small part of their wealth at very high risk in the hope of very high return, to back an innovator's ideas. They would do so in the knowledge that none of them could suffer any penalty greater than the loss of his own small stake in the venture. Britain led the way with the Limited Liability Act of 1855, and the Joint Stock Companies' Act of 1856. France followed quickly, in spite of the fact that the new system involved a degree of independence of Government which was foreign to the French tradition. What happened was that a treaty with Belgium in 1855 included certain provisions for reciprocity, and for extending these to other countries. This was done in respect of Britain in 1862. Once British *Companies* were able to operate in France, French business men argued that they were at a disadvantage without Limited Liability, and so Acts were passed to introduce this in 1863 and 1867.[3]

Spain followed in 1869, and then came Germany in 1870, and Belgium in 1873.

The remarkable social innovation of the Limited Liability Company greatly facilitated the channelling of capital into business. By increasing investment in productive assets, it raised the level of capability market power, and consequently of innovation. This type of market power is particularly suited to the underwriting of incremental innovation. For a business man, the extra investment required to incorporate a small improvement in one of his existing products or processes is small in relation to his main investment in his plant; since it is the definition of incremental innovation that it emerges logically out of existing technology, the change will be in line with, and come from, what management and workforce already know and understand; and even if a competitor soon succeeds in matching the innovation, there is probably no actual loss. Capability market power, however, is not nearly so attractive if what is required is a means of protecting originative or radical innovation. The logical sequence for this is laboratory work, testing, pilot plant and full scale plant. Apart from the fact that failure is the norm at every stage except the last, each stage also offers opportunities for any new information generated to 'leak away' to competitors who have risked none of their money at all. For them, the market power of capability is only a serious barrier when the innovator has reached the final stage of an operating, full scale plant. Consequently, some other means of protecting investment in the generation of new information, other than capability market power, is necessary if innovation is not to be restricted to the incremental type. In theory, the Patent system is this other means, but as will be stressed throughout this book, practice is very far from corresponding to theory in this case. The principle of Patenting was never applied to more than a small part of economic activity; even within that part, the protection it actually conferred was extremely uneven; it was only taken seriously by business men for a period of less than half a century; and if it had not been for the growth of the modern pharmaceutical industry as a result of the innovation of Penicillin, it might not even have survived until now in several countries. In spite of this poor record in practice, this type of Specific market power has such potential for future development, that it is of the greatest importance that it should be widely and fully understood.

Invention and innovation both produce information (that which reduces uncertainty). But 'by the very definition of information, invention must be a risky process in that the output (information obtained) can never be predicted perfectly from the inputs'. Unless, therefore, positive law steps in to create property rights in information, enabling the owner to exert control over its dissemination, no investment in the production of information could possibly be justified on the part of private individuals or of industry. In technical language, there is need for a means of "internalizing" the "externality" that exists in freely available information. The Patent system was historically the means by which positive law did act to enable individuals and firms to internalize the externalities involved in the production of information. It does so by controlling the use of information rather than by preventing its dissemination. Patents granted through the world to-day are not too greatly different from those recorded in Renaissance Venice. The principle of Patenting is a kind of bargain between the inventor and the State. In return for disclosing his invention to the public instead of keeping it secret, the inventor gets the exclusive right to make, use and sell it for a limited time, which in practice can be anything from 14 - 20 years, depending on the country. On the face of it, this should benefit everybody. The inventor has a prospect of a period of control over the externalities of any information he produces, enabling him to charge a high price for the use of this information and so get a return on the risky investment needed to produce it. The public obtains information which otherwise might never have seen the light of day, or which, if produced at all, would probably have been kept secret. But although others are prevented for a time from making, using or selling the product, the Patent monopoly does not − and very likely cannot − cover all the externalities that arise from information production. From the public's point of view, these residual externalities are of great importance. The newly-produced information, for example, can be used to build upon; to a competing inventor or firm it may open up a line of further investigation which would never have been thought of otherwise. It quite frequently happens, indeed, that use by others in this way of the part of an inventor's disclosed information which is not internalized by the Patent system results in further advance which makes the internalized part worthless. This is only one of a number of ways in which the Patent system is an inadequate protector of investment in information production. There are many others. It seems impossible to administer a Patent system that is not open to the charge that 'it tries to parcel up a stream of creative thought into a series of distinct claims'. Very often, the novelty examination carried out by Patent Offices misses the real novelty, in commercial terms, of the invention for this reason. Many Patent Offices, including those of the U.S., West Germany and (from 1977) Britain, have despaired of ever being able to define 'invention' in terms which both give the concept its full range of meaning and allow it to be manipulated administratively; and so have fallen back upon a working definition of it which relies upon the absence of 'obviousness'. In practice, this amounts to whether the Patent examiner, having studied the invention claimed, can rebuild it by putting together pieces of documentary evidence. All these various parts of the invention are then assumed to be known already to a hypothetical person 'skilled in that particular art or the art nearest to it'. Further, this person is assumed to be able to put the elements together in every possible combination.

It is probable that there are sociological and demographic reasons why the examination system in Patent Offices developed in this particular way. Patent Examiners are Civil Servants, and they are neither recruited nor paid to take the high level of individual responsibility that we require, for example, from judges. If every Patent granted really conferred a large possibility of money-making (which would be the case if Patentable novelty really coincided with commercial novelty) then the level of responsibility which would be carried by individual Examiners (and which would be seen to be carried by them) would be unacceptably high. It is only the use of common sense by all bureaucrats that whenever they are given a task which they consider requires too much individual responsibility from them, they invariably re-define it. This means changing it in ways which ensure that no individual's career is seriously engaged in any particular case.

For Patents, this could only mean turning away from the inventive step in all its commercial reality, to some more abstract definition of it. Hence, the introduction of the fiction of the individual who is supposed to have, not alone access to all the Prior Art, in the whole world and in all languages, but also the capacity to make all possible combinations of it.

Even if the technique of 'mosaicing', as it is known, is not taken to extremes, it is clear that this general approach materially reduces the capacity of the Patent system to internalize the externalities of the production of information, and so provide a basis for prudent investment in it. Another factor which seriously reduces the capacity of Patents to provide a sound basis for investment in information production, is that the Courts in most countries apply more stringent criteria than the Patent Offices to questions of Patent validity. It is true, of course, that the Courts generally have more material, including that brought to their attention by opposers of the invention, on which to base their decisions. Such stringency has increased to the point of an anti-Patent bias during the present century; also, the higher the Court, the less chance a Patentee has of keeping his protection. This cannot attract a presumptive investor in research to face the uncertainty as to whether he is ever going to be able to prevent competitors from gaining at least as much from the information produced as he does, and at no cost. It should be remembered, also, that virtually all Patent Offices now work on a basis of absolute novelty, which means that publication of the invention anywhere in the world puts it into the public domain, where it is consequently no longer subject matter for a Patent. Information even comes into the public domain when the Patent Specification is opened to public inspection in another Patent Office, even if this is at the other side of the world, and the information has never been translated into any other language. If a Belgian inventor does not patent his invention in other countries very soon after doing so in Belgium, the fact that that country opens applications to inspection quickly may easily prevent him from getting much protection abroad.

It must be evident, then, that there are enormous drawbacks to the international Patent system. The expense of litigation, as well as patenting costs, are rightly chargeable to the Research and Development budget, since the full cost of producing information must include the cost of protecting it, if it is to come into any proper investment equation. Information which cannot be protected at all is worthless, and there can be few poorer ways of investing a firm's funds

82

than in the production of worthless information. When the certain costs of Patenting and the probable cost of litigation are added to the costs of the research itself, and a proper rate of discount applied to the anticipated return, the result justifies investment only in the rarest cases. Add to the other disadvantages that there is a long delay before the Patent is granted, which means that even the inadequate protection a Patent gives can be absent just when it is most needed, at the outset of a product's life. At present, the average delay in the U.S. Patent Office is two years and five months; in some countries, the Patent does not issue until nearly 5 years protection have passed, even though the application becomes open to the public after 18 months, and there is no means of advancing the procedure if a competitor is using information to the production of which he has contributed nothing whatever.

In Britain, the 1883 Patents Act established the Patent Office and eliminated the tangle of red tape which had flourished up till then. Patents per decade per million population in Britain, which had been 1,006 in the period 1852-1881, trebled to 3,116 in 1882-1901. The rate had only been 200 in 1822-1851, showing that in spite of the inconvenience during the period when grant of a Patent was largely a matter for the Law Officers of the Crown (whom Dickens pilloried for their love of red tape in "A Poor Man's Tale of a Patent") there was a great upsurge in patenting activity in the years immediately before the Patent Office was established. When, in 1902, a search for novelty was introduced in Britain, this further improvement in the Patent system increased the number of patents per million population to 4,432 in 1902-1911. Thus, adjusting for the increase in population, Patents were being granted at a rate five times faster after 1851 (the year of the Great Exhibition, which is supposed by some historians to mark Britain's industrial climacteric) than before it. The rate trebled again with the establishment of the Patent Office, and after 1902, when the examination for novelty was introduced, it accelerated further, by almost another 50%. This was the peak, however. Although in the years after the first World War, absolute numbers of Patents granted continued to grow, this increasingly reflected a rise in international patenting, especially of the inventions of United States firms. Never again did British Patents granted to Britons and British firms attain the pre-War level. American statistics confirm the drastic decline in the relative importance of the Patent system as a means of protecting investment in innovation.

This decline has been less noticed by the public than it should have been, because of the intrinsic interest of some of the success-stories to which Patents undoubtedly contributed.

Patents certainly underwrote the growth of the German chemical industry on the basis of scientific research. (In the 1880s there were more chemists researching in Munich alone, than in all the universities in the United Kingdom). Those who invested in Edison's earlier inventions (all protected by Patents) obtained returns which were well up to the dreams of avarice. (Edison's Menlo Park establishment was the first applied research laboratory in the world). Patent protection for one of the key inventions in electricity generation as well as in ship propulsion, the steam turbine, made Sir Charles Parsons one of the very few in history actually to reap the fabulous rewards that every inventor is sure are just at the end of the rainbow. In the period 1870-1900 the greatest number of innovations in steel-making were in Carnegie plants, and Patent protection was important to them. Carnegie himself bought the rights to the Thomas-Gilchrist process, which opened up the use of phosphoric ores. But in spite of such successes during its hey-day, the Patent system (at least in the way it developed historically) was generally found unequal to its task of internalizing the externalities of information production. If this was all business men could depend on to protect the results of research, we would not have much of the innovation which we do in fact enjoy. The statistics which show that Patents have indeed been declining drastically in relative importance underline this point.

Gilfillan developed and charted a number of indices of inventive activity for the U.S. between 1880 and 1960, such as output of Chemical and Engineering Abstracts, number of Physics and Engineering doctorates, organized research professional staff, amount of Federal and Industrial Research Funds, and so on, and found the same trend for both inputs and outputs: 'With striking agreement and steadiness, these graphs plot rises of 105 fold in output and around 340-fold in annual inputs or efforts to invent, during the period 1880-1960. In the same years, the count of Patents to Americans rose only 3.3-fold, little more than the population'.[4] What then, has underwritten the unquestionably large growth in inventive and (more importantly) innovative activity there has been, since it clearly has not been the Patent system? This great upsurge in spending on research has been controlled by sane and prudent financial men, so it is certain that this has not been done without some means of internalizing the externalities involved. In one way or another, the information resulting from the investment of these funds must be under the control of those who have made the investment, that is, since information of its nature spreads freely, they must have a monopoly of it. This is partly given by Government, partly by the market power of capability, and partly by the third type of market power, that of Persuasion.

To deal with the Government contribution first, it is undoubtedly true that in all advanced countries, the State's part has been increasing rapidly. For the U.S., Terleckyj calculated that even by 1960, the Federal Government supplied 62.5% of all research funds. The Baruch Commission reported in 1979 that 70% of the $4 billion spent on University Research was funded by the Federal Government, as against only 3% by Industry (the 1953 figures had been 55% and 7.5%). [5] Not alone is modern Government a powerful factor in research in its own right, it also provides the money for much of the research and development work that is done by firms in the private sector: 'In the military field almost entirely, and in civil progress largely, American invention takes place to-day because the Federal Government desires and supports it'. It must not be forgotten, however, that Government's capacity to pay for research and development in the military or any other field, can come only from its capacity to tax, that the prey of taxation is Rent, and that it is market power that has raised a modern economy's ability to pay taxes (by generating Rents) to levels beyond the dreams of any Colbert. Even, therefore, if Gilfillan's index of inventive inputs is reduced by two-thirds to eliminate the effect of research paid for by Government and other public sources, there is still an increase of well above a hundred-fold over the period 1880-1960, during which time Patenting increased only by 3.3 times, in line with population. If capability and persuasive market power did not exist to explain this overwhelming discrepancy, there would be no way at all of explaining it.

The alternative system to Patents of internalizing the externalities of information production, is a combination of secrecy with capability and persuasive market power in a vital third element, the 'flying start', or 'lead time'. In so far as marketing power is power to *accelerate* events (the use of advertising as an accelerator has been referred to in Chapter II) the 'flying start' is simply another way of looking at this acceleration. The firm which uses it starts from the marketing end, with information about a need which can be articulated into want-for-a-product (*knowledge* of markets is an important part of marketing power). Research and development is then carried out to develop the product, secrecy being maintained at every stage. Once a product that 'works' is ready, the firm's persuasive market power comes into action, and the element of decisiveness about committing large resources to build up a market quickly, on the basis of a registered Trade Mark, plays a major role. The flying start thus obtained represents a formidable barrier to entry on the part of competitors. If secrecy has been successfully maintained, by the time its rivals are starting their research and development, the originating firm is well on the way to having the product established in the distribution channels. Having been first in the field, it has had a choice amongst all the possible advertising approaches, whereas those which come after it will have to select approaches which differentiate their products from it, and the originator will have done everything possible to pre-empt the best. Is it any wonder that this alternative system to Patents is now so much more widely used as a means of capturing the externalities involved in the production of information?

The advantages possessed by the two other types of market power combined with secrecy, compared with Patenting, will become very clear by listing point for point, what each system of protection offers. The Patent system does not offer protection of all the information which research and development produces, but in fact, through its publication arrangements, assists the spread of both protected and free aspects of an invention. A Patent never protects the result, only one particular way of achieving the result. There are many cases where the result is the important thing, and the real core of the invention is to be found in it and not in one particular way of reaching it. What made the aeroplane a practical reality was the use of the low power-to-weight ratio of the internal combustion engine as prime mover, not just one way of doing this. Selden's Patent for the automobile simply had to be found invalid, because in this case it did cover the core of the invention, and too much upset of investment and jobs would have ensued otherwise. If the Patent system is used for protection, competitors can start using at least part of the information generated by the originating firm with little delay. There is another aspect to this. It is the very greatness of an innovator who is successful, that disqualifies him from taking the next innovative step, probably because in some way, and for that particular problem, the effort of getting the new thing done has drained him of psychic energy. So it frequently happens that the first practical breakthrough is not the best solution to a problem, even though it may be the only solution open to the first person who championed an attack on the problem and forced it through to success. Someone else, whose psychic energy has not been spent in making that initial advance, starts fresh on the basis of the original invention as published through the Patent system, and may have little difficulty in finding an alternative way of attaining the same result, which does not infringe the Patent monopoly. He has capitalized upon the positive externality of the first innovator's investment in the production of information (in particular, his psychic investment) and the Patent system encourages him to do so. It can easily be seen, therefore, what a poor justification for investing in information production the Patent system is, even if considered only from the aspect of the large area of positive externality in this activity which it leaves untouched.

Secrecy, the system associated with both the market power of capability and with persuasive market power, is in sharp contrast. In the Patent system, publication is automatic and out of the originator's control (and occurs in some countries quite soon after the application is made). If secrecy is being used for protection, and it can be maintained, the time of publication can be just when it suits the originating firm. Presumably, this will be when everything is ready for the product's launch. The tendency for Patent Offices to open applications to inspection earlier (18 months after application is now quite common) combined with the length of time it takes to get a modern product from concept to working and tested hardware, means that a competitor can start to move in the same direction well before the launch of the first product in most cases, if the Patent system is used for protection. If secrecy is used, the first a competitor may know about the innovation is when it appears in the market, and the originating firm is throwing in heavy reserves to consolidate its lead. Moreover, secrecy is not subject to any of the limitations which legal necessity or administrative convenience have imposed on the Patent system. It can cover the 'whole stream of creative thought' without any need to express it in claims or to test it for novelty or obviousness, and of course without limiting it to "arrangements of matter", as in the case of the Patent system. What secrecy does, it does as well for a 'unique selling proposition' as for a machine or a drug, and it covers all the commercial results of the invention, not just one way of attaining them. Above all, it gives no positive externality to a competitor until it is very expensive for him to catch up with the originator, if indeed he can ever fully do so, because the originator's uniqueness of advantage in terms of capability market power, is strengthened so much by his "lead time".

Secrecy also gets better treatment from the Courts than Patents do. There is a well-developed law of Trade Secrets which is unequivocally on the side of the secret-owner. In the case of Patents, the Courts have to balance the monopoly grant to an inventor for something that is new, against the public's right to be free to use anything that is old; most decisions on the validity of Patents turn upon whether or not they claim novelty for something which was already 'in the public domain' or "obvious". In the case of Trade Secrets, the Courts do not have to hold any similar balance. It is axiomatic for them that the public interest is best served by individuals and firms being able to keep their secrets from being pirated. The firm that uses capability or persuasive market power plus secrecy, therefore, as means of internalizing the externalities of information production, can rely on a favourable legal climate for the protection of its advantage, once the product has emerged into the light of day. Company registration fees are generally no higher than Patent fees, and Trade Mark fees are much lower. Capability market power is almost proof against being legally questioned. Trade Mark infringement actions are far less frequent than in the case of Patents, and generally less costly (expert witnesses, for example, play a much smaller part). With these means, therefore, the cost of litigation to protect the results of research bulks much smaller in the investment equation than it does if the Patent system is chosen as the means of protection. Delays in Patent Offices often mean that an invention does not start to get protection until well after it has been made known to the public. In contrast, secrecy gives protection at the time when it is most needed, right at the beginning of the product's commercial life. This advantage of Secrecy over Patenting becomes increasingly important as technology and communications develop and the life-cycle of products becomes shorter. It is not only that physical products are more quickly superseded (for example, the time-lag between the emergence of soap powders and synthetic detergents was less than half that between the powders and mass-market bar soaps) but where there is also a psychological ingredient – generally, that is, where advertising is involved – the effective life of a product is shorter than it used to be. If a product has an expected life-span of only a few years, for example, after which time it is anticipated that it will be superseded by something better, then secrecy will give it almost complete protection. By the time it is launched, it will be too late for a competitor to catch up in this generation of the product. If Patent protection were used, this would only be beginning to come into effect in some countries, because of Patent Office delays, at a time when the product was well on the decline. It could then continue for a further decade or more when it is not needed. This would be an extreme case, but it illustrates an aspect of the comparison between secrecy and Patents that has roots in reality. Only half of all Patents are kept in force for more than 6 years, only one-tenth for more than 13 years, and some of this pattern must be due to obsolescence of products, or components of products, which would have been better protected by secrecy before and during their short effective lives.

A dramatic growth in industrial research resulted from the shift from Patenting to a combination of Capability and Persuasive market power, as the main means for protecting investment in information production. In combination with secrecy, this provided a far better basis for prudent investment in information production over a far wider range of human activity than the Patent system ever did. The change led inevitably to concentration of industry and to multi-product, multi-plant, multi-national firms of enormous size. These can even invest in basic or near-basic research in anticipation of eventual, but still unforeseen, practical applications. The more than 100-fold increase in innovational outputs reflected in Gilfillan's indices refers to the period 1880-1960. It is predominantly the growth of science-based innovation that can be seen in these figures, and this growth-rate just would not have been possible without capability and persuasive market power, coupled with secrecy, as means of protecting investment in information production. Just as the Patent system reached its climax before the first war, the influence of the alternative system does not become fully apparent until well after it, but once under way the growth in its importance was dramatic. The percentage ratio of U.S. research and development expenditures to Gross National Product increased ten-fold between 1927 and 1958. The association of these expenditures with industrial concentration is clear: The largest 20 firms account for more than half of all research and development expenditures; the largest 40, 80%; the largest 300, 91%. In 1930 the Federal Government put up 14% of all research funds, but 63% in 1953-62. From this it appears that there was an increase of about 90% in spending by firms from their own resources on research in the period 1931-1961. As Patents to Americans did not increase significantly, virtually all of this must be attributed to the market power of capability or to persuasive market power, or to both in combination, for the reasons given earlier. It is also reasonable to assume that other advanced countries followed U.S. experience at a distance. On the U.S. figures available, around one tenth of the total expenditure is on basic research, a fifth on applied research and two-thirds on development.[6] Business's own funds are no doubt least important in the basic research proportion, are probably rather more so in the case of applied research, and are at their most important in respect of 'development'.

However, it must be the alternative types of market power that are responsible for there being any basic research done by private firms on their own account at all, and for much of their applied research, because of the inadequacy of the Patent system as a means for protecting investment in information production. Furthermore, the research and development of related capital goods sectors is underwritten at one remove by the persuasive market power of the firms which advertise. There is not much industrial research and development in the tobacco industry as such (although it is one of the biggest users of *marketing* research) but there is a great deal in the fields of cigarette-making and packaging machines, carried out by the firms which sell production equipment to the tobacco manufacturers. If there was no market power in tobacco, there could be no research and development in such firms. In the same way, much of the development of the use of plastics in containers has been the result of the growth of pre-packaging in the consumer goods industries. This is a secondary result of persuasive market power, so that it is reasonable to assign the same cause to much of the research and development behind the technical side of the packaging revolution also.

Since over the period measured by Gilfillan (1880-1960) the Patent system in the U.S. effectively grew only at roughly the same rate as population, its contribution to innovation was all the time becoming relatively smaller. It probably would have been even less, if it had not itself made an internal adjustment which is revealing in this particular context. For more than a century of its life from its establishment in 1836, the U.S. Patent Office looked for a 'flash of genius' in an invention, for it to be patentable. This, requirement became increasingly irrelevant in both Office and Judicial practice, as inventions for which Patents were sought became science-based. In the 1952 U.S. Patent Act, the change was reflected in the phrase that 'invention shall not be nullified by the means through which it has been achieved'. The 'flash of genius' approach was in tune with the first thrust of the industrial revolution − with Watt suddenly seeing what the separate condenser could do for the Newcomen engine, with Goodyear realising what had happened to the rubber dropped on to the hot stove, with Bessemer having the good luck of using pig-iron made from non-phosphoric ore for his steel experiments. The same 'flash of genius' was irrelevant, partially to the inventions of the second thrust and almost wholly to those of the third thrust, where improvements are based upon a great deal of carefully-assembled knowledge. A modern drug, for example, is far more the result of the painstaking repetition of laboratory and clinical tests, designed to explore every possible application of a change in formula, than it is of any 'inventive spark' in the traditional sense. The change in the 1952 U.S. Patents Act can be seen as a belated attempt to bring the Patent system into line with the requirement for the protection of information acquired through purposive research.

The Patent system was the typical means of protecting information production, only in the second industrial thrust, and this often led to the foundation of a new firm for exploiting Patents. Interestingly, this was Schumpeter's model of the innovation process, expressed above all in his concept of 'creative destruction', where firms newly founded to exploit innovation provided 'the competition that strikes at the foundations and at the very lives' of the older ones. When he later recognized that these ideas needed modification in the light of the growth of the multi-product firm, his thought was reflecting the swing back to a pattern of growth through expansion of established firms. This was being brought about by the replacement of Patenting by other types of market power plus secrecy as the main source of protection for innovation. In the third thrust of the industrial revolution, secrecy combined with marketing power justified a 'deepening' of research effort in the direction of basic research, and led to large research budgets and large industrial laboratories. Because of the form that information protection now takes, the new things get done within existing firms, rather than by the formation of new firms. Industrial concentration thus inevitably tends to accelerate.

The decline in use of the Patent system as a means of protecting investment in innovation is partly due to the availability of alternative means of achieving the same end, but is also partly caused by the way in which that system has evolved, and to the way in which Judge-made law in respect of it has affected its usefulness to business men. Judges are affected by the conventional wisdom of their time, and especially that of the time of their own education. It would be difficult for any contemporary judge not to have been affected by the great tide of anti-monopoly sentiment which has risen in all Western countries. The first sign of this may be said to be the Sherman Act in the U.S. in 1890, and later results include the various national attempts to control monopolies, and the Competition Policy measures of the E.E.C. Patents have suffered particularly as a result, since Patents are explicitly monopolistic in intent. Judges have consequently become progressively more reluctant to leave real market power with the Patentee in infringement actions, to the extent that half of the Patents tested in the U.S. District Courts, and two-thirds in the Appeal Court, are found invalid. Other types of market power which do not look so monopolistic, but are in fact more so, have not suffered from this bias. Persuasive market power, for example, largely escapes from criticism because its techniques — advertising, etc. — give all the *appearance* of competition, even though their real function in business terms — as was demonstrated in the previous Chapter — is restricting it! So much of the Law relates to Property in its various forms also, that Capability Market Power is never considered by Judges solely in terms of monopoly, and so emerges largely unscathed. But Patents *look* like monopoly, and so bear the brunt of the adverse criticism. Firms, especially the largest, have not been slow to realize that Patent Law in actual practice, has increasingly failed to protect the Patentee. The result has been a growing readiness to infringe Patents and risk the consequences as a matter of deliberate policy. What happened to one of the main colour TV Patents, where there was barefaced infringement, and to the Patents for the E.M.I. brain-scanner, where litigation costs were enormous, are two revealing examples. In such cases, even though the Patents may be held to be valid and infringed, the eventual financial outcome can fail to reflect the real cost to the innovating firm. In the E.M.I. case, the firm attempted to use the Patent system internationally as its means of protecting its investment in innovation. It did obtain several Patents, in spite of great difficulties in some countries and after long delays in others. Some of these Patents, after extremely costly litigation, did eventually result in royalties on a very large scale. But for E.M.I. these were too late, since it had fallen victim to a take-over bid, which, it is safe to say, would never have happened if the firm had kept away from innovation. The inadequacy of the Patent system had the result of severely penalising the originator of the most important advance in diagnostic technique since X-rays, instead of rewarding it.

Capability market power in the modern sense, in which the barriers to entering a market are such as to keep out all small competitors, is a function of the number of components in a product. In the first thrust of the industrial revolution, even though skills were scarce, products did not have many parts, and their manufacture could be organized effectively in small units. Joint stock companies and Limited liability were innovated at just about the same time as interchangeable parts and the great advances in measurement and precision machining (especially grinding) of the third quarter of the nineteenth century.[7] Without the social innovations, the spread of the technological innovations would have been much slower, but because one type reinforced the other, new technologies of vastly increased complexity became possible. In terms of number of components, the precision of their dimensions, and their interchangeability, the change is illustrated by comparison of a steam engine with an internal combustion one. Only a large manufacturing unit can produce an internal combustion unit at all, much less efficiently, and the cost of its plant requires the investment of huge sums of risk capital. At least up to the end of the first World War, it was technological advances that offered the widest range of innovatory possibilities. As the scale of industry, and the degree of its complexity grew, the barriers to entry by altogether new competitors were correspondingly strengthened. Where new products within industries were concerned, however, the same trends were actually *reducing* the level of entry barriers as between those firms with capability. The development of machine tools meant replacement of human skills by machines, thus greatly adding to the availability of skill, which was in any event growing through the extension of apprenticeship and formal training. The growth of specialized component manufacture and sub-contracting, together with mechanical drawing and copying, also made it easier, where the basic resources were available and supplemented by substantial capital, to imitate and compete with an innovating firm's new product. Hence the need for a sophisticated Patent system to enable more of the externalities of investment in the production of new information, to be kept under the control of those who made the investment.

This is a second reason why the development of the Patent system was distorted (the first reason is 're-definition' by Civil Servants, referred to above). The large firms which possessed capability market power found that the system could be used as a second 'currency' for handling transactions between themselves which related to technology. This currency was of course, only available to those with new technology to exchange, so that it became increasingly linked with the practice of "cross-licensing". Consider the position of a firm with a profitable technology which it is not convenient for it to exploit directly itself in a particular national market. Of all the firms in that market which might be selected for licence of this technology, the most attractive must obviously be the one which can offer a licence for equally valuable technology in exchange. This explains the growth of cross-licensing, Patent pools and similar reciprocal arrangements. Consider further the nature of the document which would have to be the basis for each such licence, if the Patent system did not exist. It would have to disclose the new technology in question, and would also have to define very precisely, what its limits are. These, in fact, are the two components of any Patent, the Specification being the disclosure, and the Claims defining the boundaries of what is held to be new.

Consequently, if Patents were not available, firms involved in licencing would have to develop a form of documentation that would resemble them very closely. The international Patent system is therefore very convenient for these firms, who have become the biggest users of it. The authorities who administer the system naturally defer to the requirements of their best 'customers', all the more so because these coincide with the need to re-define the system so that it does not ask Patent Examiners to accept too much responsibility.

The inevitable result is that Patents developed in a way which has made them a reinforcement of the capability market power of the largest firms, instead of contributing to the establishment of a stream of new firms, founded by new men upon new ideas, which would constantly challenge the existing firms, and make life difficult for them. Schumpeter's 'creative destruction' demands a dynamic Patent system. The historical development of Patents, however, has 'domesticated' them in the interest of established firms, and of bureaucrats, with the result that their relative importance to innovation has been progressively diminishing. As the Specific market power of Patents lost ground, Persuasive market power gained it. The legal root of this third type of market power, as explained in Chapter II, is the legislation providing for Trade Marks registration. Marks found on Roman and Greek artifacts were not Trade Marks, and medieval marks were imposed by authority to prevent fraud on the public. As one writer has put it, 'like the fingerprints taken to-day by the police, they established a liability rather than a right'.[8] These marks were generally required under criminal laws, with penalties for failure to comply. They can probably be viewed most intelligibly as fulfilling a parallel function to the description of contents and list of ingredients which legislation in many countries to-day forces manufacturers to print on their packages. Frauds on buyers have always been actionable under the Common Law, and have often been punishable also under specific enactments, e.g. the French law of 1824 repressed false indications of origin. When products bore an identifying mark, it always represented a definite attempt on the part of the authorities to protect the public by having the origin of the goods traceable. Right up to the present, the function of indicating origin is essential to a Trade Mark. The firm of Thermos, Inc. itself frequently referred to its vacuum bottles as 'Thermoses' instead of as 'Thermos brand vacuum bottles'. In 1963 the U.S. Courts held that it had therefore destroyed the 'identification of origin' element in its Trade Mark, which it had then to dedicate to the public. Recently the 9th U.S. Circuit Court of Appeals ruled that 'Monopoly' had become a generic name for a game, which did not any longer identify its origin as the firm of Parker Bros. The Supreme Court refused to re-consider this decision, and so Monopoly joined a list of well-known names which were once the exclusive property of one manufacturer, but which can now be used by anybody: aspirin, cellophane, milk of magnesia, kerosene, super glue, the escalator and the zipper.

However, as invariably happens, official actions and attitudes had results which were neither intended nor foreseen. In the case of marks of origin, the most significant of these results was the emergence of property in Marks. In goods such as cloth and cutlery, from the fifteenth century onwards, there was an evolution from marks of origin to marks of quality, and hence what began as a liability tended to change into an asset. Certainly, amongst cutlers a sense of value of a mark and even of property in it, can be detected at the earliest stage of this evolution. By 1801, in Britain, a freeman of the Cutlers' Company could bequeath his mark to his widow, who could continue to sell under it throughout the rest of her lifetime. Although this made the mark into property, it did not do so in defiance of the Mark's function of protecting the public by indicating the origin of the goods which they bought. The character of the work coming from the workshop of a particular Cutler would scarcely change immediately on his death. Presumably, the team of craftsmen whom he had assembled and trained would not leave immediately but would probably maintain his standards of quality in the product for some years. This time-lag is analogous to that found in the earlier Patent Acts, and reflects the realities of manufacturing of the time in a similar way. The fourteen year term of a Patent grant is believed to have come about because it corresponds to two successive terms of apprenticeship, which might thus be considered as justifying the investment in training necessary 'to establish the new manufacture within this realm'. As long as making and selling was mainly a local affair, the question of property in any particular Mark could not be of very great importance. It would never be the Mark alone which would link the product with its maker, since the product would probably have been bought from him without any intermediary, by a neighbour or near-neighbour who either knew a good deal about its manufacturing, or was in a fair position to find out. It is significant that the two areas where scholars detect the first emergence of property in Trade Marks, cloth and cutlery, relate to products which were traded widely, even internationally. With these, the ultimate buyer was separated both by distance and by intermediaries from the maker, and needed to be able to rely on the maker's Mark as a guarantee of what he was buying. In these circumstances it is easy to see how a Trade Mark could turn into a valuable asset, from being originally a liability, in that it made it easier to sell at a distance. When the physical barriers to selling at a remove were dramatically reduced, firstly by canals, then by metalled roads, and eventually by railways, there was a parallel explosion in the asset-value of identifying marks for all sorts of products. So Trade Marks can be observed as coming increasingly under that part of the law which is known as Equity. This began as a way of compensating for inadequacies in the Common Law, but as time passed, it became increasingly concerned with Property. To the extent that business practice is governed by the Common Law, proof of fraud is essential, but a court of Equity will act on the principle of protecting property alone. In Britain, indeed, it is possible to plot the change in legal emphasis regarding Goodwill in terms of the time-scale of improvements in communications brought about by the railways: In *Sykes* v *Sykes* (1824 − the year before the first steam-operated railway, between Stockton and Darlington, was opened) a plaintiff succeeded in protecting his Mark because the articles made and sold by the defendant under it were clearly inferior to his own, i.e. the public was defrauded. In *Blofield* v *Payne* (1833) the jury found for the plaintiff even though they held that the goods made and sold by the defendant were not inferior to his, i.e. the public was not defrauded in buying them, only deceived as to their origin. *In Millington* v *Fox* (1838 − the year when travel from London to Manchester via the London and Birmingham and the Grand Junction first became possible) an injunction protecting a Mark was given even though infringement of it had been due to ignorance and there was no attempt at all, to defraud. The line of evolution of of the Courts' mind is clear − and by the standards of the Law, unusually rapid. Well before the century was half-way through, then, property in Goodwill was a legally recognised fact of business life. There was some degree of legal protection for *established products,* but this did not extend far enough in practice to cover the development of new products or new *markets for them*, that is, not far enough for innovation. And, with transport so much improved, it was development of new markets which preoccupied business men. Because the flow of capital to the large production units which went with larger markets was greatly facilitated by Limited Liability and the Companies' Acts, these also strengthened the tendency for Goodwill to be embodied in a Trade Mark, by replacing an individually responsible maker by a group of anonymous investors, few of whom would have any personal connection with the product. The growth of 'the firm' in the modern sense in replacement of the individual maker, whose Goodwill was due largely to being personally known by his customers, played an important role in making Trade Marks the effective embodiment of Goodwill.

With new markets ripe for development because of the transport revolution, with money to be made through the economies of scale in manufacturing for these markets in larger plants, with capital for such plants forthcoming through the Limited Liability and Company legislation, it is clear that the one block to development lay in the inadequacy of the law of property in Goodwill.

France started the world-wide movement with its Act of 1857.[9] In Britain a Trade Mark bill and a Merchandise Marks bill were introduced in 1862, and a Select Committee of Enquiry of the House of Commons, after hearing submissions on these, recommended that a public Trade Mark registration system be established, in which registration would be *prima facie* evidence of ownership. This would eliminate the need to prove in Court that the public associated a Mark with a particular maker, and so give legal protection during the period when Goodwill was being built up, and not only when it had been established. The Government was slow to accept this recommendation, the only immediate result being legislation in 1862, which made 'passing-off' a criminal offence. It was not until 1875 that the first Trade Marks Act was passed in Britain. By it, a special way of writing a name could be registered, but not words unless they were old Marks or were linked with a visual symbol of some kind. In 1883, the second registration Act allowed 'fancy' words to be registered, these being held to be words 'obviously non-descriptive' or 'obviously meaningless as applied to the article in question'. In 1888, 'invented' word was substituted for 'fancy' word. Until 1937 in Britain, property in Trade Marks was always associated with the Goodwill of the business – an evident hangover from the earlier tradition of the Mark existing for the benefit of the public rather than its owner. Consequently, no sale of a Trade Mark without the business Goodwill associated with it was legal. On this basis, a purchaser would have had to buy all the original owner's business to obtain control over his Trade Mark; the buyer probably did not want the business, and the seller may well not have been interested in selling anything except the Brand. The 1938 Act, which permitted the sale of Trade Marks without Goodwill attached, represents yet a further stage in the development of property in Trade Marks which began in Britain in 1824. "Trafficking" in Marks as such, is still prohibited.

The development of marketing and Trade Mark law in the U.S. is particularly interesting. A federal trade mark Act was passed in 1870, only to be held unconstitutional by the Supreme Court in 1876.[11] This was because the Constitution provided no explicit basis for Trade Marks legislation, as it did for legislation covering Patents and Copyrights. Development of brand names on the basis of State trade marks only intensified pressure for a federal mark to facilitate the growth of nation-wide brands. When this came, in 1903, it was based upon the Government's power "to regulate Commerce between the States and with the Indian tribes". It is an intriguing hypothesis that marketing techniques – in which the Americans were subsequently to lead the world – were later in developing in the U.S. than in Europe, because of the later legislation for Trade Mark registration there. No U.S. marketing man in the last quarter of the nineteenth century stands out as a master of these techniques to the extent that W.H. Lever did in Britain. It was Trade Mark registration, therefore, which provided the basis for what may fairly be called the marketing revolution and an immense amount of economic innovation. As the law stood before Registration, Goodwill could only *follow* actual sales; the goods had first to be sold, so that their maker could build up a reputation for making them, and for which he had a legal right to protection under the Common Law. Registration of a Trade Mark, on the other hand, is possible before the goods the Mark is intended for, are put on the market at all: 'The Common Law protection against 'passing-off' will protect established lines of goods from imitation, but will not provide a shield behind which new Goodwill can be built up... (but).... since registration gives almost an absolute right to stop others zom using a Mark or a Mark like it, Goodwill can be built up behind the protection given by the Trade Marks Act.'[12] The consequences of these Acts have been incalculable, because through them property in Goodwill in the Trade Mark is made absolute. As Judge Salmond pointed out, *it is only by registration that a Trade Mark becomes property.*[13] At the time of the Select Committee enquiry, one perceptive lawyer pointed out that registration meant

'an entire change in the law. In contrast to Copyrights and Patents, where the public received something which had never existed before in exchange for the monopoly granted, in the case of Trade Marks as proposed, there would be no parallel "consideration".

It was the creation of a monopoly, he held, and 'against the spirit of the great statute against monopolies'.[14] He also argued that creating a property right that could be sold, would mean that people might not know that the maker whose product they thought they were buying was no longer so in fact, 'and the public may not in some case discover the cheat for years after it has been perpetrated.' Thus the creation of a transferable property right would 'legalise mis-representation'. At least one other witness, and even some members of the Select Committee, were also aware that what was at issue was an extension of the rights of property, not merely a means of protecting existing rights.

There was, of course, no shortage of evidence of how widespread 'passing-off' was. The deposit paid by customers on bottles of Bass beer was sometimes returned to them only on condition that the labels were in sufficiently good condition to allow the retailer to use them again, this time to sell his own brew under their name. Much English brandy (!) was exported to France to be sent out again as if from Cognac. Hennessy's, in particular, suffered from 'passing-off' of this kind throughout the Colonies. File-makers in Remschied in Germany put the names of Sheffield makers on their own second-grade product. J. & P. Coats, the thread-makers, had to meet competition from reels bearing labels identical with their own, except for giving the maker's name as J. & T. Coats and omitting to state what length of thread was on the reel. One piece of evidence which must have carried special weight, was that a French printer, whose display at a Paris Industrial Exposition showed how well he could copy any firm's label, carried off one of the prizes at it. However, it was agreed that this had been in the bad old days before the commercial treaty with France, and that now that registration of Trade Marks was possible in France even for English merchants, things were much better.

As long as trade was local, any question of fraud could only relate to the physical product. When customers became separated from producers by geographical barriers, however, defrauding of buyers by providing them with false information regarding a product's origin – or false 'psychological ingredient' – became possible for the first time, and judicial interpretation of the Common Law adapted to the changes. From this standpoint, the *Blofield* v *Payne* case deserves special attention. It will be recalled that there was no argument that the physical aspect of the goods sold by the Defendant was in any way inferior to those of the plaintiff, but that infringement had taken place because the buying public had been deceived as to their origin. Since whatever benefits the public gains from knowing the source of the goods it buys can only be psychic benefits, that legal decision must be the first which recognized 'psychological ingredient' in products.

From this standpoint, it is premature to see the emergence of a new concept of industrial property in the development of the law of 'passing-off' up to and beyond the first half of the nineteenth century. All that was taking place was the modernization of the Common Law to take account of new factors in products that had not been there before. The law was still concerned to protect consumers from being deceived, not to give property rights to producers. These property rights came, not so much through progressive judicial decisions, as through the Trade Marks Registration Acts. In England, these were the Trade Marks Acts of 1875 and 1883, which made reputation a matter of Equity rather than Common Law. Before them, protection of a Trade Mark could only be through a passing-off action and depended upon *established* reputation. It was only reputation that added a second, psychological part to a physical product. A product in respect of which the public possesses no information whatever cannot be the subject of a passing-off action, of which the essence must be the provision of information which is false. It is only possible for B to 'pass off' his own product as coming from A, in so far as the public is aware of A; it is only advantageous to B to do so in so far as the public *is already* aware of A as maker of this type of product in a favourable sense. This is why Common Law protection of a Trade mark demands evidence that the public does in fact associate a particular Mark with a particular maker. It is because the Common Law is concerned with frauds on the public, not with the rights of property. It is significant that the pressures from the interests concerned had little difficulty in getting the 1862 Act passed – but failed to achieve complete registration of Trade Marks for another twenty-one years.

Trade Mark registration was a radical break with the past, establishing a quite new type of property under the protection of the law. The Queen's Counsel who gave evidence to the House of Commons Select Committee was perfectly right: Trade Mark legislation in the second half on the nineteenth century, added a quite new dimension to property. He could not, however, envisage how far-reaching the consequences of that new right would be, because he could not foresee how much it would bear upon the growth of mass communication, and how much, in turn, this growth would make possible an unimaginable increase in concentrated wealth and power. Barriers to entry are the stuff of which monopolies are made, and product differentiation is now one of the most important of all barriers to entry. This in turn builds upon the Trade Mark, which brings the sanction of law to barrier-making. 'Restriction of competition is the legal content of monopoly; control of the market is its economic substance'.[15] It is this legal sanction which turns what goes on behind the barrier into property, since if this sanction did not exist the results of this activity could be appropriated by outsiders. It is perfectly valid, therefore, to attribute the economic results of this activity (which is always of course *selling* activity, designed to develop the preferences of customers for a particular brand) to the Trade Mark on which it is completely dependent.

For products of this type, the registered Trade Mark is *the* productive factor, since it is the one on which the power of all the others to generate a surplus over costs (the normal rate of return on money being considered as a cost related to the capital employed, in this context) depends. What is this surplus? Clearly, it is not altogether what it is normally called, profit, since it is only very partially a return in respect of a decision made under uncertainty. The part that is not entitled to be called profit cannot be attributed to any of the other factors either, since these have all been accounted for as costs. It can be nothing else than a *rent* imputable to the Trade Mark. The revenue which results from a Trade Mark, indeed, is rent in the purest sense of the word. Considering rent as the return to a productive factor in its best use compared with its alternative uses, a Trade Mark has one use and one only: To provide a foundation on which a barrier to entry to a market by newcomers, can be built up. Such a market is in fact defined in terms of the Trade Mark itself. A Trade Mark can have no alternative use other than this. It cannot relate to any other brand name. Nothing can be done with the registered Trade Mark 'Exxon' except build up the brand name Exxon, not any other brand name, on it. Apart from this the Trade Mark is utterly and completely useless, however enormously valuable it may be in what is otherwise simultaneously its best and only use. If the rent aspect of a Trade Mark is examined in terms of the actual return realized, compared with the return necessary to call the factor into existence, or to direct it to one use away from alternative uses, the result is the same. All it needs to bring this factor of enormous productive potential into existence is to pay the Government fee, which is invariably nominal; the Mark thus registered has but one possible economic use, so the value of its alternative use is zero. All the surplus, then, from persuasive market power, with the exception of the trivial sum needed to keep the Trade Mark registered, must be attributed to the Trade Mark as rent.

This may also explain why welfare economists have never been happy with product differentiation and all that goes with it. What they may be objecting to in Trade Marks is the creation of rents which are not social — since no *social* rent is imputable to artificially created scarcities, and no scarce resource can be more artificially created than a registered Trade Mark. One economist who did see this point was G.C. Archibald, who wrote that income from Patents, Copyrights, Brand Names etc., is a rent or quasi-rent (although he wrongly gave credit for this idea to Roy Harrod in the latter's *Economic Essays*).[16] Nordhaus, as another example, quotes with approval Schumpeter's idea that a continuing flow of inventions is the only source of quasi-rents.[17] Persuasive market power, as was shown in the previous Chapter, is now a most powerful means of securing such a continuing flow of a particular type of 'inventions', or 'new things'. Moreover, to the extent that it depends upon a Registered Trade Mark, product differentiation as a source of funds does not wear out, and persuasive market power is often more valuable for a firm even than its market power of capability. The Trade Marks Acts resulted almost inevitably from the legislation allowing the formation of limited liability companies. Had production remained substantially local, the Common Law approach to protecting Goodwill would probably have satisfied both business men and the public. But when larger manufacturing units became possible in terms of capital supply and organisation, the area of distribution had to become correspondingly wider. It could then be argued that something more was needed even to protect the public, who were now being offered the product of a factory they had never seen, and whose owners they did not know, in competition with that of the small local firm with all aspects of which they were probably familiar, and whose owner had a personal identity for them. From the point of view of the larger manufacturer with anonymous shareholders, of course, what was even more important was that he could take steps to extend his distributional area without having to fear imitation of his goods or having competitive products 'passed-off' as his. This was especially important as the law stood, since before his product could be well established in a new area, he might be faced with the impossibility of winning a passing-off action, as he would be unable to produce witnesses who would testify that they linked his manufacture with the name of his product. Another way of looking at the situation is in terms of transport. From Adam Smith onwards, economists have known that transport costs, more than anything else, limit competition. When transport innovations made it possible to overcome physical barriers to the movement of goods, they created another problem. The goods, once they had been moved physically, now faced *psychological* barriers, of inertia, of strangeness, of lack of awareness of their qualities, of xenophobia even, and these too had to be overcome. Transporting goods across physical barriers; transporting people across psychological barriers; for the first time the two sides of the modern marketing coin were apparent on a large scale.

All the limited liability acts in themselves could do was to facilitate the flow of capital to large-scale industry — they were a necessary but not a sufficient condition for growth in scale. However, without Trade Mark registration, there would have been clear limits to that growth. No matter how great are the economies of scale in making goods in a larger plant than has ever been envisaged before, no matter how effective are the means available for transporting them physically over a greatly enlarged area of distribution, there still remains the problem of persuading people to buy them – the problem of transporting people over psychological barriers. It was the Trade Marks Acts which enabled this to be solved. They relaxed the constraints on sales which kept plants from becoming bigger and more efficient, and the consequent constraint upon the growth of capability market power. Just as steam power opened the door to massive economies of scale in production, the Trade Marks Acts opened the door to economies of scale in communications. Without Trade Mark registration, all the ways of using mass media with which we are so familiar today could not exist in anything like the same form, and certainly in nothing like the same quantity. Trade Mark registration created a quite new kind of monopoly power: The power to realise scale economies in communications related to a particular brand. This is all the more important, since empirical studies have shown that scale economies on the production side of industry are less important than used to be thought. For many firms, over quite a large range of output, the long-range average cost curve is not falling, but horizontal. In fact, it has been suggested that the argument that only large firms can afford the research and development costs involved in innovation to-day, has arisen as a justification of 'bigness' in parallel with the discrediting of the idea of production scale economies.

In contrast to production, it is certain that there are great advantages to scale in both research and development and in communications, and it is on these advantages that the modern giant corporation, especially the multi-national corporation, is founded. In the case of research and development, they justify investment in applied research with a long time to pay-off, or even investment in basic research. For example, the invention of the transistor is thought of as a piece of advanced applied research, particularly as the Nobel prize went to Shockley and Brattain, who were immediately concerned with it. But the fact that these two were working in that area at all was due to an earlier decision by Kelly, the head of Bell Laboratories, that the whole semi-conductor area was ripe for a major advance. Although it could not be foreseen where the likely breakthrough would occur, Bell and Western Electric have such resources, and their range of interests is so wide, that no matter where it happened, and no matter how long it took, they would be able to exploit it. Given the inadequacies of other types of protection (especially of Patent protection) it must be accepted that size – or perhaps more correctly, size coupled with diversity of interests, is a necessary condition if any basic research or very long-term applied research is to be a profitable use of resources.

Size, of course, relates not just to the capacity to develop and make products, but also to market them. Just as the power to make the products is rooted in Joint Stock Companies' and Limited Liability legislation, so the power to market them goes back to the Trade Mark Acts. These Acts enable a brand to be distinct from the firm which owns it, and to have an individual image built up for it. Among the benefits of this to a firm, is that it allows two or more brands to be run in competition with one another, and this is a considerable help towards expanding the total market. This would be impossible if the only form of protection available was Common Law protection, since under this it would be necessary for consumers to be able to associate both products with their proprietor firm. Once brand name registration comes in, this is no longer the case, and buyers happily choose between competing products, in ignorance that they may all be under the same ownership.

So far all discussion of the legal roots of market power has remained at the national level. International trading, however, made its influence felt early on – for example, Trade Mark legislation was urged on the House of Commons Select Committee in 1862 in order to enable traders to obtain protection for their marks in other countries on a basis of reciprocity. Serious discussions of a general arrangement between countries about Industrial Property took place at the Vienna Exhibition in 1873, and two conferences on the subject were held in Paris in 1878 and 1880. These led to the International Convention for the Protection of Industrial Property, the Paris Convention of 1883. The small group of countries which signed it originally included some from South America which are certainly not leaders in technology to-day. Britain ratified it in 1884. The Swiss wanted no part of it, but were threatened with sanctions against their chemical exports to Germany, and finally capitulated. In all probability, no other international agreement, not the General Agreement on Tariffs and Trade, not even the Treaty of Rome, has had more world-wide economic consequences than the Paris Convention. Its longevity in substantially identical form to the day it was signed, is almost certainly due to its absolute simplicity. Each adhering country is free to have any form of industrial property regime it may prefer, only binding itself, as far as Patents and Trade Marks are concerned, to treat nationals of all other adhering countries in exactly the same way as its own. Thus, for example, Italy is unusual in not granting Patents for pharmaceutical products. There is no objection to this under the Convention as long as there is no question of Patents being granted to Italian, but refused to foreign firms. On the other hand, Italian pharmaceutical firms are free to obtain Patents for their products in the United States and virtually all other Convention countries, on exactly the same terms as local firms.

Administratively, the Convention operates by what is known as priority. Once the first Patent or Trade Mark application is made in any Convention country, the clock is stopped in all other Convention countries for a year in the case of Patents and six months in that of Trade Marks. During this 'priority' period, nothing that happens in any of these countries (for example, lodgements of an identical Patent or Trade Mark application by another) can affect any steps taken to obtain protection of an invention or Trade Mark, by the original applicant. The latter therefore has the whole of the priority period in which to decide which countries warrant seeking for protection, and to take the necessary steps. Nothing can be more obvious than the way in which the Convention shifts the area of operation of an innovative company (whether the innovation is in technology or in psychological ingredient, that is, in marketing) from the individual country to the world. The multi-national corporation is most intelligible, therefore, as a vehicle for exploiting its own innovations on world markets, and the Paris Convention is, without doubt, the Charter of International Business.

At the international as well as the national level, the market power of Persuasion and the Specific market power of Patents can be seen as rooted in a legal enactment. Persuasive market power is still further protected internationally by the Berne Convention (1886) and the Universal Copyright Convention (1952) both of which were intended to protect literary works. With the growth in importance of advertising, however, it became valuable for firms to be able to prevent their successful advertising campaigns from being plagiarised. At the present time, for example, it is standard practice for U.S. advertising agencies to lodge copies of all their clients' material, whether print or film, in the Library of Congress, as is required there to obtain copyright protection. When the investment in research and creative work behind any one of these campaigns is taken into account, it can be seen how advantageous it could be to a competitor in another country to copy and use it before the originator did so, but this is prevented by the international arrangements. Between the Paris Convention, which protects Trade Marks, and the Copyright Conventions, which protect advertising, it may be said that Persuasive market power is intrinsically world-wide in its scope.

This is much less the case with Capability market power. With Patents or Trade Marks, the benefit of the Persuasive or Specific market power is hardly lessened if manufacture of the goods in question is dispersed, even to many factories in different countries. The market power of Capability, however, is very much related to a plant which has an agglomeration of skills, economies of scale and other advantages which would be lost by dispersion. Since the slump of 1873, following which protectionism emerged widely, and even more after the slump of 1929, when it became a world-wide phenomenon, Capability market power has faced tariffs, quotas and other barriers to the free shipment of its products to other countries. Free Trade is always advantageous to the country which leads in technology at any particular time, which is why Britain was its foremost advocate during most of the nineteenth century. After the last War, the country whose innovative industries were best suited to the markets for consumer and consumer-durable goods that were entering upon a period of rapid world-wide growth, were those of the United States. It is not surprising, therefore, that it was the U.S. which took the initiative in measures to promote freer trade internationally. The General Agreement on Tariffs and Trade (G.A.T.T.) was the result. It was signed in 1947, and, together with what is known as the Kennedy Round, it had considerable success in making protection unfashionable until the explosive growth of Japanese exports. As might be expected, as G.A.T.T. comes under strain from the latter, it is Japan which sees most merit in preserving it.

As to the Specific market power of Patents, international protection is patchy, since all that the International Convention does is give access to national systems, and these vary widely from country to country.[18] A Patent is only a licence to litigate, since a Patentee has to proceed against an infringer in the civil courts. The value of a Patent is therefore measurable in terms of the probability that a court will uphold its validity, and this in turn depends upon the thoroughness and range of the examination carried out by the Patent Office of the particular country before issuing it. The Dutch examination is so stringent that many firms do not even try to get a Patent in that country. German Patents have always had a strong chance of being vindicated in a court action, those of the United States, significantly less so. At the other extreme are Patents issued by countries such as Belgium and South Africa, where no examination of content takes place at all, and where, consequently, there can be no presumption whatever of validity in advance of a court ruling. Although the strength of protection available internationally for the different kinds of market power varies widely, both as between countries and as between types of market power, in every case the differences can easily be traced to the provisions, national and international, of positive law.

The keynote of the 1883 Paris Convention and the 1947 G.A.T.T. was reciprocity as between countries. There should be nothing except economic advantage in this, as indeed in any reciprocal arrangements, as long as there is substantial equality between contracting members. When what moves between countries are products incorporating factors that are scarce in one country but plentiful in the other, all the participants are theoretically better off as a result of such trade than they would be without it. This can be readily granted in the case of physical products, or raw materials for the physical ingredients of products which may also have a psychological ingredient; but what about the case when what moves between countries is only, or almost only, the psychological ingredient in what the consumer buys? The question is of cultural as well as business importance, because inevitably such a movement between countries will be very unbalanced. The less developed countries will want the psychological ingredients in the products of the more developed, and will have few, if any, products with psychological ingredients that are of interest to consumers in the advanced countries. International trade then becomes the 'demonstration effect' in action.

All agreements that are truly reciprocal are, to that extent, partnerships. It is a matter of common experience that the most successful partnerships are those in which the rights and duties of the partners reflect the true balance of their respective strengths. If two men get into partnership on a basis of equality, even though one is ten times as rich as the other, it may scarcely matter as long as things are going well. But when stresses arise, the legal document which lays down their equal status is poor counterbalance to the relative weight of their real resources; in the long run, nothing can prevent the discrepancy between them from this point of view from imposing itself on events. The International

Convention, by the reciprocity between countries for which it provides in respect of Patents, Designs and Trade Marks, is a sort of partnership in which the legal document completely ignores the real relationship between them as far as economic strength is concerned. The United States and the State of Upper Volta are members. Can anything be imagined that could possibly be further apart, in terms of the subject matter of the Convention – Invention and Brand Names? What possible resemblance to an economic balance could there be between these two member states, or between Britain and Chad, or West Germany and the Republic of Niger? But, someone from any of the advanced countries may say, 'we do not get more than we give. Is it not only fair that we can get protection for our inventions and Trade Marks in Upper Volta, on terms which are no better and no worse than the local law allows to an Upper Volta citizen, since the citizens of Upper Volta get in return the same protection for their inventions and brands in our countries? The markets to which we are offering them access,' he might add, 'are vastly more valuable than their local markets are to us'. But for what inventions? For what brands? The poorer countries have found the Paris Convention to be an extremely bad bargain.

It is a remarkable thing that the Convention, for all its overwhelming importance to the world's economic life and trade, has never until recently had its workings in practice studied in any detail. Virtually nothing is known about the economic balance between member countries on the Trade Mark account. On the analogy of the relative importance of these within individual countries, however, it is safe to say that the money involved in Trade Marks is very much more important than in the case of Patents. On Patents, a little is now known, and this can provide some clue as to what the overall balance may be like. All Patents statistics must be read with caution, because it is in the nature of Patents that there is no necessary correlation between numbers and value. Most of them never earn their cost; a very few produce really outstanding returns. With all the reservations possible, however, one cannot be blind to the implications of a pattern in which the percentage of Patent grants to foreigners is in the high nineties for countries such as Pakistan and Ireland, but only 37 for Germany and 16 for the U.S. In taking the enquiry a stage further, Ireland is a very suitable country for special study, because it can be regarded either as one of the richest of the poor countries or one of the poorest of the rich countries. A comprehensive analysis of Irish Patent statistics is believed to be the first attempt anywhere to make a rigorous assessment of the way in which the International Convention works.[19]

Ireland joined the International Convention shortly after gaining independence from Britain in 1922. Because it operates a system of renewal fees for its Patents, it is possible to weight its Patent Statistics so that they reflect value of Patents and not only numbers, to a useful extent. Murdoch found that, during the period of his study, 15% of applications were native, but only 4% of the grants, and 2% of the 'significant' patents. The total number of native 'significant' Patents was only 33 (out of a total of 1621). In just over a quarter of these, no Patent applications were filed abroad, but in two-thirds of the cases the International Convention was used to obtain Patents in other countries. But only for one-third of the native inventions did Patenting abroad bring any financial return at all, and in the vast majority of these, this was insignificant. For example, 9 of the 33 native inventions were patented in the U.S., but none of these produced any return whatsoever. Therefore, in return for giving Patent monopolies to 342 'significant' U.S. inventions, Ireland got precisely nothing from the U.S. under the reciprocal provisions of the International Convention. If the same pattern applies to Trade Marks, and there is no reason to doubt that it does, then what this study of the Patent system discloses is no more than the tip of the iceberg as far as the financial results are concerned: As Chamberlin said, 'merely to suggest such a comparison is to raise serious doubts as to whether the monopoly element in Patents is even quantitatively as important as that in Trade Marks.'[20]

On the face of it, therefore, in so far as Ireland is a typical small and fairly poor country, membership of the International Convention looks like being all loss and no gain. Actual − and presumptively valuable − legal monopolies were granted to inventors and firms in other countries in exchange for the mere *possibility* of reciprocal monopolies − a possibility which, at least as far as these statistics go, was altogether unrealized. Membership of the International Convention involved an exchange of substance for shadow. There is no reason to think that the pattern for that country in other years, or for other, even poorer, countries at any time, is any more favourable, so that the working of the Convention is overwhelmingly advantageous to advanced countries at the expense of the poorer ones. It may be argued against this, that without Patent protection under the Convention, firms in the advanced countries could not afford to sell their machines to countries which need them if they are to manufacture competitively by international standards and so export and earn foreign exchange. There are two replies to this: Firstly, given the nature and intensity of international competition, is it really likely that a producing firm would have to go without, simply because its country did not subscribe to the Convention? Is it not more probable that alternative suppliers of what would be very close substitutes indeed would rush in to satisfy the demand? And would not the fear of their entry to its market, cause the original firm to forget about its need for Patent protection in the country concerned? Another argument is that without an Industrial Property system a poor country will not be able to attract the foreign investment that it needs. Further research in the Irish statistics, however, suggests that except for the Chemical sector, Patents have little relevance on this score.[21]

Fear of entry to a market by newcomers, as was seen earlier, is every bit as good a disciplinarian of monopoly practices, as actual, realized entry. It is possibly economically better as well. There are as yet no data with which to answer these important questions definitively, which underlines how badly empirical research into the way in which the International Convention works in practice, is needed. However, the commonsense answers all point in one direction. Secondly, and paradoxically, the economic growth of the poorer countries, and their capacity to stand on their own feet, is probably being adversely affected by the protection available under the International Convention. This protection makes it advantageous for firms in the advanced countries to sell the products of the newest technology to the poorer countries, even though this may not be what they need or can use. Everyone with experience of the 'under-developed' world, reports the vast gap which exists between the equipment available and the skills, the 'feel' for equipment of this kind, and the infrastructure of related techniques, systems, instrumentation and organization that would make the equipment economically viable. The contrast in an Asian hospital between the presence of an advanced microscope with no-one capable of using it properly and no real pattern of profitable use for it, and an almost total lack of the simplest and most easily used instruments for sampling culture media, springs vividly to mind, but it can be parallelled in a thousand different ways. Almost all foreign aid to these countries is spent by Government agencies, and is therefore not subject to the discipline of profit and loss; the "demonstration effect" has virtually free reign. But one of the few outstanding successes — as long as it lasted — among poor countries in post-war years was the explosive growth of the Peruvian fishmeal industry, which was started on a basis of secondhand plants bought from the United States. However, this is the exception rather than the rule, and it seems almost certain that the gap in most poor countries between the productive capacity they have and the productive capacity of which they can make effective use, is at least partly attributable to these countries' membership of the International Convention. Everything that has been said applies with even more force, if that were possible, to the balance between rich and poor countries in Trade Mark protection. This point will be developed further below.

Any definition of an advanced country in the free world, corresponds to one where monopolistic competition operates over a major part of the economy. Third World countries, similarly, are those which tend to be primary producers, whose output cannot evade the discipline of the market in the same way. Consequently, most of what they buy, or want to buy, is the subject of 'administered' prices, returning a strong element of rent to the producer; most of what they have to sell is traded in the form of undifferentiated commodities, and so the price is a competitive one, with no rent element. And the 'third world' countries have no hope of relative improvement through purely economic activity, any more than the farmer within an advanced country, for three reasons: Improving their productivity cannot help, because this is merely translated in their case into lower prices, whereas when it takes place in the industrial sector of an advanced country it turns into higher wages and salaries and retained earnings, which in turn lead to yet more purchasing power; the lack of rent element in the revenue obtainable from products that are traded simply as commodities, means that there is no surplus available for investment or for research and development. It might be thought that because of their low levels of disposable income, Third World countries are spared the full blast of marketing resources directed towards articulating their needs into want-for-products. This is not so, because the media themselves, by their dependence upon advertising revenue, come to resemble advertising and to perform the same functions even in their editorial material. To the extent then, that third world countries import free world media material – for example in the form of canned T.V. programmes – they are pushing their own patterns of consumer expenditure in a direction which is opposed to that of their national income. This means that there is a low propensity to save in the private sector, with all the consequences this has, together with pressures making for inflation. Economists have long recognised the tendency of consumption patterns in a poor neighbour to ape those of a richer country, but the importance of this has been powerfully reinforced by the spread of the audio-visual media, especially since, unlike print, these need no formal education to give them capacity to transmit information. Although the analogy with farmers in advanced countries is valid, the situation in third world countries is relatively worse, because although they do possess numbers, there is no world-wide political system within which numbers can be translated into political power and so be a counterbalance to wealth. Some alleviation comes from international measures to mitigate the workings of the market as far as commodity prices are concerned, such as the Commonwealth Sugar Agreement, and aid of one kind or another, resulting in transfer payments from rich to poor countries. But the evidence is that much of this aid ends up in paying the rent element in the products of the monopolistically competitive industry of the free world, and most of the rest goes towards reinforcing the growth of bureaucracy. These steps to reduce the imbalance between rich and poor countries, even if they were fully effective, cannot be compared with the transfer payments made in advanced countries through taxation, between industry and agriculture. Redistribution of this type is based, not only on the political power of numbers of those who live on the land, but also upon cultural factors – for example, belief in the intrinsic goodness of country living or the attractions offered to business men by hobby farming. So, while in the advanced countries, the urban-rural economic balance continues uneasily, the third world countries, so far from catching up with their free world models, have for some time been seen to be getting further and further behind, and their lack of marketing and market power is a major cause of this.

One of the first things an emergent nation does is to apply for membership of the International Convention, even though there can be little doubt that the Convention binds such countries into an international economic system that is not in their interest. If there is no advantage, but actual disadvantage for the poorer countries in the International Convention, why then do they join it? The most likely reason is this: What the independence movement in all these countries has been fighting for, is, above all, recognition of the equality of members of the particular nation with members of other nations, especially the imperial power from which they are striving to be free, together with the right to run their own affairs. It is precisely these provisions which form the pith and marrow of the International Convention. A citizen of the newest and poorest country which joins, is to be treated by all countries (even by its former imperial 'oppressor') as equal with their own citizens as far as Industrial Property is concerned. So membership of the International Convention implies powerful confirmation that the revolution has achieved its objectives and that a country has taken its place among the nations of the earth. The fact that the Convention relates to a citizen of the new state only in so far as he is an inventor or a Trade Mark owner, is overlooked. It is forgotten that international agreement limited to industrial property is of small account to men who have little or no property of any kind. A second reason why such countries join the Convention is the belief — which is of course justified as far as it goes — that it is through industrial property legislation and international trading that the advanced countries have become rich. Thirdly, bodies such as the United Nations and the Secretariat of the World Intellectual Property Organization in Geneva have used their influence to this end. And, fourthly, poor countries think it will help them to get investment from abroad.

Where marketing is concerned, the advantage of firms from countries which have had most turns of the "spiral" is overwhelming when they get involved in international business. As there is more rent in their home environment, the amount of psychological ingredient in their products is greatest. But as their home markets have reached this stage of development along the spiral path, such firms have in their "corporate memory" the knowledge of how to operate successfully in a context of less rent and therefore less psychological ingredient in products. In a developed market to-day, Unilever may be selling up to a dozen specialized cleansing products to a typical housewife, including toilet soap, soap flakes, synthetic detergent, washing-up liquid, scourer and specialist products for dishwashers and automatic clothes washing machines. These are all specialized developments from the original "Sunlight" bar soap, and their markets are segments of the market which Lever exploited with that product in the 1880's. His firm will not have forgotten how to sell bar soap, if that is what is appropriate to any particular market, where, because of many fewer twists of the marketing spiral and little rent in the economic system, there is no demand for anything more specialized. As explained earlier, the firm also has the advantage of knowing what mistakes were made in the past, so a venture abroad which involves moving back to an earlier point on the marketing spiral, is like a re-run of the original development, with all the advantage of hindsight. Inevitably, the tendency is all one way, from rich to poor, in contrast to the reciprocity that is implicit in the International Convention.

Naturally, to call attention to the overall trend is not to deny that individual products from poorer countries may be able to develop by marketing in richer ones, and this may be helped by the reciprocal elements in the International Convention. The growth of market segmentation in the advanced countries does provide opportunities for firms from the poorer countries which are prepared to specialize in satisfying one or a few segments. But these are the exceptions; the rule remains that the overwhelming tendency is the other way. The persuasive market power of the advanced countries is extended to the less advanced. Moreover, firms having marketing power in the advanced countries have a vested interest in the growth, through derived market power, which creates the purchasing power which will make it profitable for these firms to exploit their products in foreign countries also. This they can do under the International Convention. If the Convention did not exist, a firm which wanted to develop a business in a foreign country would have to be content with whatever degree of market power it could build up locally on a basis of satisfying some particular objective requirement of local demand. In doing so, it could eventually obtain some sort of legal protection such as that under Common law. This, however, is a slow and uncertain business, and it offers little attraction or scope for a firm whose business at home is based upon marketing power. It provides no opportunity to such a firm of using its own special advantage: Quick and confident deployment of large-scale funds into advertising and marketing abroad on the basis of knowledge and experience of the past performance in the home market of its products, especially its superseded ones. The International Convention, and local laws providing for Trade Mark registration, make the international transfer of marketing power possible, and it is difficult to see how such transfer could happen without them. The inherent direction of transfer of marketing power is from rich countries to poorer ones, – it cannot be otherwise. The reciprocity provisions of the International Convention facilitate this mainly uni-directional transfer enormously. There is no point in explaining that the Convention is designed to be a two-way street; the reality is that the actual traffic only flows in one way, and if the street did not exist, it could not flow at all.

Just as the advantage Japan now has over all other countries can be explained in terms of Capability market power, so Persuasive market power throws light upon what is known as the 'technology gap' between Europe and the United States. Some writers have argued that this is at least a century old, others that it relates to management rather than to technology. It is now possible to see that whatever this gap consists of, a most important cause of it is the International Convention on Industrial Property. Older theories of international trade stressed that countries export the goods which contain a lot of what those particular countries have in plenty, but these theories fall down because they do not distinguish *new* information from existing information as a component of goods. The theories can be modernised by giving due importance to the different *kinds* of information that there are, and it will be clear, therefore, that a country which has plenty of 'new' information will export those goods which are the result of research and development, since these are the ones in which it has a comparative advantage over others. Marketing power combined with secrecy is now such an important source of protection for 'new' information, that the country which has most marketing power will also have the most research and development, and the widest range of goods incorporating advanced technology. Not alone will these goods be exportable in virtue of their superiority over what is available elsewhere, but their parent firms' marketing monopolies are also exportable, thanks to the International Convention. Acceptance of these goods in foreign markets can thus be 'accelerated' by the use of advertising and other marketing techniques. Once the importance of marketing monopoly is grasped, all sorts of aspects of United States economic dominance in the modern world fall into place to form a coherent picture. With it, technical economists can synthesize the Heckschler-Ohlin theory with the more modern 'technological gap', theories of Posner, Hufbauer, Hirsch and others. What is called the 'Leontief paradox' – that the U.S. exports labour-intensive goods in spite of its high wage rates – becomes similarly intelligible: Advanced technology goods are intensive in labour of a particular type, which is the labour that is associated with information production and application – that is, with innovation. The business man who knows there is a technological gap can see that this is due above all to the way in which marketing power underwrites research and development. And those who think that the gap is a management one are right also, in the sense that management to-day means skill in marketing more than anything else, and that American marketing resources abroad powerfully extend the exploitation of American research and development resources at home. Which has contributed more to the U.S.'s large share of the world's computer markets – technological innovation or salesmanship? People who know the computer business are in no doubt of the importance of the second of these. Patent protection underwrites the development of hardware, marketing that of software, and both are internationalised by the International Convention. It may be argued that Trade Mark law plays little part in whatever marketing monopoly U.S. computer firms possess. This is true, but their marketing techniques have been adapted from sectors of industry where Brand Names and mass-media advertising *are* fundamental – and these techniques would never have been developed except under Trade Mark protection. The positive law providing for registration of Trade Marks created marketing power, because it then became profitable to invest in large-scale advertising and marketing with objectives other than building up a basis for protection in the public's association of a brand with a firm. It is not the International Convention that extends this same type of positive law virtually to the whole world, but the way in which the poorer countries have hoped to emulate the economic performance of the richer ones by copying their legal systems. But it *is* the Convention that binds all these separate legal systems into one effective international one which works almost exclusively to the benefit of the richer countries.

The problem for the poorer countries is all the greater in that advance by means of marketing power means that the communications media develop in a particular way. The existence of marketing provides by far the most important source of funds for the growth of these media. When the money to finance the media comes wholly or mainly from advertising, even the non-advertising content of the media – the time or space between the advertisements – comes to partake of the nature of advertising and to reflect its flavour. More newspaper space is taken up with barely edited hand-outs from public relations firms, editorial policy is dominated by the need for mass circulation, the derived monopoly power of craft unions makes it impossible for even medium-circulation papers to survive. It is significant that those countries which have disciplined the electronic media so that the stations provide the programmes, and advertisements are broadcast at 'natural breaks' for a limited period each hour, are countries where, because of the persistence of a tradition of another approach to communications, a substantial proportion of the media's revenue comes from licence fees. In the U.S., on the other hand, where virtually all the revenue of radio and television comes from advertising, the system is one of sponsored programmes, where the advertiser has control over the actual programme content, and naturally directs this content towards his advertising objectives. On the international level, it is impossible for the poorer countries to deny the demand for communications, especially through the electronic media, since these require no literacy. Equally, they have neither the cultural nor financial resources to satisfy this demand themselves. On the other hand, the moment legal protection is given to registration of Trade Marks, the way is open for firms to use advertising and sales promotion profitably; there is therefore a ready-made source of finance for communications media from the firms whose brands may be registered. In a poor country, however, local sources of finance of this kind will not be significant, because of the fewness of indigenous brands and their lack of development.

Such will be the position until the country joins the International Convention on Industrial Property; this opens the floodgates to the international brands, and provides money for the expansion of media to an extent which could not possibly be contemplated otherwise. It also ensures that the media will develop in ways which suit advertising. Since so many of the international brands are American, and since the process of extending their marketing power internationally is one of re-enacting the marketing experience of the brand in the home country, it is inevitable that there will be pressure towards having the programme content similar to the programme content which has provided a successful vehicle for the brand's advertising in the U.S. Thus, even if the international salesmen for American canned radio and T.V. material did not already exist, the existence of U.S. brands internationally would bring them into being. Originally intended for creative writers, Copyright is now widely used in the protection of all aspects of advertising. It is unnecessary to stress that the Copyright Conventions reflect the same situation of legal equality, practical inequality, as obtains in the case of the

Industrial Property Convention. The balance of advantage is overwhelmingly on the side of the advanced countries as against the poorer ones, because the flow of monopoly is almost exclusively one way.

By enacting Industrial Property laws which parallel those of the advanced countries, and by joining the International Convention, therefore, the poorer countries make it profitable for the firms of richer ones to develop their marketing power in them by the use of advertising and sales promotion; this in turn provides finance for the growth of mass media, especially radio and television, which creates a demand for programme material which will be suitable for filling space or time between advertisements; and by joining the Copyright Conventions, the poorer countries make it profitable for firms from the more advanced countries to sell them this programme material. The growth of marketing power is therefore inextricably linked with the spread of a particular set of cultural values; as marketing power spreads from the most advanced country, which happens to be the United States, the cultural values which spread with it are necessarily those of the United States. And it has meant that in the third thrust of the industrial revolution, the characteristic innovations have been in the consumer and consumer-durable goods products, and mass services of U.S. firms.

Up to now, we have been considering primary market power, which can always be described in terms of the categories, Capability, Specific or Persuasive. In any actual firm, market power invariably exists as a combination of all three types. In discussing marketing in relation to innovation, reference was made to another type of market power, which is *derived* from these. It cannot exist on its own, because it is (in the precise sense of the word, and not at all pejoratively) *parasitic* on primary market power. Derived market power is a means of capturing some of the rent earned by primary market power. It appears in the form of the rent element in the factors of production used by the primary market power, illustrated in the first place by management and individuals with specialized skills that are scarce. Actuaries, for example, are vital to insurance companies, since they calculate the risks on which premiums are based. Because of their gifts and arduous training, they are rare, so their salaries include an extremely large rent element. An actuary in his best use can earn at a rate which is very many times that of any alternative use. The rent he can earn in his best use, however (in an insurance company, doing what he is trained to do) depends upon the rent the insurance company can earn from its customers and investments. The actuary's rent is derived from the primary rent of the company, and, in the unlikely event of an insurance firm collapsing, and ceasing to be able to use its primary market power to change consumers' surplus into producers' surplus, its actuary's derived rent would disappear also. Even more important than the derived market power of specialists in the firm, including its management, is the power of its non-specialist labour force. This comes about through their ability to combine so as to render the primary market power ineffective either partially or completely. The strength of this

112

power depends upon whether or not workers in combination have the power to prevent other workers from taking their places, if they withdraw their labour. If they can do so, this barrier to entry reflects a high degree of market power. It remains *derived* market power, however, since its rent-generating capacity is the capacity to divert a share of the primary rent to itself and away from the owners of the firm. If the primary power is weak, that is, if it is incapable of preventing entry to its markets by competitors, there is little rent for the derived market power to divert to itself; in the limiting case, when the firm fails, or its owners put it into liquidation, there is none.

Like all three types of primary market power, such derived market power is rooted in positive law. In Continental Europe, this takes the form of labour combinations generally being accepted as lawful, but in the Anglo-Saxon countries, there are actual Statutes protecting combination. These greatly affected the growth of Trade Unions and, indeed, made their existence possible. In the case of Britain, between 1880 and 1913 aggregate real income more than doubled, but average real wages rose by only two-fifths. Much of the lag between total real income and average real wages is accounted for by population growth, but some of it undoubtedly represents a shift in favour of the propertied classes. Such a shift was inevitable, since the Trade Marks Acts (and also, of course, the Patent Acts which were passed at around the same time) reinforced the advantages given to Capital by the earlier introduction of Joint Stock Companies and Limited Liability. Without the Industrial Property laws, the earlier provisions would not have been as important as they did in fact become, enabling rents to be generated out of industrial activity on a totally unprecedented scale. Also, it was the Trade Marks Acts, probably more even than the change of balance between the roles of technology and science, which provided the stimuli, partially for the second thrust and largely for the third thrust, of the industrial revolution. If the laws rendering it possible to make money out of marketing had not been developed, the capacity to make things, vastly increased by technologies based upon science instead of on pragmatism and trial and error, would have been worth little. Ways of selling things were developed as a result of the energies released by the Trade Marks Acts, and these inevitably tilted the balance of economic power in favour of those who controlled these ways, however much ordinary wage-earners may have improved their absolute position compared to what it had been before. What happened, therefore, was an intensification of an existing imbalance in the laws relating to property which John Stuart Mill had noted as early as 1848. By the end of the nineteenth century, however, this imbalance had grown too great. The industrial property laws had enormously increased the relative power of Property as compared to Numbers, even when the great extensions of the franchise during the last third of the century are taken into account. In Britain, indeed, as long as the House of Lords retained its power, giving more power to Numbers by giving more people the vote was largely an empty gesture, and the power of the Lords was not broken until 1910. By that time, no less than 69% of the personal wealth of Britain was owned by 1% of the population and one-tenth of the people owned 92% of all personal wealth. To that extent, the Lloyd George budget and the Parliament Act, not the Reform Act of 1832 nor Disraeli's extension of the franchise in 1867, represent the definitive breakthrough to democracy. Earlier, however, pressures had been building up against the great accretion of power to Property, and a step of enormous importance in redressing the balance, or at least in preventing the imbalance from getting any worse, is represented by the Trade Disputes Act of 1906. This was passed as a result of the manifest unfairness of the Taff Vale judgment in the previous year, in which members of a Trade Union were held responsible for damage suffered by an employer through their strike actions. The 1906 Act effectively prevented Union members from suffering in that way, by exempting them from the provisions of the Common Law as it applies to causing damage to another. It was the Charter of Trade Union activity, and it is to this piece of positive law that Unions in Britain (and in those countries which have followed British example) owe their strength, and the power to use their strongest weapon, the picket. It marks the beginning of the swing of the pendulum from the side of Property to that of Numbers, and there is a very real sense in which the Trade Disputes Act of 1906 is the counterpart of the Patent and Trade Marks Act of 1883. Industrial Property as we know it, and Trades Unions as we know them, reflect aspects of market or marketing power, and both are involved in a continuing dialectic of politics and positive law. These developments perfectly illustrate Galbraith's doctrine of 'countervailing power'. The British example has been quoted in this connection, but the same pattern is also to be found in other countries. In the U.S., the Unions were later in receiving protection from the Law. In many ways, comparable legislation to the Trade Disputes Act is not found there until the National Industrial Recovery Act of 1933 and the National Labor Relations Act of 1935 (although Woodrow Wilson, from 1914 onwards, had been responsible for some improvement in the Unions' position). This is fully a quarter-century later than in Britain. Is it altogether fanciful to see this time-lag as parallel to the similar difference between the two countries, noted earlier in the matter of country-wide Trade Mark laws?

As Unions have become more developed and sophisticated in economic terms, their leadership has come to take increasing account of the monopoly strength they share with the firms which employ their members. The firm is concerned to exploit its market power, to maximise the rent element in its sales; the Union is concerned to capture as much of the firm's revenue as it can, to maximise the rent element in its members' wages; there is a real sense in which both firm and Union are in partnership to exploit the consumer: 'The more fundamental clash of interests in any labour dispute is between labour and the consumer of the product involved, not between labour and the businessman or the corporation who employs it.'[22] The common interest of Labour and Capital in exploiting monopoly, results in a formidable combination, and all sorts of results flow from it. The firms with the most monopoly power are those most capable of conceding the Union's demands on wages without harming their own power to grow. This means that what primarily matters in wage negotiation is the monopoly strength of firms. Firms with most control over their prices can afford to give in to Union demands most easily. It is within these firms, therefore, that the largest and most frequent wage increases are granted. These set the pattern for other firms in the economy, which have to follow suit, even though they themselves have less market or marketing power with which to pass on a corresponding price to the public. Their margins are squeezed, they have less resources to devote to advertising and sales promotion themselves, so they fall behind relative to the leaders. Leadership, it is clear, is increasingly defined in terms of monopoly or market power. This tendency must lead to one or a few firms getting out in front of the others, and staying there. Nothing succeeds like success, and it is easy to see why market power is such an important factor in the growth of concentration in industry. Empirical studies show also, that this is positively associated with Trade Union strength; but there is an even more important consequence.

Wage increases, of course, which are really a sharing in the rent earned by the primary market power, are frequently justified in the name of 'productivity', but this is misleading when the context is a monopolistic one. The productivity of a plant depends upon the success or otherwise of the marketing side of the business in keeping the plant employed at or near its optimum level. If, in the context of a particular firm, a new opportunity of exerting its market power is found and successfully exploited – that is, if there is 'psychological' innovation – productivity, as at present measured, automatically goes up. The workers can claim increases based upon the notion of 'productivity', but in reality such increases represent, not greater power or facility to produce goods, but a share in greater power to 'unmake the market' for them, and thus to obtain a rent for the brand name under which the goods are sold. The results, therefore, of so-called 'productivity' bargaining, are to increase the rent element in wages and salaries in the firm or industry concerned, reflecting and sharing in the rent element in the revenues of the firm with market power. Much, therefore, of what 'increased productivity' means as a basis of wage increases, is nothing else than 'increased primary market power' on the part of the firms concerned.

It is by no means only Unionised workers, of course, who share in the rent-creating capacity of the monopolistic firm. There is also a strong and positive correlation between executives' salaries and the market power of their firms. The 'rent' element in the salaries reflects the 'rent' element in the firm's sales, as Sylos-Labini pointed out. Since market power is such a powerful source of this pattern of income transfer, it must be granted a major share in responsibility for the growth of a class which very often has economic power without corresponding economic responsibility. Before Limited Liability, property and management were inseparable. With the separation of ownership from control which Limited Liability brought about, the status of hired management improved to a remarkable extent. A species of quasi-property developed, reflected in the quasi-rent element in salaries and wages. Even though he might own no shares in the business, a man could be stimulated to initiate a successful development, because he could count upon being able to appropriate some of the continuing fruits of the innovation over time, through the increased rent element in his salary. Often, too, this would continue beyond his own lifetime, in that by getting his sons advantageously into the firm or into an associated business, he was putting them also into a position of access to rent in the form of salary. As a result, Limited Liability extended the reality of private property in a way which has been extremely fruitful for innovation.

An interesting example of how the Trade Mark Acts did the same, can be seen in the advertising agency commission system. Many attempts have been made to replace it with straight fees, but it remains virtually untouched and seemingly impregnable. If ideas were all that were needed for successful advertising, the fee system ought to work every bit as well, but it is not ideas that are needed, but *developed* ideas, ideas to whose embodiment in actual advertising individuals have committed themselves, and which they have sold both to the personnel of the agency and to the client. The commission system gives a continuing return over time to the Agency whose advertising 'works'. The Agency's commission is a quasi-rent which is derived from the quasi-rent arising from the firm's marketing power in its brand. It shares in the success in a way it would not do if it was paid on a fee basis, and it is this sharing in success that makes it worthwhile for innovators to work in advertising in preference to many other businesses.

The importance of derived market power in the context of innovation arises from the way its growth changes the nature of the new ideas that it makes economic sense to invest in. If there is a lot of rent in the system, then, to the extent that this is to be found in wages and salaries, it will be profitable to invest in persuasive market power and in those innovations that can be protected by this type of market power. This type of rent, of course, is not only to be found in the remuneration of employees of firms which have primary market power. To an ever-increasing extent, the rent which is the target of marketing men is in the salaries of those, who, in one way or another, are supported by the State. In order to take adequate account of this, it is necessary to extend the vocabulary beyond simple derived market power.

In the private sector, the market power of employees with specialist skills, or of other employees in combination, can never be more than a reflection of the primary market power of the firm which employs them. If the firm fails, their market power disappears also. But if the firm in question is owned by, or backed by the Government, still more if the employer is the Government itself, similar failure cannot arise – and this primary strength is carried through to whatever is derived from it. In this case, it is not accurate to speak of 'market power', either primary or derived, although the final result is discretionary income, which is all that matters to the marketing man. Is there any sense in which it can be correct to describe the State's power to tax, as *market* power? Obviously it is monopolistic, as a Patent is monopolistic, and the power to exclude is perfect, since no other institution has the power to tax, except in so far as the State delegates it, to Urban Councils, for example. But market power carries the connotation of choice, however limited, or of abstention from purchase altogether. The Courts and the Civil Power cannot be brought in to force someone to buy in even the most monopolistic market, as they can be to force people to pay their taxes. The power that Government employees have to extract a share of this tax is 'derived' in precisely the same way as the capacity of employees in a private firm to extract a share of the rent accruing to the firm's market power is 'derived'. In both cases the derived power arises from specialist skills or abilities, on the one hand, and combination, on the other. Many countries permit State employees to strike in the same way as other workers. Perhaps the best nomenclature to use is 'derived taxing power'. This contains the notion that the power is dependent upon some anterior force, reflecting the fact that the rent element in a civil servant's salary (which is very large indeed, since his earnings in any alternative employment are likely, in the majority of cases, to be very much lower) would virtually disappear in the unlikely event of his losing his job. At the same time, use of the word 'taxing' indicates that the derived power is able to act upon a source of funds that has the ultimate sanction attached to it. Because of this, derived taxing power is a much stronger economic force than derived market power, even though both may operate in exactly similar ways. The rent element in each turns into demand for products with psychological ingredient when it comes to be spent.

Outside the Civil Service proper, many States have establishments which they fund by direct grant. Although in theory any of these could be closed down at any time, and consequently the position of their employees is theoretically less secure than that of members of the 'core' Civil Service, the chance of such a closure is so remote that the employees' derived power is scarcely any less, so it is not incorrect to call this, too, 'derived taxing power'. Nationalized industries are less easy to categorize, partly since they take so many different forms. In general, however, they are characterized by obtaining their revenue partly from selling goods or services and partly by State subvention. The publicly-owned organization that requires no help from its owner is the exception rather than the rule. In a sense, therefore, employees possess a mixture of derived market power and derived taxing power. It is probably more precise, however, to think of such a firm as having specific market power from whatever Statute or Ordinance sets it up. When this is combined with whatever other market power it possesses, such as capability, it is clear that its primary market power is exceptionally strong. It is *reinforced*, in fact. Since derived power reflects the strength of primary power, there is an advantage in calling the derived power of employees in such cases 'reinforced' derived market power, to give weight to the 'Statutory' aspect. (Being employees of a monopoly often also increases the market power of employees in such organizations).

The same can be said of firms, which although still private, are of such importance to a Government that it is inconceivable that they could ever be allowed to collapse. Even if such a guarantee is only implied, and there is no formal statement of it, the firm has a corresponding 'notional' taxing power (in the sense that taxpayers' money would, if necessary, be used to support it if its operations in its markets turned out to be unsuccessful). In this case, too, little precision is lost by calling all of the power of employees, 'reinforced' derived market power, for convenience. It will be realized that although the same word is used, the 'reinforcement' in this case is somewhat less strong than in that of an industry which has actually been nationalized.

In terms of their effect on innovation, derived taxing power and reinforced derived market power have acted in the same direction as derived market power itself. They have accelerated the marketing spiral, and in some countries they may now be the most important factor in domestic demand, having increased the amount of rent in the system by much more than ordinary derived market power has done. The consequence has been a major intensification of the bias towards innovation that is either wholly psychological ingredient, or the type of physical change that is best protected by a combination of persuasive and capability market power, with or without secrecy as well. Thus, the expansion of the public sector in all countries over the last half-century, has contributed mightily to the growth of the giant multi-national corporation, which characteristically deploys these types of market power to soak up consumer surplus. To take account of this growth of state involvement, therefore, the working vocabulary has had to be extended to include derived taxing power, as well as 'reinforced' primary and derived market power. These extensions to the vocabulary are essential for the task in getting to grips with the contemporary crisis, in the next Chapter. This crisis owes much to the extension of the area of influence of the State in economic life, which has distorted and stifled the capacity of economies to innovate.

This extension of rent in economic systems has clearly identifiable roots either in law or Ordinance, and it is impossible to understand what has been happening to innovation without taking account of it. Derived market power impinges upon innovation in two ways. In the first instance, the stronger derived market power becomes, the less must be the residual to the owners of a business. This can only increase their risk-aversion, and progressively eliminate innovation from consideration by them. In the extreme case, a combination of strong derived market power and high taxation leaves owners with no more than the return appropriate to static businesses. They are be virtually defenceless against innovatory foreign firms, and this has been the actual situation in which many firms in the Western world found themselves during the 1970's. Secondly, as the derived rent, whether from taxing power, reinforced market power or 'simple' market power, is all discretionary income when looked at

118

from another angle, its growth, as the marketing spiral illustrates, opens up opportunities for a different kind of innovation. But the spread of innovations that are solely or largely in terms of psychological ingredient, is achieved at the cost of correspondingly increased rigidity, and lack of innovation in other areas. It is possible for an economy to go on increasing its 'rent content' whilst at the same time failing to generate real new wealth. The primary cause of such a distorted pattern of innovation can only be some by antecedent distortion of the positive law which underwrites all market power, and thereby makes innovation possible.

As Keynes pointed out, 'the ideas which politicians, civil servants and even agitators apply to current events are not likely to be the newest.' Consequently, the authorities are still a long way from recognizing, still further from understanding, the connection between the pattern of market power and the pattern of innovation. Throughout the present century, in an increasing number of countries, attempts have been made to bring market power under control. These have been based upon a most inadequate understanding of it, and this is particularly evident in that all attempts have been *ex-post* in character, rather than *ex-ante*. That is, a particular type or modification of market power is permitted to develop from its root in positive law, to a stage where certain aspects of it come to be considered abusive. Then, institutional means are brought into being to discipline it. From the aspect of the innovation which results from market power, there is therefore a double distortion: Firstly, a haphazard pattern of market power, resulting from many bits of legislation whose consequences for innovations were only fractionally understood and foreseen, could result in nothing else than a haphazard pattern of innovation. Secondly, this pattern is rendered even more incoherent by piecemeal institutional arrangements for controlling market power *after the event*, whose impact and effectiveness differ widely as between one institution and another. The results are important factors in contemporary economic problems, and will be discussed in the next Chapter. The advantages of controlling the excesses of market power, and consequently of obtaining a more desirable innovatory pattern, will appear in Chapter V.

Notes

1. Rowley Charles K: The British Monopolies Commission. London (1966) p. 47.
2. Landes David: The Unbound Prometheus. Cambridge (1970) p. 16.
3. Ripert G.: Aspects Juridiques du Capitalisme Moderne. Paris (1946) pp. 59-62; Landes op. cit. p. 197.
4. Gilfillan S.C.: Invention and the Patent System. Washington D.C. (1964) p. 8.
5. Report of the President's Commission on Technological Innovation (Baruch). Washington, D.C. (1979) p. 205.
6. Ibid. 152.
7. Rolt L.T.C.: Tools for the job. London (1965).

8. Schechter F.I.: The Historical Foundation of the Law Relating to Trade Marks. New York (1925).

9. cf. Beier F.K.: Basic Features of Anglo-American, French and German Trade Mark Law. In Information Review of Industrial Property and Copyright (1975) No. 3.

10. Cornish W.R.: Intellectual Property. London (1981).

11. Schechter op. cit. 140.

12. Blanco White T.A.: Industrial Property and Copyright. London (1962) p. 88.

13. Salmond J.W.: Law of Torts 6th edn. London. (1965) p. 565-6.

14. Hindmarch W.M.: in House of Commons Report of Select Committee on the Trade Marks Bill (1862) (212) XII paragraphs 2771-4; 2822-6.

15. Mason E.S.: Economic Concentration and the Monopoly Problem, Cambridge (Mass.) (1959) p. 334.

16. In *Review of Economic Studies* (1961).

17. Invention, Growth and Welfare. Cambridge (Mass.) (1969) p. 22.

18. Hiance P. and Plasseraud Y.: Brevets et Sous-Développement. Paris (1971).

19. Murdoch H.J.P.: Invention and the Irish Patent System. Dublin (1971).

20. The Theory of Monopolistic Competition, 6th Edn. London (1949) p. 62.

21. Collins Patrick: Unpublished Dublin University M.B.A. Dissertation (1982).

22. Chamberlin E.H.: Towards a More General Theory of Value. New York (1957) p. 263.

CHAPTER IV

The contemporary crisis

Every civilization is a definition in practice of the nature of hope, and there are times in the life of every civilization when hope and confidence in the future are undermined by events. For Western men, the present is one such time.

Any list of the symptoms of malaise would include inflation, unemployment, breakdown of law and order, ugliness in the man-made environment, conspicious waste of resources and lack of joy in work. Two further items are having a particularly corrosive effect upon Western self-confidence at the present time. The first of these is an increasing acceptance of the superiority in terms of production and technology of Japan, and, to a lesser extent, the countries of the Confucian world. This is especially humiliating because for so long these areas of achievement were thought to be characteristically Western. The second item is the growing fear that economic problems are now so great as to be beyond the power of Parliamentary Democracy to cope with. Again, this institution is so typically Western, that the fear strikes particularly deeply, and is intensified by memories of what happened in Europe the last time authoritarian systems of Government were adopted out of despair.

Such times of troubles have in fact recurred over the past two hundred years with such regularity as to revive discussion concerning "long" economic cycles, each lasting about two generations. For many years after the last War, speculation about these was in abeyance, because of the dominance of Keynesian thinking. Although Keynes concentrated on the cycles of shorter duration, the 'ordinary' or 'Juglar' business cycles, his teaching seemed relevant to all types. Slumps, or troughs of a cycle, according to this, were due to inadequate demand. By increasing demand through spending by Governments at such times and reining-in spending at others, the peaks and troughs of cycles could be flattened out, and steady economic growth attained. Although for obvious reasons, democratically-elected governments ignored the 'reining-in' part of Keynes's thesis, this approach appeared to work for three decades, to the extent that discussion of economic cycles dropped out of sight. It was almost as if to raise the topic was felt by economists to be impertinently questioning the outstanding achievement of their discipline in the real world, where

Keynesianism had relegated Trade Cycle theory to the attention of economic historians. This confidence has been shattered, however, firstly by the way in which Keynesianism as practised led to wholesale debasement of currencies, and secondly by its failure to cope with the problems of the present slackening in economic activity.[1] In fact, all that the attempts of many countries to spend their way out of recession have done in this case, has apparently been to intensify their problems.

It is hardly surprising, then, that there should at present be a strong revival of interest in Business Cycle theory. The great depression of the 1930's is within living memory; most economic historians agree that there were very similar conditions in the 1870s and 1880s, and that a major slump also followed the Napoleonic wars. The name of Kondratieff, which had scarcely been referred to throughout all the years of Keynesian dominance, is now mentioned widely again. Although the theory of long business cycles had in fact been elaborated in 1913 by the Dutchman, van Gelderen, it is Kondratieff's name that has become associated with these cycles, because the influence of Schumpeter's writing on the whole subject. Kondratieff analysed a number of indicators, almost all related to prices − including wages (the price of labour) and interest rates (the price of money) and found that they oscillated in a remarkably regular way.[2] There is substantial agreement amongst students of the subject as to the timing of all but the most recent of these cycles, and also about what causes the end of an "upswing" (a sharp reduction in the rate of profit). Why then, do they not similarly agree that the end of a "downswing" is caused by a movement in the opposite direction, that is, by a sharp *rise* in profitability, as is held by the Marxist economist Mandel?[3] The reason is again the influence of Schumpeter, who took up what is almost a throw-away line in Kondratieff's paper, and made it a key element in his large work, *Business Cycles*.[4] Kondratieff saw his task as that of recording and collating, but he did observe that

> 'During the recession of the long waves, an especially large number of important discoveries and inventions in the technique of production and communication are made, which, however, are usually applied on a large scale only at the beginning of the next long upswing... the development of technique itself is part of the system of the long waves.'[5]

Schumpeter developed this into a theory that innovation has a tendency to "cluster" at certain times, and that it was this clustering that produced a major surge of economic activity at intervals, thus giving rise to the long, or Kondratieff cycles.

Schumpeter's argument has recently been taken up and expanded by Gerhard Mensch in "Stalemate in Technology". The importance of innovation as a dynamic element is indicated by the book's sub-title, "Innovations Overcome the Depression".[6] However, Mensch is at pains to stress that his is not a cyclical theory. He develops what he calls a "metamorphosis model" of long periods of growth and relatively short periods of "turbulence". According to this, instead of continuous movement along a sine curve, "the economy has evolved through a series of intermittent innovative impulses that take the form of successive S-shaped cycles". The first claim for his approach which Mensch makes is that it leaves room for a degree of regularity in the movements of economic life, without trying to force this into a rigid pattern of repetitive change. "The wave model incorporates a deterministic recurrence of phase transition; any metamorphosis model does not. It allows for speed-up and slowdown of change".[7]

Secondly, whereas stagnation is 'buried' in the wave model, in the metamorphosis model it is incorporated 'implicitly as a separate force'. The model can therefore encompass both the effects of stagnation on innovation and the feedback with which innovation influences stagnation."

Mensch's work has been subjected to rigorous but appreciative criticism by the Science Policy Research Unit of the University of Sussex.[8] Their verdict is that the case for the long cycles and their association with innovation is 'not proven', mainly because of the limitations of the list of innovations which Mensch used. W.W. Rostow (unlike Mensch) accepts the existence of Kondratieff cycles, but sees their principal cause as "relative shortage and relative abundance of food and raw materials," resulting in changes in the relationship between their prices on the one hand and the prices of industrial products on the other. Innovation is secondary, although

"the rise and fall of the great innovations did leave their marks on relative price movements. The story of the Kondratieff cycles must be told, then, by weaving together the impulses imparted to the world economy by periods of relative scarcity or overabundance of food and raw materials with the saga of technological change."[9]

Yet another writer on the subject, Forrester, sees no need at all to bring in innovation to explain the long waves. He came in fact to study these cycles from experience of computer simulation of the U.S. economy. This showed that growth and collapse could be expected over a 50-year time-scale, because "capital plant throughout the economy is overbuilt beyond the level justified by the marginal efficiency of capital".[10] Similarly, in Depression, investment is even less than is justified. Forrester accepts that innovations are 'clustered', even though he grants no causal value to them or to this clustering. What the long wave does, he holds, is to compress technological change into certain time intervals and offer opportunities for innovation. Schumpeter wrote that 'innovations carry the Kondratieff' and Forrester's position may fairly be expressed as 'the Kondratieff, at a certain point, carries innovations'.

Fascinating as it is in the terms in which it has been carried on up to now, the 'long cycle' debate is lifted to an entirely new level of interest and intelligibility, if the definition of 'innovation' is widened. 'Getting new things done' is not just a matter of technology: The most important innovations of all are social innovations, since it is upon these that so many other factors, including technological innovation, depend. If an institutional change increases the prospect of profit, there is nothing surprising about a consequent surge of investment to innovate inventions that may have been vainly awaiting support for years previously. Since it is market power which makes investment in innovation possible, it is essential to study the times at which technological innovations were made, with reference to the institutional and legal changes which generate or modify market power.

The vocabulary developed in the previous three chapters will be helpful in this, as will also the idea of three industrial revolutions advanced in Chapter III of *Innovation*. Whether the latter terminology is used, or whether it is preferred to think in terms of three 'thrusts' or 'impulses' of the one movement, a valid periodicity can be established in terms of the type of market power which characteristically underwrote economic innovation. In the first impulse, until well into the nineteenth century, this was the market power of capability, in which advances were made empirically, working without Science: "Thermodynamics owed far more to Steam Power than Steam Power ever owed to Thermodynamics". During this period, organized R & D, Government support of R & D and market or marketing research were all either non-existent or extremely rare. These were the conditions under which numerous innovations led to a huge growth in textile manufacturing, in steam-powered transport and in metal working. For much of this period, the nature of technology was such that capability alone captured much of the externalities. Knowledge, in the industrial sense, was less of a type that could be written down and therefore copied, than what was embodied in the skills of identifiable individuals. In one sense, this impulse's typical example of technological transfer was the way America obtained mechanical spinning – through the arrival *in person* of Samuel Slater, who had memorized the construction and operation of Arkwright's spinning frame. The sense in which this is typical is the embodiment of the knowledge and skill in an individual, not the way in which Slater used his position to his own great advantage. The businesses that were pioneering technology during this period, do not seem to have had much difficulty in keeping their own skilled men from taking their skills and knowledge to competitors. Certainly, although Boulton and Watt suffered much from pirates, there is no evidence that the pirates were ever able to gain by regularly hiring away workers who had Boulton and Watt's special skills and secrets. It is likely, too, that in an era when men tended to work in the firm where they had been trained, the traditional injunction in the apprentice's Articles that he should "his Master's secrets keep" maintained moral pressure throughout a working lifetime that it needs an effort of imagination to grasp in our own times.

Although the range, both actual and potential, of capability market power had earlier been extended dramatically by the Joint Stock Companies' and Limited Liability Acts, towards the end of the nineteenth century this type of market power on its own was no longer an adequate protection for technological innovation. Skills which had been rare had become, if not commonplace, at least widely diffused. The possibilities of disseminating the valuable informational content of an innovation in a form other than as embodied in individual knowledge and skill had been greatly enlarged. Interchangeable parts contributed to this, but even more important was the spread of mechanical drawing. (Aspects of this in which it was superior, had been regarded as amongst its most important secret weapons by the French Army). Also, the nature of the knowledge which pertained to technological innovation was changing. Technology was moving in directions which brought it into contact with more generalised concepts than it had been concerned with hitherto, as witness the way in which firms sponsored research into metal-cutting techniques in the 1880s. Science was beginning to be applied too, illustrated by the way in which the German chemical industry developed out of University research. If Samuel Slater stands for the beginning of the era, Robert Mushet stands for the end of it. He lived like a hermit whilst carrying out the experiments which led to Bessemer's steel-making process being made to work in practice. This secrecy was presumably because of awareness on his part that by then, for capturing the externalities of new information, "capability" alone was no longer enough.

By most accounts, the slump at the end of the second Kondratieff cycle, in the years around 1885, was a good deal deeper than that at the end of the first, around 1848. Certainly, this owed much to a slowing-down in railway-building, which is the traditional explanation given by students of the long cycles. But at least a contributory explanation is surely that the evolution of technology had reached the limit of rational investment in innovation on the basis which had been adequate for the best part of a century – capability market power. Rostow has suggested that "in a sense, the second Kondratieff downswing was ended by the United States reaching the end of its agricultural frontier, given existing agricultural prices and technologies":[11] From what has been said above, it will be clear that a "frontier" of fully equal importance can be constituted by the end of an effective way of protecting investment in innovation, and that one of these was reached in the 1870s. Profits shrank, and prices fell

> "on average by about one third on all commodities. It was the most drastic deflation in the memory of man. The rate of interest fell, too, to the point where economic theorists began to conjure with the possibility of capital so abundant as to be a free good."[12]

What was the social innovation that enabled that frontier to be crossed? The outstanding candidate for this distinction is the modern Patent law, which appeared to compensate for many of the deficiencies of capability market power as a means of justifying investment in the new industries which owed something to science. These included steelmaking, organic chemicals, and electrical equipment. Organised R & D began, early in Germany, much later in countries such as Britain (the first 'in-house' research department there, in Brunner, Mond & Co., was only set up in 1907). Although Government support of R & D was meagre outside the Defence field (as late as 1929, the budget of the British Department of Scientific and Industrial Research was only £500,000) Governments and private firms used the Patent system to advantage.[13]

As was noted in Chapter III, however, this system, too, reached its 'frontier'. From the first World War onwards, business men no longer had the same confidence in the capacity of Patents to protect their investments in the generation of new information as they had in earlier years. This disillusionment remained a reality in spite of the fact that the growth of the modern pharmaceutical industry, after the second World War, gave Patenting a new justification, since Patents do give really valuable protection to Chemical inventions. But that was far in the future, and in the 1920s and 1930s, Patents did not appear to investors to offer the kind and strength of market power that they needed to make money in the new conditions which prevailed. There is a parallel here with Henry Ford's innovation of mass production in 1912, which gave capability market power a new lease of life. Even if this had come a generation earlier, it would still have offered no help to investors faced with the problem of capturing the externalities of investment in industries which depended partly upon scientific knowledge. This is because capability market power on its own is a poor means of protecting information – such as scientific information – which is abstract, as opposed to being concrete or embodied.

In the protection they attempt to give, Patents seek a degree of abstraction, by covering alternative 'elements' or ways of attaining particular 'steps' in an invention. The difficulty, as has been seen, is that unless the abstraction is complete, 'inventing around' becomes possible, with the result that the commercial value of the invention 'leaks away' to competitors. It took time for this weakness in Patents to be appreciated in practice. In the discrediting of the Patent system, indeed, the growth of Accountancy must surely have been a contributory factor. The spectacular scale of the prizes which were won from investing in some Patents, caused business men, as long as they were working on their own judgement and intuition, to over-rate their chances of success. Once their Accountants began to look coldly at the real odds, however, Patenting seemed far less attractive, and they began to seek for protection elsewhere.

In the third 'thrust', therefore, the characteristic type of market power was Persuasive. If there is one feature which characterizes the industries which were responsible for recovery from the Depression of the 1930s above all, it is that they related to mass markets. This does not just apply to consumer and consumer-durable goods; it is equally evident in services, such as financing (hire purchase and credit cards and facilities) and above all, house-purchase mortgages; insurance (especially pension schemes); entertainment and information, which include the mass media, and tourism. All these must be included in the list of industries that sustained the long period of prosperity from the end of the last War until the late 1970s.

Another characteristic of these industries was their increasing tendency to be organized on a global, rather than just on a national basis. The multi-national corporation, deploying management as well as investment throughout the world, a most effective vehicle for spreading its own innovations, is typical of this era. Because all these industries and services were directed at mass markets, they depended upon the techniques which make mass markets possible, especially advertising. Since advertising in this modern form, as was seen in Chapter II, depends upon Trade Mark registration law, it can only be this that is the social innovation, at the national level, which can claim credit for recovery from the 1930s low point. Moreover, to the extent that these markets have not only been mass-markets, but *international* mass-markets as well, they have depended upon other social innovations: The internationalizing of Trade Marks by the Paris Convention, and similar protection of advertising form by the Copyright Conventions. The reason why these social innovations have been used to such advantage by United States firms, to the extent that multi-national corporations are predominantly of U.S. origin, is, of course, due to the advantage which accrues in any mass-market to the firm from the country which has had most turns of the marketing spiral. For them, as also explained earlier, expansion to less-developed foreign markets is a 're-run with hindsight'.

This, of course, does not mean that the only industries that were important during this third thrust of the industrial revolution were those which served mass markets, using advertising and salesmanship made possible by Trade Mark registration law. Industries whose characteristic method of protection was capability also prospered, such as those producing the materials of which the new consumer-durable goods were made; aircraft manufacturers and hotel builders benefited from tourism, as well as Travel Agents. In the same way, the dramatic post-war expansion of the Pharmaceutical industry, based upon antibiotics, relied heavily upon Patents, as well as on marketing techniques. But the generalisation that the 'locomotive' industries during the period were those which would not have had their characteristic form without advertising and the law which makes advertising in its modern sense possible, remains valid.

An obvious difficulty arises in regard to this theory, and must be dealt with. It is not too difficult to grant that the Companies Acts contributed to recovery from the slump (or slumps) of the earlier part of the nineteenth century, and Patents Acts to that of the later part. But how can it be claimed that Trade Marks Acts did the same for the slump of the 1930s, since the latter Acts were all passed in the period 1857 (France) to 1903 (U.S. Federal)? Further, how can it be claimed that the Paris Convention was also an important institutional factor, in view of the fact that this dates from as far back as 1883?

The answer can only be that the effectiveness of registered Trade Marks had to await the growth of the appropriate demand. Marketing power can only form a basis for investment where there is pre-existing consumer surplus available to be captured and changed into producer surplus. The source of the consumer surplus that can be captured by marketing techniques, can be nothing else than rent in salaries and wages. This, in turn, results from derived market power. Trade Marks could therefore not become an institutional factor for underwriting a cluster of innovations to lead economies out of depression, unless and until derived market power had become widespread.

This implies anterior capacity to generate wealth by innovation, made possible by primary market power. Unless primary market power itself results in rent, there is nothing for derived market power to capture from it. It is perfectly possible, for example, to register an international Trade Mark in Chad, since that country is a member of the Paris Convention. Doing so offers no basis for investment, however, since Chad is a subsistence economy. No rent to speak of can accrue to any primary market power, so even if derived market power existed, there would be no consumer surplus in wages which could be exploited by marketing based on the registered Trade Mark.

In the advanced countries, however, derived market power did result in the growth of a substantial rent element in wages and salaries, since the system did have primary rent. Initially, the main mechanism for changing this into derived rent was the legally-endorsed power of unskilled workers to combine. Without this power, their wages would be set according to a *lateral* norm, reflecting the alternative employment opportunities available to them; with it, the norm is a *vertical* one, reflecting, more than anything else, the employer's capacity to pay. This, of course, is because of the rent from his primary market power.

Now, an important cause of the Depression of the 1930s was precisely the mismatch of wage rates with perceived opportunities for investment. This was particularly the case in Europe, where by that time wages had come to contain a significant rent element. Note also that the 'low propensity to invest' on the part of European entrepreneurs was perfectly justified. The traditional areas of business which they understood, no longer offered potential returns commensurate with the risk of investment, because of competition, and because so much of any gains would be captured by derived market power. New opportunities for investment were indeed opened up by the discretionary element in remuneration, but these were not opportunities so much for local European producers, as for the American ones that were operating from the advantage of experience with more turns of the marketing spiral. Consequently, it was inevitable that they should come to dominate the new consumer and consumer-durable goods markets on the basis of a 're-run with hindsight' as explained in Chapter II. Moreover, European business men were quite right to foresee that they would do so, and to be cautious about investment in competition with them.

This caution, in the event, was compensated for by the widespread adoption of the Keynesian solution, by which Governments stepped in to stimulate investment and demand. What is of interest for the present argument was that this in itself increased the importance of derived taxing power, reinforced derived market power, and 'ordinary' derived market power, and thus of mass rent in the economic system, by a full order of magnitude. Of its nature, every intervention by Government in an economy has the effect of intensifying the rent element, and cannot do otherwise. If a Government borrows more, the revenues of rentiers, in the form of interest, are increased. If it raises taxes, those with market power, either primary or derived, increase their prices to absorb them. The rents attributable to their market power go up correspondingly. When Government spends more, much of the increase goes to its own employees, whose salaries are almost all rent, and the rest is captured by the primary market power of contractors, thus adding to their rents. When Government re-distributes, whatever reaches the recipients is most intelligibly regarded as rent attributable to their voting power. And if it prints money, the resulting inflation is to the advantage of all those with market power, and is again reflected in increased rents.

Although there is some evidence of the beginning of the trend earlier – Procter and Gamble's move into Britain by the purchase of Thomas Hedley, for example – the real surge of investments to exploit derived market power was a post-War phenomenon. It was also, as could be expected, accompanied by a fundamental shift by many United States companies from national to global operation. The growth of the U.S. multi-national was undoubtedly facilitated by the advent of world-wide air transport, but its roots were in the Paris Convention. Together with the use of registered Trade Marks by national firms, 'marketing-oriented' investment grew to correspond with the discretionary incomes generated by derived market power. This investment played a major role in pulling the advanced economies out of the 1930s Depression, and in sustaining a high level of economic activity until the 1970s. It depended upon Trade Mark registration legislation, but this legislation could only have its 'locomotive' effect when derived market power had brought discretionary incomes to a sufficiently high level to justify investment in products containing substantial psychological ingredient. This accounts for the delay between the enactment of Trade Mark legislation in most countries, and the flow of marketing activities at a rate sufficient to have a beneficial effect upon long-term economic trends.

Say's law is always lurking in the background of any discussion of market power. Galbraith claimed that Keynes had killed this law, but it seems to be more true that he mis-stated it, and his mis-statement had unfortunately become widely accepted. According to W.H. Hutt, Keynes's version of the law was that 'supply creates its own demand' whereas what Say actually held was that 'supplies in general *constitute* demands in general' – not at all the same thing.[14] In the present context, rent on the supply side, has to equal rent on the demand side, and it is then quantity, not price, which moves to bring about equilibrium. The corollary of this is that if anything happens to reduce the rent accruing to the Primary market power, and if derived rents are prevented by institutional factors from accepting a corresponding reduction, the whole burden of adjustment falls upon output, and this process is cumulatively damaging. It is what turns Recession into Depression, and, as will be seen below, it has been very clearly demonstrated in the contemporary crisis. In fact, a case can be made that the higher the rent element in the system, the more rapidly and effectively investment is cut back to ensure a reduction in output corresponding to the setback to Primary market power. If entry barriers are low (i.e. if Primary market power is low) it is indeed likely that investors will plunge too heavily at one stage, or cut back too much at another, simply because of their natural tendency to look for reassurance in numbers. No business man's judgment can ever remain unaffected by the sight of his colleagues either making money or losing it. But if entry barriers are insuperable for all practical purposes, as they are in markets with high advertising 'thresholds', then investment will be adjusted much more accurately to the precise opportunities for it.

There was a canal-building mania and a railway mania, when investors, stimulated by awareness of profits being made by others, lost all rationallity. Both of these sets of excesses, as well as countless parallels in exploration and commodities, handsomely confirm Forrester's thesis of 'over-shooting'. But there has never been a comparable "detergents" mania or a "Cola drinks" mania or "anti-biotics" mania, because of the oligopolistic nature of these industries. Dewey's theoretical proof that once entry of new firms can be prevented by some means, the industry will move, in the absence of some legal restriction on freedom of contract, to a technically efficient monopoly, and that this will take the form of a profit-sharing cartel, is most apposite.[15] So is the argument in Chapter II that even where there is an active anti-monopoly regime, industries where advertising appropriations are relatively large, can still give the reality of membership of a cartel without the appearance of it. An important aspect of the technical efficiency of any such cartel lies precisely in the tailoring of investment to the opportunities for it. To the extent, therefore, that industry is oligopolistic, because of the existence of entry barriers, the Forrester thesis is weakened, and clustering of innovations is left as, at the least, a very likely source of long-term economic fluctuations. And if legal change is not the actual cause of 'clustering', it is, at the very least, the necessary catalyst.

Is it possible to go as far as Mensch, however, and claim that "innovations overcome the Depression"? Mensch's case rests upon his identification of a statistically significant clustering of basic innovations in the economic periods of mid-1820s, mid-1880s and mid-1930s. He found no similar clustering of *inventions*, and since there is a long time lag between invention and innovation, what characterizes the 'innovatory' periods must be a speeding-up of the practical use of already existing scientific and technical information. Mensch has been criticised on the ground that the list of innovations he uses is far from comprehensive and greatly underestimates the number of basic innovations in the post-War period, and also probably in the period 1900-1920.[16] It should also be added that any list which is limited to technology is inadequate for attempting to measure the economic significance of innovation. What weight, for example, should one give to Lever's innovation of branded, pre-packed, mass-advertised soap in 1883, bearing in mind that this grew into a company employing huge numbers of people all over the world, whose raw material requirements are highly significant to the economies of several African states, and which has been responsible for several further innovations of great economic importance? The criticism has particular force when it is borne in mind that Mensch's list of basic innovations contain items such as Cinerama and the Zip fastener, which, however interesting they may be, have hardly had an enormous impact upon economic life. In view of the importance of marketing in the third industrial thrust, as argued above, the limitation of using technological innovations only, as a measure of "getting new things done", has a particularly distorting effect during this period. For example, in terms of employment given, sales, profits, work subcontracted and taxes paid, the economic impact of the innovation of selling cosmetics door-to-door by the Avon Company world-wide, must rank higher than many quite famous and praised technological innovations.

Counting innovations without being able to 'weight' them accurately, encounters the same difficulty that bedevils all research with Patent statistics. This arises from the fact that whereas only a very few inventions indeed ever earn any money at all, some of these earn huge sums. Consequently, work based upon raw patent statistics is worthless. Moreover, the difficulty of assessing the importance of any innovation in economic terms must be intrinsically greater than that of a Patent, which at least has definite limits both in geography and time. Consider the innovation of refrigeration, for example, which is fairly unexciting in strictly technological terms. This could be measured in terms of sales, profits, etc., of firms manufacturing refrigeration equipment. But its true economic importance is far greater, since without it, the vast resources of the Southern Hemisphere for meat production could never have been opened up to take the pressure off European supplies. Since cheap food played a major part in the third Kondratieff upswing, refrigeration on its own can claim corresponding credit for overcoming the depression of 1873-96. Yet in Mensch's list, it counts only equally with Iodoform antiseptic, safety matches and the plaster cast.

Although Schumpeter was attracted to Kondratieff's theory of the long cycles, Mensch's 'metamorphosis model' is, in fact, more in line with his own thinking. A cyclical approach implies that an earlier impulse has to die away completely before the next upturn can start, whereas Mensch's model illustrates them as partially contemporaneous. This, in fact, is what they would have to be for Schumpeter's process of "creative destruction" to operate, and it may be useful to recall what this is. Schumpeter envisaged 'a powerful lever' in the economic process, for expanding output and bringing down prices. This lever consisted of innovation, thought of as being carried through by firms which are themselves new, and whose aggressive competition therefore 'strikes at the very lives' of the established businesses. This type of competition – from 'the new technology, the new commodity, the new source of supply' – he likened to an artillery barrage. Compared with the effect of this, 'ordinary' competition (by members of the Club between themselves, according to rules they have mutually, even if tacitly, agreed upon) is unimportant.[17]

As a description of the dynamic aspects of a situation where barriers to entry depend upon Capability market power, this is indeed attractive. It is far less so, however, when Persuasive market power becomes a factor to be reckoned with. Indeed, when towards the end of his life Schumpeter recognised that his ideas needed modification if they were to be applicable to the new multi-product, multi-national firms, he was perhaps adverting to the way in which the coming of Persuasive market power had altered the nature of the problem.

It certainly raises a difficulty for the view that what brings one economic cycle or impulse to an end, is the competing away of profit, or the shift from monopolistic to pure competition. If, as the Schumpeter-Mensch school holds, that impulse was initiated by innovations, it can only have been because investors had some kind of monopoly position which they could see extending into the future, to give them a return which they regarded as commensurate with the risk. Given the time lags between invention and innovation which Mensch tabulates, and bearing in mind the costs of B-phase innovation after the initial major breakthrough, it is obvious that investment in few basic innovations can ever have been undertaken in reliance only on whatever protection may be available for them from Patents. If they were, there would indeed be an immediate shift from monopolistic to pure competition on the day the patent expired, say 17 years from its issue date. But this rarely happens, and is not expected to happen, because innovation is protected by capability and persuasive market power as well. Investment in the innovation originally will also have been made on the assumption that the capability developed during the life-time of the Patent will long outlive the Patent as a barrier to entry. It may also be anticipated that marketing will grow in importance as a means of protecting the investment. Therefore, there need not be any shift from monopolistic to pure competition. Firms will come in to compete, certainly, but they will also be concerned not to depress the profits in what may now be called an industry, and they and the originator will collude, overtly or covertly, to this end. Such collusion very probably gives a far better return on investment than the type of competition that "strikes at the very roots" of the existing firms. 'Live and let live', as Sylos-Labini noted, is a typical decision rule of business men.

It is very important to realize that such men invest in innovation, not primarily to achieve new technology, but to generate rent. To the extent that all innovators share the values and psychology of the artist, as they must do, their objective may indeed be the excitement and satisfaction of seeing an idea become embodied and taking on a life of its own. But this leaves an *investor* cold; what he is after is the power the innovation will ultimately have, because of the barriers to entry which surround it, of extracting rent from whatever consumers' surplus can be captured. What investors in any successful innovatory thrust want more than anything else, once their own innovation dominates the market, *is* a stalemate at this point, technological or otherwise. One aspect of such a stalemate, of course, is that barriers to entry are highly effective. What follows naturally from this, is that as the firm or firms move along the learning curve, their output becomes more efficient in the use of both capital and labour, contributing to lower interest rates and less employment. Their own prices, in contrast, will be kept up by collusion of one type or another. On the macro-economic level, what else is a combination of high product prices with low demand for both capital and labour, than firstly, Stagflation, and, in the extreme case, Depression?

It is most important to note the vital part played in this by the element of market power. If barriers to entry are weak, then the system has possibilities of being self-compensating, even if the psychology of business men does cause 'overshoots'. Low demand for capital from established businesses makes it that much easier to raise capital for a new firm which wishes to challenge them. Low primary market power means low derived market power, with the result that any new firm is not prevented from starting by having to face a general wage level that is too high. And low primary market power also means that the established firm is vulnerable to *price* competition. Even if the newly-established firm does not compete on price alone, the fact that it does so at all, or even that it *can* do so, prevents the rents earned by the established firms from becoming too high. It is clear that under this set of circumstances, the fluctuations of economic life have a limited amplitude, since the success of any innovation automatically generates the conditions for limiting its economic effect. Conversely, when barriers to entry are strong, they first cause rapid growth, but eventually deep depression. To the extent that the areas covered by earlier waves of innovation are impregnable, the task of getting the economy out of depressions falls entirely upon radical innovations in quite different fields.

Therefore, the capacity of innovations to overcome a depression will be high if market power is low, but low if market power is high. In the slump of 1873-1896, an undoubted factor was the pressure on food supplies from the massive growth in population which the first industrial thrust had stimulated. The population of England, for example, *doubled* from 9 to 18 millions between 1800 and 1850. Even though agricultural productivity increased – illustrated by the yield of wheat per acre increasing from around 20 to around 30 bushels over the same period, it is clear that the balance of the evolution favoured farmers. Without imports of food, they would have been able to push prices sky-high. The innovation of the steamship made grain imports technically easier from the 1840s onwards. The market power of the farmers was of the Specific type, from the existence of the Corn Laws, which expressly forbade imports. Repeal of these laws in 1848, eliminated this barrier to entry. Since

British figures are so important to the empirical work which led Kondratieff to formulate his cycle theory, it is interesting to speculate how far this change on its own, contributed to the 'prosperity' stage of the second Kondratieff, which Kuznets dated as 1843-57.[18] Landes is in no doubt that food imports from Southern Hemisphere sources were a cause of recovery from the trough of 1873 onwards, and the essential part played in this by refrigeration has already been mentioned. These examples vindicate the views on cyclical movements of both Rostow and Mensch. Rostow's explanation of Kondratieff cycles focuses

> "on the relative prices of food and raw materials on the one hand, indus-
> trial prices on the other. Other forces were, evidently, at work, but, at
> their core, I believe that what we observe in these cycles are periods of
> relative shortage and relative abundance of food and raw materials".[19]

The opening up of the grain resources of North America, and of the meat potential of Australia, New Zealand and countries such as Paraguay and the Argentine, however, would not have been possible without the innovation of steamships and refrigeration. In both cases, a technological innovation was a necessary condition for righting an imbalance. And, if the imbalance is so extensive as to amount to a depression, then it could perhaps be envisaged that – as Mensch argues – sufficiently extensive innovatory activity could over-come it. Obviously, though, there is another necessary condition, which is that the process is not frustrated by established market power. The Corn Laws were the specific market power of the farmers of Britain and Ireland. From the repeal of these laws in 1848, these farmers had to face competition from imported cereals but prospered greatly from their capability market power in respect of meat, especially beef. Had restrictions on imported food still been in existence in 1880, refrigeration might still have been innovated, but it would certainly have been prevented from making its important contribution to keeping food prices under control in Britain in subsequent decades.

Because market power has been increasing since the start of the industrial revolution, it follows that the capacity of technological innovations on their own to bring about recovery out of a slump can only have been corresponding-ly decreasing. This is clear from the Depression of the 1930s, when derived market power was so strong that investors saw little prospect of profit any-where, much less in innovation. Much of the derived rents earned in the new high-productivity industries went into housing. It was only when public expenditure began to grow strongly, at first under the threat and actuality of War, then, after the War, by Keynes-inspired interventionism, that the par-ticular innovations of the third thrust were able to contribute to growth. These were especially innovations involving psychological ingredient, or those of the B-phase or incremental type that can be protected by a combination of per-suasive and capability market power and secrecy. All of these found their markets expanding rapidly in Western countries, largely because of the growth of what became known as "the mixed economy". In this, the part played by the State grew steadily, until, in the years after the first Oil Shock of 1974, it accelerated very rapidly indeed. Irrespective of what form government intervention took, it had the effect of adding massively to the amount of rent in the economic system. Innovatory efforts therefore became directed towards the new products and new (mainly psychological) ingredients in products, which could exploit this rent. This was all very well as long as the raw materials (especially energy) which went into making the physical components of two-part products were cheap, and no serious competitors dared to act outside the 'covert cartels' erected by large advertising appropriations. But when external challenge arose on both these fronts, which could only be met by large-scale innovation at the technological, not psychological level, the available innovatory resources were found to be quite the wrong ones for the task, and the system was also found to be too inflexible to change with anything like the rapidity required. The resulting build-up of economic pressure has been so great as to call into question the actual survival of democracy in the worst-hit countries. When democracy has collapsed before, as in the case of the Weimar Republic, it was primarily through inability to cope with economic problems. The problems of this type which Western countries face to-day are fundamentally two, one of which has been encountered before, and the other being quite new.

The 'old' problem is the contemporary version of something which, if Rostow is right, has been found in every Kondratieff cycle at the recession and depression stages − a worsening of the terms of trade for manufactured goods vis-a-vis raw materials. In the present case, of course, this was brought about suddenly in 1974 by the quadrupling of oil prices by the OPEC cartel. Drastic as this was, its harmful effect on the West was limited by the opportunities it opened up for increased sales of Western manufactures to the Middle East. Western Germany, for example, was particularly well placed for this as a capital-goods exporter, and actually increased its exports to the OPEC countries by more than the increase in cost of its oil imports. After the second oil shock, however, it became impossible to hope to absorb the OPEC surpluses by increased trade. The whole Western world became involved in their re-cycling (which had affected the weaker economies from the start); and that re-cycling has done far more damage to world political stability and economic life than the price increases themselves ever did, for reasons which will be explained below.

Looked at from the standpoint of market power, it should be pointed out that the position of the OPEC cartel is precisely what ought to be the expected end of any major wave of investment in innovation. There were huge risks involved in exploration, in developing the processing technologies, and in opening up markets for the product. For investment in the early days of oil to have been fully rational, investors should have been able to anticipate some approximation of OPEC's degree of market power eventually, at least for a period, so as to earn returns commensurate with the risks run. It is true that in the OPEC case, those who are enjoying the rent from the innovations are not those who made the original investment at high risk. In terms of the market power balance, however, the advantage of the oil-rich countries is comparable with that of cotton producers in the depression stage of one Kondratieff cycle, or of local cattlemen in the same stage of another. What *is* different, is that today the West is apparently incapable of producing the innovations that would draw the sting from OPEC's market power. Innovation of Whitney's Cotton Gin opened up vast new sources of supply for the rapidly expanding textile industry, thus eroding the market power of the original sources which were enjoying a seller's market. When supplies were interrupted because of the American Civil War, entrepreneurs and bankers swiftly turned to Egypt as an alternative source.[20] In the next cycle, innovation of refrigeration opened up vast new sources of meat for the rapidly-expanding populations of the industrializing world, thus eroding the market power of the local farmers who were enjoying a seller's market. In the past, innovations have always defeated market power, but there is no sign as yet of the innovatory thrust that would erode the seller's market of OPEC. The capacity of the oil cartel's market power to generate rent on a massive scale, has so far been adversely affected more by the reduction in the West's oil usage from a lower level of economic activity, than by the development of new energy sources. And the West's failure is clearly more one of innovation rather than of invention. The answer to market power in oil must lie in successful exploration, in conservation and in the development of the techniques of alternative energy. Yet progress on all these fronts has been painfully slow, with little evidence of the dynamism with which the 'long cycle' crises of the nineteenth century were tackled and overcome. The reason is clear: Economic innovation depends upon economic freedom. The larger the public sector becomes, therefore, the more sluggishly an economy will move to respond to external challenges. In the case of the OPEC cartel, the way in which the oil countries' surpluses were recycled, resulted in an explosive growth of the public sector in all OECD countries, which meant that power to respond to the challenge was greatly reduced. Movement towards the Hydrogen economy, for example, apart from inherent advantages this energy source possesses, is essential if the most promising of the techniques of alternative energy, such as Ocean Thermal and Wave, are to reach their full potential. It has hardly begun.

It must be stressed that the harm done to Western economies by the OPEC cartel has been far more through the way their surpluses accelerated the rate of public sector growth, than through the price increase itself. It is also more permanent, because oil price reductions in themselves, brought about by a shift to a lower level of economic activity in the West, cannot dismantle these harmful accretions to the public sector. The extra recruits to this sector during the period when the eager salesman of Western banks were pressing loans upon all-too-willing Governments, are either impossible or extremely difficult to dismiss; the increased remuneration gained by the use of Derived Taxing power and Reinforced Derived Market power, also funded by external borrowing, cannot be clawed back. Neither can any reduction in the price of oil in itself change the fact that a dead weight of debt which has to be serviced and repaid, is the legacy of the spendthrift times.

The OPEC cartel, however, is only one of the pair of millstones that have been grinding the economies of the West. The other is Japan. The impact of Japanese firms on Western economies is due to the fact that in their Keiretsu-Zaibatsu relationships, they possess the most perfect vehicle for B-phase or incremental innovation that the world has ever seen. This impact is all the more devastating for individual industries in the West, because it is selective.

Japan's Zaibatsu and Bank-centred Groups are giant holding companies which operate world-wide and include banks, insurance and shipping firms, and trading companies, in addition to manufacturing. Some of the best-known Japanese names abroad, such as Mitsui and Mitsubishi, are Zaibatsu. Keiretsu stands for the way in which these giant enterprises organize sub-contracting upstream of their own operations, from huge numbers of small firms. This Keiretsu relationship is far closer and more complex than anything known in the West, and provides the small firm with orders, management consultancy and finance, without destroying its autonomy. In a way analogous to the life-time employment which a Japanese worker can expect from the firm to which he gives his total loyalty, the small Keiretsu firm can expect to be helped through difficulties by the large one, which will seek out business in a new field for it, if demand falls off in its traditional line. Thus, the Japanese small manufacturing firm is integrated into the *world* market by its Keiretsu links with its paternalistic Zaibatsu, which trades world-wide.[21] The orders which the small firm gets are for products, sub-assemblies or components of products which have been developed in accordance with the unrivalled Japanese commercial intelligence system, so they enable it to perform far better than it could ever do if it had to rely only on its own resources. Its management can devote all its capacity towards improving its performance and its products. B-phase, or incremental innovation, is most successfully achieved in small firms, because it depends upon the closeness of the management to the shop floor, to the processes, and to the workers. The small changes which are trivial in themselves, but which cumulatively add up to the commercial advantage that alone makes economic sense of the spectacular breakthroughs, are not made by expansive strategic decisions in boardrooms. They arise from "learning by doing", in which people who are intimately involved with the product and its manufacture, see how small design changes could make access for maintenance easier, or the advantage of using a magnesium die-casting instead of a zinc one, or the savings from injection moulding a part instead of fabricating it. This relentless search for improvement in detail, both of products and of processes, has given Japanese goods their well-deserved reputation for reliability and value.

Against such a system, Western economies are virtually defenceless. In these, the relationship of large firms with strong market power to their sub-contractors, has typically been predatory, not paternal. Morris, for example, deliberately maximized his use of sub-contractors when building his great motor business, so that they, and not his own firm, would have to bear the cost of cyclical unemployment.[22] Many Western countries are now making strenuous efforts to build up their small firms' sector, a typical example being the West German Small Firm Law. No matter what is done, the effect, even on B-phase innovation, cannot hope to emulate Japanese success; simply because in the individualistic tradition of the West, sub-contractors will always be sacrificed to short-term exigencies. The present encouragement of small firms in Western countries, which has been widely acclaimed, and from which politicians have promised great things, will, in the absence of measures to be proposed in Chapter V, only result in widespread failure and despair.[23]

The way in which Japanese firms have selected their targets, has given full weight to the effect of market power. Better capability results in lower unit cost, which *could* be translated into price competition. When the marketing spiral is expanding rapidly, however, as a result of the growth of derived taxing power and derived market power of both reinforced and ordinary varieties, there is the opportunity instead, of changing producer surplus into consumer surplus by delivery of psychological ingredient. In grasping this opportunity, Japanese firms have the advantage, through their lower costs for the physical part of their two-part product, of being able to invest more in persuasive market power than their competitors. At a time when rent in the system has been increasing rapidly in Western countries, this has meant that Japanese products have been better matched to the market than others, and so gained share, often becoming brand leaders, with the extra benefits which that brings. Lower costs for the physical part of the product, also mean the capacity, in markets where personal selling through the distributional chain is important, to give higher margins to dealers and higher commission to salesmen, thus obtaining the best representation. Japanese advantage in dealer networks abroad, begins with Japanese manufacturing capability at home.

As in the case of OPEC, the West seems to be paralysed in the face of the Japanese challenge. This is intensified by awareness that, harsh as the effects have already been, there is more pressure to come, not alone from Japan, but eventually also from the whole Confucian world. There is also fear of the impact of increasing Japanese attention to A-phase or originative innovation, and to basic research. This shift is being signalled by a rapid change from English to Japanese as the technical language, which will ensure that Western countries will encounter great difficulty even in monitoring developments, much less keeping pace with them. The apprehension is all the greater because of the financial time-scale to which their system permits the Japanese to work, which is so much longer than anything which applies to the West. Large Western firms where management and ownership are separated, put pressure upon management to produce dividends quickly. In contrast, at a time when all the economic arguments about the international division of labour were against any attempt to develop an automobile industry in Japan, the experts of

MITI (Japanese Ministry of International Trade) argued strongly for it. They did so, not primarily on the grounds of the value of such an industry in itself, but because without it, a sophisticated machine-tool sector could not be built up.[24] The results are now only too apparent, when Japanese robots are being used to make robots. Another illustration is the way in which Japan's steel industry achieved unequalled levels of yield and quality in rolling steel under computer control. This "involved reviving basic research on the theory of plasticity which had been initiated and later abandoned by the Max Planck Institute in Germany."[25] The time-scale for results from applied research was too long for the Germans, but not too long for the Japanese.

Against Japanese pressure, the only recourse of Western countries is apparently to retreat into protectionism. This is especially embarassing for the U.S., since the General Agreement on Tariffs and Trade (G.A.T.T.) was inaugurated and developed on U.S. initiatives. Free trade has always been championed by the countries with most economic power. In the nineteenth century, it was Britain which pressed the arguments for free trade, because Britain had most to gain from it. The United States, which built up its first industries behind tariff barriers, was converted to free trade as these industries became stronger. In the immediate aftermath of the War, when the capability of U.S. firms was clearly far ahead of competitors in Europe and elsewhere, the United States put its influence behind the organization of the GATT in 1947. It is this agreement that internationalizes capability market power, just as it is the International Convention for the Protection of Industrial Property that internationalizes the specific market power of Patents and the market power of persuasion, based on Trade Marks. For the U.S. to seek abrogation of freedom of access to its markets by Japanese firms under GATT rules, therefore, would be to admit formally that industrial leadership had passed from it. Yet there are other signs of stagnation, which have not been lost on the U.S. Government. Investment has been declining in real terms since 1968, and so has spending upon Research and Development. The decline in innovation became so evident, that in May 1978, President Carter set up the Baruch Advisory Committee to enquire into the subject. Baruch reported in September 1979, and amongst the findings were, that investment had grown by 3.8% a year in real terms until 1970, but only by 0.9% a year since then, that after-tax returns on investment had been halved from the 8% rate in the 1960s, that less fundamental research was being done by corporations, although industrial R & D was growing at between 2 and 3 per cent annually, that the share of U.S. Patents issued to foreign applicants had doubled in 14 years, that although small firms did only 3% of U.S. R & D, they produced 24 times more major innovations per dollar than did large firms, and that uncertainty about regulatory processes is a serious inhibitor of innovation.[26]

The reason for the increasing inability of Western countries to innovate, even under the stimulus of deadly thrusts from outside, is simply stated. It is the growth of bureaucracy, in the first instance through expansion of the State, but also — in ways that are detrimental to innovation — in banking and finance generally, in giant firms and in conglomerate organizations. The rapid increase in State interventionism during this century has many roots, but the growth of market power itself has certainly been a major factor in it. This is because the pattern of economic life that is associated with the growth of market power, has been increasingly felt to be an inhumane one, out of tune with the values on which Western culture is based. Since this pattern was apparently built upon private property, many people concluded that a private property system could evolve in no other way. They rejected this way, and turned to Socialism as an alternative. The central theme of the writings of Wilhelm Roepke was this lack of a moral content in twentieth-century capitalism, and without this, he felt, it could not survive. Schumpeter forecast the end of Democracy also, as a result of intellectuals turning against it.

The truth is that from the start of the first industrial thrust, Innovation, Private Property, Democracy and Market Power have always been inter-related in a close and complex way. Originally, they were mutually supportive, and the result was a prodigious outpouring of technological advance, growth in wealth, and extension of individual freedoms, as reflected in widening of the franchise. Progressively, however, the balance between them was lost until to-day there is nothing short of antagonism in their relations. Market power, as it has in fact evolved, is now destructive of true private property, of democracy, and of civilised innovation. Humane values in innovation are also progressive-ly less to be expected from the way democracy is evolving, and the line of the latter's development is increasingly replacing true private property with a spurious version. The capacity of innovation to generate real wealth is suffer-ing from the erosion of private property, from democracy in its current form, and from market power as we know it at present. Finally, if democracy is destroyed, this will be caused by a distortion of private property brought about by uncontrolled market power; by too little technical innovation, which can relieve the destructive pressures arising from such a distortion by generating additional wealth on a substantial scale; and by lack of the *social* innovations that would remove, or at least partially correct, the distortion itself.

The reason why bureaucracy and innovation are altogether incompatible lies in the nature of decision-making under uncertainty. Decisions can only be rational in so far as they are based upon information, and, to the extent that in-formation is complete, decisions actually tend to make themselves. However, a situation of fully complete information is as abstract an ideal as the economists' perfect competition model, in which full knowledge is added to pure competition. In the real world, decisions have to be far from complete ra-tionality, because information is always lacking; consequently, for a decision to be made, an element of imagination has to be brought into play to make up for the information that is missing. To be a 'good decision-maker' is precisely to be able to supplement rational assessment, based upon whatever facts are available, with imagination to compensate for the unknown elements in the situation. In the nature of things, decisions involving innovation will require most imagination, because these have most unknowns. Now, the more complete the information, the less room there is for different decisions by different people, and, at the limit, complete information would force unanimity by making a completely rational decision possible. The exact opposite is true of that part of any decision which depends upon imagination because of the absence of information. For this part, there are as many possibilities as there are individuals, because imagination in any particular case depends upon an individual's genetic make-up, education, experience, and even state of health or mind at different times. Consequently, wherever innovation requires the deployment of resources beyond those which the innovator himself commands, as in the case with all economic innovation, what decides whether those resources will be made available or not is whether the innovator's imagination finds a match in an investor's. The chance of this happening is greater if many individuals control the resources the innovator needs, so that there is a wide diversity in imagination. The degree of uncertainty that there has to be in all decisions regarding innovation, makes it essential, if these are to be positive, that there be a large number of decision-points. Although investment is only one aspect of the necessary deployment of resources outside the innovator's own, the extent to which its availability met this criterion goes far to account for the flowering of technological innovation throughout the eighteenth and nineteenth centuries. "Those economies", as Landes put it, "grew fastest that were freest".[27] In marketing, there is no point in articulating inchoate need into want for a specific product unless availability of money is joined to want to form demand. In the same way, there is no point in the multiplicity of imaginations resulting in a meeting of minds between innovator and someone who grasps intuitively what the innovation is and what are its possibilities, unless that second individual has money to support his vision. It was once commented by one who had very special experience in the field, that Britain's industry gained enormously in the early days from the fact that so many of her landowners, who were the source of its capital, were used to racing and betting on horses. This contributed something to their experience that helped them to be able to invest at high risk with the hope of high reward, in innovation.[28]

Maximizing the number of decision-points, therefore, is an inescapable requirement, if we want to have innovation. Bureaucracy means the exact opposite, *reducing* the number of decision-points, and in the case of the bureaucracy of the State, reducing the number of decision points to a single one. This alone would be enough to explain why State involvement and innovation are mutually contradictory, but there are other factors as well. By definition, a bureaucrat's performance cannot be subject to the profit measure, or to anything like it. If the bureau where he works is a public one, it is funded out of taxation; if it is in a large private firm, shareholding and management will long since have been separated. In neither case can there be an outstanding reward for executive success, so equally there can be no justification for taking large

risks. In contrast, where profit is either not in question (as in the public bureaucracy) or goes to the shareholders (as in the private one) opportunities for
promotion within the hierarchy become all-important. Promotions are decided
less by success than by absence of failure, so, for a bureaucrat, there is a fundamental imbalance in his reward/punishment environment in favour of caution.
Since the answer to the question "What will I get from this if it succeeds?" is
always "Nothing that is commensurate with the risk to my career", the
question to which a bureaucrat addresses himself necessarily becomes "What
will I lose if it fails?" Where there is any kind of residual risk, his main interest
will be in devising means whereby blame for failure can be transferred to some
other individual or Agency, an activity which is known as the search for
"cover". "Cover" rules the life of a bureaucrat as "Profit" rules the life of a
business man who invests his own money.

Because of this, there can never be a meeting of minds between a bureaucrat
and an innovator. However polite the surface exchanges, at heart the true
bureaucrat suspects, envies, hates and fears the innovator, and at heart the true
innovator despises the bureaucrat. The "unknowns" to which a bureaucrat's
imagination is directed, are not those of business or technology, but of the
problems of following a career path within his organization. His underlying
interest dictates this, and it also controls the food his imagination receives from
his subconscious mind. That imagination consequently cannot be available to
be sparked into vision by the innovator's project. Moreover, because
bureaucrats are able to contribute so poorly to decisions requiring imagination, they inevitably tend to limit the activity of their bureau to decisions that
do *not* require it, i.e. to decisions concerned with anything other than
innovation. Nothing is more striking than the way in which an organization
distances itself from the kinds of decisions it comes to learn that it cannot make
well. One way of doing this is to re-define the task, as was discussed in the case
of Patent Offices. Because they turn their backs upon decisions involving large
amounts of uncertainty, and convince themselves that it is possible to live in the
world by limiting decision-taking to those areas where there is enough
information for seemingly rational assessment, bureaucracies are constantly
being surprised and affronted when some external agency acts in such a way as
to change all the rules that have been so assiduously learnt. Such a changing of
the rules will always be the result of imagination confronting uncertainty, and
overcoming it, in an innovatory act. It is sobering to reflect how often in
history that external force has been from outside the society in question, and
destructive of that society. There are only two ways of remunerating members
of any organization: Either they are a charge on the organization, or they are
paid from what is left over after all charges have been met. Those who are paid
from the residual naturally want to see that this is as large as possible, so they
will be vigilant about costs, especially about management and personnel costs.
Those who are not so paid, are just as concerned to see these costs expand,
irrespective of what this expansion does to the residual. They do not care about

what is left over, because they do not share in it, but more staff and more management posts mean more opportunities for promotion, weightier arguments for salary increases, and an easier and more comfortable working environment. By definition, bureaucrats are not remunerated from the residual, and consequently their energies naturally go into expanding the bureau's activities and range of influence. In the public bureaucracy, this also increases the derived taxing power of bureaucrats, since the more goods and services are directly provided by the State, the more vulnerable politicians are to the same kinds of pressure as are brought to bear on business by derived market power. Growth of the bureaucracy within a business tends to be held in check by the limits of the firm's market power, the relevance of the profit measure to its activities, the desire of shareholders for dividends, and by the shape and effect of reward schemes for top executive performance. No such automatic external checks exist in the case of the public bureaucracy. For reasons which will be discussed below, political control of the Civil Service has been weakening everywhere throughout this century. There has also been a remarkable shift in the demography of Civil Services, which removed a factor which acted as a strong internal restraint on bureaucratic growth right up to the first World War. The United States, indeed, had no permanent civil service at all until the last quarter of the nineteenth century, every elected official appointing his own staff. It was only after the assassination of President Garfield by a disappointed office-seeker that a permanent corps began to be recruited. Even to this day, the extent to which the tradition of movement between the public service, business and academic life, persists, is of enormous advantage in keeping the American public bureaucracy in touch with economic realities, even if it still finds it extremely difficult to cope with innovation. Yet, this bureaucracy too, has grown quite disproportionately in recent decades, causing the same malaise as in other countries.

In France also, at the top level, there is movement between business, the civil service and politics. This is because of the educational system of the Grandes Ecoles, in which the top echelons of so many aspects of French life are formed. Recent perceptive work has shown that this can cope well with areas where decisions can be made rationally on the basis of adequate information, but still demonstrates inability to deal with innovation.[29]

The British Civil Service differs from both the U.S. and the French, in being a closed world, with interchange of personnel between it and other aspects of national life the exception rather than the rule. From the aspect of 'permeability to ideas', the contrast is not between Britain and the other countries, but between the calibre of higher Civil Servants in all the European countries in the nineteenth, as compared with the twentieth century. Not the least of the ways in which the Great War destroyed what remained of the old Europe, was in the virtual elimination of a particular cadre of higher Civil Servants. The 'leaven and example' of this elite corps came from men who had private means and character to match it. Their place was taken by 'new men' from an altogether different demographic background. For them, advancement could only mean expansion of the power of the State with consequent growth in the bureaucracy. This new bureaucracy is incapable of sifting the kernel that is in the national interest from the submissions of special interest groups, because it is a special interest group itself. It has none of the permeability to ideas of its predecessor. It is no accident that the one set of ideas that it did take to heart, those of Keynes, were precisely those which provided comprehensive intellectual justification for the very policies which were in its own interest to follow.[30]

Of the advanced countries, it is probably in Britain that the new bureaucracy has made most progress. Consequently, it is hardly surprising that there the public sector now controls over half of GNP, two-fifths of all new investment and an even higher proportion of existing fixed assets, and pays one-third of all wages and salaries – and that the country's record in respect of innovation has been the despair of its economic leaders. British R & D expenditure in relation to national income has always been very high by international standards, but it has never had a comparable effect on innovation. This is partly due to the way it has been biassed towards Defence, especially aerospace, but even more to its organization through Government-owned research establishments. The United States system, which uses Government contracts to private firms instead, has been demonstrably very much more effective. Even in the United States, however, with the growth in power of the public bureaucracy, the tendency has emerged for this bureaucracy not only to decide what research is to be done, *but also to manage it.* This has been especially noticeable in the response to the OPEC energy price increases. It will be clear that in such an emergency, the State has two alternatives open to it. One approach is to devise means whereby the prospects of profit from innovation are increased. This will take the form of legal changes which will generate market power. It has the great advantage of mazimizing the number of decision points, which is necessary for innovation. An example, though trivial in its effect because of the inadequacy of the Patent system to confer the needed degree of market power, is that the U.S. Patent Office now advances Patent applications for energy-related inventions out of their turn for examination. The 'prospects of profit' approach, however, has the disadvantage for the bureaucracy that it offers little or no scope for expanding its own numbers and influence. In the political circumstances of the present time, therefore, the second approach was in fact adopted in the U.S., of putting Civil Servants in de facto *managerial* control of many aspects of energy innovation. The result was the explosive growth of the Energy Department, with no proportionate advance towards solutions to the problems.

It is, in fact, intrinsically impossible for Civil Servants of the new type to develop the social innovations that are needed to permit private enterprise to innovate effectively. This is because *it is not in their interest to do so.* To the extent that law is well devised for generating the conditions within which individual initiative can be effective, it is a direct alternative to interventionism, and thus stunts the bureaucracy's growth. Creativity and imagination are essential to the work of constantly re-shaping the legal structures, but these depend upon subconscious energies which will only be released when an individual's own interest is at stake. Since the interest of the modern Civil Servant lies in fact in the opposite direction, the case for market forces operating within a framework of positive law, will never be advanced with anything like the same vigour as that for some form of intervention, since this will expand the bureaucracy. Douglas Hurd, who had a unique opportunity of observing top Civil Servants in action when he was the British Prime Minister's Political Secretary, observed that:

> "It was the Ministry rather than the Minister which mattered, the general administration of the country rather than the ambitions of each fleeting group of politicians, allied to which attitude is a firm belief in the merits of action by the State. A Minister who proposes a new form of government activity will find himself promptly served. He will quickly find in his red box the requisite scheme for a new Board, a new Bill for Parliament, a new network of offices in each town and city. The Minister who wishes to dismantle part of the machine of the state has a much harder task...[31]

Another aspect of bureaucracy's brake on innovation is the the area of controls. The pharmaceutical industry has been particularly affected by this. It complains, for example, that certification trials now waste seven years' Patent protection. No one denies the necessity for controls, but the difficulty is that for the bureaucrats who administer them, the need for "cover" is paramount. It is worth remembering that Penicillin, as originally innovated, which saved the lives of countless thousands, could scarcely have *begun* to obtain certification under the present-day control system. The difficulty is that since officials cannot share in successes, but will be blamed for failures, they are so concerned that they will not be responsible for another thalidomide tragedy that they must certainly be depriving mankind of other remedies that might be as important as Penicillin.

The problems caused by the growth of the public bureaucracy can be seen at their worst in the absurdity that this bureaucracy is now actually concerned with innovation itself. As the public sector has grown, innovation has inevitably become less profitable and feasible, up to the point where Governments have become alarmed. Not being aware of the extent to which bureaucracy is the very cause of the problem, they have actually expanded the bureaucracy to try to deal with it. A large number of countries now have sub-departments of the Civil Service or State-controlled organizations which are concerned with the encouragement of innovation, and it is not difficult to explain why they are not, and indeed cannot be, successful. Because they are part of the State machine, they inevitably favour approaches with will involve the State actively in the innovation field, over those which will simply improve the economic environment within which innovation can take place as the result of unpredictable initiatives. This centralizing bias is destructive of the multiplicity of decision points upon which innovation depends. People with the capacity to innovate are not typically those who join the Civil Service, or if they do, they either leave it or are broken by it. Those who staff the section of the public bureaucracy which is given the task of dealing with innovation, therefore, can never be in more than very partial sympathy with innovators. Their conditions of employment, providing absolute security and relieving them of any need to commit themselves to a project (indeed, actually preventing them from doing so) are exactly the opposite of those which must apply to an innovator. Any innovation can only be successful as a result of an innovator's total commitment to it, and this commitment has to involve him in substantial personal risk, not only in economic terms, but in personal and psychic terms as well. The bureaucrats' need for "cover" so that their career paths within the system cannot be damaged, inevitably pushes them in the direction of second-grade projects, since it is these that offer most "cover" and lowest risk. At the international level, this search for "cover" actually leads bureaucrats from different countries to the *same* projects. At one OECD meeting, for example, when a perceptive official totalled up the projections from a number of Government innovation groups of their countries' *shares* of world markets for certain new technologies which had State encouragement, the figure was several times the most optimistic estimates of the *total* world market!

There is another factor which makes it inevitable that when the public bureaucracy concerns itself with innovation, the results will be economically disastrous. The point has been made earlier that in the first thrust of the industrial revolution, all the major advances were achieved without the benefit of a scientific explanation for them. Even in the later thrusts, when innovation has become increasingly science-based, the basic principle remains valid: All practical advances are ahead of the theory which fully explains them. The current difficulties in genetic engineering, for example, where bacteria which co-operate well at the laboratory level, actually become mutually antagonistic when scaled up to commercial quantities, cannot rely on a developed body of theory for their solution. The theory, it may be expected, will eventually emerge from whatever solutions are found in practice. The relevance of this point to public bureaucrats becoming involved in innovation, is that they cannot fail to have a strong bias towards projects which they can fully under-stand, which means projects which emerge out of the existing body of scientific knowledge. This is, after all, a most important part of a Scientific Civil Servant's 'cover'. Such projects, of course, will always be in the second or even lower rank of innovation, because the first rank projects will be ahead of the theory. If and when the 'publicly selected' projects reach the stage of com-mercialization, therefore, they will be trailing behind the real innovations of countries where the profit measure is still permitted to operate, and where, as a consequence, genuine 'leaps into the dark' can still be made.

Every bureaucracy, therefore, follows its own inner logic. It is not only that the over-riding objective of "cover" in treading a career-path within an organization, presses for the accumulation of information to make decisions "safe", or, if uncertainty still remains, to postpone them. This information-gathering function as also labour-intensive, and thus contributes to the second element in the expansion of bureaucracy, which is that promotion and power depend upon the staff budget for which an individual is, or could be, responsible. Operation of the profit measure, in its various ways, acts in the private sector to keep the growth of bureaucracy in check, although clearly its effect is inversely proportional to the strength of derived market power. This is why firms which are State-owned, where derived market power is consequently of the reinforced type, tend to be more bureaucratic than other firms. In the case of the public bureaucracies, the only constraint must be the decisions of the Governments which fund them. Why have Governments been unable or unwilling to curb the growth of bureaucracy, with all the harmful effects this had had?

To answer this, the nature of the interactions between democracy and market power must now be examined. Marx said contemptuously of parliamentary democracy that it was only 'the committee of the bourgeoisie'. To-day we are desperately at grips with the question: 'Can it ever be anything else?' Consider first an obvious contrast – between the country where democracy works most and best, and those countries where it does not work at all.

Nowhere are public affairs run through the ballot-box more than in Switzerland, where not just questions of foreign loans, but even issues such as the lengthening of the runways at Geneva airport are the subject of a referendum. But even without crossing the Iron Curtain, to where political choice does not exist at all, the countries where the Colonial powers left one-man-one-vote quickly replaced it with some form of authoritarian regime. Consulting the electorate is as much a sham in the third world as it is everyday reality in Switzerland, and the contrast is no less stark because of Swiss unwillingness in the past to give votes to women, nor of the existence of a large group of foreign workers who do not have the franchise there.

Next, consider a second contrast between Switzerland and the same countries, this time in terms of wealth. The differences are not so much in terms of total wealth but of its kind, and of the way in which it is distributed. In no country in the world are property and incomes so independent of the State as in Switzerland; there is widespread belief in market forces (as a corollary of which ownership tends to be widely distributed) and the owners of this property have shown themselves to be highly capable of generating real new wealth. In the ex-Colonial countries wealth depends almost completely on the State; it is highly concentrated and linked to government corruption; and it has little power to generate further real wealth. Even where the oil riches of Nigeria, for example, spill over into private ownership, it is as a result of individual or family connections with the State machine, which effectively controls virtually all the national income. In Switzerland, on the other hand, the State's proportion of national income is only one-fifth – vastly lower than even in any other European country.

These are extremes, but whether one looks at them or the countries in between (the U.S., closer to Switzerland; the poorer OECD countries, with the public share of national income more than three-fifths, to the ex-Colonial States) there is no escaping the correlation between the two contrasts: *Democracy is a property system.* It can be seen to work where it is a counterweight to property, giving power to numbers qua numbers, to balance the power which property that is independent of the State must always possess. It can be seen not to work when it is introduced where there is little or no independent property which needs to be counterbalanced, and – what is the vital question now – it ceases to work if the amount of property to be counterbalanced is reduced, or if it becomes less independent of the State, with the power of numbers remaining undiminished.

Correlation is not necessarily cause, but in this case the way in which democracy developed as part of the vast extension and expansion of wealth in Western civilization was convincingly demonstrated a generation ago by Schumpeter. From this analysis, it is clear that Marx was perfectly right to sense that democracy is part of bourgeois achievement, but then, as Schumpeter also observed, no writer has ever been so much aware of what that achievement was and what is has meant to humanity, as Marx. Innovation is indirectly involved in this relationship between democracy and property, in terms of both correlation and causality, and the lines of intellectual battle can now be seen to be drawn between those who see democracy as part of a balanced system, workable only in so far as, and for as long as, numbers act as a counterweight to a primary source of power, and those who think they can do away with property to a lesser or greater extent and still enjoy the benefits which democracy confers. Among the most important of these benefits is an environment in which innovation can flourish. It is probably not unfair to say that this second group includes Marxists, most Socialists, and not a few Liberals. This is in line with the historical evolution of democracy. It is altogether a travesty of this to think that the counterweight of the franchise (the power of numbers simply as numbers) is something which has only been wrung by violence or, even more, by the fear of violence, from those with the primary power of property. There is a significant sense, the record shows, in which it can be claimed to be the conscience of Property, which has prevented the owners of wealth from using its power solely in their own interest; so much has democracy's evolution owed to men who could, had they wished, have had their hands on the levers of the primary source of power, but who devoted themselves to developing the counterweight to it. The middle-class contribution to many European Parties of the Left is only one example.

In the 'property-numbers' balance it is not just property in which title is invested in individuals that matters, but the extent to which such property is genuinely independent of the State. Obviously, the very first condition that requires to be fulfilled for this is that the wealth has not come about because of the State's direct administrative action. This is not just because it is in this area that the opportunities exist for corrupting politicians and public servants, but because those who make money in this way do so by conforming to an economic pattern and a set of objectives which are set by the Government. Since these can only reflect the 'numbers' side of the balance, property which exists only by conforming to them is a mediocre counterweight. It could even be that it is a misnomer to call wealth which has this origin private property at all, even though it is individuals who have title to it; rather is it an extension of the State apparatus, a form of public property given into private hands. Next, the effectiveness of property as a counterbalance to the power of numbers, is inversely proportional to its dependence upon legislation which establishes complete or partial monopolies. These are not only the Acts which provide for Joint Stock Companies or Limited Liability or Industrial Property. All legal provisions which enable professional groups to set up barriers to entry, whether by requirement for registration by the group before admission to practice or otherwise, are monopolistic. Lawyers, Doctors, Architects and Accountants are among the groups which escape this this way from the constraints which market forces would otherwise impose on them. Such legislation allow the beneficiaries to earn Rent in their remuneration, which frequently makes them very wealthy indeed. It greatly narrows the pyramid of income distribution in society, and makes movement up this pyramid more difficult. It is obvious that the greater the inequality in Society and the more impenetrable the legal and institutional structures on which this inequality is based, the more the power of numbers will be directed towards undermining or overthrowing them, irrespective of the fact that there will be even less equality and social mobility in any authoritarian system that might replace the property-numbers balance of a democratic one. The only force capable of tempering the success of men of capacity who are determined to become rich and powerful, is the energy of similar men, similarly motivated. Although the operation of the free market appears to give opportunities to those who have already been favoured by Nature or Chance, to distance themselves still more from their fellows, paradoxically, it is market forces that also restrain them. These forces are in reality the guardians of whatever degree of equality is possible in society. And to the extent that there is a level of inequality which is incompatible with a democratic system, the degree to which market forces operate is also a necessary condition for the survival of democracy. Those who own property which has its origin in any form of arbitrarily-granted market power, are beholden to the State machine and to that extent are unable to act independently of it. This is a second reason why their property is therefore a counterweight to numbers in the democratic balance only in a limited sense. It is underlined by the change in the type of person who is a typical owner of wealth in such a system. Just as in an inflationary situation those who survive are the money-manipulators rather than the producers of goods (this was a major factor in the hatred of the Jews in Hitler's Germany after the inflation of the 1920s) so in a society whose economic life is characterized by market power, the owner of wealth is typically a *rentier*, whose money has come easily and who is not respected in any way for possessing it. Furthermore, such people even lose belief themselves in a system which makes them wealthy be preventing the market from operating. In Gibbon's great *Decline and Fall of the Roman Empire*, the first three chapters clearly express his view that in the later days of the Empire the owners of property (which by then was overwhelmingly of the type that depends upon State administrative action) would not fight to protect it, as if they saw its spurious nature. In our own time, Schumpeter called attention to the way in which 'the bourgeois order no longer makes any sense to the bourgeoisie itself, and when all is said and nothing is done, it does not really care'.[32] It does seem that property that is truly private, that is independent of the State, and that men will fight to preserve, will invariably be found to have been achieved under the discipline of the market. This is one reason why men who actually work the land have always clung so tenaciously to it; no economic activity historically has been so much subjected to market forces as agriculture. Where the market is operating, money is made by labour, risk and foresight, and men feel that have justly earned it; It is where there is State administrative or other action that disrupts the market that there is the 'quick buck', the big 'killing', opportunities for financial manipulation, and, above all, rich men with no conviction that their wealth is deserved. If, parallel with this, much power is given to numbers simply as numbers, there is nothing for this power to balance against and democracy must run riot. When that happens, as Aristotle pointed out, the outcome inevitably is that mob rule (ochlocracy) destroys all forms of order, thus paving the way for tyranny.

It is very easy to see, then, why Switzerland can operate such a highly democratic system (there is a lot of property that is independent of the State and therefore an effective balance) and why the ex-Colonial countries cannot have one at all (private wealth depends virtually completely upon State administrative action, so *any* weight to numbers would overwhelm it). It is also easy to find examples of extra weight being given to the 'numbers' side of the balance to maintain some kind of equilibrium with property, and therefore economic and political effectiveness, over a period when wealth was increasing. In Britain, the Reform Act of 1832, the further extension of the franchise to universal suffrage in 1867, the curb on the power of the House of Lords in 1910, are all intelligible as increases in the force numbers could bring to bear, corresponding to the prodigious growth in real wealth during the nineteenth century. In contrast, there seems to be no case where a decline in real private wealth has been accompanied by a deliberate restriction of the power of numbers so as to maintain equilibrium, and the consequent effectiveness of a democratic system. In fact, the lowering of the voting age to eighteen, coming as it did in Britain when property independent of the State was actually declining, was a move in the opposite direction. There is nothing automatic about the equilibrium upon which a democratic system depends, and indeed there is an innate tendency in such a system towards self-destruction because of the way in which the power of numbers can be used to erode independent property.

This in fact has happened in Western Democratic States several times during the present century. The destruction of independent wealth in Germany by the inflation after the first World War made the operation of Weimar democracy intrinsically impossible and an authoritarian regime was thus made inevitable. In France, what General de Gaulle castigated as 'the nefarious regime of the Parties' was a system where there was more democracy (i.e. more weight on the 'numbers' side) than the amount and distribution of 'independent' property in France could stand. As his partial cure, the Presidential system of the Fifth Republic gives less weight to numbers as such than the Parliamentary system did – and France's political stability, coupled with her unprecedented prosperity after the change, is evidence of the effectiveness of the better balance. At the present time it is the capability of some of the weaker OECD countries to survive as democracies that is increasingly being questioned, because of the way the balance has been shifting to 'numbers'. The most perceptive observers of what has been happening, rely heavily upon Schumpeter's ideas. Events have provided strong evidence of the power of these ideas to predict, and in the social as well as the natural sciences this is still the only test of sound theory. He pointed out as long ago as 1943 that the only explanation of the actual working of democracy that made sense was that politicians offer policies to the electorate, competitively, in just the same way as businesses offer brands of goods, competitively. A political party 'is not, as classical doctrine would have us believe, a group of men who intend to promote public welfare upon some principle on which they are all agreed' but 'a group whose members propose to act in concert in the competitive struggle for power'.[33]

There are, however, differences between 'dealing in oil' and 'dealing in votes', and one of these is crucial, as Peter Jay observed:

"In the economic market the coin in which the chooser casts his vote – the money he pays for his purchase – is also the resource, or at least a claim on the resources, which the supplier needs to continue and maybe to expand the process of supply. In the political market, while votes are the basis of power, they are not the material which power uses. The command over the resources of power comes from the taxing power which is awarded by a plurality of votes. There is no mechanism for ensuring that a plurality of votes implies a commitment by the voters of the quantum of resources required to fulfil the programme on which the winning political team has won an election. The pure marketplace requires the citizen to exercise his choice and to commit the resources required to fulfil it in the single act of purchase whereby he parts with his money."[34]

The type of electoral system in use naturally has a bearing upon the property-numbers balance. The first-past-the-post system needs less independent property to counterbalance it than does any form of proportional representation. But no matter what the electoral system, it is obvious that the competitive battle for votes by parties can hardly be other than an auction of the use of the State's monopoly of force to shift resources from the 'property' to the 'numbers' side of the balance. As the bids in this auction become higher and higher, this has the progressive result that the amount of democracy a country can stand, and still operate efficiently, is reduced. Since there is nothing in the system which will correspondingly reduce the power on the 'numbers' side to maintain a balance with the diminished 'property' side, the only possible outcome is that the system will accelerate towards less efficiency, especially in economic terms. For a long time this process operated rather slowly; there was tacit agreement between parties that certain things were not part of the auction; as long as the administrative class of the Civil Service tended to come from the side of 'property' rather than from 'numbers', this had a moderating influence on policies; and the effect of the genetic losses of two World Wars took time to be fully reflected in the average calibre of politicians. In recent years, however, all democracies have had their balance disturbed. In some, even, the retreat has become a rout, the bids in the 'auction' ever more frenzied, the erosion of property that is independent of the State machine more rapid, and the inefficiency of the system more intolerable. Since all of these things reduce the amount of democracy a country can stand, the politicians who are responsible for them are making their own avocation increasingly obsolete, hastening the day when some form of authoritarian system of government must replace them. In this apparent death-wish, their self-abandonment to the Party in its mindless rush for votes, resembles the extraordinary migrations of the lemmings, those strange little animals of Norway, which have as their only object their own destruction by drowning in the ocean.

The destruction of the democratic balance has followed an easily understandable sequence. Governmental action which initially eroded property made the system less capable of satisfying economic expectations; further governmental action to fill this gap was inevitably inflationary; since inflation means the abandonment of sound money, one of the greatest of human inventions, making money corresponds less and less to generating real new wealth, so the gap between expectation and reality widens again. Indigenous industry was progressively forced to operate in an economic climate in which it is impossible to invent and innovate competitively, so expanding and giving more employment. Where the State stepped in directly it invariably failed, since publicly-owned corporations have never, anywhere, shown themselves capable of innovating, and hardly ever, indeed, even of competing, in conditions that are really free. Consequently, Governments turned to the multinational corporations for the innovation, the foreign exchange earnings, the investment and the employment which they had made it impossible for locally-owned industries to produce. The growth of the State sector in mixed economies, in fact, creates by far the most fruitful environment for the spread of the multi-national Corporation, and this type of firm is now the prime means whereby countries with more economic freedom are enabled to exact tribute from those which are less free.

It is not too difficult, therefore, to identify the origin of the vast expansion of discretionary income, arising from rent in the system, which has been the counterpart of Trade Marks and the Paris Convention in the third thrust of the industrial revolution. The uncontrolled growth of market power had greatly intensified economic inequality. In the first instance, the imbalance was between those with property and those without; once Trades Union power was fully legalised, as a means of redressing this imbalance, another type of inequality was added, between those with strong derived market power and those with little or none (the latter including the unemployed). The discrediting of property rights generated the right conditions for the growth of the State. Such growth coincided with the interest of Civil Servants, but they were inhibited in expressing this as long as they were without an intellectual justification for it. Keynes, of course, provided exactly the justification they were waiting for. He did the same for democratically elected politicians. In this way was forged an unholy alliance between politicians and bureaucrats which intensified collectivism everywhere. This alliance was favourable to large-scale market power, since this is the cause of rent in the economic system, and high rents offer the possibility of high taxation. It was also completely vulnerable to offers of loans from the bankers who were re-cycling the OPEC surpluses. What politician does not want to be popular by spending money? What Civil Servant is going to argue that the State ought not to borrow, since the money will be spent in ways that extend his own empire? The only problem was that the activities of the alliance left economies incapable of innovating to meet the external challenge from the Japanese, as well as burdening them with deficit situations that in some cases amount to technical bankruptcy.

Lest this analysis might be considered to exaggerate the threat to Democracy, let it be subjected to an independent check. A useful vocabulary for dealing with the economic preconditions for democracy has been developed by Professor Dan Usher of Ontario.[35] In this, anything that makes democratic government work better is entitled to the adjective "political"; the word "assignment" covers any process which society uses to differentiate among people, and "equity" means any "non-political" means of "assignment". Using this vocabulary, and game theory, Usher is able to show most convincingly that

> "sooner or later, a society where the economy is run on socialist principles would come under the control of the administration class, which, being organized as a hierarchy, must necessarily place supreme authority in a king and emperor or the chairman of the only legitimate political party."

He then goes on to examine what is substantially the property-numbers balance discussed above, from several aspects, and concludes:

> Democracy, on the other hand, which may be the real prerequisite both for continued advancement of science, and for the maintenance of a degree of equality in the income distribution, requires that a substantial proportion of income be assigned outside the political arena. This requirement cannot, so far as we can tell, be met except by an economy run more or less on capitalist lines.[36]

But what is meant by capitalism? Usher's argument runs very much in parallel with that advanced above, that one essential characteristic, at least, is the extent to which property is genuinely independent of the State. Neither should it depend exclusively "upon the State's interference with market forces through the legislation which makes partial monopolies possible". Usher's comparable statement of the case is:

> The extent to which incomes are assigned in the legislature rather than by the market increases with the amount of monopoly in the economy. Perfect competition has a perfectly feasible system of equity. A world of monopolies... contains no system of equity. Somewhere between perfect competition and pure monopoly is a line beyond which the system of equity is not sufficient for democratic government to continue.[37]

"A world of monopolies" is, of course, the world of market power and high rents which has been analysed in earlier chapters. Monopoly, however, has the positive potential of making economic innovation possible, and to the extent that it is used effectively for this purpose, the line 'beyond which the system of equity is not sufficient for democratic government to continue' is presumably shifted: Innovation has some power to preserve Democracy.

Democratic government and market power (possibly even a lot of market power) are compatible as long as this market power is resulting in economic innovation and therefore prosperity. When the market power means no more than a high rent, high tax, bureaucratic system, the resulting poverty, unemployment, inequality and social rigidity are then the factors which make Democracy unworkable.

The test of whether or not market power is being used for innovation is the 'permeability' of the economic system to new ideas. This, in turn, is reflected in whether or not finance is available for innovation, and the poor response in Western countries to the energy challenge from OPEC and the incremental innovation challenge of Japan, strongly suggests that they are in deep trouble from this point of view.

In the lack of funds for the financing of innovation, the combination of high taxation with high derived market power has been particularly damaging. It has almost completely eliminated private sources for this purpose. This is particularly the case with funds for very long term investment, which many innovations need, and which played such an important part in the earlier thrusts of the industrial revolution. Banks can never be a substitute, because employed managers, like public sector bureaucrats, have to make decisions on the basis of 'cover' rather than 'profit'. A favourite device of employed investors is 'Third Party Cover', in which support is made conditional on the involvement of an established firm with assets and a reputation. Experience shows that this is no guarantee at all of ultimate success in innovating the idea in question. From the employee investors' point of view, however, it has two great advantages: It avoids associating them with immediate and outright rejection of ideas. This is what is in fact taking place as far as the Banks' own unsupported commitment is concerned, but the 'Third Party Cover' device prevents this being signalled publicly. Such signals might raise questions as to the adequacy of the employee investors for their task. It also shunts commercial and technical responsibility away from them, and enables it to be loaded on to the firm that is the Third Party. In the event of failure, therefore, it is possible to hide from responsibility for it, behind the status and expertise of the firm in question. This procedure indeed eliminates danger to career paths within a financial institution, but the consequences for innovation are very damaging. It means the replacement of profit as the criterion of investment in innovation, which can only mean that the ideas actually innovated will be the poorer ones. The best ideas can only emerge from a regime whose failure rate is far higher than any form of 'cover' in decision rules can permit. The historic decline in the profitability of industry in many Western countries can only reflect in some manner the resulting misallocation of resources in the face of competition from innovating industries elsewhere which have kept the profit measure. In the worst case of all, 'Third Party Cover' means that the decision as to what innovations there will be, is effectively abdicated by Institutions set up specifically to facilitate innovation, *and passed to established firms.* Even the best of these will be the worse for not having to withstand Schumpeter's "gale of creative destruction", whilst the worst are thus enabled to survive in senility long after their creative spark is extinguished.

Nothing concentrates the mind of management more wonderfully than the thought that rejecting a new idea may not be enough to prevent it from coming to life in the hands of another; but if the Institutions will only contribute their support within the context of established firms, then these firms are denied this most valuable stimulus. If the top management of a firm can be virtually sure that there is no chance of people lower down finding finance to get out and do it themselves if their ideas are not taken up, then it is under correspondingly less pressure to do something about their new ideas. And the time-scale of innovations is such that it is almost never possible to pin the blame for missed chances on anyone. As far as the financing of innovation is concerned, there is little difference between publicly owned Institutions and Banks, even if the latter are responsible to shareholders rather than to a Government. The problem has the same root in both cases, that is, the replacement of investors who are spending their own money, by investment managers who are dealing with other peoples'.

The first result of this historical change is a drastic reduction in the number of decision points for investment in new business. As explained earlier, because such an investment involves uncertainty, every decision involves an emotional element, and this emotional element can only result in a positive decision (i.e. to make an investment) if there is a sufficiently large number of potential decision-makers. Only then can the emotional factors work *for* a decision instead of *against* one. Unless there is empathy between entrepreneur and investor, there will be no investment. Consequently, any individual investor is only capable of investing in a very limited range of projects – those that strike *his* particular imagination. If investment is to be possible across a broad range of projects, therefore, the range of investment 'perceptiveness' must be correspondingly wide. This can only be the case if there is a very large number of people who can actually make investment decisions. Reducing the number of decision points, as has been done, must correspondingly reduce the number of decisions to invest in a new business.

The more emphasis there is on rationality in decision making – as the 'institutional' element grows – the less this can result in positive decisions under uncertainty, such as positive decisions to invest in innovation or new business. As financial organizations become more bureaucratic, those who succeed in them do so by a learning process that is quite different from the learning process of the characteristic innovator. As more investment decisions fall to be made by people who 'have never done it' the possibility of intuitive backing of the right innovations is lessened. With growing awareness of this, the bureaucratic financial organization, too, then tends increasingly to distance itself from the sort of decision that it senses it cannot make well. This leads to avoidance of projects which involve innovation.

As a result of these trends, backing for *individuals*, has virtually disappeared. Yet the empirical evidence is overwhelming that wherever there is successful innovation, there is always an identifiable individual without whom it would not have happened; even where there is a strong 'team' element, the individual 'leadership' element is even stronger. For every successful firm there is an identifiable founder. The replacement of profit by "cover" as the main criterion for investment, however, results in –

i.   Setting a minimum level for investment that makes every decision a Committee one. (Most new businesses in fact need relatively small amounts of money, well within the limit of individual 'signatures' in many Banks).

ii. Setting a minimum level of profit on the part of a business before it will be considered for equity investment.

iii. "Third Party Cover", as explained earlier.

It must be stressed that these trends do not mean that the executives of Banks and similar organizations are without ability, training and experience. But these can be no substitute for the reality that they are not spending their own money. The way in which they dispose of the money entrusted to them cannot escape being measured by the criterion of "cover" rather than "profit", because the criterion must reflect their career situations. Anything else would be quite irrational on the part of anyone who is not remunerated out of the 'residual'.

Moreover, venture capital is quite rightly regarded by financial institutions as a way of losing money, not making it. It is something they get involved in at all only as a means of demonstrating their readiness to perform some kind of Community Service. No ambitious executive with plans to achieve the top post in his Bank, picks its venture capital arm in which to demonstrate his powers. Where innovation is concerned, failure, not success, is the norm. The only possible way of at least breaking even in financing it, is to have a sufficiently large portfolio, in which any single item, if it succeeds, is enough to pay for the losses from several failures. Given the inadequacy of legal means for capturing the externalities of the innovation, and the amount of whatever is captured that will be taken by derived market power and by taxation, such a balance has always been extremely difficult to achieve, and is now virtually impossible. Much of Chapter V will be devoted to means of rectifying this situation. The problem is compounded by the difficulty fo distinguishing between what may be called a 'terminal' failure, and the type of failure which is a necessary stage on the road to success. 'All successful innovation is a combination of courage and resources: Courage to get things wrong the first time; resources to get them right the second'. Firms are sometimes able to follow this prescription as far as their own activity is concerned, but no financial institution has ever been able to develop an investment system to correspond with it.

It is also important to bear in mind that there is no shortage of bad experience to make Banks and other Institutions disillusioned with investment in any kind of innovation. In Britain, the 30 Banks and Insurance Companies that originally invested in Technical Development Capital Ltd., had to share a large loss before it was taken over as a face-saver by a vehicle of the larger Banks. Worse, European Enterprises Development S.A., in which 17 major European Banks had shares, and which had most prestigious management and associates, actually failed a few years ago. And the fact that the name of the Bank that originally backed Whittle's jet engine is no longer to be found in the Banker's Almanac is only one of the horror stories about innovation in Bankers' folklore, almost all of them true. The effects of all these factors on innovation are altogether harmful, and this applies not just to technology, but also to that most important innovatory activity, formation of new businesses. The private sector cannot be healthy without the constant establishment of businesses that are really new, not just affiliates of old ones. Familiarity has perhaps blunted our awareness of how right Schumpeter was in that famous passage where he stresses the necessity of 'the perennial gale of creative destruction'. It will be recalled that he held that 'competition in the ordinary sense' was unimportant:

> 'the powerful lever that in the long run expands output and brings down prices, is in any case made of other stuff'.

'Expands output and brings down prices...' Experience of static output and inflation, now forces us to look seriously at the argument that the major cause is precisely the absence of this Schumpeterian 'lever'.

It is altogether naive to think that his second and more important type of competition can be brought to bear without the constant formation of new firms. Established businesses have little to fear from one another – from 'competition in the ordinary sense' as Schumpeter put it. Apart from the inherent tendency amongst businessmen to conspire against the public which Adam Smith recorded, every Marketing course to-day at least indirectly teaches the advantages of 'implicit collusion', and the 'covert cartel' described earlier. The only effective deterrent against putting up prices, and keeping them up, is the fear of being undercut by a new firm, hungry for business. Managements are only spurred into activity to bring out new products by the fear that if they do not do it, some other firm will. Both deterrent and stimulus are absent unless there is a constant flow of new firms which are founded by new men upon new ideas. But it is precisely this for which it is virtually impossible to obtain finance any longer. Stagflation, therefore, must be due in significant measure to the reduction of the Schumpeterian gale to a Zephyr, or even in some areas of industry, to a flat calm. Whether or not Mensch is right that 'innovations overcome the Depression', it must be true that lack of them helps to cause it.

It must be insisted that any fault here lies only in the institutional arrangements, not in individuals. The basic truth is that there is a limit to the risk which an employee should be asked to take, and if he is asked to do more, we must expect that he will, in self-defence, re-define the task so as to reduce the risk to his career, as the Patent Examiners did. An interesting and topical financial example is to be found in the special Funds for helping to set up small businesses in the U.S. To please their political masters, the employed managers of such funds know that they have to strike a balance between having too few of their investments fail (which would indicate that the Fund was not filling a vacuum left by other financial institutions, and having too many failures (which could imply that they were poor project assessors). The observed behaviour of such managers, is to invest up to the 'balance' level in projects that will almost certainly fail, but which have some ethnic or 'minority' aspect which suggests that that failure is in a good cause. With the 'failure' proportion thus conveniently out of the way, the fund managers can then have a comparatively risk-free life by applying ordinary banking criteria to the main bulk of their investments, and this is precisely how they are behaving.

The problem can be illustrated in another way from experience with the British Government Guaranteed Loan fund for small businesses. One recommendation made for the administration of this, was that access to such public funds should be given only to Banks which agreed to invest a specified, very small, proportion of their total lendings each year in new businesses.[38] As actually instituted, the Scheme gives *automatic* access, without such a condition, for four times' a Bank's own investment in a project. But the burden of decision about the Bank's part still remains with the local Bank Manager, who naturally has to tailor the risk to his own career path, with the result that virtually none of the Government money has found its way into innovatory projects. Had the recommendation referred to above been adopted, responsibility would rest, in the first instance, with the Board of a Bank, which would have to decide whether or not access to the Government money was worth the risk of having to make a commitment to invest a small amount of the Bank's own resources in new businesses. Once that is decided by the Board, however, the position of the individual Bank Manager, with reference to investing in innovation, is transformed. He and his colleagues *must* dispose of a certain amount of money at high risk if the Board's decision to take up the Government funds is to be made effective. His risk is at an acceptable level, in just the same way as any R & D manager *has* to spend at high risk, a budget for the passing of which his superiors have taken responsibility. This point has been grasped in the United States in the Small Business Innovation Act of 1982. This requires 10 Federal Agencies which do 99% of Government R & D, to allocate a small proportion of their budgets to innovation in small firms. This proportion is only 0.2% to begin with, but it will rise to 1¼% quickly, so that eventually $½ billion will be available each year under this programme. This will fund about 2000 Phase I awards of up to $50,000 each and 1000 Phase II awards of up to $500,000 each. It will be obvious that even though this imaginative scheme does not overcome the 'multiplicity of decision-points' problem in the financing of innovation, it does deal with the problem of 'cover' on the part of employed investors. Even if all the awards turn out to be for projects that fail, no blame can attach to the personnel of the funding Agency, since the Law forced the Agency to spend part of its budget in supporting them.

The way in which weakening of the independent property pole of a system that depends upon balance, progressively stifles spontaneous innovatory activity, therefore, is by drying up multiple sources of finance to back imagination. Attempts by government to make up for this, inevitably fail, both because of centralized decision-making and of the replacement of profit by "cover" as the measure of what is to be decided. Progressively, as the system ossifies, economic activity ceases to be about any radical attempts to solve the underlying problems, especially the technological ones. Instead, it becomes increasingly channelled into areas dominated by the State, where it becomes less and less productive. "Making money" comes to have less and less to do with making things. Mensch holds that in the technological stalemate, "the profits that entrepreneurs and stockholders could reap from improvements or even expansion of the existing operation cannot compare with the profits the financial market can offer."[39] It is, of course, only because of the public sector's appetite for funds that this is the case, and the result is to divert both money and creative energy into the least productive areas. One detailed study of the OECD countries over a number of years showed that for every 1%

expansion in share of the State-controlled sector, an economy's real power to grow was reduced by .2%.[40]

This process has been greatly accelerated by the successive oil 'shocks'. Even with their reduced capacity for innovation, Western countries could have coped with the multiplication of energy prices brought about by OPEC. What has overcome them has been, not the price increase, but *the recycling of the OPEC surpluses*. The increased cost of energy falls mainly upon private individuals and firms, but only partially comes back to them in terms of OPEC orders for goods. The surplus comes back as loans to Governments, most of which are dissipated in higher public sector remuneration and uneconomic investment. Consequently, in almost every Western country the oil crises have resulted in a major increase in the size of the public sector, which means in turn that the very innovatory power that is required to deal with the problems, is destroyed. The outstanding exception has been Japan.

Not alone were the oil shocks prevented from unleashing an explosion in public sector growth there, but the Japanese have had notably more success than others in adapting to higher oil prices through conservation, changes in technology, and above all, structural changes in the economy. The contrast with Western countries which attempted to avoid changes by expanding the public sector and by deficit financing, is stark. Worse still, the gap is not one that a reversal in the trend of oil prices will narrow − in fact, it can only widen still further. Japan, with so much of its economy still dependent upon free enterprise, will react swiftly and appropriately to the new situation; the Western countries will be all the slower in reacting, the more they have moved towards centralized control. Worst of all, resources drawn into the public sector in attempts to evade the consequence of the oil price increases, cannot be returned to the private sector where they might be productive under the changed circumstances. We may be in the process of discovering − as the Romans certainly did before us − that the process of bureaucratic growth is irreversible.

The contemporary crisis, therefore, is a crisis of innovation and productivity, of which public sector growth is both a symptom and a cause. The extent and the forms of the growth of market power, however, cannot evade a substantial share of the blame.

Stagflation is the simultaneous presence of stagnation and inflation, and some types of inflation are just not possible without market power. Consider the imposition of a tax on firms that do posses this power. By definition, these are capable of escaping the market seeks to impose upon them, above all the constraint which would make them price-takers. Having market power, they are price makers, so, faced with a new tax, in virtue of membership of a formal cartel, or of an informal cartel of advertisers, or some other means of exercising their market power, they will increase their prices, not only to recoup the tax, but also increased costs incidental to it, such as Accountancy. Where there is market power, therefore, tax or any other imposition on the firm by the State will simply go straight through into inflation. Growth of taxation alone, in the context of strong and widespread market power, is enough to account for much of the world-wide phenomenon of inflation during the present century. However, this is only the beginning of the effect of market power, because persuasive market power has contributed to inflation in several other ways that deserve particular consideration.

By articulating needs into wants-for-a-product, marketing increases consumers' expenditure at the expense of personal savings, and it may even increase demand at a rate which is beyond the intrinsic capacity for productivity growth of an economy. The impact of commercial television, for example, is primarily to stimulate wants at the fastest possible rate; this can easily be a faster rate than the rate at which society can adapt itself to produce the means of satisfying them. It is obvious that in a number of countries the introduction of commercial TV increased wants at a faster rate than their economic growth, and not surprisingly strains followed.

The Trade Mark laws underwrite marketing power; which makes advertising in the modern sense possible; which both causes explosion of the mass media, and modifies even the material they use between the advertisements in the direction of enthroning the "consumer society". The nett effect is increasingly to articulate needs in the form of specific wants. When wants are backed by money, they become effective economic demand, and the spiral entrenches marketing power still further. Since firms which possess this power can meet demands for increased wages by putting up their prices, the more market power there is, the more immediately inflationary must the effect be. Where Government expenditure bulks large in the total, the pressure of derived taxing power is very difficult to resist. This comes from its own employees, who are, of course, like other consumers, under advertising pressure to spend up to, and beyond, their means. It also comes from the increased cost of what the Government has to buy itself, and from the heightened expectations of the public at large. These are partly a reflection of the way in which the non-advertising content of the mass-media tends to reflect the values of advertising. All such forces build up into a level of pressure on Government to solve its problems by printing money or by any of the equivalent ways of credit creation which are open to it today, that is virtually irresistible to democratically-elected politicians. Since only a small part of the public sector activity is 'sold', the State cannot react to increased costs and wage demands by a price increase; since raising taxes is electorally unpopular, it increases the money supply.

It is an observable fact that the largest modern firms are able to finance by far the greater part of their growth from their own resources. This must be attributed frankly to their market power. The reason why General Foods, du Pont de Nemours and Coca-Cola are able to finance practically the whole of their capital expenditure from internally generated funds is quite simply that, through skilful use of persuasive market power, they are in a position to disregard the traditional concept of value and sell their products at an arbitrary price, which is not at all related to the cost of production. They have monopolistic control over their own price, and they can count – because of 'mutual dependence recognised' (membership of the 'covert' cartel) on their competitors not using price as a weapon against them. If the total volume of money is kept in proportion to the volume of productive resources actually available, this can only mean resources are captured by the firms with market power, and these resources are not available for alternative uses. This amounts to cornering of a nation's saving capacity by the firms which possess market power, thus starving other sectors of the economy of the money they need for their own development. It is the real source of the 'private affluence and public squalor' which Galbraith has noted. The large pharmaceutical firms are able to pay for an immense amount of research and development, absorb heavy marketing costs, and finance rapid growth almost completely from their own profits and depreciation provisions, developing and selling a multiplicity of products, many of which are straight substitutes for one another, all largely on the basis of the Industrial Property Acts. In contrast, local authorities are everywhere at their wits' end to obtain funds to build and maintain their hospitals – simply because they do not have access to money on the same basis. A system which allows manufacturers to charge an arbitrary price, not related to the cost of production, is one in which there is an element of rent in the price, and in the manufacturer's surplus of revenue over costs. There is rent also in its workers' remuneration, and even more in that of those who work directly for the State. At the limit, virtually all the pay of Civil Servants is rent, because they can rely on derived taxing power for it, and not just derived – even 're-inforced derived' market power. Basically, inflation is putting money into circulation to meet this rent element. Company saving, through its 'rent', 'non-value' or 'super-profit' components, has – except in Japan – replaced private saving, relegating the capital market to a minor place in financing investments. This relative reduction in volume of the capital market, makes it almost inevitable that a Government under democratic pressure will expand the supply of credit, thus assuring inflation. To-day, a balanced system of the old kind, in which currency represented goods and disappeared as these goods became available on the market, has become an impossibility. Instead, it has become necessary continually to create new money to enable demand to keep pace with supply at a price which includes the manufacturer's rent due to his primary market power, his workers' rent due to their derived market power, and the rent in public sector wages due to derived taxing power. Much of this rent turns into demand for psychological ingredient in products. Central Banks are subjected to the same pressures as democratically-elected politicians, and, since there is no reason why their Directors should accept vilification for being the cause of unemployment, they will provide the commercial banks with new reserves to enable them to generate new means of payment which correspond to this rent element or psychological ingredient in products.[41] In turn, Central Banks themselves are unable to turn their backs on any mechanism – such as foreign borrowing – that will keep them supplied with reserves. And when (because, for example, no further borrowing abroad is possible) fiscal rectitude is forced upon politicians and Central Banks, and they try to get the money supply under control, the resulting slow-down in the activity of the economy hurts the weakest elements in it most. The rent element in the revenues of firms with market power will be largely untouched (having control over price, they will almost certainly raise their prices to compensate for any drop in turnover). Galbraith has shown how in the downturns of the short business cycles, it is the small business that pays the price. Even in the Depression of the 1930s, firms with market power were able to keep up their prices. And as with firms, so with workers. Those with most rent in their remuneration, meaning those with derived taxing power, reinforced derived market power, or derived market power in firms where the primary market power is strong, keep their secure jobs through recession and even depression, whilst those with least rent in their pay, join the dole queues. If the disease is market power, efforts to deal with inflation are directed only at a symptom. If the available market power structures are such as to underwrite innovation broadly in the discretionary income area, and if the external challenge demands a set of responses that involve originative innovation, then attacking the symptom is even more pointless. All that will happen is that the system will continue to function in the old way (which has been rendered obsolete by the external challenge) with the one difference that it is functioning in a progressively slower motion, an embodiment of Sylos-Labini's monopoly theory.

It must be recognised that a large part of the pressure on elected politicians to increase expenditures, originates – even if at one remove – with the firms which possess market power. Persuasive market power, in particular, puts the voters under pressure from the mass media to get and spend. At the same time, two things happen to the savings of the community, which make the Government's position worse. By articulating wants in ways that result in immediate expenditure, marketing reduces the public's propensity *both to save and to accept taxation*; secondly, the way firms with market power can exact rent from consumers, makes it possible for them to grow from internally generated funds, i.e. depreciation and profits. Growth, for firms which possess market power, is the result of using the power of self-financing to invest in areas which lend themselves to an extension of marketing power, leading to more power of self-financing, and so the marketing spiral grows. People under marketing pressure to spend, will use their voting power to ensure that they are not taxed too heavily; the Government thus increasingly has to look to the business sector for its direct tax revenue, and so comes to have a vested interest in the extension of market power, since this generates taxable rent. But at the same time the fact that the funds they need for growth reach monopolistic firms directly, so that they are relieved of the necessity of competing for them in the capital market, also means that the capital market is smaller than it would otherwise be. Since it is this market which must provide the Government's capital needs, its contraction puts pressure on Governments to expand the money supply.

It is hard to avoid the conclusion, therefore, that inflation is endemic to the consumer society as we know it. Market power inevitably means that all the possible users of capital – public authorities, firms which possess little or no market power, and individuals, among them – do not start on level terms. The firms with market power are able to siphon off a large amount of the funds before these ever reach the capital market. Interest rates, being a matter of supply and demand, are consequently forced up. Thus a bias is introduced into the economic system which causes growth to take the direction of increased market power. Those without one of the alternative monopoly systems, have to pay more for the capital they need, which reduces their power to grow. The Government, whose workers always look for "parity" with the most monopolistic sector to justify their own wage increases, is under almost irresistible pressure to print money in one way or another. From the theoretical point of view this can be seen to be inevitable: Say's law, which was for so long the basis of political economy, only applies when there is no rent element in prices; if there is, it is because new income has been generated in the form of rent in wages. This rent, it should be noted, does not mean any real extension of buying-power, but simply enables wage-earners to pay the monopolistic price charged by producers. In this we must to-day include the Rent element in everything that is supplied – whether it is wanted or not – by the State. The link between 'wage-push' inflation and market power, therefore, seems just as clear as it has been in the case of 'demand-pull' inflation, arising from the inability of Governments to withstand both the voting and financial pressures on them to expand the money supply. It seems ironical that so much of Government's troubles in the financial sphere, should be attributable to the positive law for which they themselves were responsible, especially the law of Trade Marks which underlies marketing power. The connection in time between the growth of marketing power and the growth of inflation historically seems to fit reasonably well. Moreover, the way in which the importance of gold as a medium of exchange has declined as that of marketing power has increased, reflects the way all monopoly is a means of escaping from the constraints which the free market (of which gold has always been the characteristic currency) seeks to impose. These points are especially striking because it is not being claimed that market power alone is responsible for inflation, only that it is a very significant contributory factor. And this factor may also work in indirect ways. For example, a democracy in which communications media are financed largely by their own sales, will be different from a democracy in which they are financed by advertising; leaving various extensions of the franchise out of it altogether, therefore, Governments and parties depend upon the media to-day to an extent that was not so in the past, and they have to adopt the skills and techniques of advertising, to fit in with the way the media themselves reflect the source of their finance. The amount and nature of modern democracy, the kind of people who get elected, the trend towards 'presidential-type' Government in systems which have been historically Parliamentary, all owe much to the existence of market power. Inflation is by no means only a monetary problem, and there are more kinds of debasement than just debasement of currency.

It need scarcely be stressed how detrimental inflation is to Innovation. It is quite incompatible with the long time-scale of A-phase or originative innovation, thus forcing firms to limit their attention to incremental innovation, and even then only to innovations with a short time to pay-off. It results in the dominance of Accountants over Technologists (of whatever kind) which means less room for the imaginative element that is essential for investment in innovation. It expands the State sector, thereby shifting resources towards consumption and wasteful capital projects. Worst of all, it destroys property that is independent of the State, thus undermining Democracy, and paving the way for a totalitarian regime.

The way that market power has developed has also contributed greatly to that intensification of inequality which Marx predicted. If this trend continued, it would eventually make the overthrow of Democracy inevitable, and even to-day it is inhibiting the ability of the Democracies to respond to the contemporary crisis. The level of concentration of privately-owned industry is as good a measure as any of inequality, because concentration reflects market power, and market power means rent in wages and salaries. There is little need to stress how far concentration depends upon the ability to erect and maintain barriers to entry. Apart from the obvious value of persuasive market power for this, the capacity to invest in R & D also contributes to concentration. This does not arise from investment in laboratories, toolrooms, testing and measuring equipment and so on, as much as from the kind and number of people that are involved, and the need for continuity in research programmes to be maintained if they are to be fruitful. As there is a minimum level of advertising expenditure for a firm to be effectively 'in the market' at all, so there is a minimum level of research and development expenditure. Without this, the firm will not have the means to match the improvements that competitors are all the time building into their products, nor to absorb new technology as this becomes accessible, nor to be at the frontier of technology so that any invention it may make itself will be able to obtain Patent protection that is legally valid. Without this, no good team of research people can be kept together, since no group of mettle will be content to be wholly parasitic. It has been thought up to now that it was concentration of industry and the large size of firms which was responsible for the growth of the kind of dynamic monopoly which depends upon fixed costs in research and development:

'A benign Providence, who, so far, has loved us for our worries, has made the modern industry of a few large firms an excellent instrument for inducing technical change. It is admirably equipped for financing technical development. Its organization provides strong incentives for undertaking development and for putting it into use'[42]

This is the effect of capability market power, as seen by Galbraith. But it is only part of the truth. It is not the existence of large firms which has been primarily responsible for technical change, but the means for bringing about technical change, i.e. the legal arrangements for protecting investment in information production, have favoured the emergence of large firms. It is not concentration which has been the cause of research and development, but research and development interacting with marketing power which has caused concentration. Investment in research and development is investment in information production, which can only be justified on a basis of monopoly; persuasive market power combined with secrecy provides one of the best means yet devised for obtaining effective protection for information, and has increased the flow of funds into research and development enormously as a result. The increased scale of research and development becomes a monopoly element in its own right because the fixed cost element in it constitutes a barrier to entry on the part of rivals, who have to meet it if they are to be effectively competitive. The monopoly position of the firm which has market power is thus further consolidated. It is because it has market power to protect the results of its research and development that a firm is big; it is not because it is big that it has research and development. No forces making for concentration of industry are now more powerful than capability and persuasive market power, because of the basis they provide for investing profitably in research and development. Because of the International Convention, much of this force is world wide in its scope. Those who have market power, which ultimately comes from legislation, to 'unmake the market', clearly reap great advantages, but what of those who do not have this power?

In every country, the sector whose lack of power to escape from the constraints of the market is most evident, is that of agriculture. Intellectual Property has added a dimension to the old tensions between country and town; now the frontier between them also divides monopolistic competition from pure competition. Everything a farmer sells is traded as a commodity, subject to all the constraints imposed on the trading of commodities by the free market; almost everything he buys is the product of monopolistic industry, organized specifically, and with powerful resources and techniques, to *evade* those constraints. Competition there may be between monopolistic firms within industries, and between monopolistic industries, but it is competition of a quite different kind to the competition in which primary producers are involved. Competition between monopolistic industries or firms by no means eliminates the rent element from the surplus of the return they receive over their costs; competition between primary producers always does. This is the practical aspect of Sylos-Labini's point, made on the basis of theory, that because of monopoly, increases in productivity in agriculture are reflected in lower prices, whereas in industry they are reflected in higher wages and salaries. They will be reflected, too, in better and easier working conditions, increased costs in industry generally and higher and more stable "profits" –

which, of course, are really rents. It is not because they are less clever, or work less well, or are involved in something that is intrinsically harder to do, that farmers are poor compared with townsfolk, to the extent that in all advanced countries, most notably in the Common Agricultural Policy of the E.E.C., Governments transfer payments from one group to another by means of the taxation and subsidy or price support system. It is simply that by enacting the Industrial Property Laws, Governments have given such great power to industry to escape the constraints of the market, that to maintain any kind of balance, some positive law for redistributing part of the rents accruing as a result was necessary. Just as there is a real sense in which in Britain the Trade Disputes Act of 1906 is the labour counterpart of the 1883 Trade Marks and Patents Acts, so the Agricultural Subsidies Act of 1947 was the counterpart for those who live on the land, before Britain's EEC entry. Such transfer payments by Governments are all the more necessary, since the farmer is as much the subject of informational pressures arising from marketing monopoly as anybody else. He − and more importantly, his wife and family − have their needs articulated into wants-for-products by the mass media. Their consumption pattern is thus pushed in the direction of the world of monopolistic competition, a pattern which is sustainable only by a wage or salary which includes a substantial rent element, at the same time as their revenue pattern remains dominated by the iron hand of pure competition. Price is the essence of the competitive process in the things they sell; price competition is absent in most things that are sold to them. As long as positive law allows some sectors of the economy to evade pure competition, while others remain largely under its discipline, the imbalance will persist. Farmers can rely only on whatever political power their numbers give them, to wrest some countervailing financial transfer from the industrial sector via Government-imposed taxation. The imbalance between town and country in advanced countries, also exists between the advanced countries as a group and the poor countries of the Third World, but there is no World Government to take any steps to redress it.

The distortions of our patterns of market power, therefore, are at the root of our inability to respond by innovation to challenges from outside. In the broadest terms, we have large elements of primary market power which are not justified by any contribution to innovation. The interaction of almost equally powerful elements of derived market power with these, results in an inflexible economic system, devoted almost solely to the perpetuation of its own rent. Within this general pattern, the type of market power which now generates the highest and most secure rent element, is the market power of persuasion. This attracts so much of the resources of society, especially the very scarce resource of entrepreneurial talent, that little is left to cope with external challenges that could only be dealt with by men who have been trained, and have gained experience in other ways. Having advertising men in plenty is no use to us when the problems demand innovation in technology. In the cultural impact of the growth of market power, salesmanship, advertising and sales promotion are the most obtrusive elements. The number of people engaged in advertising and related fields has grown enormously since the passing of the positive law on Trade Mark registration first made modern advertising possible as a way of life at the end of the last century. But perhaps more important than the numbers, is the kind of people who earn their living in this particular way. Modern advertising offers scope for people who are skilled in the use of words as well as to people who are gifted visually, people who can express themselves in dramatic form or through music. Agencies and advertising departments of firms are big enough to require good administrators, and the problems of understanding the business of clients demands a highly trained and intelligent breed of generalist business man. As a service industry, requiring little in the way of fixed assets, it offers unusual scope for an entrepreneur to build up an extremely profitable business quickly from a base of little capital. Advertising is the first job choice of many clever students when they leave the University, and as an industry, it probably contains more able people in proportion to its size than any other – certainly a higher proportion of the 'selfstarters' who are distinguished from others by their readiness to rely on themselves, and by their keenness to 'get on'. In a good advertising agency, there is as much brain power and as much talent as in any ordinary University Faculty – and a good deal more capacity to get things done. In the best international agencies, there is more of both. Yet with all of this, many advertising men, and those generally the most intelligent, are more than half-ashamed of the business they are in.

To some extent, this can be expalined by the fact that impersonal salesmanship, like personal salesmanship, is directed towards exploiting human weakness, not strength. The way in which sexuality in advertising reflects this is too obvious to be worth detailed attention; another example is the way in which advertising works on the natural human tendency to emulate models or leaders, in ways that sell goods, ignoring aspects which by other standards, are at least as worthy of imitation, possibly even more so. The picture of bourgeois life, for example, that advertising thus holds out to the masses for imitation, necessarily leaves out all the finest things of bourgeois achievement. Wherever imitation can be used it is the same: Advertising is a force which of its nature has to work against delicacy of feeling, subtlety of expression, individual differences, intellectual complexity or 'rigour'; above all it must explicitly exclude any aspect of life that cannot be expressed in terms of what can be bought and sold. Some of the neurosis of the advertising world must be due to the fact that it contains a large number of highly intelligent people, who are unable to conceal from themselves that this is so. But another reason is that, of its nature, advertising is concerned with words, and words are above all, the distinguishing mark of Man. It is in the power of communication through words, and the capacity of formulating, marshalling and expressing thought that words make possible, that Man transcends the nature he shares with the animal world. Words, and the power of expression through words, will always be found at the very core of the tradition of civilization. And from Herbert Spencer to Teilhard de Chardin, all the great evolutionary thinkers see the world as in process of becoming increasingly dominated by words. Clearly, then, if this way of looking at things represents the best of the past as well as the thrust towards the future, anyone whose work involves the use of words, not to change the world, nor to shape culture, nor to establish and guard values, but instead to cater to the world as marketing research reveals it to be, to take mass culture as given and to be subordinate to the values of potential customers, is bound, if he has any sensibility at all, to feel uneasy. No man who has been at all touched by the culture of the West can ever get used to the idea that words are subordinate to culture; the idea that words are for changing the world is too deeply rooted for that. But advertising uses, and has to use, words in exactly the opposite way. The advertising agency which did not pay careful attention to what cultural attitudes and values are, did not accept them without reserva- tion as the material it has to work with, and did not use its resources for communication accordingly, would not last long in business. Advertising *has* to use words in a way which subordinates them to cultural values, because

> 'ad men, with their functions and techniques, always operate outside the area where the choices that really affect society are made. And the real power is exercised in those choices; this is, power lies wherever ideology is invented, summed up. woven together; wherever creative intellectual contributions elaborate ideologies which, in the hands of the elite, can move society in one direction or another'.[43]

What can be said, then, about the existence in modern society of a large number of clever and able people, making their living by using words in a way which runs directly counter to the most fundamental thing in their own cultural tradition and the most dynamic elements in the intellectual life about them? It will not be surprising if some of them are unhappy about their situation, or even neurotic; the quest to set things right by energetically pursuing 'advertising's duty to the public' becomes completely understandable; the way in which advertising mens' lives reflect fashions in everything from their shirts to their videos earlier than any other group, is seen to be nothing more than an aspect of the inversion of the traditional roles of words and the world which is intrinsic to the advertising business. What effect on modern society is produced by the existence within it of a group of substantial size which is composed of people with above-average intelligence, ability, energy and creative capacity, who are themselves uneasy about the purposes for which their gifts are being used? Certainly, since confidence is a factor in all positive cultural achieve- ment, the inverse correlation that there is between confidence on the one hand, and intelligence and sensibility on the other, in the advertising world, renders this effect unlikely to be constructive.

It is probably actually destructive. Will capitalism die because the intellectuals reject it, as Schumpeter thought? Advertising men are not hard-core intellectuals, and they are certainly not in revolt against society – anything but. However, any definition of the intellectuals which leaves them out altogether is too narrow because of the kind of people they are, of the kind of work that they do, and of the effects of that work. Even if they are far from being in active revolt, their position is one of neutrality on the question of values in society since, as Buzzi has pointed out, advertising must accept contemporary and local values, whatever they may be, and any attempt to change these values is out of the question. This is a form of abdication. Western society is not being destroyed by advertising, nor by advertising people; but its destruction is being made that much easier because advertising represents so much that is good, so much humanity, so much intelligence, so much creative energy, diverted into accepting and expressing the values of contemporary society, rather than into creating them. Born leaders, it has been said, have no business at the head of lost causes, but the place for leaders, whether born or made, can hardly be on the sidelines either, if they are to escape being charged with a new form of 'trahison des clercs'. The sterilising of so much power to shape culture which the number and kind of people employed in modern marketing represents, arises only from the existence of marketing power. As such it is a clear result of the Trade Marks Acts, which make modern marketing possible.

However, important as it is, it may even be less so than the growth of the mass media, with which many of the people who are employed in marketing, are intimately concerned. This, too, is directly attributable to the Trade Mark Laws, since advertising in the modern sense would not be possible without them, and advertising is the economic basis of the mass media as we know them.

The defenders of advertising always used to include a claim in its favour that without it, newspapers and magazines would cost twice as much or even more. Since a free Press was regarded as one which was financially independent of the Government, advertising was therefore a major factor in having a free Press. Less is heard of this argument now, and the tendency to forget it seems to have developed alongside of the growth in the broadcast media, especially television. This is rather odd, since whereas the Press media get between three and four-fifths of their revenue from advertising, much of television is financed *wholly* from advertisements, and the trend is strongly set in the direction of this method of financing television throughout the world. So that if without advertising, there would be fewer and more expensive print media, without advertising there would not, in many cases, be any television at all. To have free broadcast media, especially T.V., might well be regarded as more important even than free print media. Certainly politicians take it very seriously.

To the extent that media are financed by advertising, they must share the characteristics of advertising. In particular, they are involved in the same subordination of words to culture which is essential to advertising if it is to be effective. Thus there is no room for 'conspiracy theories' of faceless men in the media manipulating the values of society at their will. The media men would not survive long if they ceased to pay attention to what their mass audience wants to hear and see; the media reflect the values of society, not the other way round. However, the particular values in society which a medium will reflect, must be decided by the way the medium is financed; a medium financed by mass-market advertising must reflect those particular values which are shared by the mass of people. The very nature of its financing inhibits such a medium from being a force through which the values of society are changed. This is the big argument in favour of the financing of media by advertisements: To say that TV as we know it, for example, has little power to change the values of society is not to say that it could not be used for this purpose, if its financing were different, since it is an information-spreading means of great technical power. Limiting this power to spreading information concerning things-that-can-be-bought is probably the least harmful way of using it, and this is done by financing it through advertisements.

However, not all the effects of financing mass media through advertising can be regarded so benevolently. The nature of their financing, and its amount, change the nature of the media themselves. The amount of advertising that people will stand in a medium, especially one towards which they have to pay something directly themselves, is not unlimited. Increased advertising revenue therefore creates a demand for more news and features to fill the spaces between the advertisements, or for more material to fill the transmitting time between the commercials. The first result of advertising growth, then, has to be trivialisation of the medium's editorial material, since this material is quite literally and precisely stop-gap. What is required of broadcast material is in economic terms no more and no less than that it will keep a listener or viewer from switching off before the next commercial comes on, and what is similarly required of printed material, whether news or features, is that it will keep a reader turning over pages so as to be 'exposed' to advertising. Moreover, the communication process requires some contribution from the reader, listener or viewer himself – he cannot be completely passive. Such a contribution takes energy, and the amount of this energy available is quite limited. It would therefore be a mistake to allow it to be used up in attending seriously to anything else, when it is the advertisements which are the raison d'être of the whole process. Catharsis, supposing it could ever happen through TV drama, would be nothing short of catastrophe, because it would leave the viewer un-receptive during the commercials. Trivialisation, then, is an intrinsic part of the financing of mass-media through advertisements. If U.S. TV, for example, is indeed the 'wasteland' it has been called by a former head of the Federal Communications Commission, this is due primarily to the way it is financed. This in turn goes back to the Trade Marks Acts that underwrite advertising in its modern form. The task of 'filling the spaces (or times) between the ad-vertisements' also opens the door to the Public Relations man. The activity of

Public Relations, which, like Advertising, has made valiant but equally unsuccessful efforts to turn itself into a profession, is measured, whatever those
who practice it may say, by the amount of space in print media or air time in
broadcast media, that can be directed towards particular products in ways
other than by paid advertising. From this comes the press conference, the news
story that is a disguised advertisement, the sponsoring of sports and other
events to the extent that it no longer seems possible for any of the pleasurable
human activities that are publicly engaged in, to take place except in association with a brand name. People may be indifferent to this, or they may dislike
it, but in either event they ought to be aware that they owe it to the positive law
which supports brand names and brand advertising.

One of the most important effects, however, of the media having so much
time or space to fill between the advertisements, and of their constant need to
maintain their readership or viewership, is the inflation of news items, and of
people associated with them, to many times their intrinsic importance. The
media act as a source of stimuli which cause people to live their lives at a heightened level of excitement. They steep them in crisis after crisis, political,
monetary, personal; crises of authority, of the age gap, of a footballer's
marriage; involving them, as James Morris has so beautifully put it, in

> 'the progress of perpetual change, which stimulates the spirit too far,
> cuts us off from the springs of certainty, and leaves us spinning
> nervously and testily from unnecessary challenge to trumped-up re-
> sponse'.[44]

Freedom of the media historically has meant freedom from Government
control through freedom from Government subvention; this was achieved
through the growth of advertising as an alternative source of revenue, but this
makes the media no more free to communicate values that are in conflict with
those which assist the effectiveness and growth of advertising, than they were
to attack their earlier paymasters. What is at stake here is not the crude exercise
of influence on editorial content by a large advertiser. This does happen
occasionally, as everyone who works in the media knows, but it rarely needs to
reach the stage of being overt, thanks to the awareness media people have of
where their money comes from. It is concern with the size of readership or
audience, not as a group which shares the articulated views of the medium in
question, but as a target for advertisements, that betrays the medias' lack of
freedom, and that ultimately makes even their editorial content have an
advertising flavour, and serve an advertising purpose. To the extent that the
space or time between the advertisements is filled with material provided by an
advertising agency (e.g. in the case of sponsored TV) or by a Public Relations
department or firm, the media's editorial matter is performing an actual
advertising function. Looked at in this way, it is nonsense to decry the mass
media for failing to provide education, or instruction, or entertainment; their
function is none of these. Instead, it is to provide advertising, and no one can
deny that they do this well. How prescient was that phrase of Disraeli's in

which he refers to events tending 'to enthrone the commercial principle', and his fears for the result! If the mass media reflect enthronement of the commercial principle, it is only because the commercial principle is enthroned amongst the values of society at large; and it is these values which are expressed in the positive laws which provides the mass media with such a gigantic source of revenue. The media, then, have to inflate news and people in importance to fill the ever-growing amount of space or time between a mounting volume of advertisements. The results of the existence of mass media, both good and bad, arising from editorial content as much as from paid advertising, all go back to advertising as the source of the medias' revenue, and through this to the Trade Marks Acts which make this kind and this amount of advertising possible.

A most important cause of the contemporary crisis may therefore be rejection of the pattern of innovation that has actually emerged, as part of rejection of the business culture that is responsible for it. Indeed, one very characteristic aspect of contemporary economic reality is the widespread unease there is about it; there is a bitter taste from all the wealth that is being generated at an unprecedented rate. A typical example comes from the Harvard Program on Technology and Society, the economic research of which has been

'in response to a wide range of contemporary critical analysis implying that the present economic system fails to counter adverse effects of technology, fails to meet major social needs which are inadequately reflected in the feed-back process of the market economy, is far less competitive than is generally claimed, is biassed against the development of demand and production in 'public' goods, is dominated by advertising, creates unnecessary wants and excessive product diversity, stimulates bellicosity and commits many other crimes. It is traditional to regard the economic system, given the relatively simple basis of company law on which it is founded, as possessing the property of naturally responding to society's developing socio-economic needs. The work (of this program) demonstrates that in the present circumstances that view is simply wrong'.

Since the existing pattern of innovation is associated with the existence of private property, its rejection has resulted in a turning away from the institution of private property, with consequent tolerance of growth of bureaucracy. Those who for one reason or another do not like the economic world that they see, conclude that this is the inevitable, natural result of the principle of private ownership on which it rests. What they see, they think is in some way part of the structure of the universe, incapable of being other than it is because of some form of inescapable cosmic law. They are, of course right to think that business and innovation rest on a foundation of private property, but wrong to assume that the form they take to-day is the only possible form a system based upon this principle could have taken, or could still take in the future. Every bit as much as those who are enmeshed in the system, its critics fail to recognise its man-made nature, man-made in that it has been shaped by men in the mass and by individual men, by what men have thought as well what they have done, above all, by the laws they have made, modified, repealed and allowed to fall into desuetude in accordance with the shifts over time in thinking and in social pressures. Because of this failure, since its critics think that the principle of private property can only be expressed in one set of concrete terms, and they disapprove of these, they conclude that it is the principle that is wrong. It is thus rare enough to-day to find reformers who are not Socialists to one degree or another. Whether they espouse collectivism completely, and demand the absolute elimination of private property, or whether they allow property some residual role in an economic world where State activity will dominate, they are united in believing that the present system is damned irretrievably, and in calling for action to put it out of its agony.

As the distortions inherent in the system became more and more obtrusive, people came to think that the system based upon private property was irredeemable, and consequently turned to Socialism as an alternative. Their logic echoed Brecht's question. 'What is the crime of robbing a Bank, compared with that of owning one?' Opposition to the criterion of 'the market' in economic matters grew, because the results of the operation of 'the market' were considered to be so monstrous. The 'profit motive' was decried as the dynamic for industry, because the industry which it created was considered to be on an inhuman model and scale, with Man alienated amidst artifacts. Increasingly, therefore, the forces making for reform have become antagonistic to the very principle of private property.

During the present century a chorus of questioning has swelled, as the shape of the world which has been built upon thse extensions of the meaning of property that have been discussed earlier, has become apparent. Questioning turned into rejection, and led to proposals for reform, but almost always the originators of these proposals have taken as absolute what is only relative; they have confused a principle with what is only one particular way of realising it in concrete terms; they have concluded that results of man-made positive law could not have been other than they are. Taking it for granted that the system was rotten to the core, and based upon an unsound principle, they have striven to replace it by one degree of Socialism or another. It is not necessary to discuss here whether a collectivist system or one based upon private property is more capable of organising the resources of the world to the end of human happiness. What is certain is that whether it does in fact contribute to their happiness or not, men want to see new things done, they want to see ideas turned into concrete reality, they want innovation. What is equally certain, confirmed by history, experience and common sense, is that Socialism cannot match private property where innovation is concerned. It cannot match it because innovation is the result of human creative energy, and nothing has ever equalled private ownership as a means of releasing this energy into economic channels and dedicating it to the task of getting new things done. No Socialism of which we know anything, either through direct experience or from the record of history, has been able to operate without bureaucracy. And bureaucracy, whether of the State or of the large firm, is incompatible with innovation because it cannot foster individual creativeness. Corporate responsibility may be able to hold ground already gained, – although contemporary Western experience casts doubt even on this – but it cannot break *new* ground.

Although not many would question that the extensions of private property by legal changes during the nineteenth century have resulted in an unprecedented amount of innovation, there is now widespread doubt as to how much of this has been worth while, taking into consideration the accompanying disadvantages, since no change can ever be wholly for the better. There is even more apprehension concerning the direction with economic development is taking for the future under the stimulus of this innovatory pattern. Politically, these doubts and fears find expression not only in the strength of socialism in terms of votes and parties as well as in ideology, but also in the way in which parties which espouse the principle of private ownership are forced to adopt policies involving State intervention and the growth of the bureaucracy. In fact, there is a rather widespread consensus that the disadvantages of the present system of private property have increased, are increasing and ought to be diminished. Up to the present, however, only Socialists have had thorough-going and coherent proposals for achieving this, because those who accept the principle of private property have been slow to see that the actual expressions of this principle in practice that there are at present, represent only a very few of its possibilities. As a consequence, their proposals for reform tend not to go beyond tinkering with established arrangements, when what is needed is a radical reconstruction. To quite an extent, this is because conservatives tend to rely upon the rule of laws in society rather than to try to run society as a machine is run, by plans and measurements in an exact framework. In doing so, they can too easily overlook the extent to which law, being man-made, introduces its own distortions into life, and is therefore always in need of correction. Nowhere is this more true than it is of the laws which derive from the principle of private property, and which act as the dynamic element in this or that sector of economic life. It can be foreseen with certainty about such laws that they will be followed by innovation, because they will release human creative energy into the corresponding area; but nothing can be known in advance about the precise form the innovation will take, nor about the direct and indirect affects it will have. The meaning of the law only emerges gradually over time with the working out of its consequences in practice.

The meaning of the series of legal enactments during the nineteenth century which extended the range of economic life in which the principle of private property could operate, was thus almost wholly concealed from the men who were responsible for these enactments. They did not foresee the results of Limited Liability; they did not consciously set out to create Industrial Property according to some comprehensive philosophical model. They were concerned to make changes in laws so that some practical disability from which business was suffering was removed, or so that things would go more smoothly in some particular direction. Few forces have done more to shape the twentieth century than those nineteenth-century laws. They transformed the way of life of every country in the world, in a movement which is even still gathering strength. Even the Communist-bloc countries have been affected by it. Economic innovation comes about because of monopoly, but the amount and sort of innovation that does in fact take place reflects the extent and type of monopoly there is. In the modern world, there is more innovation in the psychological ingredient of products than at any earlier period of history because of the range of market and marketing powers available; equally, because of the nature of these particular powers to escape the constraints of the market, the results of this innovation have a particular balance between advantage and disadvantage when assessed by humane standards. All this innovation takes place only in those areas of life where one type of monopolistic business operates; not alone are other areas starved of innovation themselves, but they have to pay additional costs arising from the pattern of innovation there is. The result has been a reaction which expresses itself sometimes in a belief that socialism is the only hope of redressing the present imbalance, sometimes — as with much student revolt — in a move towards anarchy. In all this process, the growth of the mass media and the reversal in the traditional function of words which is implied in the advertising man's role, reflect cultural disintegration.

Just as it was out of his own creative energy that Marx recognized the creativeness that there was in capitalism, even though his name was destined to become the very symbol of enmity to it, so the rest of mankind, in different ways and on different levels, recognizes creativeness and responds to it wherever it may be found. For the last two centuries that means responding to a great deal of what is involved in the industrial and marketing revolutions. It may indeed be that the very fact that human creativeness expresses itself in this way rather than others reflects a declining culture; no one who has read Rostovtzeff can fail to be impressed by the case he makes that the flowering of capitalist organization and its attendant material benefits was characteristic of the Hellenistic world in the stage of decline, not growth; nor to mark the parallels for our own history. What seems certain is that for the last two centuries the same kind and degree of creative energy has been directed into economic and technological activity, as went into the fine arts and literature during the Renaissance, into Liturgy — in the broadest sense, which includes the buildings or settings for worship — during the ages of Faith, into survival and reconstruction during what historians used to call the Dark Ages, into speculation and prayer whilst the grandeur that was Rome was turning into something to be escaped from and rejected. Marx's own special contribution to historical analysis, by its success and limitations, confirms that. It can throw no light on the mysterious, early, creative stages in cultural growth, on how a new spiritual principle emerges and eventually moulds whole areas of human life in its own image. But in the later stages of culture, when the sap has gone down, when the particular formulations of the spiritual insights which shaped it no longer have the power to move the minds and hearts of men, when social forces cease to be confronted and modulated by religion, because the old gods have shown themselves unable to protect society against the barbarians – for such periods of history, the economic interpretation is more intelligible than any other. The common element through the best of times and the worst of times, the age of wisdom and the age of foolishness, is the creative energy of man; it expresses itself in different ways at different times, there is no escape from responding to it, and for two centuries now that has meant responding to the Industrial and Marketing Revolutions.

Marxist strictures are valid, even though Communist remedies are not. There *are* tremendous imbalances in the Western pattern of innovation, and these reflect the positive law which underwrites the monopoly structure that makes innovation possible. The nineteenth-century legislation upon which so much modern market power depends, has never been modified in any fundamental way, and the reason probably is that the power to innovate in economic affairs is so new and so powerful a thing in human life, so manifestly absent in all the ages of history before the modern one, that anything proved to be the source of such power has strong claims to be let alone, lest a mechanism which people know to work even if it is not understood, may be impaired. Thus, in the United States, although anti-monopoly legislation goes back to the Sherman Act of 1890, it was only with the Procter and Gamble/Clorox case in the 1960s that the Federal Trade Commission first grappled with some of the problems posed by persuasive market power. In Britain, successive amendments of the 1883 Trade Marks act tended to strengthen the capacity of that Act to confer this type of power over market forces. Only with the very recent Trade Description Act has there been any decisive swing in favour of buyers as against sellers. Another reason why market power and the laws which bring it into have been let alone, of course, has been the belief that its results were simply the unique and inescapable working out of the principle of private property, instead of simply being one of many possible ways. Because of this belief, the forces making for reform turned increasingly towards elimination of private property itself to one degree or another, and ignored any possibility that alternative ways of expressing the principle of private property might be an improvement. On balance, however, the main reason why things have gone on as they have done, is that the common consensus of humanity has been that the game is well worth the candle. From the ordinary man's point of view, the positive side of market power consists of its contribution to innovation, and even when the negative aspects are listed, the net balance favours it strongly. Although 'it is just not possible for the economist to establish a positive link between economic growth and human welfare', the average sensual man is not at all unaware that growth and progress have their dark side, but he nevertheless takes the view that on balance there is more to be said for them than against. C.P. Snow is speaking for him when he says in the essay that sparked off a famous debate:

'It is all very well for us, sitting pretty, to think that material standards of living don't matter all that much... In the advanced countries, we have realised in a rough and ready way what the old industrial revolution brought with it. A great increase in population because applied science went hand in hand with medical science and medical care. Enough to eat, for a similar reason. Everyone able to read and write, because an industrial society can't work without; health, food, education; nothing but the industrial revolution could have spread them down to the very poor. Those are primary gains – there are losses too, of course. It is worth remembering that there must have been similar losses – spread over a much longer period – when men changed from hunting and food gathering life to agriculture. For some, it must have been a genuine spiritual impoverishment.'[45]

However nostalgic we may be for Burke's 'unbought graces of life' or Algernon Cecil's 'high courtesies of citizenship', or Tallyrand's 'sweetness of life before the Revolution' (life always seems to have been sweeter before any revolution, including the Industrial one) we are forced to recognize the positive aspects. Even at the level of sensibility, all has not been loss, although "What was the GNP of Venice?" remains a real question for those who want us to stake all on economic growth.

Since all monopolies are particular (for what else can the 'uniqueness of advantage' that is monopoly, be?) imbalance must be accepted in any economic system which uses monopoly and which consequently has innovation. The innovation justifies the imbalance. To say this, however, is not to accept one kind or degree of imbalance as being no better or no worse than another, nor to pretend that the system of market power which characterizes the modern world is the best that can be obtained. It is very far indeed from being so. Probably there will never be a time when monopoly systems correspond precisely to what is needed, because business men are quicker to act than academic men are to note and reflect, or than politicians and civil servants are to legislate. It is also probably true to say that the gap between the positive law there is and the law that is needed, is to-day wider than it has ever been. The vested interests opposing reform do not consist only of the large firms which benefit so obviously from laws of property which go so far beyond the principles upon which the institution of private property rests. These interests also include the bureaucrats whose power would be greatly diminished or even extinguished completely, in a world where market forces were permitted to operate, and politicians who are unable to think beyond the next election. But the present system cannot last. Too many of its results are being questioned as obviously having no part in civilized life, at the same time as it is manifestly failing to give the innovation needed to cope with challenges from the Near and Far East. Of course the system is defended by those who are paid to do so. But thoughtful people no longer defend it. Consequently, there is a widely-felt feeling of being in a trap, with all economic activity condemned to become progressively more dehumanised as it becomes less effective. The horns of the dilemma are a collectivist system which provides an unsatisfactory context for creativeness in economic affairs, resulting in the need to abandon hope of much innovation, and a system in which innovation is plentiful, certainly, but less and less concerned with generating real new wealth, and increasingly incapable of coping with external challenge, such as that posed by Japan and the Confucian world. Can we be surprised if there are prophets of doom, who believe that if things continue as they are, economic activity will become increasingly imbalanced, until Western civilization comes crashing down in successive waves of disillusionment, weariness and revolt?

This may indeed happen, and we know enough about the contemporary crisis to be able to discern trends that could progressively lead to it. If market power remains uncontrolled as at present, the rent element in Western economies can only increase. One consequence of this is that even more of world manufacture and trade will come under the control of multi-national corporations. A second consequence is that the growth of primary market power will be paced by that of derived market power, i.e. wages and salaries, too, will incorporate a larger rent element. The contrast between being in or out of work will be starker than ever, yet at the same time, derived market power will prevent wages moving downward under pressure from market forces, so unemployment must increase. Innovations will be even more factor-saving and less output-increasing. They will be even less those that can generate employment by increasing real new wealth, and even more those that are able to capture some of the rent in the system, than they are to-day. This means that investment will concentrate upon *marketing* innovations, i.e. those limited to psychological ingredient. Such a pattern of innovation will expand wants at a faster rate than economies are capable of satisfying them, and the pressure on politicians for money to turn want into demand will fuel inflation. Inequality in society must become more marked than ever with the further growth of market power. Belief that the existing pattern of property, firms and industrial organization is the best that a free enterprise system can do, and strengthening contempt for this, can only help the cause of collectivism. This cause will be actively promoted by the public bureaucracy, which stands to gain from it in the short term, and by politicians, ensnared as they are in the vote auction. Growth of the State will make innovation less possible; the State will attempt to cure what it has caused, not by ceasing to interfere, but by setting up public institutions to encourage innovation. This must inevitably fail, because it ignores the basic reality that innovation depends upon individual creativity: Creativity diffused at the macro-level can never substitute for, or even make contact with, creativity concentrated at the micro-level. Lack of innovation must lead to lack of investment and foreign exchange earnings, as well as to unemployment. One of the consequences will be that products from countries which have kept the profit measure and restrained the growth in their public sector, will increasingly dominate the markets of countries that have opted for Socialism. A second consequence will be that politicians in the latter countries will take the soft option of trying to keep up the voters' standards of living by deficit financing. The external borrowing which this will call for, will make their burden of taxation a crushing one. If history is any guide, final bankruptcy and revolution will be preceded by some attempt, à la Necker, in France in 1789, to reform the taxation system without tackling the even more fundamental problem of the existence of Rents to tax.

What the contemporary crisis comes down to, then, is that we are running high-rent, high tax economies, when it is only the forces of the market that can give us prosperity. It is only the forces of the market that can reconcile the highest values of our culture and our economic activity. It is only the forces of the market that act to produce whatever degree of equality can in fact be achieved in any society. Interference with market forces is necessary if we are to have innovation, but such interference must be deliberately and precisely related to the innovation that is required, and limited correspondingly. The contemporary crisis is due, more than anything else, to the way in which we have got the priorities exactly reversed − an unplanned pattern of interference with market forces leading to innovation and wealth of kinds that have given economic freedom a bad name.

In the final chapter, therefore, an attempt will be made to show how market power could be modified, so as to give a pattern of innovation that would be truly humane, and which would reconcile the values of high culture with those of business and technology.

Notes

1. Buchanan J. Mc G. and Wagner R.E.: Democracy in Deficit: The political legacy of Lord Keynes. New York 1977.
2. Kondratieff N.D.: The Long Waves in Economic Life, in Review of Economic Statistics XVII (1935) p. 105.
3. Futures 13 No. 4 (Aug. 1981) p. 332.
4. Business Cycles. New York 1939.
5. op. cit. 111, 112.
6. Mensch Gerhard: Stalemate in Technology, Cambridge, Mass. 1979.
7. ibid. p. 73.
8. Clark, Freeman and Soete in Futures 13 No 4 (Aug 1981) p. 308.
9. Rostow W.W.: Getting from Here to There. London (1979) p. 25.
10. In Futures 13 No. 4 (Aug 1981) p. 323.
11. Rostow op. cit. p. 33.
12. Landes David: The Unbound Prometheus. Cambridge (1970) p. 231.
13. Tizard H.W.: A Scientist in and out of the Civil Service. Haldane Lecture, London 1955.
14. Hutt W.H.: A Rehabilitation of Say's Law. Athens, Ohio (1974) p. 3.
15. Dewey Donald: The Theory of Imperfect Competition: A Radical Reconstruction. New York (1969) p. 18.
16. Freeman C. In Futures 13 No. 4 (Aug 1981).

180

17. Schumpeter Joseph: Capitalism, Socialism and Democracy. London (1943) p. 84.
18. Kuznets S: Economic Change. New York (1953) p. 109.
19. Rostow op. cit.
20. Landes David: Bankers and Pashas. London 1958.
21. Yoshino M.Y.: Japan's Multinational Enterprises. Cambridge, Mass. 1976.
22. Overy R.J.: William Morris, Viscount Nuffield. London 1976.
23. cf. Centre for Environmental Studies Research Series No. 32. London, 23 Chandos Place. 1980.
24. National Economic Development Office Industrial Policy Discussion Paper No. 7: (Japan). London (1980) p. 51.
25. Gold Bela: Productivity, Technology and Capital. Cambridge, Mass. (1979) p. 279.
26. Advisory Committee on Industrial Innovation Final (Baruch) Report. Washington, D.C. 1979.
27. Landes D: The Unbound Prometheus. Cambridge (1970) p. 19.
28. Norway Nevil Shute: Slide Rule. London 1954.
29. Zysman John: Political Strategies for Industrial Order: State, Market and Industry in France, Berkeley, California 1977.
30. Kingston W: Ideas, Civil Servants and Keynes, in Journal of Economic Affairs, London, January 1983.
31. Hurd Douglas: End to Promises. London (1979) p. 29.
32. Schumpeter, J.A.: Capitalism Socialism and Democracy. p. 161.
33. ibid.
34. Jay Peter: Employment, Inflation and Politics. London 1976.
35. Usher, Dan: The Economic Prerequisite to Democracy. Oxford 1981.
36. ibid. p. 193.
37. ibid. p. 73.
38. Kingston W: In Industrial Innovation. London (1979) p. 42.
39. Mensch op. cit. p. 63.
40. Smith David: In National Westminster Bank Review, November 1975.
41. Buchanan. op. cit. p. 123.
42. Galbraith, J.K.: American Capitalism. London (1975) p. 86.
43. Buzzi Giancarlo: Advertising, Its Cultural and Political Effects. Oxford (1968) p. 133.
44. Morris James: The Great Port. London 1970.
45. Snow C.P.: The Two Cultures and a Second Look. Cambridge (1959) p. 25.

CHAPTER V

Proposals for innovation

In the previous chapter, it was claimed that many of the difficulties which Western countries face, are the result of inadequate or distorted patterns of innovation. If each of these difficulties is analysed individually, it will be clearly seen how much the innovation factor contributes to it, and when they are all added up, the indictment is a damning one. It is because we can no longer carry out B-phase innovation as well as the Japanese, that we are losing ground in export markets and are seeing our home markets penetrated increasingly by their products. To the extent that we were slow to innovate in the energy field, we left ourselves similarly at the mercy of the OPEC cartel. The resultant OPEC surpluses, recycled through the international money markets, have been an irresistible temptation to politicians who have elections to win. Whatever chance these might have had of resisting the lure of external borrowing under 'normal' conditions, they had none at all of doing so under the combined pressures of Japanese capability, greatly increased energy prices and the salesmen of the international Banks. The resulting major acceleration in the rate of growth of the public sector reduced Western productive and innovative capactity still further, making the crushing effect of the external forces still more devastating. Since democracy itself depends upon a substantial proportion of economic life being independent of the State apparatus, this public sector growth has lessened the capacity of democratic systems to survive. The weakest countries now depend so much on external borrowing, in fact, that disaster could be reached for them – and for the international banking system – with an end of the availability of OPEC surplusses for recycling, as a result of less usage causing a drop in the price of oil. Japan's free enterprise flexibility will gain from such changes, but countries with inflated public sectors will not. They will be too rigid to adapt.

Even without these special comparatively recent factors, however, the innovatory patterns of the West have themselves been contributing to the growth of collectivism for a long time. These patterns have come to be judged by more and more people, not to reflect a humane vision of economic life. To the extent that this happened, people came to look to the State rather than to individual enterprise for economic development that would accord with genuine human needs and hopes. This change in public attitudes was naturally used energetically by those with most to gain from centralized power, the politicians and the bureaucrats. These attitudes were based upon the belief that capitalism, a free enterprise system, or economic arrangements based upon private property, could only result in one kind of economic development, the one which we have actually had. Because people found this progressively less defensible, they either turned to Socialism, or felt themselves without intellectual and emotional weapons with which to resist encroachments by the State. Sometimes, these were initiated by politicians, sometimes by bureaucrats, but in every case the other group provided willing accomplices. On this point it is important not to be deceived by the carefully nutured myth of the civil servant with no axe to grind, loyally putting into effect policies devised by his political masters, or, as the British tradition puts it, having as his principal duty "keeping his Minister out of trouble". No civil servant, any more than anyone else, can avoid having his thinking affected by his own socio-economic background. If he depends completely upon his career for his status in society and his spending power, as modern Civil Servants do, he simply cannot be indifferent to what will improve both of these. This is expansion of the bureaucracy of which he is a member. Note that the assertion does not impugn in any way the moral quality of the bureaucrat. He may be an ideal husband and father, and a loyal citizen. He may be convinced that in all he does, he has nothing but the common good at heart. He will certainly be offended at any questioning of his motives, especially if it arises from the side of free enterprise or capitalism, where the motivation is so evidently greed. And this is the precise point. It is perfectly possible to be quite realistic about free enterprise and to accept openly that greed is its dynamic, because if market forces are permitted to operate, they channel the energies of business men into serving their fellows as customers, and taming their excesses as competitors. The bias against the market is now so strong, that it can never be said too often that it is only market forces that can bring about whatever degree of economic equality is possible in human societies. In contrast with the frankness of the free enterprise approach, the bureaucratic approach depends upon a falsehood: That because they serve the State directly, Civil Servants are therefore exempt from being tainted with greed, and that what they propose and endorse is consequently the result of objective assessment.

It is not, and the fact that it is not has very important consequences for innovation. We now know enough about how ideas are communicated, and about how they need to be given psychic life by emotion, to be very respectful towards subconscious factors. Self-interest plays such a powerful role in these, that it acts as an extremely effective 'censor' for ideas impinging from outside. In the typical modern bureaucrat, this means that emotional energy will never be put behind ideas that will cut the size of the bureaucracy, since that is not in his interest. But ideas which can foster interventionism *will* be supported by the necessary emotional energy, because they are, directly or indirectly, to his advantage. The alternative to collectivism is a system of positive law, within which private agents are free to operate. Any such legal system, to be and remain effective, must be continually refined and updated, in accordance with new demands upon it, and greater understanding of its workings. In the nature of things, it is idle to expect this work to be done by Civil Servants. It demands creativity of the highest order. Like all creativity, this will depend greatly upon subconscious forces for the release of the necessary energy. These forces, however, will not be released, because it is not a better legal framework, but more intervention by the State that is in the interest of the Bureaucrat. And it is towards more intervention by the State that the all-important forces in the subconscious minds of all but the very rarest Civil Servants, inevitably work.

Every student of public bureaucracies is aware of a watershed at some point within the last half-century, when their ethos changed definitively in the direction of intervention. This is not to say that in some countries, France for example, the 'State' element has not historically been stronger than in others. But the 'old' Civil Servants were nevertheless able to extract 'common good' elements out of a mass of self-interested lobbying, and draft laws as a result, which released undreamt-of energies from those who were free to act within those laws. The whole of the nineteenth century, as Chapter III showed, was characterized by this type of creative law-making. One of the worst legacies of the Great War and the inflations which followed it, was the near-destruction throughout Europe of the class which had been capable of so much creativity, but so strong was the tradition which this class left behind it, that it imposed itself to a large extent upon the 'new men' of the post-War period. But the interests of these new men were not the same as their predecessors, and when Keynes's thought provided plausible intellectual vindication for the intervention which coincided with those interests, the underlying reality took control. From then onwards, little energy was available for the type of legislation which had formerly been so fruitful of innovation, and the great nineteenth century laws of capital deployment, of Patents and of Trade Marks were allowed to ossify, instead of receiving the constant development and modification they needed. The process was cumulative, because failure to develop these laws meant that business continued to operate in a legal regime which became progressively out of date – the "unacceptable face of capitalism" became inevitable. The worse free enterprise looked, of course, the less likely collectivist measures were to be questioned.

In seeking to develop solutions to the contemporary crisis, therefore, the motivation of the modern Civil Servant must be brought under keen scrutiny. The advice he gives to his Minister is not unbiassed. He can only have arrived at the position of giving advice by a process of promotion which reflects his success in absorbing the prevailing ethos of his Service. With the best will in the world, therefore, he must favour proposals that bring about an extension of its power over those which do not. The best will in the world can also be lacking.

There is no shortage of case histories which show how civil servants have manipulated politicians in ways that have greatly increased their own opportunities for extended influence. Equally, when at times of financial stringency, politicians come to power on a platform of cutting public sector expenditure, they frequently find that such "cuts" as their civil servants offer, are those that will have the maximum damaging impact in terms of votes. If, in spite of this, the politicians press ahead, they invariably discover that any "cuts" will leave the bureaucratic establishment itself untouched.

Any policy for innovation, therefore, that is not based upon a clear-sighted vision of the anti-innovation bias of the public bureaucracy, is bound to fail. By "anti-innovation bias" is not meant, that this bureaucracy will fail to have policies and proposals for encouraging and bringing about innovation. It will have no shortage of such policies. What is being asserted on the basis of logic as well as of history, is that these proposals will – indeed *must* – tend to central-ize decision-making, instead of multiplying the number of decision points. Add to this the replacement of the necessary emotional input of individual innovators who are involved in personal gain or loss, by the relaxed position of bureaucrats who will not be affected personally by results. Add also that investment decisions where the bureaucratic approach is adopted, must be based upon the criterion of "cover" rather than that of "profit", and it must be perfectly clear how, if we want innovation, we must turn our backs decisively on bureaucracy. And Western countries both want and need innova-tion very badly at the present time.

Bringing the self-interest of the bureaucrats out into the open, however, is only the start of the task. There must also be positive action to remove the elements in the alternative which are repugnant to public opinion, so that not alone is there innovation in plentitude, but that economic innovation also corresponds to truly human values. Since all innovation is the result of market power, and all market power is rooted in positive law, this can mean nothing else except changes in legislation. These changes must affect property rights, especially those property rights which originated in the nineteenth century, including those relating to investment (Joint Stock Companies and Limited Liability) and intellectual and industrial property. In so far as what has been called in earlier chapters 'derived market power' is also a problem for Western democracies, increasing costs and replacing investment by consumption, it can best be dealt with by modifying the primary market power on which it depends. Similarly, 'derived taxing power' and 'reinforced derived market power' which are even more – much more – dangerous for the democracies, will be eroded automatically by replacing the power of the State by a private property system that has been purged as far as possible of the elements that have progressively caused its rejection. Although it is only in the present century that this rejection has become widely evident, John Stuart Mill saw with deadly accuracy what was happening as long ago as 1869: 'The laws of property' he wrote:

'have never yet conformed to the principles on which the justification of private property rests. They have made property of things which never ought to be property and absolute property where only a qualified property ought to exist. They have not held the balance fairly between human beings, but have heaped impediments on some, to give advantage to others; they have purposely fostered inequalities and prevented all from starting fair in the race. That all should indeed start on perfectly equal terms, is inconsistent with any law of private property; but if as much pains as had been taken to aggravate the inequality of chances arising from the natural working of the principle, had been taken to temper that inequality by every means not subversive of the principle itself; if the tendency of legislation had been to favour the diffusion instead of the concentration of wealth — to encourage the subdivision of the large masses instead of striving to heap them together; the principle of individual property would have been found to have no necessary communion with the physical and social evils which almost all Socialist writers assume to be inseparable from it.''[1]

It is very easy to relate Mill's comments to innovation. Because there is more effective market power in some parts of the economy than in others, there is an unprecedented explosion of innovation in some areas of life, *but only in some areas*. The way in which the resulting innovation is uncontrolled is strikingly analogous to what biologists call a 'wild' growth, that is, a multiplication of certain cells at a rate which is out of balance with the rest of the organism. Indeed, the multiplication of cells is the model of all innovation, which is the realization of ideas in concrete form. The 'new thing' or 'idea' is the information programmed into the existing cell, and the new cell, which is structured according to this programme, is 'the new thing done', the concrete realization of this 'idea', or its innovation. A 'wild' growth of cells is nothing else than innovation out of control. All the signs of a parallel 'wild' growth are to be found in modern economies where market power is characteristic of business, and the effects are felt throughout the entire world. No system, on no less authority than that of Marx himself, and even in the Communist Manifesto, has been more innovative than free enterprise. It is worth reflecting, inded, on the extent to which Marx's followers have taken so many of his insights which make a part of a problem supremely intelligible, and applied them to the whole, where inevitably they break down. Just as Marxist history gives the best clues to understanding recent centuries (we might expect, after all, that the economic interpretation of history would make a good deal of sense of an era characterized by 'enthronement of the commercial principle') so there is a sense in which Marxist economics is right when it says that the problem of capitalism is its 'chronic inability to absorb as much surplus as it is capable of creating'. This sense emerges once the substantial equivalence of Marxian 'surplus value' with Rent (including quasi-rent as defined by Marshall) is recognized. Capitalism *as it has developed* is manifestly unable to absorb all the effects, both direct and indirect, of too much Rent in its own structure. When there is a strong rent element in wages, for example, the forces tending to clear the labour market are prevented from operating, and unemployment results. It must be stressed that this applies only to the results of one particular complex of positive law, generating property rights according to one particular pattern. It is not the single, inevitable outcome of adoption of the principle of private property. It results from the present *system* of private property, which gives too much innovation in some sectors of life and too little in others. A different system based on exactly the same principle, by giving a more balanced pattern of innovation, would remove the surplus value difficulty correspondingly. If the legal arrangements for granting monopoly so as to enable innovation to happen, resulted in innovation in all areas of life, instead of only in some, as at present, one of the most telling criticisms of capitalism in the Marxist canon would be eliminated. Such a change would deal simultaneously with the problem of absorbing surplus value in some areas, and with that of 'creating wealth at one pole, poverty at another' − the latter because of the way in which market forces tend to diminish inequality.

Joint Stock Companies and Limited Liability are legal devices which extend the range of economic activity in respect to which private property can function as an agent for the release and direction of creativeness. The Industrial Property Acts, above all, the Trade Marks Acts, reinforce them powerfully. Between them, these various refinements, extensions and reinforcements of the basic principle of private ownership, have been responsible for an unprecedented outpouring of human creative energy into business, which is unmatched, not only in history, but also by any of the alternative economic systems which exist in the contemporary world. A solution to the problems created by market power which depends upon turning our back on all this positive achievement is unthinkable, for many reasons. By no means all of these are materialistic. It is a matter of experience and observation that it is in exercising his creativeness that man is most himself, is most aware that there is an order in his universe, a meaning to his life, and that he is in touch with both. It is not necessary to claim that the exercise of creativeness in business is creativity of a very high order (in fact, the bulk of business activity involves very low-order creativity indeed.) The point is still valid that for many people this is the only contact with creativeness they possess through the immediacy of their actual experience. It is none the less real for being low-order creativeness, and is their means of contact with a wider and deeper world. Once this contact has been experienced, at however superficial a level, there can be no going back from it, and there has been too much experience of it in the Western world for a voluntary change to a way of organizing economic activity which reduces the amount of creativeness involved, to be at all acceptable. As a means of directing innovation to humane ends, collectivism has nothing to offer people formed in the Western tradition. For just the same reasons, Western countries, bred to individualism, cannot hope to meet the challenge of Japan by attempting to copy arrangements which reflect the social cohesion of that country.

A second question, however, which has some links with the first, is whether the huge and unbalanced growth of innovation in some areas of economic life where market power is plentiful, is beyond the capacity of Western society to cope with, or is the growth too much for that society to be able to survive? Put bluntly, is the problem some form of economic cancer? Not all 'wild' growth is aggressive, in the sense of invading neighbouring organs. What distinguishes a cancerous growth is precisely that it *is* aggressive in this sense. It is uncontrolled innovation invading nearby territory. Is there any analogous aggression to be found in the uncontrolled growth of innovation? Consider, for example, the secondary effects of marketing monopoly. If one of these effects is not only to inflate the communications media to an extent that would be unthinkable otherwise, but also to modify their 'editorial' content, can this be regarded as innovation 'invading' a neighbouring area? Is invasion of the right to privacy by the media not an aspect of their need for circulation or viewership at any cost to keep up their advertising revenue? Invasion of the countryside by posters, of suburbs by noise, invasion of the capacity for eroticism by the obtrusiveness of sex in advertising, invasion of childhood by salesmanship (two forms of destruction of innocence) – do not all these count as aggressiveness? And what makes them economically possible, if not marketing monopoly? If aggression on the part of the uncontrolled innovation is established, it makes little difference whether it is directed against a body physical or a body politic. The 'wild' growth innovates at the expense of the organism as a whole. With cancer, there is always the question of whether or not it is terminal, as the technical term is. In the Western world, there is no lack of ancestral voices prophesying doom for society, and it is undoubtedly true that the widespread reaction against the results of the existing pattern of market power, looks to many people who have a sense of history, as symptomatic of an approaching end. The apparent (and increasing) inability of the system to cope with the problems of structural unemployment in the advanced countries and the relatively increasing poverty in the underdeveloped ones – Sylos-Labini, it will be remembered, saw both of these as having a common cause (the entrenchment of monopoly in the economic system); the destruction of the environment as the apparently inevitable by-product of the outpouring of new things; growing contempt, even among those who benefit by it (sometimes among those who benefit *most* by it) for the values of the consumer society, especially among the young, to whom it fails to offer 'an ideal, an élan and a hope' – all these are weighty factors against an optimistic prognosis. Marx, of course, saw private property withering away before the State did. Schumpeter thought that the end of Capitalism would come about because the intellectuals it had created would turn upon it; Galbraith and his followers hold that the system is already dead to all intents and purposes, and that future generations will look back with wonder at the naiveté of any belief that in our times it still had claims to be called a free enterprise system. And, as mentioned earlier, those who have read Rostovtzeff cannot fail to be impressed with the parallel between the present and the growth of large-scale capitalism which was associated with the beginning of the end of the Hellenistic world.

Yet the fact that a growth is 'wild' does not mean that it necessarily has to be fatal to neighbouring parts of the organism, and even when it is found to be aggressive, surgery can frequently bring it under control. The object of this final chapter, then, is to prescribe the surgery: To suggest what steps are needed in order to eliminate the harm from market power by bringing it under control, into balance with the rest of social life, and into harmony with true human needs, whilst preserving as much as possible of its beneficial aspects.

This condition demands that any proposals should be for a non-socialist and non-bureaucratic alternative to, or modification of, the present system. Enough is now known about how innovation is brought about to make it clear that what must be preserved above all are the right economic conditions whereby new things can be done. The production of new ideas in itself appears to be so much a part of human activity, that it may not even need a particular environment or economic climate to stimulate it. Psychology has taught us a good deal about the way in which new ideas come, and linked it with the instinct of play and with spontaneity to such an extent that we can almost say that it is the absence of positive activity *at the conscious level* that is the important element. It may be, of course, that however much spontaneity ideas may need for their birth, the kind of new ideas and the area to which they relate will reflect some form of direction, some setting of boundaries. Presumably even the most ardent advocate of free-association or of brainstorming sessions, if he is concerned to get new ideas that can be used in business, tries to orient the technique in a corresponding direction. Even if this is so, it does not compare in importance with the part environment and attendant conditions play in turning the idea into concrete reality. There is far less need to worry about the new ideas, than there is about the provision of support to innovate them. There will always be inventors, just as there will always be artists, no matter how unfavourable the conditions for their emergence may seem to be. But innovators are a very different matter. They stand between the idea and the resources it needs if it is to become a concrete reality, and they have a perception of what it is possible to achieve. Unless they can see a good chance of obtaining the backing they need, men of this type will not devote themselves with the singlemindedness that is needed to overcome the difficulties inherent in innovation. There are many witnesses to the fact that historically such men need not be very intelligent, not brilliant organisers, nor well-educated in either the humanist or the business sense; but they must have courage, they must have doggedness, *and they must start out with some rationally-based presumption of success.* Many an innovator, when he comes to his goal of the concrete realisation of an idea, has been willing to admit that this eventually came about only because he had been too stupid and too stubborn to give it up. And it is nothing else than widely diffused private property which (in Western society at least) can both produce innovator-types, and provide them with the resources which they cannot do without.

The basic problem, indeed, is one of property rights. It was the progressive emergence of these after the medieval period which enabled freedom of contract to play its essential role in the industrial revolution.[2] Extension of such rights to whole new areas during the nineteenth century produced innovation on an unprecedented scale. But, as Mill observed, this involved making 'property of things which never ought to be property and absolute property where only a qualified property ought to exist''. The reaction against the consequences reversed the trend of centuries, and, in Belloc's words, represented 'that general movement from free contract to status, and from the Capitalist to the Servile State, which is the tide of our time'.[3] In this reaction, alienation of those who worked without property or hope of it, in contrast to the concentration of wealth and industry into big units, made the extension of State activity electorally acceptable as a supposed counterweight. With the coming of the multinational corporations, many of which deploy more resources than a good-sized State, it should be obvious even to those who benefit most from the existing Laws, that reform is necessary if the creature of legislation – market power – is not to outgrow and ultimately destroy the political power which made it. The issue for Western society comes down to this: If market power continues to remain out of control, then it can be foreseen that present trends will continue; World trade will eventually be overwhelmingly dominated by relatively few firms, all with headquarters within the most advanced countries, the gap between rich and poor (effectively between those whose salaries and wages will be mainly rent on the one hand, and those who are technologically unemployed and unemployable, on the other) will be greater and more unbridgeable than ever, as will the parallel gap between rich and poor nations; it will be less and less possible to finds a means of living which does not involve complete acceptance of the prevailing economic system. A job with little or no rent element will be hardly worth having; to lose a job (meaning access to rent) will be a total disaster. The commercial principle will be enthroned, and the social world will be less and less worth fighting to preserve, because of a complete divorce between art and life. Add to this the degradation of the environment at an ever-faster rate, the disillusion of the intellectuals, the inevitable further growth of bureaucracy, both business and Government, and it seems certain that some form of revolution would bring down the whole monstrous structure. If mercenaries could never keep a king on his throne, what must be the fate of a system whose only defenders will be the public relations men? So that the worst may not happen, the first task is an educational one, to get people – and especially politicians – to see the issues, and the possible methods of dealing with them, clearly.

When Alfred North Whitehead said that the supreme achievement of the nineteenth century was 'invention of the method of invention' he was, of course, thinking of inventions which had been successfully taken from the idea stage to that of actual working embodiments. Consequently, at least an equal achievement must have been 'invention of the method of *innovation*' which was a set of ways of internalizing the externalities of information production. In at least one sense, this corresponds to the most vigorous traditional definition of invention, requiring the 'flash of genius', the unexpected result, 'the inventive step'. This is because no one could possibly have foreseen how successfully the new legal system, leading as it did to large-scale market power, was to provide just such a means. It has been a serendipitous benefit of positive legislation on a prodigious scale. And even though not many people have adverted to the results of legislation to this effect, especially at the theoretical level, there is a sense in which business men do indeed know the score. Indeed, they may not know in any formal sense what particular Acts underpin by far the most effective part of any business they may be in. Nevertheless, they do know that big firms have advantages over small, that it pays to advertise, that it is better to be a multi-product rather than a single-product company, that research and development has to be protected against industrial espionage, and that Patents are of dubious value. In other words, for them the results of the Trade Marks and similar Acts are exactly the same as prose was to M. Jourdain – he had been using it all his life without knowing it. Moreover, the true entrepreneur reacts to a change in the prospects of profit with quite extraordinary rapidity. When the 1883 Trade Marks Act was passed, W.H. Lever was on the point of giving up business, as having no further interest for him. When he grasped the implications of the new legislation, however, he acted so decisively that "Sunlight" was registered, and his great enterprise under way, within a matter of months.[4] Given that business men will always try to make whatever money is to be made out of any particular scheme of positive law, if so much innovation has come about from a system which was never properly designed for the purpose, what possibilities must lie in store if the whole industrial property complex can be remoulded successfully in the light of what we now know about how innovation takes place? Producing the innovations to overcome the current recession should only be the least of these.

It makes a good deal of sense to see innovation as an exciting toy in the hands of the human race. Nothing, perhaps ever, certainly for generations ahead, will be able to replace man's confidence in himself as the hub of the universe, shattered as it has been by successive blows from Copernicus, Darwin and Freud. If anything can, it is likely to be the exhilaration of the power he now knows himself to possess increasingly, of actively and purposively shaping the future. Excesses of meretricious gadgetry and sales promotion may perhaps be regarded merely as symptoms of an initial ineptitude in handling an experience which, after all, is quite new to humanity and which carries with it enormous intrinsic excitement. Something is now known about how to get new things done; man cannot remain indefinitely on the level where his 'new things' do not transcend the advertising message or the computer game. An unbalanced pattern of innovation reflects an unbalanced pattern of market power, so market power must be controlled. How should this be done?

The first general principle to be followed is that control must be on an *ex ante* rather than *ex post* basis. All the attempts which have been made during the present century to control monopoly in a number of countries, have been *ex post*. That is, the policy appears to be to allow the monopoly to grow up, and then to create some form of mechanism or organization to deal with it, such as the Federal Trade Commission in the U.S., the Monopolies Commission in Britain, the Fair Trading Commissions in several other countries, and the Directorate General for Competition Policy in the E.E.C.

Attempts to control market power began in the U.S. The activities of what were known as 'The Trusts' led to the passing of the Sherman Act in 1890, which was the beginning of anti-monopoly legislation. The Trusts were holding companies with majority interests in competing firms which enabled them to co-ordinate production and prices profitably. The Sherman Act made all contracts in restraint of trade illegal, and every attempt to monopolise, a misdemeanour. It was a most radical break with legal tradition. Before, in Common Law, peaceable combinations, however restrictive, were immune; enforcement of contracts imposing "direct" restraints on trade, turned on "reasonableness", and the law gave no relief to victims of unfair competition. In applying the Sherman Act, the Courts interpreted 'combination in restraint' liberally, and so they ended the Trust form of market power, and led to the holding company form. This Act was followed up in 1914 by two important Acts – Clayton, which outlawed price discrimination, exclusive and tying contracts, and cross-holding of directorships and stockholdings; and Federal Trade Commission, which prohibited unfair means of competition. These new Acts divided responsibility for the enforcement of the Sherman provisions against market power between the Justice Department and the Commission. Since until 1938 the Commission's orders had to be confirmed by a Federal Court, it had little real power.[5] In 1936 the Robinson-Patman Act strengthened the price-discrimination element in Clayton. One significant tendency in U.S. industry as a result of the anti-Trust laws had been that towards mergers, since cartels were outlawed. Any law against cartels and the like leads to growth of integrated firms, and the 'enhanced development of giant corporations and the relatively heavier expenditures on product innovation and brand-sales promotion'. Underlying the Sherman Act was the desire to protect incentives to competition, rather than to disperse existing market power. Uncompetitive behaviour, not monopoly as such, was considered to be the enemy, but neither Clayton nor the Federal Trade Commission Act did much to change this. The contrasts between the Sherman and Clayton Acts are instructive. Where Sherman was general, Clayton was explicit. Sherman dealt with monopoly as fact, Clayton was more concerned with the *means* of *attaining* monopoly. Where Sherman stresses punishment, Clayton stresses prevention.

The problem of whether practices tending towards monopoly are intrinsically harmful or not, has exercised lawyers for a long time. The whole history of combination cases represents a protracted struggle between the principle of common honesty in private transactions and the stern rule which forbids restraint of trade. Before 1890 there were few cases where third parties sought relief from, or damages for, contracts in restraint of trade. In the Mogul Steamship case, Lord Coleridge spoke of 'the line which separates the reasonable and legitimate selfishness of traders from wrong and malice'. The majority of the Court of Appeal then held that an agreement in restraint was void only and not illegal. A Court decision in 1946 – the 'Tobacco' case, – laid it down for the U.S. that monopoly could be established by evidence of power with intent to use it – actual evidence of exclusion of competitors was unnecessary. It also referred to 'conscious parallel action' between firms. (This decision is the obvious legal counterpart of Sylos-Labini's theoretical point that it is concern with the actions of rivals which is the essence of oligopoly).

The establishment of the Federal Trade Commission in 1914 introduced a new factor into the control of market power. Efficiency and progressiveness enforced by the market, rather than dispensed as largesse by publicly-minded custodians of private power, have been the traditional objectives of American anti-Trust policy, and the division of responsibility for these objectives between the F.T.C. and the Justice Department has been the cause of some friction and ambiguity. In contrast to the Courts, for example, the F.T.C. has always been suspicious of size. Conglomerates were once considered to be harmless, but observation of the tendency towards reciporal buying on the part of conglomerate member firms caused the F.T.C. to change its mind. The different approaches of the Courts and the F.T.C. are reflected in the question of 'soft' competition, which the F.T.C. is widely believed to want, in order to protect small businesses. But 'hard' competition seems to be necessary for technical advance, as is illustrated by the history of U.S. Steel, which at one stage competed 'softly' and so rapidly fell behind technically.

What effect has anti-Trust in fact had on concentration of industry and monopoly in the U.S.? The authorities differ. For Galbraith, anti-Trust is 'a charade':

> 'Anti-Trust...wages a fairly effective war on small firms which seek the same market power which the big firms already, by their nature, possess... In each case, the anti-Trust laws effectively protect the large business from social pressure or regulation by maintaining the myth that the market does the regulating instead. Also, the anti-Trust laws cannot positively alter the basic structure of a capitalist economy... or make satisfactory contact with oligopoly.'

The Reconstruction Finance Corporation, which was liquidated in 1950, was, in his view, probably a more effective contributor to freedom of entry than the anti-Trust laws.[6] There has always been great difficulty even about the scope of legislation. For example, the Robinson-Patman Act deals with firms' actions relating to price only, all the other aspects of non-price competition being outside its scope. Since marketing in the modern sense uses sales promotion rather than competition by price, it is hardly surprising that Kaysen and Turner should conclude that this Act has contributed little towards solving the dilemmas of monopoly control. Keysen agrees that the present anti-Trust set-up cannot cope with market power created by jointly acting oligopolists.[7] But for Dewey, anti-Trust policy has perceptibly reduced concentration. Monopoly, he thinks, has certainly not increased, and has probably decreased, since 1910.[8] J.S. Bain claimed that concentration had been stable since about 1935. Although D.A. Worcester Jr.'s sophisticated empirical enquiry found more concentration in the U.S. than most previous studies did, he discovered no significant evidence of a trend towards further concentration.[9] And the relationship between competition and concentration is complex. Even though there was only one producer of aluminium in the U.S. until after the last war, competition from copper nevertheless drove down the price. In fields such as chemicals or building materials, the number of different product fields in which the firm has a stake may be more important for industry leadership than the percentage of any single product market it holds. Dewey's summing-up is that although the five-fold increase in the anti-Trust Division's budget between 1938 and 1942 was worth more than all the Sherman amendments ever passed, nevertheless the pattern at least to the mid-point of the century was 'legal victory, economic defeat', and the rule that the Courts will not enforce a private agreement that restricts competition remains the supreme achievement of anti-Trust policy in the U.S.[10]

Outside the U.S., the country which comes closest to the American approach to control of monopoly is France. That is, the French use prohibition and provision for invalidity of agreements in restraint of trade instead of what has been described as 'the Principle of Publicity'. This takes its origin from the general European view that limitation of competition is not intrinsically harmful. Some countries, such as Norway, where anti-Trust legislation goes back to 1926, become officially concerned about monopoly only when what is known as a 'dominating enterprise' controls more than a quarter of a market (less if it is the subsidiary of a foreign firm). Others, such as Holland, go so far as to give the Government power to set up compulsory cartels. Activity of this type by Governments originated in Germany, where the first step was taken in making memberships of a failing potash cartel compulsory. Germany, of course, is always associated with cartel-formation, not surprisingly, since the number of cartels there grew from 4 in 1865 to 395 in 1905, although many of them had short lives. This method of organizing industry is so strongly entrenched in German tradition, that the occupying powers even failed in their attempts to outlaw cartels in Germany in 1947.

In Britain, the Commission set up under the Monopolies Act of 1948, seems never to have developed a clear-out set of principles for dealing with the problems:

> 'The Monopolies Commission has not been impressive, on the whole, in its handling of oligopoly enquiries. The Commission has tended to neglect an examination of such critical inter-relationships as those between advertising and potential competition, between brand promotion

and industrial concentration, and between price rigidity and indirect forms of price competition... The Commission has considered a measurement of rate of return on capital to represent the most valid criterion in assessing the public implications of price levels'[11]

And the judgement of the Courts has reflected a prevailing climate of public opinion in which mergers and bigness are acceptable and even approved.

The years of depression between the wars influenced politicans, economists, businessmen and the judiciary in their open encouragement of the rationalization process. 'Under changed post-war conditions the judiciary has shown itself to be least well equipped for a flexible renewal of its inter-war attitudes.'[12]

The impression left from a study of the authorities on how Governments have sought to control monopolies in practice is not one of any great success. The results achieved by anti-Trust activity are meagre compared with the amount of effort which has been devoted to it throughout this century. All the controls that have been instituted operate only *after* the event, and the bringing in of a controlling element almost seems to be effective confirmation that the dynamic area has by then shifted elsewhere. Examples are the way mergers grow when cartels are outlawed, and how sales promotion intensifies as an aspect of a tacit agreement to avoid price competition. There seems to be widespread confusion about both objectives and means to achieve them, and a good deal of evidence that the actual outcome of policies has often been very different indeed from what was intended. In no area has this been more evident than in that of innovation.

What is involved here is an important aspect of the relationship between economic innovation and politics. The authorities are evidently ambiguous in their attitudes towards monopoly, and the most plausible reason for this is that innovation is considered to be important, and contemporary innovation is demonstrably associated with large firms. Where products are traded internationally, a native large firm will be handled gently, so as not to reduce a country's capacity for innovation, with consequent harmful balance-of-payments effects. This attitude is in fact given express legal form in the U.S. by the Webb-Pomarene Act of 1918, which specifically allows firms to perform all the 'collusive' acts abroad, for which they would incur severe penalties at home. It is also significant that in Japan, the Government has power to force firms into cartels for the purpose of penetrating export markets and that these powers are used.

The record of such attempts to control monopoly after it has become established, therefore, is a sorry one. However many civil servants are employed in the task, they are always going to be less dedicated to it, less well led and less flexible in their ways of meeting changed circumstances, than the opposition. For these reasons, a Civil Service body is particularly incapable of controlling market power. The Civil Service, by the nature of its organization and recruitment, is only able to deal with those areas of public life where there is an established body of theory and where the activities are well understood.

This is why public bodies have some ability to control areas like building standards, fire and disease prevention and so on. But in entrepreneurship, the successful practitioners have to be well in advance of the theory, and it is only in retrospect that they can explain what they are doing, if indeed they can ever explain it at all. This is no area in which to expect successful control by a Civil Service, nor has it ever been obtained. We can never know the factors in market power, especially those in marketing, which are bringing about the important changes, until these factors have been superseded by something new, and have become part of a settled body of accepted theory. If there ever was a case of trying to catch your own shadow, it is trying to control monopoly by policing it *ex post*. For example, this type of policing has been powerless to prevent the emergence of the 'virtual cartels' which modern marketing makes possible. None of the 'peaks' of anti-trust achievement during its first half-century – Standard Oil in 1911, U.S. Steel in 1920, American Tobacco in 1946, du Pont 'Cellophane' in 1956, IBM in 1963, related to marketing monopoly. It is only with the Procter and Gamble/Clorox case in 1967 that the Federal Trade Commission can be seen clearly extending its concept of competition so as to take in explicitly the condition of entry to a market as a dimension of market structure. The ultimate Supreme Court judgement in this case took account of two factors which have been noted earlier as important in marketing monopoly – entry barriers and *potential* competition. Yet the exponents of marketing monopoly always seem to be one step ahead of the regulating agencies. It has been suggested that the 'hard' policy towards 'horizontal' mergers between two firms, both of which are market leaders, and 'vertical' ones that involve significant foreclosure, had led to the growth of conglomerate firms, where the products of the acquiring and acquired firms have no apparent economic relationship to each other – Radio Corporation of America's take-over of Hertz Rent-a-Car being an example. If and when the anti-trust authorities become capable of dealing adequately with conglomerates, the dynamic area will presumably be found to have moved elsewhere. In market power's contribution to the growth of bureaucracy must be included the bureaucracy which is concerned with the will-o'-the-wisp of controlling that very power itself.

To get proper control into this area of the economic system, then, there is need to review the whole complex of capital deployment and industrial property legislation, including its extra-national aspects. There is need to place it close to the centre of policy-making, instead of on the periphery, where it is now. And there is need to devise some means of making it continually more sophisticated, so as to keep in step with economic reality as this evolves in practice. There should be all the more concern to achieve this last objective because of awareness that so many current problems exist specifically through failure to do this in the past. This failure, it is insisted, owes much to the way in which Civil Servants abandoned their traditional role as framers of legislation within which others could act fruitfully, in exchange for the one (which paid so much better) of becoming actively involved in extending the role of the State. It is analogous to Benda's *Trahison des Clercs*.[13] It means that no modern Civil Service can contribute to the solution of the problem, since it is itself a major part of the problem. Any solutions will have to come from outside, and they will have to reckon with opposition from forces that should, in truth, be the continuing source of legal reform.

Before offering some practical steps towards such solutions, it is necessary to pay some attention to the claims of two approaches which have the merit of being non-collectivist. The first of these argues for elimination of intellectual and industrial property legislation altogether, in order to achieve, as some people naively think, a return to the competitive system. This is easily dealt with. The competitive system in this sense is an economist's abstraction. It never did exist, and never could exist, in the real world. Monopoly, in its true definition of *any* uniqueness of advantage, there always has been, and without it, what is there to get the economic process started at all, since uncertainty is built into the human condition? Innovation, as has been stressed from Chapter I onwards, depends upon markets *and* upon interference with markets. The second alternative which sometimes calls itself the 'Libertarian' one, attempts to get balance and dynamism into the economy by urging 'market forces' as the means whereby the evident distortions and imbalances resulting from a large State sector can be eliminated. The difficulty is, of course, that the 'free' markets which this approach recommends, are not free, because they have been brought into being by fundamental distortions of market freedom caused by positive law. Markets of the modern type could not exist if positive legal enactments had not created massive capacity to escape from the constraints of market forces, and it is precisely the unbalanced results of this that constitute the problem. The weakness of Liberalism has always lain in overlooking the restrictions on absolute freedom which preserve the liberties which are so highly valued by those who profess it. The freedom which the citizens enjoy, exists solely and precisely because freedoms are denied to the barbarian at the gates. Since the 'market' approach under discussion is a form of economic liberalism, its influence is weakened by characteristic liberal ambiguity. For example, it is against State interference with industry, and argues that business will serve the common good best if it is left alone. This is to ignore the fact that the business almost certainly depends upon a very definite interference by the State in the form of the positive enactments which create special types of property. The same approach is against monopolies, specifically the Patent system, but it accepts the Trade Mark system without question. Yet, as has been seen, Patents are now relatively unimportant compared with Trade Marks. The approach is in favour of advertising, because advertising 'makes for competition' and especially because it has been

> 'predominantly a supporting instrument for successful innovation and its aggressive role in breaking down the established market power of existing products has been persistently stronger than its defensive 'barrier' effect'.[14]

This, of course, begs the important question, what is the value of the type of innovation which is advertising-related? Competition of this kind is competition between elements of the economy that are already greatly privileged by being placed in a position to escape from the constraints which the wider market seeks to impose upon them. The real issue, it is now clear, is not what goes on within these privileged areas where marketing monopoly operates, but *the very existence of these areas in their present form*. If a privileged class is created by positive law, which is more important, the way the privileges are shared out within the fortunate group, or the way the community's resources are divided between the privileged group as a whole, and the others? What really matters is the way in which there is less innovation than is needed in those aspects of economic life to which the Industrial Property laws do not apply, because innovating power is being drained off into those aspects where these laws *are* effective, there to raise the level of activity to a frenetic pitch — 'throwing us from unnecessary challenge to trumped-up response'. Since this is the problem, it is of comparatively little importance that advertising plays a role in the bringing about of competitive innovation within a 'notional cartel'. Such "innovations" do no more than satisfy wants that have been articulated *for* people instead of being articulated by people themselves. The competitive struggle which produces them is unimportant compared with the competition for resources between those sections of the economy which possess market power, on the one hand, and those which lack it, on the other.

It is also characteristic of the same type of intellectual approach to attack the market power of Trades Unions, and to argue for measures which would reduce this power unilaterally. But, as has been seen, the power of Trade Unions is derived, not primary. W.H. Hutt has in fact argued convincingly that they really are unable to force those who have the primary market power to part with more than they think necessary, once decisions whether or not to invest are being made with full knowledge of what the Union's demands will be.[15] Whether this is so, or not, the problem is really what may be called "adversary collusion" between employing firms and Trades Unions, with the objective of extracting as much consumer surplus from the public as possible. It may very well be the case that the derived market power of Trades Unions is a powerful deterrent to investment in innovation, since owners of primary market power may frequently judge that too much of any anticipated return would be diverted to the derived rent of the productive factors, and to taxation. Nevertheless, in setting matters to rights, derived market power cannot be the first target. If the primary market power is brought under control, then whatever is derived from it must automatically be disciplined as well. In the same way, it is the growth of political acceptance of State interventionism that underwrites both derived taxing power and reinforced derived market power. Such acceptance has as a major cause, patterns of innovation and market power in the private sector which are judged to be inhumane, and consequently cause voters to endorse collectivist policies. There will be no shortage of advocacy for these, from both politicians and bureaucrats who stand to gain from their adoption. But if the offending primary market power is removed, a reformed free enterprise system cannot fail to be preferable to socialism. In this, the State apparatus would wither away, until it became matched to those tasks which only the State can perform. Reinforced derived market power would be automatically stifled as a consequence, so that it would eventually become practical politics to deal with the even more serious problem of derived taxing power.

The weakness of Economic Liberalism, from which ideas of the type under review spring, is that it does not look closely enough at its own assumptions. In Economics, as in Politics, indeed, Liberalism is a flower; not a root; it is only possible within a context that it is incapable of constructing or even of keeping in being, on its own. Consequently, in the contemporary crisis, just as the extremes will not do as a solution, neither will tinkering with the existing system on the Liberal model. Reform must be at the level of the foundations, as von Hayek, who is in so many ways the Liberals' mentor, expressed in words that echo Mill:

> 'It seems to me beyond doubt that in these fields (Patents, Copyrights, Trade Marks) a slavish application of the concept of property as it has developed for material things has done a great deal to foster the growth of monopoly, and that here drastic reforms may be needed if competition is to be made to work'.[16]

And yet, however drastic the reforms have to be, they must preserve the one tremendous gain of the haphazard and hardly understood arrangements there have been until now, which is the capacity to turn ideas into concrete realities, or 'The invention of methods of innovation'. Even if the full range of the necessary reforms is beyond any individual's power to visualise at this stage, it is at least possible to outline certain changes that could be of immediate benefit, and which fit within certain general guidelines.

Of these guidelines, by far the most certain is that solutions must be non-bureaucratic. It should be clear from everything that has gone before that where innovation is concerned, any attempt to impose real control by the establishment of regulatory agencies is likely to be doomed to failure. And the evidence, recited in earlier chapters, including the judgement of such experts as Galbraith and Dewey, is that it has failed. Galbraith, it will be recalled, holds that all that anti-trust succeeds in doing is preventing smaller firms from reaching the impregnably privileged position of the giant firms, and Dewey has argued convincingly that its operations involve an actual welfare loss:

> 'The thrust of these diverse views (of Galbraith, Berle and others) is much the same: anti-trust is a monumental irrelevancy. At best, it does nothing but squander a few million dollars of resources annually. At worst it has the capacity for considerably more mischief.'[17]

This is the actual situation, since as soon as a member of a regulatory agency shows himself to be a serious threat, he is enticed into the opposing ranks by the vastly greater rewards open to him there. The example of the individual who was enticed into the President's chair of Pan-American airlines from his job as head of the Civil Aeronautics Board, is only one of many that could be quoted. Also, although the following comment relates directly to pollution; it has a much wider application:

'As long as cleaning up pollution is left to the politicians, there is grave danger that whatever Federal Pollution Control Commission is set up will go the way of the FCC, the FDA, the ICC, the CAB and virtually all other federal, State and local licensing agencies. In case after case, the ordinary citizen has seen the regulators quickly become tools of those whom they supposedly regulate. Corruption and the protection of special interest creep in, and public service drops to last priority...whenever possible the price system for pollution control should be instituted *not* by administrative means, but by modifications of our legal system and the extension of the property rights of individuals.'[18]

There is also the cost aspect. With the present system, the public is paying twice for excesses which it does not want at all, firstly for them to be perpetrated, secondly for the attempts to control or eliminate them. In many countries, publicly-financed advertising campaigns have been mounted to persuade people that smoking is a health hazard, i.e. to counteract the advertising of the tobacco firms. This is highly illogical, considering that these firms' power to invest in advertising in the first place, is a direct result of the positive law which enables them to register their Trade Marks: Government provides the essential legal condition for the creation of a monopoly; when the results of this monopoly are proved to be harmful to the public, Government then spends money, raised from the public through taxation, to counteract the results of the monopoly which it has itself made possible through positive legislation. It would obviously be vastly more effective, and would save two sets of costs, to exclude cigarettes from the benefit of the Trade Marks Acts. If this were done, advertising in the modern sense would instantly become impossible as far as cigarette brands are concerned. Whatever the basic human need to which smoking caters, may be, the resources of the mass media would no longer be able to be used for articulating it into 'want for a particular brand of cigarette'. The psychological pressure from the cigarette firms would be relaxed, the market would drop off in so far as it depends upon this pressure, and Governments' objective of protecting the health of the public from an adverse influence, would be achieved without increasing their costs.

Note also that with this method, there has been no diminution in either individual or corporate freedom. Nobody who wants to smoke cigarettes is prevented from doing so; no firm is prevented from making cigarettes and selling them to him. Nor is such a firm prevented from building up its reputation, and using advertising to do so, under the protection of Unfair Competition law, or Common Law. The process, of course, would be much slower than it is now, and the advertising would be different, since its objective would be to build up a link between the firm and the brand in the public's mind, so as to enable a claim to exclusive rights to the brand name to be sustained in the Courts. It could be foreseen, too, that this type of litigation might become a substantial cost item in the firm's accounts. For these reasons, new brands would be infrequent, trade would tend to be local rather than national, and more national than international, as far as the finished products are concerned. The market for cigarettes would be seriously constrained by competition from alternative products which contribute to the satisfaction of the same basic need, such as sugar confectionery. The makers of these alternative products would retain important advantages in that their advertising, relieved as it is through Trade Mark registration from the need to build up any link between a brand name and a firm, could still be directed towards linking the brand name with other things which have a positive selling value, such as manliness, or sex, or prestige. Naturally, the cigarette firms would feel that they had been unfairly treated, but what has been taken away from them is a privilege, not a right. Any unfairness can then consist only in taking it away from the cigarette firms without doing so for all firms, and this could be justified in their case on the ground that cigarettes have been proved to be harmful to health, whereas the other firms' products have not. What Government would be effectively saying is this:

'The monopoly created by positive Industrial Property law is an essential technical economic device for ensuring that there will be innovation. In the present circumstances of the tobacco industry, this means innovation in 'psychological ingredient', on the selling side rather than on the production side; that is, it largely means finding new ways of articulating some human need or a combination of human needs, into demand for a particular brand of cigarettes. Because of what our scientists have told us about smoking and health, we see no justification for innovation on the selling side in this industry, and therefore will no longer extend the privilege of Trade Mark registration to it.'

The example of cigarettes quoted is a simple and clear-out issue, on which politicians could easily decide, almost in the way that the Crown Law Officers in England, or the President's Office itself in the United States, decided about Patents before the setting up of the Patent Office. But for any general use of the *ex ante* method of control, there must be regulatory agencies, which would, of course, be concerned with the issue of monopolies before these have been embodied in concrete reality, and with policing them as they grow, rather than vainly trying to do this when they are fully mature, with all the indirect political power which they can then bring to bear. Immediately, this raises the spectre of a regulatory agency itself getting out of hand; 'If democracy resolves on a task which cannot be guided by fixed rules, it must become arbitrary power'.[19] This danger must be squarely faced.

The model for all such agencies must be the Patent Office, since this is the institution which already has most corporate experience of dealing with monopolies *ex ante*. The process of shifting the mechanism of control from after the fact to before it, would make all the existing *ex post* regulatory agencies – Federal Trade Commission, Monopolies Commission, relevant sections of Departments of Justice, Fair Trade Commissions and the like, more like the Patent Office. What it would be essential to preserve, however, would be a multiplicity of agencies with the capacity to grant market power. Only in this way can some element of the discipline of competition be brought to bear upon their bureaucracies. There can be no doubt, for example, that negative attitudes which those who have advocated various reforms of the Patent system in the past, have faced, are due to the fact that in every country, the Patent Office is itself a monopoly. The danger of misuse of power by any of the monopoly-granting agencies, would be further lessened if money could be made the measure of any such grant, instead of time. This point will be developed further below.

The choice seems to be between market power which *is* out of control, and a regulatory authority which *may* become so. The Courts, after all, in many countries, are a regulatory force whose power may be regarded as unlimited in one sense, since it can constrain Government itself by declaring its actions 'unconstitutional'. Yet there is no agitation for the abolition of the Courts, based on their misuse of this power. The method of recruiting the men who exercise it, the Judges, sometimes involves selecting them from the ranks of practising lawyers. Lawyers may be no worse than other people, but they are certainly no better. If men capable of exercising such great power can be recruited from amongst lawyers, then they can be recruited from the practising body of any profession. There can be some optimism, therefore, that extension of the powers of existing regulatory bodies would not break down on the single ground of the calibre of the people administering them, *especially if they were exercising these powers ex ante instead of ex post*. Also, the decisions of these bodies would presumably remain subject to ultimate review by the Courts, as they are at present. Part of any reform package would have to be means whereby this appeal to the Courts does not continue to be the tremendous advantage to large firms that it is now. The small firm's or individual's Patent, for example, is very much limited in value precisely because of this power of appeal. If a large firm infringes the Patent, the legal costs of defending it, coupled with the low probability of success, will probably intimidate the smaller firm from taking legal action, especially if the larger firm's management makes it clear that they will use the very many stratagems open to them for making the litigation more costly for their opponents. No form of free legal aid is likely to be the answer, as this would clog up the Courts by making appeal the rule when it ought to be the exception. A better approach might be an independent public body whose function it would be to provide a continuing process of clarification of all Monopoly laws by prosecuting cases in the Courts to test the validity of industrial property grants. Infringement of a Patent, for example, might be dealt with originally under the Patent Office's own internal appeal system. A firm or individual that was dissatisfied with a decision there, could then bring the case to the independent review body, especially if clarification of some aspect of the decision could help to produce a better Law. The review body would then decide for or against bringing the matter before the appropriate Court. In a sense, it would be adding to the present widely-used arrangements for 'leave-to-appeal', the necessary provision for granting 'resources to appeal', without which they are largely pointless.

For the reasons explained in the previous chapter, it is difficult to see how the officials to staff such a regulatory agency could be drawn from "modern" Civil Servants. The agency's brief would deny it power of active involvement, forcing it instead to develop law in ways that provide an effective context within which men of action can operate, and in operating serve the common good; but those who formulate the law must be removed from the temptation to act themselves. Once it is known that there must be monopoly if there is to be innovation, that property can have its meaning and reality extended through positive law, and that great benefits can follow from such an extension, the task is to see that it is properly controlled – controlled, above all, with understanding of what property is, what it does, and what diverse forms it can take. The control of property in this sense is now one of the supreme tasks of any Western Government, and in a democratic society, it is a task which falls as much upon the permanent Civil Service as on politicians. Both groups have failed, because both groups at heart, now believe in Big Government. The creation, maintenance and supervision of property rights can only be performed by men who are totally convinced of the case for economic freedom and against expansion of the role of the State.

The spirit which should inform the exercise of control over monopoly, has been implicit in some law for a long time. In Britain, when the 1624 Statute of Monopolies specifically left open the possibility of monopoly grants for 'new manufacture within this realm', in what was otherwise a wholesale clearing-out of monopolies, it was recognising the intrinsic nature and value of monopoly. Its function is to provide a means of obtaining an above-average return on an investment in getting something new done, with the above-average risks that this involves, no more, no less. If there is no monopoly, the new thing cannot be done; if monopoly has no relationship to the risks inevitable with new things, it should be extinguished as was done with all other monopolies by the 1624 Statute. English law, therefore, and the law of all countries which took it as their model, already contains an explicit principle for dealing with monopoly: Either monopoly contributes to innovation, or it is harmful. Modern man now knows that the phrase 'new manufactures' can include all sorts of things and services which were undreamed of in 1624, and he also knows that these can be encouraged in many different ways besides a straight Patent grant. The relationship between monopoly and innovation, however, remains unchanged. We may know more than our ancestors, because we are standing on their shoulders, but the unknown remains every bit as daunting as ever it was, and there must be hope of big prizes to be won if prudent men are to invest money in exploring it.

Consequently, in modifying legal arrangements so as to deal with unbalanced innovation, care must be taken that the overall attraction of investment into production is not reduced. If the reforms work, policies that are now attractive to large firms, because they can count upon capability market power to protect the results of their investment, will then be less attractive to them, because that power will probably be reduced, and will certainly be restricted to fewer areas than those in which it is dominant now. But at the same time, investment in information production will become more attractive to smaller firms, partnerships and even individuals, because the power of the official means of information protection will be greater, and its range will be expanded compared with the present. Of the possible areas of reform, by far the most practical in the short term is that of Patents, because valuable changes in that area could *add* to existing arrangements instead of replacing them. As such, they will meet less opposition from vested interests. Their success could lead on to changes in Trade Mark law, to modify the market power of persuasion. In that case some existing interests could be adversely affected, but it would be possible by then to show how extension of the principle of Patenting had opened up whole new opportunities for investment, in order to overcome resistance. Reform of capability market power should be left until last, because this involves most modification of existing property rights. The 'capital deployment' laws may be amongst the hardest to change. It could be hoped, however, that by the time these come to be tackled, the evidence which will have accumulated of the value of "making property only out of things that should be property", to adapt Mill's phrase, will be so conclusive as to make the necessary changes politically acceptable.

Beginning by extending the principle of Patenting has one powerful and immediate attraction for Western countries: It puts into the hands of their industrialists their only possible means of responding effectively to pressure from Japan. This arises from the point stressed in previous chapters, that Schumpeter's dictum that monopoly is essential for innovation is also true in reverse. Wherever there is monopoly, innovation will follow, because it will be possible to invest at high risk in the hope of high reward. For this reason, any failure to develop a particular type of market power, does not mean there will be no innovation. It only means that whatever innovation there is, will be brought about under some alternative market power system. Failure to extend the Specific market power of the Patent system has simply meant that innovations have come about through capability and persuasive market power. More particularly, the world's Patent systems have progressively moved away from protecting B-phase or incremental innovation. This movement has been reflected in replacement of the criterion of relative novelty by that of absolute novelty, and by examining for "obviousness". Rejection of a Patent application on the ground that its subject-matter is already known in some other country or that it "would be obvious to one skilled in the Art" is clearly less likely to apply to the big, original breakthroughs of A-phase or originative invention. It is very likely indeed to apply to the small, often simple changes of incremental innovation, with the result that these have had to be protected, not by Patents, but by Capability market power, sometimes reinforced by Persuasive market power and Secrecy also. With its Zaibatsu/Keiretsu linkages, Japan now has an unbeatable system for using capability market power to protect its B-phase (i.e. incremental) innovations. Western countries have no hope of matching this, and thus feel condemned to see themselves progressively deprived of the power to innovate competitively. This is all the worse, because it is only over the long time-scale of incremental innovations, that the profits of the earlier originative innovations are reaped. But if the principle of Patenting can be extended so as to give explicit protection to incremental innovation, the Japanese stranglehold is broken, and Western capacity to invent is once again matched by a corresponding capacity to invest, innovate and capture the rewards of innovation. Any attempt to achieve the same end by copying the Japanese system is doomed to failure, since Western countries simply do not have the required degree of social cohesion. The Western tradition is an individualistic one, and the Patent is a classic social innovation, designed to produce rewards for individual effort. If, therefore, there is a genuine Western solution to the problem of protecting incremental innovation, it is more likely to be found in extending the principle of Patenting then in any other way.

Wherever electorates have invited even a tentative move away from big government, it has been found that the pressure of Japanese capability in home as well as export markets is still a major obstacle to rolling back the power of the State. Policy changes which do not go beyond attempts simply to return to an earlier and freer type of economy result, under present conditions of international competition, only in business decline and unemployment. Indeed, there is now a risk that the levels of these might cause voters to turn back to support for interventionism − and Japan would suffer as much from this as any country, since it would undoubtedly be accompanied by import controls. All OECD countries therefore have an interest in preventing this happening. Nothing except productive investment on a very large scale can cure recession, but this can come about only if there is the prospect of profits. This means in practice that the investment must be such as to result in new products that can be expected to compete with the best available. There can be no future in making the old products in the old ways, in a world where the Japanese have established such a lead in robotics. Even if politicians do try bravely to cut public expenditure, therefore, the needed private investment will not come about automatically. Because of the intensity of competition, combined with the damage done to economies during the long years of public sector growth, a special stimulus is necessary. That stimulus can be nothing other than some means of making innovation profitable for a vastly increased number of firms. In Western countries it can be provided by – and probably only by – developments in intellectual and industrial property.

It is clear that improvement of company profitability by weakening those factors which cut down the residual to the primary market power must be a long term matter. Nor can it be expected that the excesses of derived market power can be controlled until the distortions of primary market power are corrected. But if these factors can at least be prevented from increasing in strength, it is open to any Government to improve profitability levels at a stroke by modifying the laws which underwrite market power. Initially, such an improvement may be potential rather than actual, but it is potential profitability that matters for investment, and it is investment that is of supreme importance now.

There can be no argument as to the legal changes that are most urgently required: Firstly, those that will justify massive innovation in all aspects of energy, and secondly, those that will provide a counterweight in terms of Specific market power to Japan's unmatchable market power of Capability. Only such changes can bring about private sector investment in innovation at the rate that is needed, a rate unheard of in recent years. Nothing else has the power to sustain and expand manufacturing employment in Western countries, and, in the longer term, to arrest and reverse economic depression.

Everywhere, the way in which innovation has been the worst casualty of public sector growth can be quantified by the historically clear inverse relationship between the Public Sector Borrowing Requirement and the availability of venture capital. Investment in innovation simply does not pay, as the law stands at present, except for the very few firms that are working on the frontiers of technology, and have Capability market power to back up their patents. Lending to Governments is much more attractive.

The orginal function of patents has changed over the years in ways that make them a reinforcement of the Capability market power of established, and generally large and multinational firms, rather than, as they should be (and indeed as they were, especially at the end of the last century) the basis for the establishment of new businesses. Patents, as discussed earlier, have become a second currency for the largest firms, and cross-licensing between these keeps other firms from being able to buy into new technology simply with money – a formidable entry barrier. And this change in the nature of patents has been blindly followed by countries which are the homes of few, if any, multinationals, in disregard of their own economic interests. Nothing is easier to demonstrate, for example, than that the 'updating' of British patent law in 1977 must be of far greater benefit to the advanced technology firms of the U.S., Germany and Japan than it can ever be to United Kingdom firms in general.

In making it possible for patents to generate, in the words of the British Statute of Monopolies in 1624, 'new manufacture within this realm' on the scale required, what is needed is a means of granting a kind of legal protection that will justify investment in the innovatory process *after* the R & D stage. Even in successful cases, this may be up to one hundred times the R & D investment before a return on capital is seen, and at present, it is only the market power of Capability that can provide adequate incentives for taking the risks involved. Legal provisions requiring absolute novelty and non-obviousness limit the Specific market power in terms of patent protection that is available for this purpose. To the extent that Capability market power has now come to be held overwhelmingly by Japan, then the answer for other countries can only be to create a new type of Specific market power that will underwrite investment 'downstream' of R & D. This is precisely the kind of investment that is most needed now to cope with the recession, both in terms of scale of financing, and of the types of employment it can generate. It could be stimulated virtually overnight by extending the principle of Patenting, and no other single change has anything like the same power to improve company profitability to such an extent or so quickly, and thus give time for the other structural changes that are needed, to be made.

Extending the legal protection for investment in innovation also offers what may be the only means for rendering structural changes in economies, especially those which must inevitably reduce the derived market power of trade unions, politically acceptable. A combination of low company profitability, high taxation and trade union market power, and a legal regime that is quite inadequate for attracting investment on a large scale into innovation, only means growth in unemployment from new technologies, exports decline and import penetration. In contrast, if a link can be forged between high profitability and high investment in innovation, the spectre of unemployment on a large scale is banished, because innovation can provide all the jobs that can ever be needed. From his detailed studies of the U.S. economy, for example, Rostow is confident.

> 'that authentic investment requirements in resource-related fields exceed the levels of investment required for sustained full employment over the next decade, and would require the setting of priorities'.[20]

The only limit is the extent to which the State increases taxation and derived market power increases labour costs unrealistically, thus reducing company profitability. If the legal structure is right, then high profits will be re-attracted into investment in innovation to a significant extent. Any technological unemployment remaining would consequently be the direct responsibility of the trade unions. They cannot be blamed for it at present, because there is no reason for profits to be invested in innovation to-day.

The culprit is quite simply the fact that, under the present balance of the different components of market power, investment in innovation is only barely a rational activity for a business man, and this results in the paradox of firms that are flush with liquid assets complaining of lack of opportunities for profitable investment. No firm, for example, has shown itself better able to make money during general economic decline than the British General Electric Company. It holds huge reserves in cash, yet is notoriously shy of R & D which has anything but short times to pay-off. In remedying this situation, extension of the principle of Patenting is the most attractive option available.

Over the years, as a result of dissatisfaction with the Patent system, various suggestions for its reform have been put forward. It is unnecessary to deal with any of the changes which have been advocated or brought about by Patent Offices themselves, or by their Trade Association, BIRPPI (International Union for the Protection of Industrial Property) and its successor WIPO (World Intellectual Property Organization) which do not seek to go beyond ways of making the existing system work better. Just as the basic provision of the International Convention for the Protection of Industrial Property, the equality of the citizens of any member country before the industrial property laws of all, has remained unchanged since 1883, so the Patent systems of all countries are still to be found substantially in the Venetian law of 1474. Some incremental changes have been referred to earlier, e.g. the way in which the U.S. system has abandoned the requirement for a 'flash of genius' in invention, because of the reality that so much modern 'invention' is rather the result of uninspired, painstaking research. Others include the development of a large degree of uniformity in national Patent laws, mainly due to the existence of the International Convention's Secretariat, to the direction in which the United Nations and similar bodies nudge the legislation of the newer countries, to developments such as the Patent Co-Operation Treaty, which is the culmination of various bilateral search exchange programmes and will eliminate much duplication of searching by national Patent Offices, and the establishment of a central Patent Office for the E.E.C. All of these changes leave the fundamentals of the Patent system untouched.

During the nineteenth century, however, proposals for economic reform were advanced that involved virtual destruction of this system. In Britain, it was being so incompetently run that the opposition to it was vehement. Significantly, its strongest critics were those with Capability market power. The great railroad and steamship engineer, Brunel, claimed that it actually frustrated technological innovation. More than half of all Patents tested in the Courts were declared invalid. However, a parallel movement for reform of the system obtained an Act in 1852 which simplified administrative procedures, and the great Patents, Designs and Trade Marks Act of 1883 finally silenced the critics.[21]

In the Netherlands, the objections to the Patent system were taken so seriously that is was abolished in 1869. As the system was revived in 1912, the Dutch experience ought to provide something like a controlled experiment in the economic importance of Patent monopolies. Switzerland is a somewhat similar case, since that country was extremely dilatory about introducing a modern Patent system, and in fact only did so, under German pressure, as late as 1907. One study of both these countries in their 'Patentless'' periods found no sign that their economic growth was slower than it might have been with a Patent law, and conflicting evidence as to whether there might have been an extra spur to local inventiveness if Patent protection had been available. At first sight, this seems to conflict with the views of Ravenshear, who thought that the Dutch record showed that Patents were necessary, in that whilst that country's total exports from 1884-1904 went up 136% against 98% for U.S. and 22% for Switzerland, exports of Dutch *manufactured* products only went up 52.7%. Dutch exports of manufactures in the relevant period went up as much as they did, he claims, because they involved 'intensive' innovation (learning by doing) which is independent of the Patent system. He also states that without Patent protection, English output of wheat over the nineteenth century went from 8 to 30 bushels an acre and milk from 80 to 270 gallons an acre.[22] This can undermine his argument about Patents, since it is known that the nineteenth century was a period of rapid improvement in agricultural organization. Social innovations such as Co-operatives and also new sources of artifical fertilisers were only two of many factors in this. Looking through the figures, the reality behind them might not be a relatively poor performance by industry due to lack of a Patent system, but a superlatively good performance by agriculture. In the present state of our knowledge, then, neither the Dutch experiment nor Swiss suspicion of Patents give decisive aid in assessing that particular type of economic reform which consists in abolishing the Patent system altogether. It seems reasonable to assume, however, that since other types of market power have in any event been replacing Patenting as a means of internalizing the externalities of information production, to eliminate Patents would intensify this trend. The dependence of innovation on capability and persuasive market power would then become total.

Other reforms were proposed by Professor Plant and Polanyi and may be treated together.[23] These were based upon the belief that the need to put invention into the strait-jacket of Patent claims in order to be able to administer it at all, ran counter to the very nature of invention. Polanyi therefore revived a proposal for replacement of the system by awards made by a public body, which had been advanced by R.A. MacFie in the 1840s.[24] (To a limited extent, this was eventually done by the Royal Commission on Awards to Inventors which was set up in Britain after each of the World Wars). On the face of it, this system seems to have advantages for inventors, but it does little or nothing for investors. The problem of getting an above-average return for above-average risk remains. It can be said of the Patent system (or at least it could be said of it in its best days) that at least in some cases it does produce commensurate rewards for a risky investment. Because of the optimism of business men, the tendency is for the chances of obtaining one of these spectacular prizes to be over-estimated. However little venture capital is brought out by Patents, therefore, it is more than the overall returns actually justify. The apparent ease of obtaining money for some kinds of innovation, once investors had become aware of the fortunes made by Edison's earlier

backers, seems to be an illustration of this. The Polanyi-Plant proposals for reform might give more justice to inventors in the abstract than the Patent system
does, and yet do economic harm by removing even the present very inadequate
'baits that lure capital on to untried trails', in Schumpeter's phrase. There can
be no escaping the reality that what the public wants is not the new idea, but the
new idea realized in concrete form. Finding the oil in itself benefits nobody;
only getting it out and distributed does.

S.C. Gilfillan also worked out a set of proposals for radical reform of the
Patent system.[25] These are 'to grant Patents on more favourable terms to
licensed, semi-public, non-monopolistic trade associations, than to non-co-
operating patentees'. The advantages he claims for this approach include
making unlimited funds available for research; optimizing Patent pooling;
eliminating secrecy, invention-suppression and duplication of research; and
encouragement of small firms. There are, however, serious objections to
Gilfillan's scheme. Information that is equally available to all members of a
trade association can never be information on which a risky investment in
realizing it can be based, since there is no monopoly. Three illustrations of this
may be quoted: Firstly, the example of Tolstoy already mentioned in *Invention and Monopoly*. Because he forewent his copyrights on philanthropic
grounds, nobody could afford to publish his work until his wife took the
matter in hand, and had his quixotic gesture revoked. The State of Kansas used
to keep the Patents obtained by its public (mainly agricultural) research
services open for use by all comers, but found that there was no interest in
them. When it adopted a policy of granting single exclusive licences, its Patents
started to be exploited. The U.S. Baruch Commission recommended that
exclusive licences should be granted on publicly-owned Patents, since without
exclusivity they were being left unexploited by industry.

Almost all countries except the U.S. now have provisions in their Patent Law
for the grant of compulsory licences as a result of some form of abuse of the
Patent monopoly, such as not working the invention in the particular country.
Virtually no use is made of this part of the law. The reason is evident: Such a
licence does indeed break the monopoly of the patentee, but it does not give
one to the objectors. (It would be interesting to know the source of such applications as there were, to see whether a guess that they were from firms whose
real uniqueness of advantage lay in the market power of capability or persuasion, rather than in Patents, is close to the mark). Similar evidence comes
from the history of Licences of Right, which are to be found in all countries
which operate a Patent system of the British model. A patentee can save half
his renewal fees by readiness to grant a licence to anyone who asks for it, on
terms to be fixed by the Comptroller of the Patent Office if the parties cannot
agree. This provision is little used, presumably for the same reasons as apply in
the case of compulsory licences. All this evidence suggests that Gilfillan's
'Trade Association' proposals would fail because they would dilute the
amount of monopoly actually obtainable. Another major objection to

them is that they provide no opportunity for the 'champion', who has been shown to be an essential element in the innovative process. Trade Associations have never been noted for invention or innovation, and the most likely reason is that they do not provide the right 'ecology' for the innovator to flourish. A Trade Association is analogous to a convoy, whose speed has to be that of the slowest ship, whereas the innovator is like the independent raider who relies upon resourcefulness and speed to achieve his objectives. The two do not mix, and neither do innovators and Trade Associations. Gilfillan did implicitly recognise some of the drawbacks of what he had in mind, because he accepted the importance of monopoly:

> 'To distill into a simple formula our observations on custom-barred invention, we should say that the power to invent, or in any way to change things abruptly, is inseparable from ownership or control over all those things that must be changed to use the invention, including even part of the education, thoughts and activities of those who must use the novelty. If invention be thus inseparable from ownership or authority, it follows that where there is no ownership, no invention can be brought into use, wherefore no one will spend much time nor any money to invest and perfect that obviously unadoptable invention. In still fewer words, without requisite ownership or preempted control, bold invention is impossible.'[26]

Elsewhere he refers to 'large production' and the 'monopoly of the organized industry', which are, of course, nothing else than the barriers to competition raised by the firm's fixed costs, or capability market power. His reference to "education, thoughts and activities" is an interesting restatement of the concept of psychological ingredient as the characteristic of persuasive market power.

Some of the most original and thoroughly worked out proposals for reform of the Patent system ever to have been advanced are those of Dr. Hermann Kronz.[27] Firmly rooted in the belief that what is needed is protection of innovation rather than invention, these ideas concentrate on "the immediately utilizable object of the innovation and the first act of commercial exploitation". Anything that can make a 'net social contribution' is to be patentable, if it has not been used previously in the "home" territory. This territory could be larger or smaller than a country, e.g. it might be only a region, or it might be a group of countries. There would be no examination for obviousness, but objections from third parties would naturally play a large part in the examination procedure. The term of the Patent would be decided from case to case. Since the object of the reforms is to enable ideas to be realized in the concrete, it would only be appropriate to grant the new type of protection to those with the resources necessary for this. In cases where individuals or firms lack these, they can nevertheless qualify for a Patent by making a contract with a "substitute innovator" who can provide them. Much more will have to be said about Dr. Kronz's ideas below.

Of the proposals which follow, those for changing from time to money as a measure of a Patent grant and for public policing of grants, were advanced as long ago as 1967. Those which offer an alternative to Capability market power (and hence now a means of combatting Japan's unmatchable possession of this) are more recent, having been circulated privately since 1979 and first published in 1981.[28]

The first point to be made about these proposals for extending the principle of Patenting so as to stimulate investment, is that they do not affect existing patent arrangements at all. The latter are specifically directed towards protecting invention, whereas what is now needed is a means of granting monopolies that will make a rational activity out of investment in innovation, especially of the incremental type.

This must mean in the first instance, protection for 'combinations' that are 'obvious to one skilled in the art', and therefore unpatentable under present arrangements. Amongst these would be most of the improvements to products and processes which are individually small, but cumulatively of supreme economic importance. The managements of large numbers of Western firms see perfectly clearly what the next stage of incremental development of the products in their field must be. But they are paralysed by the fear that if they do design, and tool up for, the improved product, they will find themselves submerged by the capability market power of a competitor (most likely Japanese) long before any kind of return on the investment has been earned. If this fear is removed by extending the principle of Patenting appropriately, such firms are immediately enabled, not merely to match, but to leapfrog the very best of the present international competition. The consequent freeing of resources of men and money that are currently frustrated could have dramatic consequences for both investment and employment.

The primary characteristic of the new type of industrial property which is proposed, is that the monopoly granted should be explicitly linked to the making of an investment, thus pulling the system back towards its original objective of underwriting 'new manufacture'. For this reason, it was originally called an "Investment Patent". As such, although conceived in ignorance of Kronz's work, it has a remarkable resemblance to his "Patent for Innovation". A change of title appeared to be required once it was understood that there might be advantage to both types of protection system if the new one functioned in some other way than through the Patent Office. In the English-speaking world, Letters Patent and Warrants have for long existed in parallel, so the title 'Innovation Warrant' would be well rooted in history. "Innovation Certificate", as an alternative title to "Innovation Warrant", lends itself more easily to translation into other languages. The Innovation Warrant, as will be seen, could in fact be handled by whatever section of government already deals with encouragement of industry and employment. It has already been argued that any competitive elements that can be introduced into the public bureaucracy can only contribute to its efficiency, and that consequently any monopoly-granting institutions in the State should be independent of each other. According to this principle, then, the Trade Mark Office should be independent of the Patent Office, and this independence would reflect the competition between Persuasion and one type of Specific market power. If a new Innovation Office administered Innovation Warrants, this would similarly underline the distinction between invention and innovation, whilst the separate Companies Office would continue to look after most aspects of Capability market power.

Secondly, money is introduced as a measure of the monopoly that is granted. It is an indication of how poorly all patent systems have kept up with changing circumstances that their measure is still only time — substantially the two terms of apprenticeship of the early grants which were thought necessary for new technology to take root. But the true measure of any monopoly cannot be anything except money. In the early days of patents, there was obviously no practical alternative to time as a measure, but never to change from it has meant ignoring all the achievements of accountancy in the interim. However, since the proposed change is to arrangements which have persisted for so long as to be venerable it is recognized that strong arguments will need to be advanced to justify it.

These arguments begin with acceptance that one of the outstanding achievements of the nineteenth century was undoubtedly the discovery of the power of legally-created monopoly in relation to innovation. Its effect was to extend the range of legal protection of information, and thus the extent and fruitfulness of investment in information production. But in so far as there has been failure to understand what was happening, economic life has been dominated by market power and by the results of market power. This is akin to what happens in all scientific discovery, in which the scientist's early attention to a particular aspect of reality is often an experience of being oppressed by it; the excitement of discovery in science results from the replacement of this oppressive feeling by vision. Previously the research worker was dominated by his material, now he dominates it. Now, in this process of growth in understanding, which is the replacement of subjection by power, and essential tool is measurement: "We grow in pace", said Lord Kelvin, "with the precision of our measures". In the case of monopoly, one reason why there has been so little growth, is that the measures of monopoly, so far from being precise, have been very primitive, or even non-existent. In the case of Trade Marks, there is no measure of monopoly at all. The law allows registration, which is the foundation on which a barrier to entry can be built. There is no limit in the strength of this foundation to the scale of such a barrier. The static monopoly can support any degree of dynamic monopoly. Registered Trade Mark protection in Law is no different for a purely local brand, from what it would be, when, by massive investment in marketing research and advertising, use of the product sold under the brand, has been developed into a national habit. A Trade Mark can be renewed indefinitely, and the fees for keeping its registration in force are the same for the brand that identifies the output of a small workshop, as for the name which is a household word. Marketing monopoly rests on a legal foundation that involves no limit to its growth, and gives no measure of it. Once the law has provided the foundation for the construction of a barrier to entry by competitors, it is not concerned with how strong or how high this entry barrier may be. The State grants the potential for marketing power without strings attached.

This is not the case with Patents. Here there *is* a limit and a measure, but it is a very crude one indeed. A Patent is granted for a fixed term of years, irrespective of differences in technologies or need for protection. A toy which will have no more than a few months vogue, if it is patentable, will get just the same number of years' monopoly as an important 'originative' invention. In some cases, the period of protection is very much more than required, in others very much less. As technology becomes more complex, the gap from original idea to financial return becomes longer in time, but the Patent monopoly remains unchanged. Some Patent systems of the British type try to provide for this by allowing an extension in the term of the Patent for, say, up to 10 years, on the ground that the patentee has received less return during the basic period of protection that he ought to have done. An example is the 'droop snoot' of the Concorde supersonic airliner, the nose which moves downwards to let the pilot make a visual landing and upwards to minimise drag when flying at full speed. This was essential to the concept of this aircraft from the design stage, but so long was the time from original design to production even of prototypes, that the Patent protection would have expired altogether before the device could be used, if it had not been extended by the Court. The fixed term of the Patent system often therefore provides protection when it is no longer needed; in the opposite sense, the delays of up to five years in granting Patents in some countries mean that many inventions do not get protection when they most need it – in the early years. Evidence to the Baruch Committee on Innovation in the U.S., was to the effect that up to seven years' protection are now effectively lost from the Patent grant for pharmaceutical products by Certification procedures. As a measure of monopoly, the fixed term of the Patent system is about as crude as could be devised. What is worse, there is official satisfaction at this very crudeness: 'In our view' the Banks Committee on the Patent system in Britain reported, 'the Patent system is not meant to guarantee a reward to the inventor which purports to be commensurate with the merits of his invention'.[29]

As has been stressed earlier, rewarding the inventor is comparatively unimportant, because the human urge to keep on finding new things is apparently inextinguishable. The person who needs to be rewarded is the *investor*, whose action (which increasingly includes providing the inventor with the resources he needs if he is to be able to work at all) gets the new thing done. He is an investor precisely because he looks for returns that *are* commensurate with the risks he takes. Faced with an official stance such as that of the Banks

Committee, is it any wonder that sane and rational business men turn their backs on the Patent system and look to other types of monopoly for the protection they need to have? The opposite of Kelvin's dictum is probably equally true and applies to the replacement of Patenting by these other types of monopoly. We decline in pace with the *imprecision* of our measures.

It is not only that time is a quite inadequate measure of monopoly, as the Patent system shows. Since what is risked in the innovation process is measured by money, nothing except money can be an adequate measure of the outcome. Scarce resources can be invested in information production only if there will be legal protection for the information produced so that it earns a return. Von Hippel has shown that it is actually possible to predict where innovation will take place, according to where investors can capture the resulting benefits.[30] Money is the measure of scarce resources, so the proper measure of the result of legal protection for information can be nothing else than money, not time nor anything else. As long as legal monopolies are measured in terms of time, as in the case of Patents, economic life is as bound to be dominated by monopoly as a scientist who tackles a problem with a child's ruler and a kitchen scales as measuring instruments is bound to remain dominated by his material. Only when there is a start to measuring monopoly in terms of money, will there be a measure with the required degree of precision to make an advance. The first thrust of the industrial revolution would have led nowhere without the work of Henry Maudslay in developing means of precision measurement. In a parallel way, what is now required is a true yardstick for monopoly. All administrative difficulties in bringing it about are utterly unimportant compared with this.

Another reason why it is vital to move to money instead of time as the measure of Patent monopoly, is that Patents must be enormously strengthened, if they are to provide a basis for investment at high risk, that business men will take seriously. But, if they were strengthened sufficiently without changing the time measure, Patent examiners would find themselves in the position of being the effective arbiters of the destination of huge sums of money. For all the reasons discussed earlier, they could then be expected to re-define their task so as to evade this responsibility. The result could only be that the much-needed strengthening of the Patent system would be prevented from taking place in practice. In contrast, with a money measure, the automatic limit built into the system, protects the Examiner in his career and so makes it possible for him to do his job, irrespective of what strengthening of the actual Patent grant there may be during its lifetime.

Granted that it is desirable, how practical is it to think of using money as the measure of all legally-created monopolies? It certainly was not at all so, in the days when the Patent system reached its definitive shape. Then, time was probably the only practical measure available, and this was why, for example, the American constitution uses it. The intention of the founding fathers was clearly that the monopolies granted to individual writers and inventors should not be unlimited ones, and so they built in a limitation in terms of time, as the Venetians had done. The British Statute of Monopolies, interestingly enough, does not specify what the measure of monopoly is to be. However, to-day the means exist that would make it very much easier to use profit instead of time as a measure of monopoly, or instead of failing to measure monopoly at all, as is done in the case of Trade Marks. There is the universal practice in business of regular accounting, and many sophisticated techniques have been developed for allocating costs and revenues to specific departments and items. There are similar ways of dealing with the future, such as budgetary and discounted cash flow techniques. There is taxation, which has created a horde of public servants with the resources and expertise to query and understand the financial working of all sorts of companies. Above all, there are systems for the control of public money spent on contracts with firms. These have been developed further in the United States than anywhere else, mainly because of the need for supervision of large defence projects. Specifically, they include ways of administering the investment of large amounts of public money in contracts involving research and development. There is public accountability for the activities of special kinds of firms; for example, most countries have a section of the civil service which keeps the activities of insurance companies under constant review from the aspect of their solvency, not of taxation. Where price controls exist, firms are used to opening up their books to public officials, as they also are where any form of State aid is at stake. All in all, therefore, modern business is built upon the practice of measuring all its activities in precise money terms, and modern Government is used to knowing what is going on in business, in the same terms. Since this is so, what is so difficult about the idea of measuring monopoly precisely by money? Or about relating monopoly to innovation specifically in financial terms?

What is being suggested is that every legally created monopoly should be subject to the most precise measure possible, and that measure can only be financial return. An Innovation Warrant, for example, instead of being a monopoly which lasts for a given term of years, whether or not any adequate investment is made in exploiting it, would be a monopoly which depended upon the making of an investment to develop an idea, and would go on until the profit actually realised, reached a given multiple of the original investment. In the case of outstandingly successful innovations, this might be a short time, well within the present span of years of a Patent grant; in that of slow starters or poor performers, it might be even longer. There need not be only one 'multiple', in fact, there could well be a series of multiples to take account of the different amounts of risk involved in different types of innovation. Basic research has the highest risk of failure and the longest time to produce returns, together with the greatest difficulty in being protected, so that at present only a few of the very largest firms can invest in it, even on a basis of secrecy, capability and marketing monopoly. A large 'multiple' would cope with both the time and the risk elements, irrespective of size of firm. The risks involved in what

Ravenshear called 'originative' invention, though great, are nevertheless smaller than those in basic research, and this difference could be reflected by a smaller 'multiple'. Similarly, the many small improvements which he called 'intensive' invention are obtained from investment at a still lower level of risk, to which a third and still smaller 'multiple' might correspond.

Use of this 'multiple' system would have the great advantage of limiting the *arbitrary* power of Patent, Innovation, Trade Mark or even Companies' Offices. With it, there could be no question of officials handing out monopolies of known value to favoured applicants. Instead, all they would do is agree with an applicant which category of risk his proposed investment in information production falls into, and correspondingly what 'multiple' would apply to it (and their decision on this would be open to public and judicial scrutiny); monitor his investment outlays and the return on them, if any, and actively protect his monopoly until the return reached the agreed multiple of the investment. In many cases, of course, there would be no return to monitor, such are the risks of investment in invention and innovation, so that the 'watchdog' aspect of their work would relate to a large number of investments in information production, and a comparatively small number of successful products resulting from this.

Next, the criterion of what is eligible for an Innovation Warrant, would cut through all abstract questions of novelty or obviousness, and be strictly commercial, as befits a device which has no other object than generating investment and employment in viable manufacturing industry. This criterion would depend upon the answer to one simple question. Can a product with this particular new feature, or combination of features, actually be obtained in the ordinary course of trade for the type of goods in question, at the present time? If it can, then the product is not eligible, but if it cannot, then investment to put such a product on the market would be a candidate for the new type of protection. For example, the hybrid petrol/electric motor for cars is widely regarded as very promising. It is not patentable now because it is no more than a combination of known elements which would be held to be obvious 'to one skilled in the art'. But because no one can go out and buy a car with such an engine from his local dealer, investment to change this situation would be able to be protected by an Innovation Warrant. The existence of this protection, which is a new type of specific market power, would be a powerful countervailing force against the capability market power of the giant Japanese firms, in the race to put such a car on the world market.

Fourthly, an Innovation Warrant, once granted, would be irrevocable. Who would prospect for minerals if the geographical limit of his claim could be called into question at any time? Yet this is the position of every present patentee, which goes far to explain why other forms of market power have so largely replaced patents as the means whereby the risks of innovation are justified. As far as technology is concerned, what this means in practice is that no new information which becomes available later than the grant of a Warrant, can have any effect on the latter's capacity to underwrite an above-average return on the investment made in reliance on it. Related to this, is the cost of prosecuting infringers and of defending the monopoly grant. It has been seen earlier how the expense of this, weighted by the risk of having to incur it, makes almost all investment in innovation an irrational act by proper accounting standards, if Patents are the only source of protection. One practical way of dealing with the problem might be analogous to 'Title Insurance' as used for private homes in the U.S. According to this, for a regular premium, a firm (or the Innovation Office itself) would take on all responsibility for protecting the Warrant holder's rights against all others. One way or another the burden of policing the monopoly must be removed from the Warrant holder. There seems to be no good reason why it should be a crime to rob a firm of its cash in hand, but not of the value and fruits of its investment in new technology. Or why it should only be intellectual property that is excluded from the care of the Fraud Squad. A minor corollary would be removal of the protection of the capital deployment Acts such as limited liability, from Warrant infringers.

This 'active' aspect of protecting the granted monopoly is of great importance. One of the objects of the proposed reforms is to reverse the trend towards mindless growth of firms. This trend is reinforced at present, in those areas where the Patent system is still important, by the fact that a Patentee has to police his own Patent, and himself take action in the Courts against infringers. The inherent cost of this, plus the capacity of an infringer who has a long purse to spin out litigation over a period of years (during all of which, remember, a Patent granted in terms of time is a wasting asset) is a most serious deterrent to the small firm, or individual inventor. So great is the advantage which large firms have at present, indeed, that, assisted by the bias of the Courts against Patentees as a class, they can in practice ignore the restrictions which the Patent system as currently administered attempts to place on them, and can infringe with impunity when they judge it necessary. After the experience of EMI with their brain-scanner in the U.S., it must now be accepted that even the valid Patents of large firms offer poor protection for investment. Under the proposed system, pirate firms would no longer have their present advantage; the various Offices would have the duty of ensuring that the monopolies they grant do in fact work to the benefit of those who have obtained them, leaving these firms or individuals free to get on with their job of innovating. The present system places a premium, not only on size, but also upon legal competence as contrasted with, say, engineering competence; it makes for the growth of the bureaucratic element in firms.

In the case of the outstanding success story of the post-war era of a business built upon Patents, Xerox Corporation, it is highly relevant that the inventor, Chester Carlson, was himself a Patent Agent. The Innovation Warrant system would redress current imbalances, in such a way as to restore the primacy of Engineers over Accountants. This is not a trivial advantage. The strength of an economy, and even more importantly, its human quality, depends upon its primary and secondary industries; to the extent that the services which make them run smoothly become overblown, these services necessarily become parasitic. Nothing is gained for humanity, for example, by an army of tax-collectors facing an army of accountants recruited to defend business and individuals from an over-elaborate and excessively heavy tax system; it is, after all, only in the sense of money – and money which has become divorced to an extent from its function as a measure of reality in economic terms at that – that there is anything productive about tax avoidance. An innovative economy cannot be built upon a wide gap between management and tool-room, with Directors having no experience of what it is to wear overalls and to have dirty hands. German engineering is as good as it is because of the practical bias in the training which German to management has received in the Technische Hoch-schulen; the great days of British innovation were certainly linked with the system of premium apprenticeship, in which middle – and upper – class boys, after obtaining a good secondary education, paid to get the same practical training as craft workers; the great Parsons turbine business was built as much on the workers' admiration for Sir Charles, 'who could do anything with his hands' as upon his own genius for invention; rejection of Fessenden's speech-transmission inventions by the Bell firm has been attributed to the fact that bankers were in control of it from 1907. When the lawyers take control, the power to innovate moves out, as it did in U.S. Steel, so that a system which minimizes lawyers' involvement in monopoly, by that very fact is a better en-vironment for innovation. The powers of inspection of plants when it is suspected that a protected *process* is being infringed, incidentally, which the Innovation Office would need to have for its purposes, are no more than can be given at present by a Court once litigation in respect of a Patent has com-menced.

Under the proposed system, a firm would be encouraged to invest in in-formation production by the secure knowledge that it will have a real monop-oly on the results for whatever time is needed to give it a return on its invest-ment, commensurate with the risk it took originally. It would no longer anti-cipate having to fight in the Courts to defend this monopoly, since this would now be the job of one section of the relevant Office, or of its Title Insurance firm. No difficulty seems to arise in the case of success, but what about failure, which in the nature of things, will be much more frequent? Does this system mean that a firm could pre-empt a particular area indefinitely, simply because it had failed to produce anything which could give it the required return? This would have to be avoided, and one way of doing so is suggested by the system used in Canada for oil prospecting. In this, a prospecting firm obtains a six-year licence to drill for oil in a particular lot, by agreeing to direct a certain amount of resources to this end. These resources must be committed, either by guarantee from an acceptable source, e.g. a bank, or by actual deposit of the funds needed for the exploration, with the Government. Expenditure on exploration is officially monitored, and if successful, the initial licence may be changed into a twenty-one year exploitation lease of the lot in question. Applied to innovation generally, a similar arrangement would be that a firm or individual would make a proposal for investment in advancing the 'real' state of the art in some particular field. This proposal would necessarily involve expenditure over time, and there would be a degree of risk attaching to this expenditure which could be estimated only in very broad terms. The Innovation Office's function in the first instance would be to agree with the proposer which category of risk his intended investment falls into (this will decide the 'multiple' of eventual returns related to inputs if it is successful); how much money he is to put into the exploratory stage of the project, and for how long the research is to go on. Note that the only aspect in which there is a danger of arbitrariness in the power of the Innovation Office is in deciding the category of risk, and that in this the Office would be working in the full light of public awareness. One firm might possibly abandon a proposal because the Office would not agree that the risk involved is as high as the firm says, so that the 'multiple' is consequently judged by the firm to be too low to justify this risk. A second firm may then put forward a proposal that differs only in part from the first one, and the Office might rule for a higher multiple. This kind of danger is inherent in all systems of control, and one could argue that at present it is as much to be found in the powers of Patent examiners, especially in countries such as the U.S.A. and Germany, as it would be under the proposed system. However, there would only be a problem of misuse of power in those cases where the Office gets the category of risk wrong; it is reasonable to assume that as information and experience are built up, the Office's performance in this respect would improve continuously. Also, when a public servant knows his actions are going to be subject to public scrutiny, it concentrates his mind wonderfully.

There would at no stage be any question of the Innovation Office granting monopolies except where risk is involved; and the monopoly granted, while presumptively proportioned to the risk, would in every case be a limited one. But it is a limit to which no business man can object, and it is defined in terms of the measure he is using all the time: Profit. If he cannot reach agreement with the Office as to the degree of risk involved in his proposed research, and consequently as to the number of times he should be able to make profits of this amount if it is successful, before his monopoly is extinguished, he need not make the investment. On the other hand, if he does make it, he knows that in the event of technical and commercial success, he is going to have an adequate financial return. This is an enormous improvement over the present position with Patents, when to the uncertainties of bringing research to a successful technical conclusion are added the uncertainties of being able to protect the results from rivals who have contributed nothing to their production, and the likelihood of having to become deeply immersed in litigation to obtain even the most limited degree of protection. Innovators are not at home in Courts, and innovation cannot flourish where lawyers reign.

Clearly, the Innovation Warrant as proposed would be vastly stronger than a patent of the present type, and this is necessary if it is to provide an adequate basis for investment at high risk. But the use of money as its measure draws the sting from monopoly and ensures that this serves the public interest. There have been many calls over the years for the strengthening of patents, but the decisive objection against these has always been the quite excessive profits which might then be earned from the (admittedly very few) successful innovations. This objection loses its force once money, rather than time, is made the measure of the monopoly. The more valuable the development that is protected by a Warrant, the quicker its profits will reach the ceiling prescribed by the 'multiple', and the sooner it will therefore come into the public domain and be open to all comers. Profits from the monopoly cannot exceed the statutory multiple of the investment which has had to be made to earn them. The size of this multiple would be decided by the authorities according to publicly debated investment and employment objectives, and the system would be administered with the same impartiality by Innovation Offices as patents of the traditional type have been.

In the case of the bigger innovations it would be desirable that the vehicle for an Innovation Warrant should be a new and independent firm. This would facilitate monitoring of its accounts by the public by the normal workings of Company Law in respect of disclosure. It could then be made a condition of the Warrants that they automatically lapse if audited accounts, with appropriate supplementary information, are not lodged promptly in the Companies' Office. Competitors can then be relied upon absolutely to monitor them at no cost to the State. The latter's function would only be to see that the auditors of Warrant-holding firms maintained strict and consistent standards, to deal with matters to which attention is called by public monitoring of such firms' accounts, and, where a firm has a corporate parent or shareholder, to ensure that relations between these involving provision of goods or services, are on a proper "arms-length" basis. This point is important, since it would be a mistake to prevent new, Warrant-holding firms from being subsidiaries of existing firms, even wholly-owned subsidiaries. To the extent that the innovating firm has close links with others that have strong production capability and/or an international marketing organization, it might gain some of the advantages of the Japanese Keiretsu system in B-phase innovation. The dangers of financial manipulation, however, are there, and the system would have to be able to cope with them. A further reason for using new firms as vehicles for Innovation Warrants is that this would make it easier for key personnel to participate in the equity. This could justify the risk to their careers, and, unless their careers *are* at risk, their creativeness will not be fully tapped.

The examination process for an Innovation Warrant application would rely very largely upon Third Party submissions. These would have to be made within a strict time limit to be considered, and no information arising subsequently would have any relevance to the grant of a Warrant. A valuable by-product of this procedure is that it would force all firms to monitor Warrant applications systematically, lest they might miss a chance of objecting to one which could affect them. By this means, awareness of new technology would be diffused much more effectively than is the case at present. Monitoring of Patent Specifications (except by the Japanese) is the exception rather than the rule. In some countries where Third Party submissions can form part of the examination procedure, it is considered disadvantageous to object before grant of a Patent, since the system allows the Patent to be attacked later, if necessary. These procedures put no pressure on firms to use the publications of the Patent system as the valuable source of information they can be. It is axiomatic in learning theory that the need for knowledge plays a large part in its absorbtion. If a firm can be affected by the grant of an Innovation Warrant to another, its management will study Warrant applications with a degree of interest which they would not give to material whose relevance is not seen to be so immediate. This interest must stimulate additional ideas in them for their own firms. For technology diffusion, searching of new material simply has to be done by those who are most actively engaged in the solving of problems. What will pass unnoticed by an unconcerned scanner of the information, leaps off the page to one who is battling with a difficulty. The spark jumps across the brain only if there is a 'potential difference' − which is provided by the problem to be solved.

How would the system cope with a situation where a Third Party produced evidence of investment already made with substantially the same objective as that of an Application for a Warrant? Any solution should achieve two objectives: Firstly, it is desirable that a Warrant should be granted wherever possible, so as to prevent the innovation from having to take place − if at all − under alternative market power arrangements. Secondly, the loss to the losing Party for having made any investment in R & D should be mitigated as far as possible if a Warrant is awarded to another. If the Warrant system can arrange this, there will be more investment in R & D, simply because one element of uncertainty has been removed from it. This element is strong in the existing Patent system, in those countries where there is "a race to the Patent Office". Even in the event of technical success, an investment may become totally without value simply because a competitor has been fractionally earlier in lodging his Patent Application. Consequently, prudent investment in R & D has to weigh up both chances, with the result that many original projects will not be attempted, and research is pushed into 'safe' directions.

The best way of using the Warrant system in such a case, would be to bring the resources of both Applicant and Objector together. This might be done by giving the objecting firm one chance to make its own 'full' investment within a given time, in which case it would obtain the Warrant. Presumably, this could involve financial support from the Applicant firm, and it could be made known that Warrants would be more readily granted if co-operation of this kind is evident. A second approach would be for the Warrant to be awarded to the Applicant firm only if the objection is withdrawn. This would make the R & D of the objector saleable to the Applicant, in order to bring this withdrawal about, at a price which reflected the potential of the innovation. A third possibility is to grant the Warrant to the Applicant, subject to his paying a royalty to the objector over the period of his own protection, that would repay the objector's investment in R & D in real terms, but without giving him a profit. Even better solutions would no doubt emerge from experience in working the system. Those suggested, however, would permit investment in R & D to be made in the knowledge that even if an Innovation Warrant is not eventually obtained to enable the embodiment of the research to be made and sold, *some* return will probably be obtained for any new information of value that is generated. This is a big improvement on the present system, and can only lead to more R & D funding, and better deployment of these funds.

A different problem would arise when a firm has obtained an Innovation Warrant, but becomes incapable of carrying the innovation through. This could be because of unforeseen difficulties, or because lower profits from the firm's established lines cause new projects to be denied support, or even because a change in management brings about a change in policy. It is obviously against the public interest that other firms which are then willing to attempt the innovation should be frustrated from doing so in such circumstances, but at the same time the irrevocable character of the Innovation Warrant must be preserved. A possible solution might then be for the Innovation Office to announce that it stands ready to grant a new Warrant in that particular field, if the earlier one is surrendered. The most likely outcome in such a case would be negotiations between the parties, resulting in the earlier innovator getting some return from his investment in exchange for giving a clear field to the later one. It could be expected that a market in Warrants would develop in any event, through which they would come into the possession of the firms best able to exploit them, but some provision such as that suggested would be necessary in the Innovation Warrant system, in order to prevent firms from acting in a merely negative way, by blocking innovation by others that they are unable or unwilling to carry through themselves. A similar device could be used to ensure that no Warrant-holder could deliberately put off obtaining the final increments of his return on investment so as to frustrate a competitor who wishes to invest in a further stage of development of a product. The rules could prescribe that once a substantial proportion of the return has been obtained, a Warrant-holder would have to accept any offer to buy out his interest, for the unearned balance of the 'multiple', appropriately discounted.

A two-stage system, with a lower multiple in the second stage, corresponds to the realities of investment in innovation. The risk involved in bringing a product to the stage of first repeat sales, is much higher than that of subsequent periods. Such a system would be particularly useful in bringing about negotiations in cases where the Warrant holder is not being successful. If a firm is coming to the end of its first stage and is faced with the need to invest more money to extend its Warrant into its second stage, then surrendering its Warrant, handing over control to another firm, and remaining a minority shareholder, could be attractive to it.

Of the several international agreements relating to Patents, the only one that is relevant to the Innovation Warrant is the International Convention for the Protection of Industrial Property. This, it will be recalled, does not bind a country to have any particular kind of Patent system, or indeed to have one at all, only to treat foreigners, if they are citizens of member states, on exactly the same basis as nationals, under whatever system there is. Consequently, treating Warrants in exactly the same way as Patents, should not cause the slightest difficulty under the Convention. This should shift the balance of the Convention's effect in the direction of generating investment and employment locally instead of abroad. Patents for invention, as currently defined, are of greatest value to those firms which are in the vanguard of technical progress, and reciprocal international agreements therefore benefit those countries which possess most such firms, at the expense of those in the second or lower ranks of technology. Patents granted in the less advanced countries are monopolies within their boundaries which intensify import penetration. They lead a firm to try to reap the maximum economies of scale by producing in a single plant in its home country, and to penetrate export markets by the Specific market power of its Patents. Making Innovation Warrants available to foreign firms on the same basis as local ones would have the opposite tendency, since to gain the advantage of a Warrant these firms would have to make an investment, not only in the B-phase development work, but also in local production facilities.

To the extent that the cause of unemployment is seen to be foreign competition, it is inevitable that the case for import controls will be argued strongly as a means of alleviating the problem. Comparison of the likely effect of the Innovation Warrant concept with such controls is instructive, and shows that the advantages are all with the proposed new type of Specific market power. By protecting industry that has become uncompetitive with foreign rivals, import controls ossify it, and ensure that it will never again be a force in export markets. Since B-phase innovation will continue to forge ahead abroad while the pressure for it has been relaxed at home, not only must the protection become permanent, it must be made progressively stronger as the quality gap between home-produced and foreign products widens. In contrast, the Warrant, by definition, protects industry only to the extent that its products are judged to be better than the foreign competition by the market; this protection is strictly temporary (and the stronger and more valuable it is, the shorter time it will last); and it is explicitly linked to investment of the type that can lead to penetration of export markets with these improved products on the basis of capability market power.

A further advantage of the Warrant, is that it provides an incentive for firms which have fallen behind foreign competition, to invest in 'catching up'. This is particularly important, since there appears to be no other incentive available that can have this effect. Consider a firm whose product is suffering, for example, from imports which incorporate the last three incremental innovations of 'best practice'. The Warrant holds out the promise to such a firm, of getting a really worth-while monopoly of the *next* incremental innovation. Clearly, there would be no point in making an investment to produce a product which had this improvement, unless it also incorporated the earlier incremental changes which the firm had failed to make. Not alone, therefore, does the Warrant underwrite investment to bring out products that are marginally better than the existing best in the world. It also justifies the investment needed to bring products up to the best standard in the world as a preliminary to further advance, in the cases where this is needed.

For both science and regional policy, the 'multiple' of the Innovation Warrant could be an instrument of the greatest flexibility. The United States Patent Office already discriminates in practice in favour of certain types of invention (for example those relating to energy or genetic engineering) by advancing them ahead of their turn for examination. As a means of encouraging particular developments however, this device is trivial in comparison with that of offering a higher multiple than average for appropriate Innovation Warrants. Regional industrial policy based upon different multiples could be highly sophisticated and capable of rapid adaptation to changing circumstances. The need to find alternative employment quickly for a town where a steel mill has to close, for example, could result, under the Warrant system, in an exceptionally high multiple for investment there for a limited period. None of these policies would require a penny in subsidy from either national or local Government; they would be virtually costless to administer; and the distortions and misdirection of energy that are inseparable from present regional incentive schemes would be eliminated. The industrial developments thus encouraged would be as organic and as soundly based as possible, because they would be undertaken and carried on throughout under the discipline of the market. Large differential advantages would indeed be offered to firms to invest in certain types of industry or in certain places, but actually realizing these advantages would depend upon the new products being bought in preference to those offered by competitors, so that profits are earned. Moreover, if Innovation Warrants which were used explicitly to generate employment, resulted in flexibility on the part of the Trade Unions, not only would the Warrants' power to redress regional imbalance be enhanced, but they would be producing the beginning of a solution to one of the longer term structural problems of the economy.

Apart from derived market power, the other main factor which deprives an innovator of his primary rent, is, of course, taxation. Consideration should therefore be given to waiving all claims to tax on an innovatory investment until the 'multiple' has been earned as profits. It will be obvious that multiples could then be lower than they would have to be if they related to taxed profits.

Although to an investor who is using the right discount factors, there is no difference between a high multiple with taxation and a lower multiple with a tax holiday, lower multiples should be easier to handle from the political point of view. Most advantage would be gained by having multiples at the highest possible acceptable level, and bringing the innovation into the public domain as early as possible by not taxing its profits. The psychological effect of tax freedom would also tend in the direction of positive decisions to invest. Best of all, of course, would be where the grant of an Innovation Warrant meant *both* freedom from tax and a temporary suspension of all the laws which underwrite derived market power, including minimum wage and unfair dismissal regulations. Every Warrant would then constitute an 'Enterprise Zone' in a sense that could only be extremely attractive for investment.

The question of what the 'multiple' should be is a pragmatic one, and it might with advantage be capable of being changed in the light of circumstances by ministerial order rather than by statute. There are four reasons why error should be on the side of generosity:

- the urgency of the need for investment in innovation, especially of the incremental type which Patents fail to protect at present.
- the strength of well-founded conviction amongst businessmen and financiers that 'pioneering doesn't pay', which it will take very attractive terms indeed to overcome.
- the extent to which it is only when firms with Innovation Warrants are actually seen to be making money out of them that others will be drawn in large numbers to invest in innovation; and, above all
- the fact that innovatory managements will not stop with one success, so that a large part of any profits from Innovation Warrants is certain to be re-invested in developing further new products and improvements.

The attractions of the Warrant system to the managements of manufacturing firms and those who finance them are obvious. A firm which faces annihilation in both home and export markets from the quality and price of competitors' products, can now develop an investment plan, not only for improving on existing products, but also for manufacturing by the very latest techniques. Because the improved product is not yet available on the market, the project would be eligible for a Warrant, and once this is granted, the investment can be made in the secure knowledge that if technical success is achieved, then commensurate profits will follow. Every resource can thun be devoted to achieving this technical success, without the fear of sowing for others to reap, or having to provide for the expense and distraction of litigation. Although the Warrant would only cover the home market, the capability resulting from the new investment would also give an advantage in lead-time in export markets, and the concentration on technical success, also made possible by the Warrant, could only reinforce this advantage. Exports might be further encouraged by only counting home market profits against the Warrant 'multiple'.

The industrial structures of the West depend upon a complex of positive law which dates from the middle of the last century. To the extent that they are now unable to cope with pressures emanating from the Middle and Far East, new types of market power must be called into being to redress the balance of the old. The obvious source for these is the principle of Patenting, which has far more possibilities of practical application than have ever been realized in practice. It must be clearly understood that absence of a particular kind of market power will not prevent innovation happening: it merely ensures that the innovation takes place elsewhere, modified by, and under the protection of, whatever market power there is. The fact that Patents cover incremental innovation in manufacturing so poorly, therefore, simply means that such innovation will be what can be underwritten by capability or persuasive market power. The stark reality which must be faced by every one of the second – and third – rank countries is that they are now at an overwhelming disadvantage in both. This is most evident in relation to the Americans in persuasive or marketing power, and to the Japanese in capability. As argued in the previous chapter, for example, it is impossible to overstress how effective for B-phase innovation Japan's Zaibatsu-Keiretsu institutions are. No matter how inventive Western countries have shown themselves to be, none of them, not even the U.S., now matches Japan in the ability to produce 'the second invention that every invention needs – how to mass-produce it at an affordable cost'. This is why extension of the principle of Patenting is so promising. It could produce a flood of energy innovations that would finally end economic pressure from OPEC. It also offers a means of meeting the competition from Japan and the Confucian world, which, fierce as we feel it to be, is yet only at an early stage in its momentum. As a powerful and flexible instrument of specific market power, expressly directed towards increasing investment and employment, the Innovation Warrant has strong claims to be considered urgently. The cost of trying it out is trivial, and it could have surprisingly quick and valuable results for the survival, and revival, of 'manufacture within these realms'.

It is most instructive to compare these proposals for an Innovation Warrant with those of Dr. Kronz for reform of the existing Patent system. The similarities are quite remarkable for sets of ideas worked out completely independently of each other. They are even more so when the legal and Patent Attorney background of Kronz's approach is contrasted with the Innovation Warrant's roots in economics and politics. What is involved here is a *social* invention. The similarities of both approaches, indeed, could be held to be yet another confirmation of Gilfillan's thesis that no individual is essential to the inventive process, since social need inevitably evokes social response. There can be no doubt that protection for innovation is a prime social need at present. The validity of Gilfillan's thesis, it can also be argued, depends upon there being a multiplicity of points of enquiry and decision, since he refers to innovation as depending upon numbers of individuals' ability to devote time to this activity. The first important point to note is that both proposals set out to protect the actual thing made and sold, rather than the 'concept', which is the subject-matter of the existing Patent system. For Kronz, "the real problem in industrialised countries is the transformation of technical knowledge into products and investment under much more difficult market entry conditions".[31] The industrial innovation process is determined by forces that are independent of Patent protection, he thinks. These views are in complete unformity with the assumptions which underlie the Innovation Warrant, and which have been developed in earlier chapters. In particular, the argument that Capability and Persuasive market power now underwrite innovation to a far greater extent than Patents do, is exactly in line with Kronz's case. Encouraging investment, of course, is the whole object of the Innovation Warrant.

Both the proposal of Kronz and that of the Innovation Warrant turn their backs upon the examination for obviousness which is such an important part of the present Patent system. For Kronz, the required novelty is achieved if there is no previous public use in the "home territory"; for the Warrant, "if the product cannot be obtained in the ordinary course of trade". In considering the apparently slight difference, weight should be given to one of the realities of innovation, which is that success *never* comes at the first attempt. It is probably true that every successful invention is in fact a re-invention; it is certainly the case that every successful commercial product has antecedents that failed. The criterion of "current commercial availability" would not deny a Warrant on ground of lack of novelty to an application because of previous unsuccessful attempts. These, however, can and do destroy novelty where a 'prior use' criterion is in force. The former yardstick therefore appears to be more effective for bringing about innovation, which, as was pointed out in *Invention and Monopoly*, is always "the result of a combination of courage and resources: Courage to get things wrong the first time; resources to get them right the second". Contemporary Japanese prowess, incidentally, obscures the fact that their performance has been a triumphant vindication of this principle. Most of their early post-war efforts to penetrate the United States market, for example, in motor cars, failed dismally. It should be said that Kronz holds that the "State of the Art" only consists of "actual, utilized prior art", which could mean that his "prior use" criterion of novelty probably discounts earlier *failures*. If it does, it would be virtually identical with that of the Innovation Warrant.

Both approaches are in substantial agreement as to what the subject-matter of protection should be. For Kronz, this is expressed as the "economical-commercial" innovation, as long as this is "embodied", and for the Innovation Warrant approach, it is "anything saleable". In the latter, the emphasis on investment is explicit, whereas what Kronz demands is "capacity to carry through the innovation". This can be provided by a 'substitute innovator'. Since the latter is substantially equivalent to 'investor', and since Kronz presumably intends the capacity to innovate to be followed through by an attempt to innovate, which necessarily involves investment, there is no significant difference on this score either, between the two schemes.

As to the measures of the monopoly to be granted, Kronz proposes a variable term, which is clearly an attempt to escape from the disadvantages of measuring a Patent grant in terms of time, which have already been discussed. In fact, his 'variable term' is linked to money, because he proposes that the minimum term of protection should be until the investment made in the innovation has been recovered, with a maximum "when 50% of the total demand has been supplied".[32] This is uncannily close to the concept of the 'multiple' put forward above. As a measure, it is less precise, but it might well be easier to administer. The use of a 'multiple' applied to sales as a surrogate for profits, might incorporate much of the better features of both systems.

In the light of Kronz's sophisticated 'variable term', the question may fairly be asked, "Why complicate the issue by introducing measurement by money instead of time; could not the new novelty criterion be used in a monopoly which would be granted for a period of years?" And if that period was short, compared with Patents, say 5 or 7 years, would it not pacify the opponents of the other valuable feature which has been proposed – incontestability? Certainly, for the sake of getting a realistic novelty criterion into operation quickly, it would be well worth accepting time as measure of an incontestable monopoly. However, money remains the measure most worth striving to obtain, for three reasons:

Firstly, the difficulty of deciding to invest in innovation is so great, that whatever can be done to eliminate any element of uncertainty is of great value. If time remains the measure of the monopoly, an investor – even assuming technical success – can only guess at what his return will be during the monopoly period; with money as measure, using the 'multiple' he knows that at the worst he will eventually get his return – the uncertainty is reduced to how long it will take to obtain a known return. Psychologically, this is much less of a deterrent to invest.

The second reason, which may be critically important at the present time, relates to derived market power. Investment in innovation must depend upon what are perceived to be the *nett* returns to investors, after paying the rents imputable to the various factors used. Among these, the rent of the derived power will be relatively large. If investors judge that workers will use their derived market power to capture the bulk of the primary rent arising from the monopoly, they will rightly conclude that however strong the latter is in absolute terms, it does not provide an attractive investment opportunity. The 'multiple' system requires for success that there should be some limitation, either legal or voluntary, upon the exercise of derived market power. Using money as the measure would assist the achievement of binding agreements, since all parties would know precisely what the financial parameters were. It would be much more difficult to obtain Union restraint if the financial return was hypothetical, as it would be if the measure of the monopoly was time. Also, the fact that they know that they will be free to exercise their derived market power to the full once the 'multiple' had been achieved, might make it easier for Trades Unions to agree to returns for investors (in the event of commercial success) that would be much higher than those currently available.

Thirdly, in establishing the 'multiple' by law, the Government would be taking on itself the responsibility for any profits that are made as a result, by investors in innovation. The Civil Servants administering the Warrant system would be correspondingly relieved of responsibility, and would therefore be less likely to redefine their task in ways that frustrate the objectives of the scheme. Past experience with the Patent system, does not generate the same confidence in time as a measure of monopoly from this point of view, since in this case the Civil Servants felt that they were being asked to accept too much responsibility, and did re-define their task as a consequence.

Another similarly between Kronz's proposal and that being advanced here, lies in different treatment of monopoly according to regional requirements. In Kronz, protection can be granted in a region smaller or larger (the latter presumably by international agreement) than a State. In the alternative Warrant system, a different 'multiple' may be specified for investment in innovation in different regions. Both also stress the importance of third party opposition as means of establishing the true "state of the Art". Indeed, when all the similarities are taken into account, each approach receives powerful support from the other. Some combination of both would meet the urgent immediate need, which is for a type of Specific market power to protect those types of technological innovation which now receive inadequate protection from Patents. This would make it possible to invest prudently in incremental innovation, for example, on a basis other than capability market power. Almost overnight, this would greatly reduce the advantage possessed now by Japanese firms through their unique possession of this type of market power in an increasing number of fields. The Warrant system would even force the Japanese to invest in Western countries to get round the perfectly legitimate and justifiable barriers to their trading which it would set up.

In B-phase innovation, the impact of the Innovation Warrant system would be especially large and rapid. The full value of some of the system's provisions, however, will not be obtained, until they are also applied to A-phase innovation, which is generally supposed to be the domain of the existing Patent system. Kronz, indeed, considers his proposals as an alternative to Patents as they are at present, whereas the Innovation Warrant system was put forward as an additional type of protection, which would leave the existing Patent system completely untouched, and which might best be administered by some public Institution other than the Patent Office.

The provision in the Warrant system for money instead of time as the measure of Patent monopoly was in fact, originally proposed for the existing Patent system. This raises many of the same questions as does the possible application of the Warrant method to 'originative' innovation – the big, revolutionary changes that open up whole new lines of development. It also touches upon whether or not there should be Patent or similar protection for scientific discoveries. A useful practical illustration is the case of the vertical – axis windmill. When wind – power began to be investigated with more urgency as a result of oil price increases, the Canadian National Bureau of Scientific Research 'invented' this. When they applied for a Patent, however, they learned that they had been anticipated by a Frenchman, Darrieus, in 1929. Development of the Darrieus rotor has consequently been rather sporadic, for the very good reason that no firm is interested in investing at very high risk, to produce new information which its competitors can then – in the absence of Patent or other protection – use freely.

If the Innovation Warrant system was in force in Canada, the Darrieus anticipation would have no effect, since the invention had never been innovated. It would not have been possible at the time of the National Bureau's work to buy a Darrieus rotor 'in the ordinary course of trade'. Consequently, the Bureau would be entitled to a Warrant, which would justify the large scale investment which the development requires. This investment could come from the Bureau itself, from a Canadian firm, from a foreign firm which was ready to make its investment in Canada for the sake of obtaining Warrant protection (and which would be entitled to do so under the Paris Convention) or any combination of these. By whatever means, it seems certain that commercial development of the Darrieus rotor would be much further advanced than it actually is. But what of the original inventor? Wind-power was of little commercial interest throughout the cheap oil period, so presumably Darrieus never obtained backing to develop his invention before his Patent (as traditionally measured by time) expired. If money was the measure, Darrieus, or, more likely, his heirs, might still have owned a Patent or Warrant when OPEC made wind power more interesting, and a valuable 'multiple' would still be available for an investor who saw the prospect of profit from developing the rotor in the changed circumstances. It must be added that if to measurement by money were added the other features of the Warrant system (such as incontestability) the chances of obtaining backing for the invention earlier, must have been considerably stronger.

The advantage of the 'multiple' over time as a measure of monopoly is also illustrated by the way in which it could help to solve the difficulties in protecting computer programs. In these, what needs to be protected is not so much the systems software, which instructs the machine what to do, much as a non-commissioned officer gives tactical orders to his men. It is the applications software, or the strategy. This is expressed in a set of rules for solving a particular problem by a number of steps, which is called an algorithm. In 1969, the U.S. Courts allowed a Patent to be granted for a 'bundled' program, that is, as a process claim related to a computer.[33] This apparently opened up the possibility of Patenting algorithms, since a Patent would then cover the conversion of a general-purpose computer into a special-purpose computer by means of the program. Patent Offices, fearful of long monopolies, concluded that this would give too much market power to Patentees, and so took steps to have computer programs explicitly excluded from Patent protection.

Copyright, of course, applies to an original computer program, but only to the format, not to the algorithm, so it is of little use, Re-stating the algorithm circumvents the copyright, which relates to form, not content. Protection under Trade Secret law is of some value, and its increased use in the computer field is yet another example of the way in which marketing power plus secrecy has been taking the place of Patenting as a means of protecting investment in the generation of new information. Many of its disadvantages could be eliminated by addition of registration. This could have a comparable effect upon the software industry to that of Trade Mark registration upon marketing a century ago. In the 1969 IBM proposal for this, there would be a national registry for computer software, which would hold programs as trade secrets for a limited time. Enough information would be published to enable potential users to identify the programs they need. The idea of registration has been taken up by the World Intellectual Property Organization, and there are considerable hopes for development, based upon the introduction of property law concepts into the jurisprudence of trade secrets.

It should be noted that if money is used as the measure of the monopoly granted, there is nothing to prevent Patents from being used to protect algorithms. Programs could be registered, and open to all. Use of the program would require a fee, most of which would accrue to the originator. Once he had received the appropriate 'multiple' of his investment in producing the algorithm, the program would come into the public domain and be freely usable by all. The more important and valuable the algorithm, the more quickly this would happen. All fear of granting a monopoly on some vital algorithm which would enable huge rents to be extracted from users over a period of up to 20 years, would be removed by the simple device of switching from time to money as the measure of the grant. The relevance of the switch in the case of computer programs is intensified by the fact that it is the advent of computers which has made the precise analysis of costs and returns so practicable.

The question of the context of novelty is also illuminated by comparing the existing Patent system with what is proposed for Warrants. All the significant Patent Offices have now opted for an 'absolute' degree of novelty, meaning that novelty can be destroyed by evidence from anywhere in the world, in even the most obscure language. A comparable degree of novelty for an Innovation Warrant would depend upon the product's not being available for sale in the ordinary course of trade in any country, even the most advanced. Relative novelty could mean not similarly available in a group of countries, such as the Ten of the EEC, or in the Warrant-issuing country alone.

Whichever criterion is adopted, no difficulty appears to arise as long as the subject-matter of Warrants is incremental innovation. As it moves towards originative innovation, however, the amount of Research work relative to Development work increases. Since the Warrant is conditional on making an investment to produce the product, and since this cannot be done until the R & D for it has been completed, there must either be an option period before grant of the Warrant, or the two-stage 'multiple' must be part of the system. A similar adaptation of the 'multiple' could be applied to conventional Patents.

In both cases, duplication of research work would be avoided. For example, in the countries which operate a 'first to file' rather than 'first to invent' Patent system, the 'race to the Patent Office' is a very tight one indeed, so much so that some Offices, such as the French, record the time of lodgement of papers to the minute. Since only one firm can get the monopoly, the others have lost their total investment in this particular piece of research, through being slightly slower in getting their results into a form which can be expressed in the 'claims' required by the Patent Office. The race certainly puts pressure on research workers to get their results into that form with the least possible delay, but the fact that there is only one prize, that it is impossible to know the strength of the competition, the point from which it is starting, or even whether it is starting at all, and that the winner takes all, is inevitably a deterrent to investment in information production. This deterrent would be removed by the reforms proposed. There would still be a 'race to the Innovation Office', but it would be a race, not with results already obtained, but with proposals for research, that is, proposals for results *to be obtained*. The winner in this race still has to obtain the results, but he can make his investment in research in the secure knowledge that if he does obtain them, a proper financial return must follow. He will be allowed to enjoy a monopoly of their exploitation until his reward has reached the agreed 'multiple' of his original investment, and this monopoly will be *actively* protected by the State until that time. The losers, on the other hand, will not have invested any more than it has cost them to formulate their proposals to the Innovation Office; their resources for research will have been committed only a little, if at all, and they will have lost no time. Consequently, these resources, instead of being largely wasted, as they are at present, upon duplication of research, often unwittingly, can immediately be directed into alternative channels. Better deployment of research should eventually increase the aggregate amount of innovation. It will be seen, therefore, that the new system proposed achieves formally and explicitly and over the whole spectrum of 'new things', what at present takes place in a haphazard way, often by the misuse of existing institutions, with inflation of the role of Government as sponsor of research, and a bias in this research towards the realization of inventions which are directed to war.

If the overall picture of research spending is examined, it will be seen that it is only in the area of Government research and development contracts that there is any real possibility at present of avoiding duplication in research. This is not to say that this does not happen with Government contracts, because it does, and that there are not other serious deficiencies in control, because there are;

but simply that in principle centralized control of the State research budget ought to be able to distribute research and development contracts in such a way that duplication is avoided (except in so far as it is considered necessary to give firms facility in absorbing new information from outside.) This principle is poorly realized in practice, due to incompetence, political lobbying, graft, or the general blurring of the lines of control which is inescapable in the spending of public money – especially when this is 'to get new things done' rather than 'to keep things going'. Nevertheless, because of it there should be a lower amount of duplication of effort in research in the area where the work is largely paid for by the Government, than where the principle is precisely that of duplication of effort, i.e. the area where research is paid for by private sources. This means that in the technical economic sense the firms working on Government contracts are more 'efficient' than the others, because they do not have to recoup wasteful expenditure on duplication of research from the sales of their products. Since by far the largest part of Government expenditure on research in every country has a national security aspect, the biggest Government buyer of research is always the Defence Department. Consequently, it is the firms in what is known as the Military-Industrial complex which get the benefits of an above-average degree of freedom from the burden of research duplication. The conclusion is obvious: The importance of these firms in the economy is raised above what it would otherwise be, by the inadequacies of the present system of protecting investment in information production.

There are, of course, other ways in which the duplication of investment in research is avoided at present, but often these are a by-product of policies rather than a deliberate objective. For example, competitive firms made no attempt to match Philco's research on television, on the assumption that if it was successful it would be of such great importance that the Federal Trade Commission and the Justice Department could not allow Philco to reap the benefit of a Patent.[34] They were right, and economically this can be regarded as a good result, in that it avoided waste of resources by duplication. But this is not what the F.T.C. was set up to do, so that this and similar rulings, can equally be regarded as the exercise of arbitrary power, in that they involve a clear over-riding of the provisions of the Patent Law. With money as the measure of a Patent grant, the F.T.C. would not need to get involved at all. All that the tremendous value of the successful outcome of Philco's research would mean would be that the 'multiple' of its investment would be reached very quickly, and the monopoly protection would then immediately cease. Philco could not complain, in that they would have obtained the agreed number of times their original investment back as profits. This should leave them considerably better off than a situation where their due reward under the present Patent system is abridged by the fiat of the Federal Trade Commission. Neither could its competitors complain, because the larger the profits of Philco, the sooner its monopoly protection will lapse, so leaving them free to capitalise on the information it has produced, which would then come into the public domain. And the public interest is served, and prices of products can be lower generally, by eliminating duplication of research through means that are not bureaucratic.

Another advantage should be the correction, at least in good measure, of the present bias in favour of certain types of innovation, simply because they happen to suit the administrative needs of the system. It can presumably be taken from the way every national Patent Office that operates an examination system, insists that the invention be expressed in claims – the division of the stream of invention into discrete elements – that this is in some way necessary if the system is to be made to work at all, even as badly as it is recognised to do. Because some types of invention lend themselves to description in Claim terms, and others do not, this means that there is more innovation in some fields than in others, not at all because that is the pattern of what is needed, but simply because that is the pattern of what can be protected by Patents. The present system, for example, only affords protection for specific ways of solving a problem, when the real inventive step may have been the recognition of the problem to be solved in the first place, which receives no protection at all. Either rival firms can 'invent around' the originator's solution (using his information both as disclosed through the Patent system and as revealed directly from his new product and its sales) or the originator has to invest resources in devising and Patenting every possible way of solving the problem, in order to prevent their doing so. This is clearly a waste of resources if his first solution was adequate, and is really only a means of trying to get some protection for the real invention – the discovery that both a problem and a possible solution to it existed. The system proposed would not suffer from these major defects. The first proposal to the Patent Office would describe the problem to be solved, the line of investigation intended to be followed, the amount of money it is proposed to spend on the research, and the length of time is expected to take. The multiple agreed by the Patent Office would apply to any means of solving the problem, because it is largely impossible, in advance of doing the research, to say what the best means will turn out to be in practice. If the problem is solved, the monopoly as measured by the 'multiple' applies until the original risk capital has been repaid the agreed number of times. Up to that time, no other firm can offer an alternative solution to the first one by 'inventing around' it, and the originating firm has therefore no need to waste resources in pre-empting alternatives. It can be seen that this approach, with its evident advantages, is only possible when money and not time is made the measure of monopoly. As long as time is the measure, a monopoly can never be attached to information which consists of recognition of a problem, because this could give an outrageously valuable monopoly when extended to the full term of a Patent (at present generally fourteen to twenty years). Using profit as the measure, however, the previously unrecognised problem would come into the public domain just as soon as the return to the firm or individual who first invested in its solution, had reached the agreed multiple of that investment;

and it would then be open to other solutions, as well as to other users of the first one. Monopoly would then apply to the information content of recognising and defining the problem just as much as to the information content of a particular solution to it; but monopoly could never result in excessive profits, since these would be limited by the 'multiple'. At present, there is a Patent system which produce the occasional monopoly which is vastly in excess of anything which is needed to bring forth the required amount of scarce resources. That Patents for Aluminium in the U.S. led to production of this metal being controlled by a single firm right up to the end of the last war, is a case in point. At the same time, the great majority of inventions do not get a level of protection which brings them any adequate return, with the result that business men are rightly shy of investing on the basis of a Patent monopoly. What are particularly unfairly treated under the present system, are inventions which are ahead of their time, since any Patent protection measured by time will have expired before these become realized in practice. Again, as the Darrieus example indicated, using money instead of time as the measure of monopoly, deals with this difficulty, and so makes a Patent that much more worth investing in. In this area, as in others, we advance according to the precision of our measures.

Reference was made in Chapter I to the theoretical argument that a private enterprise economy will tend to invest below the optimum level in basic research. This reflects the difficulty of protecting or ('internalizing') the information produced, under the present legal system. What basic research is done in industry, is only to be found in the very largest multi-product firms, since it is impossible to tell in advance where the commercial application of a fundamental scientific advance will come, and such firms have the best chance of exploiting it when it does come, because of their spread of interests. Under the present system, therefore, a most important – possibly *the* most important – justification of sheer bigness in industry is that only in this way can industry concern itself at all with basic research, when spending its own money, and not just with applied research. It must be suspected, however, that this is only because no one has ever looked very seriously for any other way of protecting an investment in research. If an effective alternative could be found, the case for large corporate size would have one of its main supports removed. The Innovation Warrant, by strengthening Specific market power, already reduces the need for Capability market power, which is associated with firm size, for innovation. What hopes are there of finding such an alternative also, for protecting investment in fundamental research?

There was some activity directed towards establishing Patent rights for scientific discoveries in the years between the Wars, but none since. One reason for this which springs to mind is that the great expansion of research and development in industry dates from the 'thirties, when it first began to be realized that marketing monopoly, capability and secrecy provided an effective method of protecting new knowledge, at least for the largest firms. A second reason for the loss of interest may be that so much scientific research is now financed by Governments, either through their own Research Establishments, as typically in Great Britain, or through research and development contracts with the Universities and Industry, on the United States model. Nelson and Winter have established that in all sectors with strong scientific underpinnings to their technologies, institutions other than 'firms' – universities, for example – have played a major role in developing that science. Looked at from this perspective, the efforts to extend Patent rights to scientific discoveries appear very like a last spurt on the part of the Patent system, before it became definitively replaced as the leading method of information protection, by secrecy in combination with capability and persuasive market power. Now that Japanese firms increasingly have the advantage in these, this issue is becoming a live one again, raised especially by Dr. F.K. Beier, of the Max-Planck-Institute for Foreign and International Patent, Copyright and Competition Law in Munich.[35] It must become an increasingly important topic in future years, as Japan's industries become increasingly devoted to the production of goods which embody the most advanced scientific knowledge. If they have access to this without paying for it – as they had earlier to Western applied knowledge – their advantage in turning it to practical use will result in even more bankruptcies and unemployment in Western countries. The traditional freedom of scientific workers to publish and have access to information, will have to be limited so as to bring about some economic balance between what countries put into the common pool of knowledge, and what they take out of it.

It was only in France that scientists ever widely supported the idea that scientific discoveries should be patentable, and a bill to this effect was introduced by Barthélemy in 1922. A report and proposals were prepared for the League of Nations by Ruffini in the following year, and these were discussed at length, Britain being flatly opposed throughout. The line-up of countries is interesting in itself, since it reflects the traditional French concern (based on a 'natural rights' approach) to give legal protection to an idea as an extension of a personality; in contrast to the British approach, which is that the question of patenting ideas only comes up if they are to be the subject of investment. One approach seeks to protect the inventor, the other, the investor. Also in 1923, Gariel advanced a scheme of awards to scientists to be paid for by a tax on innovation. The most comprehensive study of the possibilities was that of C.J. Hamson, whose book appeared in 1929. He defined discovery as a new fact or truth capable of verification experimentally, and adding substantially to existing human knowledge other than what is the result only of ordinary technical skill. 'A discovery therefore consists in the making of one or more relations, with proper deduction or induction therefrom'[36] He proposed a body to represent scientific property as 'trustee of discoveries'. This would be a Corporation which would act to protect the interests of scientists, and which would be subject to the Courts. There would be a public register of agreements with manufacturers, listing sums paid and discoveries used. This register would be maintained by a body other than the Corporation charged with looking after the interests of scientists, probably by the Patent Office. It would only be the use of a discovery in such a way that it resulted in a physical object that would create an obligation to pay a royalty to the Corporation. Consequently, the use of information to create more information would remain unrestricted. All licences to use discoveries would be specific and particular.

One part of Hamson's proposals, it will be noted, amount to the present Patent system with automatic 'licences of right'. His idea of a Corporation to represent the interests of scientists, and to save them from having to get involved in a multitude of licence agreements, each probably involving small payments, is of considerable interest. "Patent pooling" agreements such as that of the U.S. aerospace firms, do just this very effectively in some industries. His proposals do not preclude the issuing of traditional-type Patents to inventors who used a particular scientific discovery in creating an arrangement of matter, but they would mean that there was an additional contingent liability on whoever actually used an embodiment of such a Patent, to obtain the appropriate licence from the Corporation. This would mean paying royalties in respect of the scientific information, without which, after all, the physical embodiment might never have been possible. 'Licences of Right' as was shown earlier, effectively negative the value of a Patent, by breaking the monopoly, and this is why the provision is so little used.

None of the proposals made for Patent rights for scientific discovery went as far as suggesting the grant of monopoly in the information in the sense of control as to its use or non-use. Presumably one reason for this was the thought that its value could be too vast to be contemplated; for example, if Faraday could have had an absolute monopoly over all electro-chemical applications, since these depended upon his work, this would have been giving unthinkable power to one man. Time is a most inadequate measure even of existing Patent monopolies, but it would be even more so for scientific discoveries. For every case where a scientist's ideas were turned into sales of products within the Patent term, and where there would therefore be returns so vast as probably to be socially unacceptable, there would be many others where the time gap between basic research and successful products would far exceed the life of the Patent; polystyrene and vinyl chloride were first mentioned in the 1830s, but took more than a century to become major industrial products, and Einstein would have collected nothing from the atomic energy industry in spite of the debt that this owes to the results of his famous equation $e = mc^2$. It is worth noting that using money instead of time as the measure of the monopoly, has none of these disadvantages. No matter how late the discovery became embodied in a saleable product, the 'multiple' would ensure a return on the original investment; no matter how enormous the potential returns might be, the same multiple would cut them off in practice when they had reached the level regarded by society as reasonable in the light of the risks the research had involved, and its cost.

Extension of the principle of Patenting, therefore, is as possible for basic research as for 'arrangements of matter', and the use of money as the measure of monopoly is the key to effectiveness in both. The question then arises, should monopolies in scientific discoveries be granted, or should some automatic licence system, such as was suggested by Hamson, be operated? Some will be shocked at the idea of restrictions cutting across all the traditions of freedom of the scientific community. This was why all the arguments of Chain that Penicillin should be patented were in vain.[37] However, scientists are by no means as independent as they like to pretend. As far as that part (admittedly small) of fundamental research that is carried out by firms on their own account, is concerned, it is always done in – and consequently protected by – the strictest secrecy. Next, a high proportion of basic research is done with public money, mainly for Defence purposes. In so far as this is open to all, it is much more the consequence of the reasonable premise that what the public has paid for, the public should be free to use, rather than upon belief in the freedom of the scientific world. The sources of money for scientific research seriously restrict the freedom of Scientists to pursue their self-chosen goals in practice. This leads to a link between Science and Government that is every bit as close as the link between Church and Government was in some countries in the past. Such a link forges the close connection between Science and weapons of war to-day, which has resulted in a call by some perceptive members of the profession, for 'the disestablishment of Science'.

One way of doing this, obviously, would be to give fundamental research a major source of income, *independent of Government*, through enabling it to share in the returns from the physical products which embody its discoveries. This could be done by an extension of the principle of Patenting to bring about monopolies in information, much along the lines in which Copyright law brings about monopoly in the way information is expressed. There already exists a means of protecting *form*; what is needed now is parallel legal protection of *content*. The same system of the 'multiple' that has been suggested for Innovation Warrants and ordinary Patents could apply, but it is not so obvious that any property right should be an absolute one, where basic research is concerned. If it were absolute, there could develop links between centres for fundamental research and particular businesses which might seriously restrict the applications of the research results, and lead to a re-emergence of the very disadvantages of the present market power systems all over again – especially in the advantage the largest firms would have in basic research. A contrary argument is that although it seems reasonable to assume that if research results are open to be used by anybody, their potential applications will be most widely recognised, the general experience that 'Licences of Right' are a failure leads one to be doubtful about any watering down of a legally-granted monopoly. Another factor to be borne in mind is that, historically, the best results in applied science and technology appear to have come when links with the basic centres *have* been close: The fundamental University research of Sataudinger and his school in polymer chemistry underlay the great German chemical complex of I.G. Farben. Virtually all new ideas in the aeroplane of the between-War years originated in Germany, and were due to the way basic research at the University of Göttingen was closely associated with the industry. The balance of advantage seems to lie with granting absolute monopoly and allowing such ties to develop, but at the same time counting upon the use of the correct measure of monopoly (profits by the operation of the 'multiple') to cope with any tendency to abuse. There also may well be a case for having a body such as that suggested by Hamson, to administer the Patents granted for scientific discovery, to deal with what could be a large number of small payments if they were widely licenced, and to monitor them. The suggestion has been made earlier that the Innovation or Patent Office should take over the function of policing monopolies, to the extent that it should have powers to act to protect them, as the Police can act to protect other kinds of property, on their own initiative. If this duty is not to be intolerable, the Office should in general act only upon complaints made to it by interested parties, hence the need for a monitoring function in the proposed Corporation of Hamson's. As to whether this body should be part of the Innovation or Patent Office or not, it seems in line with the principle of 'diversity' which underlies the whole set of reforms proposed, that it should, if possible, be independent of them.

As to precedents or Prior Art, there is a Corporation in the U.S. to administer the Patents obtained by Universities. Even closer to the question, there are composers' bodies in most advanced countries which look after their income under the various Copyright Acts. ASCAP in the U.S., and the Performing Right Society in Great Britain, developed along lines originated in France more than a century ago. In each country, the composers and lyric writers, together with their publishers, vest in a single national Society the non-dramatic performing rights in all their works, so enabling the Society to grant the music user a blanket licence authorising him to perform any and every work in the repertoire, paying according to the extent of the use required. A national Society is linked by contracts of affiliation with its opposite numbers in other countries, so that a licence from it thus covers virtually the entire world repertoire of non-dramatic copyright music. Moreover, a Society is able to do this at a minute fraction of the expense which the music user would incur if he tried to negotiate individual licences with the copyright owners all over the world. Taking the British Performing Right Society's method of operations as typical, it looks after the interests of about 170,000 performing right owners on a non-profit-making basis, at an administrative cost of around 11%. It licences premises where music can be publicly performed, by a system of differential royalty tariffs, and at the same time obtains listings from them of the songs and music played. The royalties received are then distributed to the Copyright owners on the basis of these listings, by a method which is admittedly imperfect, but which does have a rough justice to it. Even though the most popular composers probably do better than they ought, the least popular are still better off than they would be if the Performing Right Society did not exist.

There is no reason why a similar approach should not be used for scientific creativity, the scientific paper being analogous to the music as published, and the laboratory or development workshop to that of the premises in which performance takes place. In the case of computer programs, the program as written (presumably deposited in some form in a library) and the actual hardware that can make use of it, would be comparable analogies. All scientific information or all computer programs being handled by the Corporation would be available freely to all whose laboratory or computer was licenced, and the royalties would be distributed according to use-frequency listings provided to the Corporation by licencees. On the basis of a Performing Right Society-type operation, extension of the principle of Patenting far beyond its present limits cannot be said to be impossible or even difficult on administrative grounds; add to this the use of money rather than time as the true measure of monopoly, and objections to such an extension because it would produce gigantic rewards for some and little or nothing for others also disappear. If there is a serious desire to 'disestablish' basic research and rescue that large part of it that is currently dominated by the military-industrial complex, this is one practical way to do it.

Extension of the principle of Patenting therefore offers immediate solutions to Western countries for the dual problem posed by Japanese capability market power. Innovation Warrants provide an alternative method of capturing the externalities of investment in incremental innovation. Property rights in scientific discoveries would mean that goods which embody scientific knowledge would have to include an element in their price that would eventually accrue to the Scientific establishment. Even if Japan refused to enter into a Convention or bi-lateral treaties providing for reciprocal rights, therefore, their products would have to pay the 'Science Levy' on importation to any Western country. The impetus to innovation which better protection of investment in it would give, would also make any future attempt to organize an energy cartel, ineffective. If 'invention of the method of invention' was one of the great achievements of the nineteenth century, development of means for bringing about innovation could be one of the major advances of the twentieth.

Although the most immediately fruitful of such means is extension of the principle of Patenting, it is important that this should not result in any of the disadvantages of Patent systems, as these actually exist, being transferred to other areas of industrial property, which have so far been free of them. It has been argued, in this book, that the main objective of Patent Offices is now to ensure that what is in the Patent document conforms to certain administrative criteria of novelty and utility, and it has become virtually irrelevant whether or not it can serve as a sound basis for investment. Secondly, and again for administrative reasons, the Patent system attempts to divide up the stream of invention into discrete particles. Clearly, there would be no point in transferring these disadvantages to an area where they have not been found up to now, and where much innovation has been possible in consequence. When the Trade Mark system (linked with secrecy) underwrites information production, it does so largely in a form which justifies investment and leads to profits; it is concerned with production and money-making, not with the holding of an abstract balance between the 'new' information invented and information already in the hands of the public. It cannot happen, for example, under the Trade Mark system, that no protection whatever, even locally, is obtainable for information which happens to have been produced fractionally earlier in some distant part of the world, as occurs frequently with Patents under the requirement for absolute novelty. Consider an invention which has been laid 'open to public inspection', say, in Norwegian in the Oslo Patent Office, which will occur 18 months after an application is made there. Not many foreigners read Norwegian, yet in most countries to-day, this alone would prevent anyone who made the same invention independently but later, from getting a valid Patent. That is, no Specific market power whatever would exist as a basis for investment. Contrast this with the protection given by secrecy and capability or persuasive market power. Even if the same information becomes available to two firms on opposite sides of the world simultaneously as a result of their own independent research, each will have gained an advantage over its local competitors. The markets of a New Zealand firm and those of its Norwegian rival may never in fact impinge; even where they do, the realities of market power will ensure that neither will get all the sales. With capability and persuasive market power, there can always be *some* return from producing information of a type that can be embodied in products. With the Patent system, the return is often zero, just because the protection available is zero. Any reform which merely imported this disability of the Patent system into what other types of monopoly plus secrecy offer at present would be no reform at all.

The same is true of the Patent system's disadvantage that it seems to be necessary in operating it, to 'divide up the stream of invention', which causes a bias even within the Patent system itself. Patent 'claims' are boundaries expressed verbally, and in some types of new thing, the real inventive advance is more apt for expression in verbal terms than in others. With other types of market power, allied with secrecy, *any* idea can be protected, irrespective of how it can best be expressed. Again, it would be no reform to import the rigidity of the Patent system into marketing monopoly. The opposite is needed, to bring the universality and flexibility of capability market power and marketing monopoly into the Patent system and other legal arrangements for protecting investment in information production.

In extending the principle of Patenting it would be of the utmost importance that with the exception of certain areas which can be clearly defined in legislation, there should be no restriction in defining innovation. There can only be one criterion, if the danger of arbitrary power is to be avoided, and this is novelty, irrespective of subject matter. It would be intolerable if because a proposal was for breaking new ground in an area which the staff of the appropriate monopoly-granting authority regarded as trivial, perhaps even in poor taste, it would not receive exactly the same treatment and monopoly protection as something which they regarded as important and noble. It is never possible to say in advance which steps into the unknown will be the important ones, and what is trivial to parents may be important to their children when they in turn have grown up into quite different circumstances. Much Patent Office examination time even to-day is taken up with establishing whether or not an apparently trivial invention is or is not an advance in the state of an apparently trivial art, yet it is loyally done. One advantage the present system regarding Trade Marks has, at least, is that no moral or aesthetic judgement on the part of those who administer it is involved. A Trade Mark can be used as readily to protect a paste trinket as a life-saving drug. This freedom must be preserved in any reforms that deserve to be taken seriously.

The point needs to be stressed, because it is of particular relevance to the reform of Trade Mark law, which should be undertaken once extension of the principle of Patenting as far as Warrants has been completed. There are many areas of economic activity where the most suitable type of monopoly protection for innovation is, and will continue to be, the right to register a Trade Mark, and to make use of it. Every case, for example, where the novelty lies in the adaptation of existing knowledge simply to produce a product which is more suitable for a particular market, but without an advance in the technical state of the art, is of this type. If a firm decides that there is need for a varied range of cosmetic products with a particular psychological ingredient for a particular group of women, this is innovation if it has not been done before, it involves risk that is above average, and therefore justifies monopoly protection. How can this protection be given in a way which does not harm the interests of others, whilst at the same time being really valuable to the originator? It cannot be in the form of a monopoly to make the physical products; this would be outrageously unfair to others who may want to use them for different markets altogether, and are probably already doing so. Moreover, it is not here that the innovation is to be found, but in the change in the product the customer buys, with its mixture of psychological and physical ingredients. What is unknown is not 'can it be done'? but 'is there a demand for it?' Obviously, it can be done, since there are no technical unknowns involved; the step into darkness relates to the reaction of the market. The information to be generated can only be found by actual working in the market. It is to this that the reduction in uncertainty which is information relates, and for which monopoly protection is required and justified. Trade Mark registration monopoly meets this requirement perfectly, and there is no reason why the same principles of measuring the value of the monopoly granted should not apply as in the case of

Patents. Since legal monopoly should only be created so as to make investment possible under conditions of more than average risk, and not otherwise, its measure should be money.

The contrast in the present situation, where even the measure of time, inadequate as it is, which applies to Patents, does not apply to Trade Marks, is especially dramatic. Both Patents and Trade Marks are monopolies granted by positive law. Why should innovation in one case be granted protection for a term of years which may often be too short to produce an adequate return on the capital originally risked, when in the other it is effectively without any time limit (since a Trade Mark can be re-registered indefinitely)? The question is all the more pertinent, because the intrinsic superiority of persuasive market power may in fact mean quite rapid repayment of the original investment. The contrast is so marked that it is easy to see how marketing monopoly has become a far more important source of protection for innovation than the Patent system ever was. To achieve a balance, we must improve the precision of our measures in this area also, and since here too money is the only true yardstick of monopoly, there seems everything to be said for using the same approach of the 'multiple', as suggested in the case of Patents.

In cases where the uncertainty relates to demand rather than to science or technology, then, the appropriate monopoly to justify risk remains a registered Trade Mark. This would be granted for the exclusive use of the originator until such time as the profits gained from it amount to an agreed number of times his original investment. After this, the Trade Mark would be open to all, but Unfair Competition law would still protect the manufacturer's *reputation*. To illustrate how this would work, take the case of the glucose drink, Lucozade. Nothing could be simpler or more 'obvious' than its chemical make-up, so there could be no question of its owners, the Beecham Group, seeking or obtaining a Patent-type monopoly. On the other hand, the Group's marketing experts think that, properly handled, the product could satisfy a widespread demand for a drink for people who are unwell, especially if they feel themselves lacking in energy. It would not be for the examiners of the Innovation Office to concern themselves with a 'Which' – or 'Consumer's Report' – type of enquiry into whether or not there are any objective grounds for the advertising claim that 'Lucozade replaces lost energy'. People must be free to buy, and manufacturers must be free to sell, products which have psychological ingredients as well as physical ones; it would be quite intolerable if people who feel that Lucozade does them good should be deprived of this feeling just because in strictly scientific terms there is as much energy to be obtained from a cup of sugared tea. To give the Trade Mark Office power to decide questions like this would be to open the floodgates to arbitrary decisions, which would quickly make its work impossible. The only criteria with which the office need be concerned would be: Is the brand name new, that is, does it infringe any other Trade Mark monopoly, or has it been used before? In the Lucozade example, seen from the perspective of time before the first investment, this condition would be fulfilled. There is uncertainty on the demand side as to whether or not the psychological ingredient to be attached to this brand name will 'work'. The proportion of people which will get enough psychological satisfaction from drinking Lucozade in the belief that it is replacing their lost energy, to buy the product, is vitally important, but unknown. Such uncertainty makes investment in the making and selling of Lucozade of more than average risk, which needs monopoly to justify it. The Trade Mark form of monopoly is most suitable, and in a case like this, the Trade Mark Office would have to grant it. Not, however, as at present, once and for all, and effectively *in perpetuo*. At the outset, the Beecham Group would obtain an *option* to have a monopoly in the Trade Mark 'Lucozade'. This would be for a period of, say, three years, to enable the firm to carry out its marketing research and test market operations. If the Group is then satisfied that it has a viable product on its hands, the Trade Mark monopoly would move on to an 'exploitation' basis controlled by the 'multiple'. This monopoly will grant the Trade Mark owners the exclusive use of the Trade Mark 'Lucozade' until such time as their realized profits from it have reached the agreed multiple of their original investment. From that time on, any other manufacturer can sell an identical product and call it Lucozade, so that there might eventually be Lucozade made by several competing firms. Although Beecham's monopoly in the Trade Mark would be extinguished, their 'use or reputation' protection, arising from the public's ability to associate the product with their name, would remain. Anybody could make or sell a mixture of glucose and water and call it Lucozade; but nobody would be entitled to pretend that it was made by the Beecham Group if it had not been.

It would be essential to insist that there should be substantial physical identity of product, before a brand name could be used other than by its originator, even after the Trade Mark monopoly is exhausted, in order to protect the public. The most common defence of Trade Marks, branding and advertising has much weight in it. A brand is the public's guarantee of quality, since no manufacturer is going to invest money in trying to build up the reputation of his brand on the basis of a physical product whose quality is poor or inconsistent. Clearly, over the life of its Trade Mark monopoly, any firm would maintain the same standards in its physical product, for this reason. But once the monopoly is broken, if the requirement of physical product identity were not maintained, the opportunity would exist for fly-by-night operators to capitalize upon the association in the public's mind between the brand name and a particular level of physical quality in the product. Once the Beecham Group's Trade Mark monopoly had expired, for example, one rival might be less than scrupulous about maintaining the traditional glucose content in his 'Lucozade'. The result would be to deprive the public of something positive – the association of a name and a specification or a level of quality. Identity of product quality would therefore have to be an essential precondition for the legal use of an expired Trade Mark. A firm which builds up a brand name –

'an invented word or invented words', as the Trade Marks Act puts it – adds a new word to the language. This word has a precise meaning for large numbers of people, defined in terms of the product to which it relates, and it is its originating firm which has given it that meaning. In the hierarchy of words, it will not be very important, and the weight of meaning it has to carry will never be great; yet it deserves not to lose whatever small meaning it has, because of the importance all language has in the transmission of cultural values. Few things, indeed, are more important than that the meanings of words of all kinds be preserved. In this sense, the humble work of ensuring that the meanings even of brand names were not degraded would be a contribution of a sort to civilization. Monitoring them might best be left to the original Trade Mark owner, in whose interest maintenance of meaning would be; but the Trade Mark Office should have real powers to compel enforcement.

But just as these new words must be protected from having their meaning devalued, equally they must be allowed to come into the common vocabulary once this meaning has been defined and their creators adequately rewarded for the risks they took in defining them. The enrichment of life brought about because Lucozade existed may not be of a tremendously high order, and may even be considered by many to be of the utmost triviality. Yet it is not nothing, and it is because of the Beecham Group that the brand name has the associations and meaning it has for so many people. Is that a reason why this firm should own this new word, and effectively control its meaning, for ever? The difference between selling glucose-sweetened water and the psychological ingredients that make up Lucozade, and selling glucose and water as commodities, is remarkable in money terms, and is economic rent. It is the monopoly of the brand name that enables this rent to be extracted from the public, and since at present this monopoly can be renewed indefinitely simply by paying the nominal fees to the Trade Marks Registry, there is no time limit to the rent that is associated with it. Can a risk which is limited justify a return which to all intents and purposes is unlimited? Does not the formula proposed, in which the rent, insofar as it arises from the Trade Mark, is extinguished after proper remuneration of the original investment, taking account of the risk that this involved, hold out promise of giving much better balance in the allocation of scarce resources?

Another important advantage of granting Trade Marks for a limited period only, would be the virtual elimination of 'spurious' novelty. The symptoms of this are intensification of sales promotion, a frantic search for differentiation from competitive products which have also reached the same technical plateau, inflation of trivial aspects of the product to importance, and the proliferation of special offers, deals, couponing, banded packs and all the other apparatus of modern mass salesmanship. What all these amount to is an attempt to maintain public interest in, and excitement concerning a product, constantly at a level which is only appropriate to a period of innovation. It needs only a little reflection to realise that the root of this problem is the present practice of giving legal monopolies in Trade Marks without effective time limit. Since a manufacturer owns the Trade Mark in perpetuity, he will concentrate his product innovations on to a particular mark. All Unilever's product innovations in soap powder, for example, have tended to be incorporated in the brand 'Persil'. The pattern tends to be that where 'originative' invention is almost always expressed in a new brand, 'intensive' invention may go towards the improvement and consolidation of the older ones, or into a new brand, depending upon factors such as the scale of the market and the prevailing product life-cycle in it. In cosmetics, a new brand may be launched only on the basis of a piece of originative invention on the marketing side. Since 'originative' inventions are inevitably few and far between, and since much 'intensive' invention is below the level of perception of the consumer, it is inevitable that there should be long gaps when the absence of innovation has to be compensated for by sales promotion. Interest in the brand which has started at a high level (because at that point it really was something new and better) has to be kept up to this pitch as much as possible until the next innovation in the product comes along.

The stridency of modern marketing arises more than anything else from this. The mechanism of marketing is geared to innovation, and the fact that no real innovation is present does not change the way the mechanism operates. A motor designed for a particular load will run 'wild' and may even fly apart and do damage, if it is run without the load and without a governor; there is no 'governor' on modern marketing to control it when the load of innovation is off, and the result is the damage to their sensibilities against which an increasing number of people is reacting.

Limiting the Trade Mark to a period of time defined by profits as a multiple of the original investment involves none of these drawbacks. The Trade Mark is anchored to innovation in the first place, since it will only be granted to allow something new to be explored and exploited. While there should be no restriction on the subject matter of novelty by the Trade Mark Office, meaning that it should exercise no judgement as to whether an innovation is worthwhile or meretricious, the linking of one Trade Mark to one innovation would automatically force business men to a judgement, because only innovations of a minimum degree of importance can underwrite the development of a brand name. Once the innovation has run its course, by repaying its original investment the agreed number of times, the Trade Mark monopoly is extinguished. The next real innovation will be associated with a different Trade Mark, so that there is no need or possibility of using sales promotion, unreal differentials and the like, to bridge the time gap between them. There would be more monopoly than there is to-day for the true purpose of monopoly, which is to provide the legal basis for investment in information production; but it would no longer be possible to use legal monopoly to stimulate public interest in a product to a level which the intrinsic value of the innovation does not justify.

It may be asked whether it would not pay a firm to try to extend its effective monopoly after the legal protection has run out, by using the interest – and differentiation – creating techniques of modern marketing. The answer emerges from the earlier discussion of the different function of advertising, depending upon whether the protection available is Trade Mark registration, or only Unfair Competition Law or Common Law. Under the proposed system, while Trade Mark protection lasts, the position for an innovative product would be very much the same as it is to-day. The information content of the advertising is high, and so must its efficiency be; differentiation from competing products is genuine and clearly definable because of the innovation; and there is no need for sales promotion to stimulate consumer interest artificially. The overwhelming function of the advertising would be to articulate an inchoate need on the part of consumers, into want for this particular product. However, when the Trade Mark monopoly is extinguished (which, if the Trade Mark Office has calculated its 'multiples' correctly, should be when the product is no longer 'new' to most people and when the originator has been handsomely rewarded for his risk) the function of the advertising will change. From then on, it would be open to anyone to use the Trade Mark for a product of identical (or at least not inferior) quality. The new word will then have been definitively inserted into the language, and the Trade Mark Office's function in relation to it from that point onwards is no longer to protect the monopoly of its former owner, but to see that the word does not lose the meaning he has given it. For the originator and other manufacturers who respect this, there would be no more monopoly protection, so the function of advertising would thenceforward be to ensure that as far as possible members of the public associate a particular product with a particular manufacturer. If the originating firm tried to extend its Trade Mark monopoly by using its advertising as it did before his Trade Mark expired, it would be at the price of neglecting its ability to protect itself under Unfair Competition Law or Common Law. It may be predicted with some confidence, therefore, that with the end of monopoly, the advertising would quickly begin to reflect its changed function. Of course, there could well be a carry over of Capability market power due to the build-up of fixed costs in manufacturing plant during the period of registered Trade Mark protection. This is inevitable, it represents genuine economies of scale, and dealing with it, if indeed it needs to be dealt with at all, would be no problem. One reason is that the best way a firm could exploit its capability once its Trade Mark had expired, would be to lower its price to such an extent that it would not be worth a competitor's while entering the market at all. The public would then get the best of all worlds – the quality of a branded product at a price which included the least possible rent element. The implications of widespread adoption of this practice for reducing inflationary pressure, do not need to be stressed.

It may be argued – as in the case of Innovation Warrants – that firms would extend their monopolies over time in order to thwart competitors, by deliberately failing to realise the last few increments of their 'multiple'. This is hardly likely, firstly, because doing so would reduce their aggregate revenue from the monopoly on a Discounted Cash Flow basis; secondly, because it would mean failing to gain the maximum rent from their fixed costs on the production side; thirdly, because it would give them a less reliable foundation than they might have had on which to develop Unfair Competition or Common Law protection when the time comes. If it did become a problem, the Trade Mark Office should be equipped to deal with it, by means such as agreeing the *shape* of the growth curve of profits with the innovator at the same time as his 'multiple', or by relating multiples to the speed of bringing the new thing into the public domain, or, as suggested in the case of Patents, by opening the grant to compulsory purchase once the bulk of the 'multiple' has been earned as profits.

The more marketing monopoly is studied, the more inescapable seems the conclusion that the things that are wrong with it can all be traced back to the use of a system that is designed for innovation, for something *less* than innovation. There is no justification for legally created monopoly except that it is necessary to produce an adequate return for risky investment, above all the risky investment of information production. Making Trade Marks unlimited in time goes far beyond what is needed for this. It gives the Trade Mark owner a permanently privileged position, not only in respect of the profits to be derived from his 'originative' invention, at the psychological level, but also the profits from 'intensive' invention under the same brand name. This is so whether there is a worthwhile improvement in the product, or merely some artificially induced change inflated out of all importance – but where investment is at a much lower level of risk – by the brand's existing machinery for publicity and promotion.

None of these disadvantages would apply once appropriate measure – money – is applied to Trade Mark monopoly, and is followed through logically by extinguishing the monopoly of a Trade Mark when the 'multiple' is reached in terms of realized profits. Advertising would then always be used in the best possible way, because its information content would be high, without any need or possibility to inflate either its volume (to counteract the extent to which it is no more than 'noise') or its subject matter (by trying to give importance to meretricious aspects of the product). Sales promotion as such, in the sense of what happens to advertising when there is no longer anything new to say about the product, would not disappear from the scene completely, however. There would be certain cases where the market would reach a high stage of development before the originator's 'multiple' was exhausted. In these, it would pay the firm to use sales promotion much as it is known at present to speed up the rate of return on its original investment. This is the only thing it can do to *increase* its absolute level of return, because its monopoly advantages cease once a known ceiling is reached. On a Discounted Cash Flow basis, however, the sooner the 'multiple' is realized, the more valuable it is. Those who feel, therefore, that some of the colour of urban living would be lost if Promotion was eliminated, can rest assured that this would not happen completely under the new system. At the same time, there is no doubt that there would be far less of it. To this extent, there would also be less advertising. This would be compensated for, certainly in part and possibly even wholly, by the fact that there would be many more brands, since every marketing innovation would now have its own Trade Mark. At present this applies generally only to the most important ones. The advertising that would be lost would be the part that gives ground for the adverse criticism which the industry currently receives. It would also be the part which is responsible for the inflated importance of the communications media, with the undesirable effects which follow from this. Since an advertising medium takes on the flavour of the advertising it carries, the elimination of the advertising for the trivial aspects of products, should have a beneficial effect upon the editorial material that goes in between the advertisements. Advertising would be intrinsically more interesting, because its 'information content' would be higher – not in the sense of being more wordy, but according to the strict technical meaning of having power to reduce uncertainty. There would be more in this content than was, quite literally, news.

There is only one possible justification for allowing unlimited rent to arise from limited investment, no matter how risky, and that relates to the way these rents are put to use. The firms which originate new brands successfully and thus generate rents, do not distribute all of them to shareholders. They invest a large share in other new brands, many of which fail, and so the overall picture is one of much more modest return on capital than would be thought if only the successes were considered. Moreover, firms which have had a very favourable result from one investment, are more likely to be tempted to invest in the next risky project for that very reason. Apart from this, they have the corps of experienced innovators, and so have the best chance of getting the best results with the minimum inputs. Using the Lucozade illustration again, without the rents from this and similar products, the Beecham Group could not have invested in pharmaceuticals. Consequently, would not many people have suffered from lack of the remarkable advances Beecham Research made, especially in the Penicillin area? This is a persuasive way of stating the classical argument in favour of the existing pattern of market power. If it is accepted, it leads inevitably to dominance of the economy by large firms, to the direction of research and development into channels which can be protected by capability market power and marketing monopoly, and to all the disadvantages which have been dealt with earlier.

However, this argument does not have to be accepted. Capability market power and marketing monopoly have grown to their present importance more than anything else because they are a far better means of protecting investment in innovation than the Patent system, which was the official means ostensibly set up for that purpose. They filled the vacuum which risk-takers abhor. But, if Specific market power is reformed so that there is no longer a vacuum, then equally there is no need for excessive growth on the part of the other types. Once an Innovation Warrant or Certificate gives real protection to investment in the production of information, it will be possible for new ideas to be backed financially outside the big company with just as much prudence as to-day only applies inside it. All the academic studies of the effectiveness of Patents by firm size have completely missed the point: To the extent that a Patent or Warrant is doing its job properly, size of firm becomes quite irrelevant.

One way of looking at the modern firm which makes a good deal of sense, is as a group of people with the capacity to direct investment profitably into new things within certain clearly defined, rather restricted areas. Bankers and the public know that they cannot understand these areas to anything like the same extent, and so limit themselves to investing in firms which can demonstrate their ability to do so. For a number of reasons, size became associated with the power to demonstrate this, and so it is now generally accepted that large firms are necessary for successful innovation. This, it should now be clear, is not an absolute at all. Much of the advantage of the large firm as far as innovation is concerned, arises from nothing more than the nature of present legal arrangements for protecting information. Alternative arrangements could make firm size of relatively little importance from this point of view. Those proposed here, for example, would make it possible for banks and the public to invest in the production of new information, in many ways other than through the large firm. Returning to the earlier illustration, then, the rents of Lucozade are only necessary to the investment in research on new Penicillins, because Patent monopoly and marketing monopoly are the way they are; with a reformed system the number of firms, institutions and even individuals who could invest in Penicillin research without taking a decision which was in any way more foolhardy than the same decision taken in to-day's circumstances by the Board of the Beecham Group, would be much greater.

What applies to money, also applies to careers. Large firms are run, especially if they are progressive, by men who are perfectly capable of running their own businesses, and who would frequently like to do so. What prevents them is generally the excessive risk, as things stand at present, of committing themselves to something small and new, since this means the absence of capability or marketing power, the only really effective means of protecting the new information embodied in their products. But if the various Offices were genuinely able to hold out the promise of worthwhile protection, whether by Warrants, Patents or Trade Marks, of new ideas, the number of such men would be much greater, because the risk to their careers would be much lower.

Nothing could be of greater importance for the effective control of monopoly power. This can only mean maximizing the ease of entry by newcomers into any situation where market power is generating rent, *except where the rent is a fair return for investment in innovation*. Real means for easier entry, in turn, are a matter of availability of capital to individual entrepreneurs. At present the lack of Specific market power makes the sort of firm such people could found and run, much less attractive to financiers than large firms. Large firms, in particular, can offer 'cover'. The reforms proposed strike against unnecessary bigness in two ways: By making it easier for funds for innovation to flow to small as well as large firms, and – as a result of this – by improving the opportunities for top management to become self-employed. It would then be much more difficult for a large firm to recruit and keep the entrepreneur-manager types it needs to grow into a giant. Any slowness on the part of the large company's board to back a good idea would be likely to result in its management obtaining backing to carry it through elsewhere, so that in this way also, the new system would be conducive to more rapid innovation. Comporate lethargy would result in much quicker corporate retribution than it generally does to-day. Management buy-outs would not await the arrival of a Receiver into the firm which has failed to compete.

Irrespective of what economic arrangements are made, innovation ultimately depends upon the creative energy of identifiable individuals. If we want innovation, then, we must get innovators into the right places – and all the evidence is that they are not there now. Large firms are almost always the wrong place for an innovator, since their bureaucracy dissipates his creative energy; in fact, it is symptomatic of industrial decline that the energy which formerly went into innovation, now spends itself in finding a way forward through the bureaucracies of the State and of businesses. Neither is the innovator's own "greenfield" firm right in any but the rarest of cases to-day, because attempting to cope with all the complexities of a modern business simultaneously, will distract him from his central task. Innovation now requires access to a range of resources and skills that goes far beyond what sufficed for an Edison, a Parsons or a Marconi. No individual can be master at the same time of a particular technology, of all financial and tax aspects of a business, of marketing, of industrial relations, and of dealing with Government, not to speak of the problems of trading on a world scale, or of Patents. If he is indeed competent in several of these, then he is correspondingly unlikely to be able to offer the innovator's unique contribution: The relentless – even obsessive – pitting of his will and brains against uncertainty, in one limited area. What is required now above all, is to end the dependence of innovations on exceptional individuals, and to render it commonplace. To achieve this, we must take as many other burdens as possible off innovators, so as to leave their energies free for the work which only they can do. Some of these burdens can be lifted by making them free of the resources, in men and plant, of an existing firm; others by specialists in the field of innovation as a whole.

Consequently, a worth-while contribution might come from a number of firms which would act as catalysts between existing firms and innovators in the formation of new businesses.

These 'catalyst' firms would bring together:

1. An established firm which has been actively seeking involvement in an innovation related to its field, at least one of whose directors in personal-

ly committed to the project. Its contribution would be made mainly in kind, by providing a base for the new firm, design and workshop facilities, market research, accounting etc.

2. An innovator who is determined to commit his career substantially to the project's success, and who will benefit very considerably in the event. His contract would explicitly spell out the terms for his redundancy in the event of the project being aborted and these would be sufficiently generous to enable him, without recklessness, to take the risk of leaving his existing job, in order to throw himself into the venture.

The "catalyst" firm's expertise and experience would be wholly concerned with innovation. It would evaluate projects in the first instance, and then search out the other two parties and bring them together. It would raise external capital, bring its expertise to bear on the development as it goes forward, and be in overall financial control in the early stages. Eventually, however, it would sell control to either or both of the other two parties, retaining a small shareholding in all its projects.

A partial analogy is the case of Xerox Corporation. The inventor, Chester Carlson, agreed with the Battelle Institute that they would do the development work in exchange for a share in his very strong Patents. Independently, Haloid Corporation, which was already in the photographic business, and was actively searching for new products to invest in, asked Battelle if they could help, and so the two vital components were brought together. The analogy breaks down in that Battelle is an R & D Institute, whereas what is envisaged in the present case are firms with a primarily entrepreneurial bias, and specialist understanding of the innovation process. Also the innovators would only rarely be Patentees; they would be more likely to be creative individuals who are enthusiastic about some particular incremental innovation, or a product which is not Patentable at present because of requirements for absolute novelty and 'non-obviousness'. (If the proposals for Innovation Warrants become a reality, of course, they would very likely be Warrant holders.) Such an approach corresponds to the realities of current requirements on the part of firms, individuals and investors, for innovation to be successful. It could be expected to help to bring about a significant re-orientation of existing resources, both human and material, towards innovatory activity.

To sum up, therefore, these proposals for bringing market power under control, rest on five main foundations:

The first of these is the replacement of *ex-post* by *ex-ante* arrangements as far as possible for the control of market power. That is, monopolies arising from positive law should be limited by the laws which grant the monopolies in the first place. Every grant should have a defined cut-off point.

Secondly, the sole justification for any monopoly should be explicitly and exclusively its link with innovation, as the means of bringing about above-average financial returns for high risk in investment in the production of information. Wherever such a link is clear, monopoly is to be encouraged;

wherever it does not exist, monopoly is to be extinguished.

Thirdly, existing Patent Offices should be given rivals in the form of Innovation Offices, which would administer Innovation Warrants. Trade Mark Offices should also become autonomous, as should Copyright Offices. If proprietary rights for scientific discoveries are devised, their granting Body should also be independent.

Fourthly, profits, and not time, should progressively become the accepted measure of all monopoly, and all legally granted monopolies should be extinguished once profits have reached some given multiple of the original investment risked.

Fifthly, although monopolies in registered Trade Marks would eventually be limited by the same profit/multiple method as would apply to Patents, Warrants and other monopolies provided for by law, Unfair Competition law and Common Law protection of reputation would remain.

These proposals are designed to deal in a practical way with the problems of the contemporary crisis. They do so by setting priorities, according to urgency and feasibility. The immediate need is for ways of dealing with the threats to Western economies from outside, that is, with the threats from Japanese capability on the one hand, and the OPEC cartel, on the other. The innovation Warrant proposals offer a real alternative to protectionism – and probably the only effective one – for dealing with the problems posed by Japan's productivity. They would do so by making massive and widespread Specific market power possible, to counterbalance Japan's Capability market power. This would underwrite an upsurge in innovation, especially incremental innovation, which would then be receiving the protection which the Patent systems of the world have increasingly failed to give it. For the first time too, profits could be anticipated by any firm, not just the largest ones, from investing in developing products that are 'obvious' (in Patent terms) but which nevertheless do not yet exist. Business confidence, investment and employment could not fail to be stimulated quickly and strongly by putting these proposals into effect. Investment in Energy R & D would also be intensified as a result of these proposals, and the results of this would reduce both the power of OPEC and energy costs simultaneously.

In the long run, however, the threat to the West from internal weakness is even greater than from external forces. The source of this weakness is the growth of bureaucracy, especially that of the State, with its consequent stifling of innovation. A major cause of acceptance of bureaucratic growth is that people are progressively more repelled by the alternative, which goes by the name of free enterprise. But if nothing else has emerged from the preceding pages, it can only be awareness that this is not free enterprise at all, but an economic world actually characterized by mindless interference with economic freedom on a grand scale. This can only be dealt with by relentless application of the principle that either market power must be shown to be underwriting innovation, or it is to be ruthlessly rooted out, wherever it is found. Introduction of money as the measure of all legally-granted monopolies will help greatly in achieving this end. Its consequent destruction of entrenched positions which masquerade as the result of economic freedom will clear the way for steps to promote the widest possible understanding of the vital principle: That the operation of market forces brings about the highest possible degree of equality that can be attained in human society.

After reforming and revitalising Specific market power, therefore, the next task will be to deal with the Persuasive type, based upon Trade Mark registration. Here again, use of money as the true measure of monopoly, by ending registration of Brands once profits reach a multiple of the investment risked to bring their associated products into existence, will be the instrument.

As to the bureaucrats, the urgent task is an intellectual one: To kill, once and for all, the myth which they have fostered, that their active intervention is required and beneficial, when in fact it can only be harmful. Their true function in respect of innovation, as of so much else, is not to originate and administer so-called panaceas, but the vastly more exacting task of getting the law right. If the laws relating to innovation are wrong, none of the measures resulting from bureaucrative interference will work; if the law is right, such measures are unnecessary.

Capability market power will be left until last to deal with, for two reasons. Firstly, the Innovation Warrant proposals which offer the means of coping with external challenges, affect few local vested interests adversely, and should therefore meet little resistance. This is not the case with reformation of the laws of capital deployment which underwrite Capability market power as we know it. Secondly, much more needs to be known about how exactly these laws work in practice, if reforms are not to do as much harm as good. For both reasons, experience of the beneficial results of getting industrial property right, will be an essential prerequisite for reshaping other, older and more deeply entrenched types of property.

At the same time, Mill's words that "the laws of property have never yet conformed to the principles upon which private property rests" must not be forgotten. The effort to change the laws so that they foster the diffusion rather than the concentration of wealth must be made, if collectivism is not to triumph in the end.

These reforms would make possible a fourth thrust of the industrial revolution in which the powerful instrument of interference with markets would be used to direct innovation to humane ends in a much more conscious way than has been the case up to now. Market power would be made the servant of man, instead of the blind master which it is at present. It is a commonplace that man's control over matter has outrun his capacity for social control. Perhaps the most damaging result of uncontrolled market power has been the way it has diverted resources and creative energy into technological and marketing innovations, at the expense of *social* innovation. This reflects, it should now be clear, a system of positive law which has had results which have often been as unforeseen as they have been important. Although on balance these results have been beneficial, the record has not been as favourable as it could have been if the law had developed on a basis of more awareness of its effects. Response to the contemporary crisis must begin the task of changing the laws of property into an instrument for making innovation serve humane ends as never before. If this can be achieved even partially, the principle of individual property will indeed be found to have nothing to do with the physical or social evils which have been blamed on it. On the contrary, it will re-emerge as an essential condition if creativity in business is to find expression in ways that are fully human.

The first and essential step in changing the laws of property to the desired end, is to recognise that there is nothing sacred about the present pattern of either innovation or market power. Our immediate problems are rooted specifically in Capital deployment and Intellectual Property legislation, passed on to us by the nineteenth century with but little foresight of the enormous consequences which would follow. This legislation can be changed in the light of what is now known about its consequences. We can also progress according to our understanding of our Measures. No doubt any changes that are made will also have results that will go far beyond, and be different from, those envisaged at the time they are made. The laws will then have to be adapted to new circumstances once more, which will be a task for another generation. Any legislation which provides scope for the exercise of human creativeness must produce unforeseen results, and must consequently be the subject of unceasing review. The problems which have arisen from market power are simply due to failure to subject the relevant legislation to this continuing scrutiny. Because of the link between this legislation and "getting new things done", the political economy of innovation is an important part of that eternal vigilance which is also the price of economic freedom.

Notes

1. Mill John Stuart: Principles of Political Economy. 1909 London edn. Book II Ch. 1.
2. Atiyah P.S.: The Rise and Fall of Freedom of Contract. Oxford 1979.
3. Belloc Hilaire: The Servile State. London 1912.
4. Wilson C.: History of Unilever. London (1954) I, p. 35.
5. Dewey Donald: Monopoly in Economics and Law. Chicago (1959) p. 152.
6. Galbraith J.K.: American Capitalism. London (1952) p. 35.
7. Kaysen C and Turner D.F.: A Policy for Anti-Trust Law. Cambridge, Mass. (1959) p. 110.
8. Dewey op. cit. p. 307.
9. Worcester Jr. D.A.: Monopoly, Big Business and Welfare in the Postwar United States. Seattle (1967) p. 81.
10. Dewey op. cit. p. 305.
11. Rowley C.K.: The British Monopolies Commission. London (1966) p. 200.
12. cf Grunfield G.C.: in Friedmann W. (Ed.) Anti-Trust Laws. London (1956) p. 351.
13. Benda Julien: La Trahison des clercs. Paris 1927.

256

14. Seldon Arthur: Advertising. London 1969.
15. Hutt W.H.: The Strike-Threat System. New Rochelle (N.Y.) 1973.
16. von Hayek F.A.: Individualism and Economic Order. Chicago (1948) p. 113.
17. Dewey Donald: The Theory of Imperfect Competition: A Radical Reconstruction. New York (1969) p. 199.
18. Dolan Edwin G.: TANSTAAFL (1971) p. 36.
19. von Hayek F.A.: The Constitution of Liberty. London (1960) p. 71.
20. Rostow W.W.: Getting From Here to There. London (1979) p. xxv.
21. Batzel Victor M.: Legal Monopoly in Liberal England. In Business History 22 (1980) p. 189.
22. Ravenshear A.E.: The Industrial and Commercial Influence of the English Patent System. London (1908) p. 40.
23. Plant A.: In Economica (1934) p. 33.
24. Polanyi Michael: In Review of Economic Studies Vol XI No. 2 (1944) p. 61.
25. Gilfillan S.C.: Invention and the Patent System. Washington D.C. 1964.
26. Gilfillan S.C.: The Sociology of Invention. Boston. 1935, repr. 1970.
27. In Mitteilungen Der Deutschen Patentanwälte, March 1976.
28. In European Intellectual Property Review, May and July 1981.
29. Committee on Reform of the Patent System (Banks Committee) London 1970.
30. In Research Policy Vol XI (1982) p. 95.
31. Kronz, op. cit.
32. ibid.
33. cf. Software Protection: The Legal Protection of Computer Programs. London 1969.
34. Villard H.H.: Economic Performance. New York (1959) p. 367.
35. Beier F.K.: Problems of Economic Exploitation of Basic Research Findings. Weinheim/Bergstr. 1982.
36. Hamson C.J.: Patent Rights for Scientific Discoveries. Indianapolis 1929.
37. Wilson David: Penicillin in Perspective. London (1976) p. 237.

Appendix

An alternative approach to the "multiple"

Throughout Chapter V, it was insisted that the proper measure of any monopoly is money, not time. This led to the idea that a grant, of an Innovation Warrant, for example, should last until an innovator had earned profits amounting to a prescribed "multiple" of his original investment.

Since this will happen after a discrete period, it is tempting to think of using time *as a surrogate for the profits 'multiple',* since this would avoid the difficulties of monitoring profits. If the reward is to be properly matched to the risk, however, this would mean a variable term of grant, according to the circumstances of each case. This would involve the exercise of discretion by members of the staff of the Office, which would be open to abuse, and would certainly meet strong objections. At the least, if the argument advanced earlier is valid, these officials would be forced to re-define their task in such a way as to render it capable of being performed within the constraints of their employment conditions. Consequently, innovation protection would come to have the same faults, as have so greatly reduced the value of the traditional Patent system.

However, there is a way of combining the convenience of 'time' with much of the precision of the 'multiple', without requiring the use of official discretion. This would be by using *categories* of risk, based as far as possible upon empirical research. The following illustrates how this would work in the case of Innovation Warrants.

In a simple model, it could be readily accepted that irrespective of what size or type of firm undertakes something new, probability of financial success is highest if the objective is no more than an incremental change, and lowest if it is the first practical application of basic research. Innovation which depends upon well-understood technology transfer falls somewhere between the two. Let us assign probabilities of success of .6, .1 and .3 respectively, to these cases, as a first approximation.

Similarly, irrespective of what the project may be, it could easily be agreed that the risk which any firm faces in undertaking innovation, is directly related to the ratio between that firm's size and the resources which the innovation will require. This is certainly true of the risk as subjectively viewed by its management. It can be expressed as the ratio between the firm's assets and the innovatory investment. Translating risk into probability of success, figures which might be generally accepted are .5 where this "firm-related" risk is at its lowest, .2 where it is at its highest, and .3 for the intermediate cases.

If both the firm-related and the project-related risks are now combined by multiplying their probabilities, we get the following matrix (Table 1).

Table 1. Probability of success.

Firm-related risk	Project-related risk		
	Incremental	Technology-transfer	Radical
Low	.3	.15	.05
Medium	.18	.09	.03
High	.12	.06	.02

Then, if the length of the monopoly grant is to be the inverse of risk, in order to attract firms to innovate, for each category the number of years will be the reciprocal of these probabilities (Table 2).

Table 2. Term of Warrant (years).

Project	Type of project		
Firm-related risk	Incremental	Technology-transfer	Radical
Low	3.3	6.7	20
Medium	5.5	11.1	33
High	8.3	16.7	50

The monopoly term corresponding to each category of combined risk, means that an innovator could indeed look forward to receiving back a 'multiple' of his investment, in the event of technical success. Whilst the probability figures taken in this example are arbitrary, the resulting spread of terms, if not their absolute lengths, seems quite realistic. With growing experience and assembly of empirical data, 'multiples' should become progressively better matched to risks as these are actually perceived by investors.

A team of experts in the Innovation Office could constantly be refining its probability figures for both types of risk (and, indeed, additional ones) according to evidence supplied to it by firms as well as from its own studies.

Any individual application would automatically be assigned to its appropriate category of firm-related risk according to the general rules in force at the time, and without any discretion on the part of the Innovation Office. Similarly, the team of experts should not find much difficulty in ruling as to which project-related probability figure should be used for the subject-matter of any new application. Since to do this, they would not need to know anything about the firm making the application, its identity would be concealed from them and they could therefore never be accused of bias. Officials of the Innovation Office would then only have to combine both figures, without having any discretion as to the length of the term, and the evidence as to both components of the final probability figure leading to it would be open to public inspection. Competitors, as well as applicants themselves, would know what the term in any particular case would be. Assignment of new applications to their appropriate project-risk category should become progressively easier, indeed almost automatic, as a body of case histories is built up. Firms getting grants would be asked to provide data to assist in this. Applicant firms would have no difficulty in supplying the information needed for assigning their application to its appropriate category in terms of firm-related risk. Every firm knows what its assets are, and every applicant firm would know what it proposes to invest in the innovation. Any mis-statement would be fraud on the Office, which would make the grant void. A large firm which used a small one as a 'front' so as to get a longer term, would also be caught by this provision. If a small firm comes under the control of a larger one later on, the term automatically changes to what the large firm would have been granted if it had made the original application. If the original applicant firm obtained additional capital, however, without any change in its control, the term would remain unchanged. This feature would help small and medium-sized innovatory firms raise venture capital without sacrificing their independence.

A valuable feature of the Warrant proposals is the way the "multiple" could be varied so as to encourage investment in certain regions, or types or sizes of business. This feature need not be lost by moving to use of the "matrix", since all that would be needed is a factor, applicable by law, to the standard "firm-related" probabilities. This would again be outside the discretion of Innovation Office officials, and the resulting change in weighting would be carried through to the length of monopoly term.

Index of subjects

Index of persons, firms and institutions